# Kings, Lords and Courts in Anglo-Norman England

# Kings, Lords and Courts in Anglo-Norman England

Nicholas Karn

THE BOYDELL PRESS

First published 2020
The Boydell Press, Woodbridge

ISBN 978-1-78327-486-4

The Boydell Press is an imprint of Boydell & Brewer Ltd
PO Box 9, Woodbridge, Suffolk IP12 3DF, UK
and of Boydell & Brewer Inc.
668 Mt Hope Avenue, Rochester, NY 14620–2731, USA
website: www.boydellandbrewer.com

A catalogue record of this publication is available from the British Library

This publication is printed on acid-free paper

In memory of my father,
Jeffrey John Karn

# Contents

# Preface and Acknowledgements

The preparation of this book has been an extended process, and it has been shaped by the fundamental influence of some of the major projects of recent years. All of these are collaborative, and have involved the range of expertise that can only arise where many are involved. They are models of scholarly endeavour, as well as richly productive of ideas. The English Episcopal Acta project and its many editors are a key and ongoing influence; the AHRC-funded project on the acta of Henry I was another. Both involved detailed work on sources from the twelfth century, and led to questioning of some of the narratives and theories that used them. This book is the product of those concerns, and an attempt to try to explain some of the developments apparent in the sources but which had not been so prominent in the historiography.

Academic research benefits from the provision of resources to allow concentrated study without distractions. The contribution of funding bodies is important, and there are many debts to acknowledge. Some of the questions answered here first arose during the tenure of a Postdoctoral Fellowship awarded by the British Academy and held at Christ Church, Oxford; other parts were prepared during an Early Career Fellowship awarded by the Leverhulme Trust and held at the University of Southampton. The sustained support of the latter institution has allowed for the development of the ideas in this book. A Visiting Research Fellowship at the John Rylands Research Institute, University of Manchester, also assisted work on this project.

Many people have contributed to the making of this book, and some have made more notable contributions through recommendations and advice or through reading and responding to components of it: the late Professor Christopher Brooke; Dr Suzanne Coley; Professor Anne Curry; Dr Mark Hagger; Dr Leonie Hicks; Professor Paul Hyams; Professor Richard Sharpe; Professor Nicholas Vincent; Professor Christopher Woolgar; and many others. I am appreciative of their time and their ideas. I have also gained much from the opportunity to discuss relevant themes with students at the University of Southampton, especially those on the 'Crime and Society in Medieval England' special subject; I am grateful for their thoughts and questions. I have also derived much benefit from opportunities to present aspects of this study, at seminars and conferences in Copenhagen, Exeter, Leeds, London, Southampton, and Winchester, and from the observations, comments and debates that arose thence.

Finally, I am ever appreciative of the support of my family, who have contributed so much over the years. Sadly, my father died when this book was nearly finished; thus, it is dedicated to his memory.

# Abbreviations

| | |
|---|---|
| [1, 2, 3, 5, 6, 7, 8, 9, 10] Æthelred | Liebermann, *Gesetze*, i. 216–70: *The Laws of the Kings of England from Edmund to Henry I*, ed. and trans. A. J. Robertson (Cambridge, 1925), 52–133. |
| [2, 3, 4, 5, 6] Æthelstan | Liebermann, *Gesetze*, i. 150–83: *The Laws of the Earliest English Kings*, ed. and trans. F. L. Attenborough (Cambridge, 1922), 126–69. |
| *Abingdon Chronicle* | *Historia Ecclesie Abbendonensis/The History of the Church of Abingdon*, ed. and trans. John Hudson (two volumes, Oxford, 2002–7). |
| Assize of Clarendon | ed. William Stubbs, *Select Charters and Other Illustrations of English Constitutional History* (ninth edition, Oxford, 1913), 170–3. |
| Bates, *Regesta* | David Bates, ed., *Regesta Regum Anglo-Normannorum: The Acta of William I, 1066–1087* (Oxford, 1998). |
| Baxter, *Earls of Mercia* | Stephen Baxter, *The Earls of Mercia: Lordship and Power in Late Anglo-Saxon England* (Oxford, 2007). |
| Bishop, *Scriptores regis* | T. A. M. Bishop, *Scriptores Regis*: *Facsimiles to Identify and Illustrate the Hands of Royal Scribes in Original Charters of Henry I, Stephen and Henry II* (Oxford, 1961). |
| [1, 2] Cnut | Liebermann, *Gesetze*, i. 278–371: *The Laws of the Kings of England from Edmund to Henry I*, ed. and trans. A. J. Robertson (Cambridge, 1925), 154–219. |
| *Decem Articuli* | Liebermann, *Gesetze*, i. 486–8: *The Laws of the Kings of England from Edmund to Henry I*, ed. and trans. A. J. Robertson (Cambridge, 1925), 238–43. |

| | |
|---|---|
| *Dictionary of Medieval Latin* | *Dictionary of Medieval Latin from British Sources*, ed. Richard Ashdowne, David Howlett and Ronald Latham (three volumes, Oxford, 2018). |
| [1, 2, 3, 4] Edgar | Liebermann, *Gesetze*, i. 192–215: *The Laws of the Kings of England from Edmund to Henry I*, ed. and trans. A. J. Robertson (Cambridge, 1925), 16–39. |
| [2, 3] Edmund | Liebermann, *Gesetze*, i. 186–91: *The Laws of the Kings of England from Edmund to Henry I*, ed. and trans. A. J. Robertson (Cambridge, 1925), 8–15. |
| [2] Edward | Liebermann, *Gesetze*, i. 140–45: *The Laws of the Earliest English Kings*, ed. and trans. F. L. Attenborough (Cambridge, 1922), 118–121. |
| Faith, *English Peasantry* | Rosamund Faith, *The English Peasantry and the Growth of Lordship* (Leicester, 1997). |
| Fleming, *Domesday Book* | Robin Fleming, *Domesday Book and the Law: Society and Legal Custom in Early Medieval England* (Cambridge, 1998). |
| *Gerefa* | Liebermann, *Gesetze*, i. 453–5. |
| *Geþyncðo* | Liebermann, *Gesetze*, i. 456–9: *English Historical Documents,* c. *500–1042*, trans. Dorothy Whitelock (London, 1955), 432. |
| Great Domesday Book | Cited by folio number and reference to the numerical organisation in *Domesday Book: Text and Translation*, ed. and trans. J. Morris (38 volumes, Chichester, 1975–86). |
| Harmer, *Writs* | Florence E. Harmer, *Anglo-Saxon Writs* (second edition, Stamford, 1989). |
| Hudson, *Oxford History* | John Hudson, *The Oxford History of the Laws of England*: ii, *871–1215* (Oxford, 2012). |
| Lambert, *Law and Order* | Tom Lambert, *Law and Order in Anglo-Saxon England* (Oxford, 2017). |

| | |
|---|---|
| *Leges Edwardi Confessoris* | *God's Peace and King's Peace: The Laws of Edward the Confessor*, ed. and trans. Bruce R. O'Brien (Philadelphia, 1999). |
| *Leges Henrici Primi* | *Leges Henrici Primi*, ed. and trans. L. J. Downer (Oxford, 1972). |
| *Libertas Londoniensis* | Liebermann, *Gesetze*, i. 673–5. |
| Liebermann, *Gesetze* | *Die Gesetze der Angelsachsen*, ed. Felix Liebermann (3 volumes, Halle, 1903–16). |
| Little Domesday Book | Cited by folio number and reference to the numerical organisation in *Domesday Book: Text and Translation*, ed. J. Morris (38 volumes, Chichester, 1975–86). |
| London *Leges Anglorum* | Liebermann, *Gesetze*, i. *passim*, and F. Liebermann, *Über die Leges Anglorum saeculo xiii. ineunte Londoniis collectae* (Halle, 1892). |
| London version of *Decem Articuli/ Willelmi Articuli Retractati* | Liebermann, *Gesetze*, i. 489–91: *The Laws of the Kings of England from Edmund to Henry I*, ed. and trans. A. J. Robertson (Cambridge, 1925), 244–51. |
| Molyneaux, *Formation* | George Molyneaux, *The Formation of the English Kingdom in the Tenth Century* (Oxford, 2015). |
| *ODNB* | *Oxford Dictionary of National Biography*, ed. Colin Matthew and Brian Harrison (60 volumes, Oxford, 2004); online with supplements at https://www.oxforddnb.com/ |
| *Quadripartitus* | Liebermann, *Gesetze*, i. *passim*, and F. Liebermann, *Quadripartitus, ein Englisches Rechtsbuch von 1114* (Halle, 1892). |
| *Rectitudines Singularum Personarum* | Liebermann, *Gesetze*, i. 444–53. |

| | |
|---|---|
| *Regesta* | *Regesta Regum Anglo-Normannorum, 1066–1154*; i: *Regesta Willelmi Conquestoris et Willelmi Rufi, 1066–1100*, ed. H. W. C. Davis and R. J. Whitwell (Oxford, 1913); ii: *Regesta Henrici Primi, 1100–1135*, ed. C. Johnson and H. A. Cronne (Oxford, 1956); iii: *Regesta Regis Stephani ac Mathildis Imperatricis ac Gaufridi et Henrici Ducum Normannorum, 1135–1154*, ed. H. A. Cronne and R. H. C. Davis (Oxford, 1968) |
| rpt | reprinted |
| Van Caenegem, *Lawsuits* | R. C. van Caenegem, ed. and trans. *English Royal Lawsuits from William I to Richard I*, 2 volumes, Selden Society, 106–107 (1990–1) |
| Wormald, *Making of English Law* | Patrick Wormald, *The Making of English Law: King Alfred to the Twelfth Century* (Oxford, 1999) |

# Introduction

Before 1066, there were shires and there were hundreds; they were arenas where disputes were settled and where business was transacted. Edgar instructed that everyone should do justice to others in the hundred.[1] This relatively simple pattern did not long survive the Conquest, and there is widespread historiographical consensus that there arose new kinds of court, which embodied and protected the powers and claims that lords demanded from their dependents.[2] The pattern that emerges from the sources is that throughout the eleventh century lords created mechanisms for inserting their influence into assemblies and courts in various ways. There was no single method here; some tried to redraw boundaries so that courts consisted solely of their own dependents upon whom influence might be brought to bear, while others inserted their agents into courts so that they could have a strong influence upon them. Later, lords created units under the hundred, which mostly consisted of their own dependents and not those of other lords. Great churches acting as lords seem often to have been most active in doing this. These kinds of tactics straddle the Conquest, though most examples are first clearly evidenced after 1066. It would seem that something fundamental about lordship is being expressed through these tactics.

Where lords tried any of these methods for enhancing their influence in hundreds, there was generally a strong link to their own dependents, or sometimes to those who they thought should be their own dependents. This indicates that where lordly influence was strengthened in existing assemblies, or where new courts were set up as subdivisions of older assemblies, these developments were really about shaping the relationship between lords and their dependents, rather than mere acquisitiveness. The relationship between lords and their dependents assumed that lords would be in a position to control and discipline their dependents; this was fundamental to the better-documented lords' courts from the later twelfth century.[3] So far as can be seen, much of this business was done in the hundred before the Norman Conquest, for this was a prime location where lords

1 1 Edgar 1.

2 In this volume those who were bound to and who served lords will be referred to as dependents for the sake of consistency, lest the intrusion of variant terms with different resonances such as man or vassal is misleading.

3 S. F. C. Milsom, *The Legal Framework of English Feudalism* (Cambridge, 1976),

could manage their dependents, but also a place where those dependents were visible and accessible to the claims of other lords and even the representatives of kings such as sheriffs. Dependents could be exploited by others or even lured away if visible and accessible in these circumstances.

The extension of lords' influence in existing courts and the creation of new ones were thus effective tactics for strengthening the influence that lords had over their dependents and their capacity to manage and discipline them. It probably allowed for more rigorous access to the resources that those dependents generated, and so could have been to the material advantage of lords as they strengthened and intensified lordship bonds. The developments seen here in relation to courts are directly paralleled by the contemporary proliferation of local churches, in which lords created churches as a means of keeping as much as possible of the resource of their dependents on their lands, and so diminishing the influence and claims of minster clergy.[4] In most cases, these parallel tactics were done by the same kinds of people at about the same time. Both were driven by a fundamental desire to monopolise the resources of their dependents, and to allow for closer supervision and management without the same scope for interference from outside.

The creation of new courts can be seen especially after 1100, when they often appear with the description *halimota*. These courts seem to have been common, and maybe the norm. They were defined by lordship, and often consisted of the dependents of one lord only. Yet attendance at these courts was much wider than at later kinds of lordship courts. They included those who were free and law-worthy, and they could give testimony on oath much as a hundred might.[5] They were thus general and omnicompetent lordship courts, but, at least in the first half of the twelfth century, they worked with the communal hundred courts. As such, they must be distinguished from the hallmoots that are documented from the thirteenth century and beyond, which were essentially manorial courts, restricted to the unfree peasantry.

The changing pattern of courts from the eleventh century onwards had complex origins, but also had considerable consequences. The appearance of different and potentially competing courts, which represented different lords and different kinds of interest, generated debate over the ways in which business might be allocated to them. In this task, there was little available in terms of guidance from the past; the Anglo-Saxon laws did not set out any coherent approach towards jurisdiction and the remit of courts because the relative

chapter 1; and on the later manor see Zvi Razi and Richard Smith, eds., *Medieval Society and the Manor Court* (Oxford, 1996).

4 John Blair, 'Introduction: from Minster to Parish Church', in *Minsters and Parish Churches: The Local Church in Transition, 950–1200*, ed. John Blair (Oxford, 1988), 1–19.

5 The evidence for the work and attendance of these courts is set out in Chapter 4 below.

simplicity of the pattern of assemblies before 1066 made such a development unnecessary.[6] Debates over where business should be heard interacted with ideas about ownership and claims, that some kinds of business belonged to lords as the owners of courts and could be claimed by them as such.[7] There was thus a substantial shift after 1100 in how these matters were discussed and managed. It saw the development of norms and standards for how to describe and assert claims over particular kinds of business or instances of business, and the growth of a consensus over what would be regarded as compelling arguments in these circumstances. These developments mostly preceded the appearance of a learned legal tradition in England, but rather reflected the presence and effectiveness of debate among the wide class that participated in the law. It should be linked to the other major evidence for debate about the law in England in this period, the translations of older legal texts and composition of new ones, especially as these often reflected some of these debates.

Lords seem to have been the agents in many of these kinds of change, but they also had implications for the greatest lord of all, the king. The idea that lords should embody their influence over their dependents in the form of a court was one that kings not only embraced, but even initiated; the idea of the *curia regis* as a court, and even of the phrase itself, first appeared after the Conquest.[8] Yet, the work of lords in creating courts to manage their interests over their dependents and shield them from the public assemblies had considerable consequences for kings. It made it much harder for kings to demand their claims and interests arising from various kinds of business, because matters did not necessarily appear in a public assembly where they could be observed and where claims could be made. This meant that hundreds were losing their role as common ground where all kinds of business were raised and claimed. So, from Henry I's time kings changed their attitude towards the hundreds, and intensified their claims over them, to the extent that they claimed them as their own courts more specifically and aggressively, rather than as communal courts which did royal business. They had not done this before.[9] This allowed them to demand attendance at the

6 A. G. Kennedy, 'Disputes about *Bocland*: The Forum for their Adjudication', *Anglo-Saxon England* 14 (1985), 175–95, is the fullest analysis for how pleas were allocated to different courts before 1066, and it argues that *bocland* cases could be heard before the king or in shires without any sharp distinction.

7 Lords came to claim that courts were theirs; they could write of 'my court' and similar. That interest will be referred to here in words linked to own and ownership, for these avoid problematic vocabulary around possession.

8 Hudson, *Oxford History*, 43–6 describes how kings before the Conquest acted personally; 274–5 shows how the court developed after the Conquest, even to the extent of dealing with matters during the absences of the king.

9 Lambert, *Law and Order*, 250, on the earlier status of hundreds. This question is discussed more fully in Chapter 6 below.

hundreds as an expression of their own lordship, and so maintain an infrastructure of local courts that provided a structure for claims. At the same time, kings made a vital distinction between court ('*curia*') and plea ('*placitum*'), which had once been synonymous, and which ultimately allowed for the idea that there might be king's pleas enforceable regardless of whose court dealt with business. This is first seen consistently in royal charters from Henry I's reign, and marks a development just as important as the vocabulary for describing and claiming courts.

Yet the most visible development in how kings interacted with the law was the advent of royal justices. These were introduced by Henry I in 1107–8, and were at first local representatives whose role was to monitor their districts for incidents which might have involved the king's claims, and then pursue them. This involved accusing and summoning individuals into the king's hundred courts, but might have involved pursuing matters in other courts controlled by lords. They were not like later Common-Law era justices who took the custom of the king's court to the shires and could act authoritatively on that basis; rather, they operated within existing courts and procedures, and their role was to act as a kind of advocate or agent, claiming royal financial dues where they could. Early justices were monitors of pleas and business, and often seem to have as much in common with later coroners as with the justices of the later twelfth century.

## Courts in the Tenth and Earlier Eleventh Century

This book is built around the aim of explaining change, and change can only be a development from a chosen starting-place. The starting-place here is the relatively simple pattern of courts in the first half of the eleventh century. Kings could hear some disputes themselves, though seemingly they were involved in rather few disputes overall.[10] Before the Norman Conquest, kings dealt with disputes rather informally, and there was no term that corresponded to the later *curia regis* to give a sense of institutionalised form to the king's legal work. That developed instead after the Conquest, when the king's court quite quickly came to have an existence separate from the person of the king, so that it heard and determined disputes even when the king was absent in Normandy.[11]

[10] Hudson, *Oxford History*, 43–6. A. G. Kennedy, 'Disputes about *Bocland*: The Forum for their Adjudication', *Anglo-Saxon England* 14 (1985), 175–95 shows that kings did not claim business consistently. They did hear some cases personally, of course, such as that in the Fonthill Letter; on that see Nicholas P. Brooks, 'The Fonthill Letter, Ealdorman Ordlaf and Anglo-Saxon Law in Practice', in *Early Medieval Studies in Memory of Patrick Wormald*, ed. Stephen Baxter, Catherine Karkov, Janet L. Nelson and David Pelteret (Farnham, 2009), 301–17.

[11] Van Caenegem, *Lawsuits*, no. 7.

There were shires and there were hundreds or wapentakes,[12] and there seems to have been nothing beyond those two basic varieties of court. The available sources for their work are uneven and there are substantial gaps in what might be known about their functions. The hundred is represented well in the laws written in the tenth and early eleventh centuries, but then there are few sources for the hundred until the abundant testimony of the hundreds recorded in Domesday Book, which gives a somewhat different impression from that in the laws. The shire, meanwhile, is much less well attested in the sources, in that it is covered less fully in the laws and in Domesday Book and thereafter. The gaps in the sources mean that it is unlikely that a full history of the hundred or the shire in the eleventh century could ever be written. Though shire and hundred can be treated as comparable phenomena, and classified as courts, the term was not used at the time; they were simply called hundreds and shires, and the only Old English term used to group them into one category was 'gemot'.

*The shire (sometimes and later the county)*[13]

In origin, the shire was a share of the kingdom of Wessex, and the pattern of shires was extended outwards as the rule of the kings of Wessex expanded. The creation of shires across the midlands occurred during the tenth century, though there remain substantial uncertainties over how and when this all happened.[14] Domesday Book shows that by 1086 there were shires across most of England, except for the areas that later became Rutland and Lancashire, which were attached to other shires nearby, and except for the areas that later became the northern shires of Westmorland, Cumberland, Northumberland and County Durham, which may not even have been in England.[15] Shires were royal creations, and were run in the interests of kings. There were royal agents and representatives who co-ordinated them and ran them for the kings. Originally, these agents were the ealdormen, but in the later tenth century they were displaced by sheriffs, and then replaced by the earls, who kept a prominent role in the shires.[16]

Shires seem in origin to have been principally military in function, though their activities expanded substantially over time.[17] Once kings created a taxation

12 Hundreds and wapentakes were effectively synonymous, though the term hundred was used in much of the south, the west and the midlands, while wapentake was used in areas in the north and east where Scandinavian influence was strongest. For simplicity's sake the term hundred will be used throughout this book, though it should be understood that wapentakes are implicitly included.

13 Hudson, *Oxford History*, 48–50, 276–80.

14 Molyneaux, *Formation*, 157–64.

15 Molyneaux, *Formation*, 155–7.

16 Molyneaux, *Formation*, 172–3.

17 The most important recent work on this is Molyneaux, *Formation*, 165–72.

system in the form of geld, this was managed through the shires.[18] In terms of organisation, shires came to have courts, which were attended by the leaders of the districts over which they ruled.[19] These seem not to have transacted as much business as the hundreds, for they met less often and had a much more restricted attendance.[20] There are instances of disputes being dealt with in shire courts, but they are not numerous. Also, testimony of the shires is much less common than testimony of the hundreds in Domesday Book.[21] Yet they had a significant role in that the shires and their courts had claims over the hundreds, even to the extent that they could rearrange them.[22] Shires had some kind of responsibility over the hundreds, and were accountable for decisions and allocations within their territories. In these cases, shires were brought together, so that others would make a judgement over one.[23]

Shires were in origin royal and were run by royal representatives, and this remained the case for most shires and counties into the twelfth century and beyond. Yet, after the Norman Conquest, some shires passed into the hands of great lords, who took over the interests that had belonged to kings. This can be seen especially clearly in the case of Cheshire, where the dominance of the earls of Chester lasted much longer than the control of other lords elsewhere.[24] In Cheshire, the earls were lords of all the land in the shire, except those lands that belonged to the church and which were held directly from the king, and so

18 For an overview of geld see H. R. Loyn, *The Governance of Anglo-Saxon England, 500–1087* (London, 1984), 119–23; on its later history Judith A. Green, 'The Last Century of Danegeld', *English Historical Review* 96 (1981) 241–58; Judith A. Green, *The Government of England under Henry I* (Cambridge, 1986), 69–75.

19 Molyneaux, *Formation*, 165–71.

20 Robert C. Palmer, *The County Courts of Medieval England, 1150–1350* (Princeton, 1982), 3–8.

21 Fleming, *Domesday Book*, p. 541; note the disproportion in the size of the index entries for the testimony of the shires as opposed to the testimony of the hundreds.

22 *Leges Edwardi Confessoris*, 13–13.1.

23 *Leges Henrici Primi*, 31.1.

24 On Cheshire see C. P. Lewis, 'The Formation of the Honor of Chester, 1066–1100', *The Earldom of Chester and its Charters: A Tribute to Geoffrey Barraclough*, ed. A. T. Thacker, *Journal of the Chester Archaeological Society* 71 (1991), 37–68; David Crouch, 'The Administration of the Norman Earldom', in *The Earldom of Chester and its Charters*, ed. A. T. Thacker, *A Tribute to Geoffrey Barraclough, Journal of the Chester Archaeological Society* 71 (1991), 69–95; Graeme J. White, *The Magna Carta of Cheshire* (Chester, 2015), 7–15. More broadly see W. E. Wightman, 'The Palatine Earldom of William fitz Osbern in Gloucestershire and Worcestershire (1066–1071)', *English Historical Review* 77 (1962), 6–17; Jean Scammell, 'The Origins and Limitations of the Liberty of Durham', *English Historical Review* 81 (1966), 449–73; James W. Alexander, 'New Evidence on the Palatinate of Chester', *English Historical Review* 85 (1970), 715–29; James W. Alexander, 'The Alleged Palatinates of Norman England', *Speculum* 56 (1981), 17–27.

held claims over all who held land therein. The earls also controlled the shire court, which became something that expressed the lordship of the earls; its attendees were overwhelmingly the dependents of the earls, and the court came to include dependents of the earls who held lands outside Cheshire. Moreover, the sheriffs and other functionaries were appointed by the earls, and carried out their commands rather than those of the kings. At the same time, other royal representatives were excluded from influence or control in Cheshire. The overall effect was to make Cheshire a place where kings could not work through their usual channels, but had to work through the earls, who might act as their intermediaries. Cheshire was the longest-lasting such arrangement, but there were other cases where earls attained to positions of great local dominance, in Shropshire and Herefordshire in the decades after the Conquest,[25] and perhaps more generally in Stephen's reign.[26] Shires have not been covered at length in this book, for few lords had the wealth and networks to control a whole one.

### *The hundred*[27]

The comments in the laws mean that it is possible to describe how the hundred should have worked, at least in the eyes of those behind the laws and, presumably, those who used it.[28] The hundred was described most fully in the source known as the Hundred Ordinance, or 1 Edgar. This shows that the hundred was viewed as a territory, and also as a community. The idea was that all should take part in the proceedings of the hundred, even if the exact meaning of that is not defined; it could be taken to mean all, or merely those to whom the document might have been addressed, potentially the leaders of the hundred only. Those who attended the hundred were the ones who made decisions within it; as the Hundred Ordinance observed, each was to do justice to others, not hear justice handed down by someone else. Thus, the hundred seems a relatively flat

25 Chris Lewis, 'Herefordshire under William I', *Anglo-Norman Studies* VII (1985), 195–213; also J. F. A. Mason, 'Roger de Montgomery and His Sons (1067–1102)', *Transactions of the Royal Historical Society* fifth series 13 (1963), 1–28; J. F. A. Mason, 'The Norman Earls of Shrewsbury', *Transactions of the Shropshire Archaeological Society* 57 (1964 for 1962–3) 152–61; J. F. A. Mason, 'The Officers and Clerks of the Norman Earls of Shrewsbury', *Transactions of the Shropshire Archaeological Society* 56 (1961) 244–57.

26 R. H. C. Davis, *King Stephen, 1135–1154* (third edition, London, 1990), Appendix 1: Earls and Earldoms.

27 Hudson, *Oxford History*, 50–5, 280–4.

28 On this see Molyneaux, *Formation*, 141–55; also H. R. Loyn, 'The Hundred in England in the Tenth and Early Eleventh Centuries', in *British Government and Administration: Studies Presented to S. B. Chrimes*, ed. H. Hearder and H. R. Loyn (Cardiff, 1974), 1–15.

structure. There was someone called the hundredman or the hundred alderman,[29] who had a kind of leadership role but did not dictate how decisions were made. The role of the hundredman was to organise the operations of the hundred, to bring forward matters that the hundred should look at. Thus, the hundredman was meant to receive notifications about suspicious conduct, where someone had purchased goods without the usual processes. Perhaps, this aspect of the role of the hundredman might be likened to someone who set the agenda for a meeting.

The status of the hundred is fundamentally unclear. On the one hand, hundreds were created at the behest of kings in the tenth century, and the laws show that hundreds were intended as the principal mechanism for carrying out royal fulminations against theft and other matters. Thus, Patrick Wormald asserted that they were essentially royal in nature, and part of a developed system of royal government, in which kings created and owned the hundreds.[30] Yet, on the other hand, they cannot be regarded as simply a vehicle for the imposition of the authority of kings. Earlier arrangements for maintaining order had assigned a powerful role to the king's reeves who ran the king's lands, yet they did not rule the hundreds.[31] Recently, Lambert has characterised the hundreds as expressions of local, customary ideas about law, and as essentially communal rather than royal in nature.[32] The contrast between these two positions probably looks greater than it might have been in lived experience. Certainly, kings did not claim that the hundreds were theirs before the twelfth century,[33] but were content to leave them to do much of their business, and to use them to put their priorities into existence. Yet, at the same time, hundreds were not jealous defenders of their status against the impositions of kings, at least, so far as can be seen. The contrast between the positions of Wormald and Lambert is more one of chronology, and it is one that goes to the heart of this book. Kings only came to claim the ownership of hundreds when there was an alternative. Earlier, they could be allowed to function on their own, without any need for kings to claim them for themselves.

The functions carried out by hundreds were various, and it is likely that they developed substantially across the eleventh and twelfth centuries. The tenth-century evidence shows that hundreds were expected to deal with multiple themes in parallel. The injunction that all in the hundred should do justice to others could be interpreted to suggest that the hundred held a very broad competence to deal with all kinds of disputes and disturbances in which someone was looked upon

29 This figure should not be confused with the later hundred bailiff; see Lambert, *Law and Order*, 247–8.

30 Patrick Wormald, 'Charters, Law and the Settlement of Disputes in Anglo-Saxon England', rpt in his *Legal Culture in the Early Medieval West: Law as Text, Image and Experience* (London, 1999), 289–311, at 304–6.

31 Lambert, *Law and Order*, 246–7.

32 Lambert, *Law and Order*, 246–50.

33 See Chapter 6 below.

by others as the author of some injustice. It could include such matters as the arbitration of private disputes, though that is essentially conjectural; such matters do not show up in the sources as a key and consistent function of the hundreds. More clearly documented is the way in which hundreds were expected to take charge of processes for dealing with theft and related matters. Hundreds were expected to organise the pursuit of thieves; they were expected to carry out the processes for dealing with thieves and those of ill-repute prescribed in the laws;[34] they were expected to oversee surety groups; and they were expected to take charge of the processes involved in warranty, whereby witnesses saw to the transfer of claims between individuals.

Hundreds had a substantial role in policing society. They oversaw arrangements for ensuring they all were in surety,[35] and so bound into networks of lordship which could bring some measure of control over individuals. Hundreds also carried out the pursuit of thieves, including into other hundreds,[36] and could punish those who refused to take part in the work of pursuing and apprehending thieves.[37] Most of the business of ensuring order in society was carried out or overseen within the hundred.

The laws shows that warranty should be provided for such items as livestock,[38] but it is likely that this role in overseeing sales and ownership either went much further, or that it expanded considerably over time. There is little evidence at all for the way in which hundreds discharged their duties in warranty in relation to livestock; there are only the references to this in the laws, and the theft charms as evidence that the purloining of cattle was a matter of some concern.[39] Yet hundreds' testimony about ownership is abundantly documented in one source, making this the most richly documented activity of the hundreds in the eleventh century; Domesday Book shows that hundreds were well-informed about land and lordship, which implies that these kinds of knowledge were gathered by them.[40] Oversight over land and lordship is not mentioned in the laws, but could

34 There are very many references to theft in the laws; for instance, 3 Edmund 4; 1 Edgar 2; 3 Edgar 6.2, 7.3; 4 Edgar 2.2, 11; 1 Æthelred 1.2, 1.9a; 2 Æthelred 6.2, 7, 9.3; 3 Æthelred 4; 5 Æthelred 25; 6 Æthelred 28.2, 32; 8 Æthelred 27; 1 Cnut 5.3; 2 Cnut 4.2, 8, 21, 26–26.1, 29, 30.1, 30.9, 64, 76, 82; and on bad reputation see 3 Edgar 7; 1 Æthelred 1.1; 3 Æthelred 3.2, 4; 2 Cnut 22, 25, 30.

35 3 Edgar 6; 4 Edgar 3; 1 Æthelred 1, 4; 2 Cnut 20.

36 1 Edgar 2, 5.

37 3 Edgar 7.2; 2 Cnut 25.2.

38 Lambert, *Law and Order*, 270–3, 326–9.

39 Andrew Rabin, 'Ritual Magic or Legal Performance? Reconsidering an Old English Charm against Theft', in *English Law before Magna Carta: Felix Liebermann and* Die Gesetze der Angelsachsen, ed. Stefan Jurasinski, Lisi Oliver and Andrew Rabin (Leiden and Boston, 2010), 177–95.

40 The importance of the testimony of hundreds can be seen in Fleming, *Domesday Book*, p. 541.

be regarded as a logical extension of the instructions to oversee the ownership of livestock. Even though written records were clearly being used in shires and hundreds in the eleventh century,[41] the recollection and adjudication of claims to land was central to the business of the hundreds by the later eleventh century, and the bearing of testimony over claims may have been the dominant business of the hundreds.

## Approaches to the History of Courts

The idea that courts proliferated across the eleventh and twelfth centuries has been accepted widely in the historiography.[42] There has been a general consensus in scholarship from the end of the nineteenth century onwards that ecclesiastical courts and lordly courts developed across the eleventh and twelfth centuries, and there has been no thorough challenge to this position. Indeed, it is hard to see that a credible case could be made against it, given how completely it reflects the pattern of the evidence. If the existence of these courts and their development and proliferation has been taken for granted, there has been much less concern about how these courts came into being. There has been recognition that the appearance of ecclesiastical courts is a problem that deserves attention, and it has been stimulated by the survival of William the Conqueror's proclamation which subtracted ecclesiastical business from the hundred.[43] In contrast, there has been much less interest in how lordly courts appeared and developed, and what has appeared in print is mostly theory rather than evidence-based. Thus, the creation of lordly courts is a substantial gap in the historiography.

The question of the existence of private courts in Anglo-Saxon England has been current since the nineteenth century, and in recent decades there has developed a consensus that there were no private courts in that era.[44] The debate among Anglo-Saxonists has mostly been cast in fairly narrow terms, and is principally concerned with how far there might have been franchises, in which kings

41 Sally Harvey, 'Domesday Book and its Predecessors', *English Historical Review* 86 (1971), 753–73.

42 Not all legal historiography is covered here, merely those items that confront questions around courts and jurisdiction in the eleventh and twelfth centuries.

43 Colin Morris, 'William I and the Church Courts', *English Historical Review* 82 (1967), 449–63 and *Councils and Synods with other Documents relating to the English Church: Part 1, AD 871–1204* ed. D. Whitelock, M. Brett and C. N. L. Brooke (2 vols, Oxford, 1981), i/2, 620–4.

44 See T. B. Lambert, 'Royal Protections and Private Justice: A Reassessment of Cnut's "Reserved Pleas"', in *English Law before Magna Carta: Felix Liebermann and* Die Gesetze der Angelsachsen, ed. Stefan Jurasinski, Lisi Oliver and Andrew Rabin (Leiden and Boston, 2010), 157–75, and the historiography and debates cited therein.

granted that others could hold and manage courts or other regalities. This debate has not really been about the extent to which private courts existed; rather, it has been about the powers, limitations and capabilities of kings and the Anglo-Saxon state, which has been one of the principal frameworks for understanding pre-Conquest England in recent decades.[45] Private courts in this view could be seen as a derogation from and limitation of the power of kings, and as such problematic for the theory of the overwhelming power of the later Anglo-Saxon state.

The assumptions behind this view are somewhat problematic. It draws on the later idea of franchise or regality, in which jurisdiction is seen as something that should originate with kings, and in which any developments therefore had a direct impact on royal power; jurisdiction was thus a zero-sum game. It has recently been shown that kings did not claim control or ownership over all assemblies and courts in Anglo-Saxon England, and that the hundred in particular was an assembly of locals, not a royal court.[46] It is not clear that there was a conception of ownership that could be applied to courts and assemblies; instead, it would be better to think of how lords and others could make claims in courts, through controlling the behaviour of attendees, through the ability to summon them, through managing the business of the court through their agents, and so forth.[47] These kinds of claim can be shown before the Conquest, and in many cases were later turned into claims to own the courts involved. Private courts were the end of this process, not the start of it, and there were many intermediate positions between those two extremes.

There is some consideration of the problem of lordly courts in Pollock and Maitland's influential but dated *History of English Law before the Time of Edward I*.[48] The chapters in which these points are made were those where much of the work seems to have been done by Maitland, and so presumably represent his thought more than that of Pollock.[49] Maitland saw that the origin of lordly courts was a problem, but he confessed to his inability to see a solution to the problem:

> Whether the right to hold a court can only be conferred by the sovereign's grant, or whether it arises from the mere relation between lord and tenants, is a

[45] For instance, James Campbell, 'Observations on English Government from the Tenth to the Twelfth Century', rpt in his *Essays in Anglo-Saxon History* (London, 1986), 155–70.

[46] Lambert, *Law and Order*, 148.

[47] Lambert, *Law and Order*, 127.

[48] Frederick Pollock and Frederic Maitland, *The History of English Law Before the Time of Edward I* (second edition, Cambridge, 1898).

[49] Patrick Wormald, 'Maitland and Anglo-Saxon Law: Beyond Domesday Book', in *The History of English Law: Centenary Essays on 'Pollock and Maitland'*, ed. John Hudson, *Proceedings of the British Academy* 89 (1996), 1–20, at 2.

> question to which we get no certain answer for a long time after the conquest of England, whether we ask it of England or of Normandy.[50]

Maitland's perplexity is perhaps understandable. Any answer to this problem must depend on a mass of diverse and scattered sources, especially charters, rather than on the rolls of the royal courts which formed the real heart of Maitland's work. When Maitland worked, much less of this material was available in print than can now be found in published form; moreover, much of it was still in private hands, for there were as yet no local record offices. There is also the sense that these questions were not central to Maitland's mission. He was really concerned with the law of the thirteenth century, when there was a common law of the kingdom of England, and when there were central records that reflected activities within that legal framework. Maitland is generally much briefer and less specific about the earlier twelfth century than he was about the thirteenth.[51]

Elsewhere, Maitland took categories and ideas from the thirteenth century and applied them to earlier ones.[52] This fitted well with the scope of his book, where the focus lay on that epoch. Thus, his analysis of the jurisdictions of lords takes their later status as a norm, and uses their later typology as a means of explaining their origins:

> According to the legal theory of the thirteenth century seigniorial jurisdiction has two roots – (1) the delegation of royal powers, (2) the relation between lord and tenants. Jurisdictional rights are divided into two classes. On the one hand, there are the franchises and regalities (*libertates*, *regalia*) which, at least according to the opinion of the king's lawyers, can only exist in the hands of a subject by virtue of a grant from the crown. On the other hand, there is jurisdiction involved in the mere ownership of a manor or in the mere fact of having tenants; we may briefly characterise it as being of a civil, non-criminal kind.[53]

50 Frederick Pollock and Frederic Maitland, *The History of English Law Before the Time of Edward I* (second edition, Cambridge, 1898), i. 73; Frederic W. Maitland, *Domesday Book and Beyond: Three Essays in the Early History of England* (revised edition with an introduction by Edward Miller, London, 1960), 110–14. For a critique of Maitland's position see T. B. Lambert, 'Royal Protections and Private Justice: A Reassessment of Cnut's "Reserved Pleas"', in *English Law before Magna Carta: Felix Liebermann and* Die Gesetze der Angelsachsen, ed. Stefan Jurasinski, Lisi Oliver and Andrew Rabin (Leiden and Boston, 2010), 157–75.

51 Though his thoughts on the eleventh century and earlier can be found in Frederic W. Maitland, *Domesday Book and Beyond: Three Essays in the Early History of England* (revised edition with an introduction by Edward Miller, London, 1960), 110–39, 307–45.

52 This regressive method is also seen in Frederic W. Maitland, *Domesday Book and Beyond: Three Essays in the Early History of England* (revised edition with an introduction by Edward Miller, London, 1960).

53 Frederick Pollock and Frederic Maitland, *The History of English Law Before the Time of Edward I* (second edition, Cambridge, 1898), i. 571–2; Frederic W. Maitland,

Maitland later observed that in the thirteenth century a lord's jurisdiction over his dependents by itself allowed a lord to hold a court, regardless of the position of the king.[54] Though this legal doctrine formed the basis for thinking about lordly courts at that later date, it has considerable problems as an account for their origin. Lords and tenants or dependents had been linked together in all kinds of ways into the distant past, long before the thirteenth century. Yet, only at certain points in time did lords feel the need to create courts as arenas for dealing with matters arising among their tenants or dependents. More fundamentally, when a lord created a court, how did this affect other kinds of legal assembly? Was the business later done in the lords' court subtracted from another court, or was it simply not done at all before? Was the business previously done in an extra-legal setting? If so, why did lords feel the need to use courts to discharge it? During the twelfth century, lords' courts can be seen carrying out functions concerning the ownership of land, including witnessing the transfer of land and adjudicating disputes. These functions seem earlier to have been carried out within the hundreds. Maitland did not engage with these kinds of question, and was content to use the legal theory of the thirteenth century without any attempt to apply it to the circumstances of the eleventh and twelfth centuries. There is a gap here. It is an understandable gap because the problems between which it lies were not central to Maitland's project, and would have distracted from it.

Other scholars who have looked at the problems of lordly courts have followed Maitland in examining how they worked and how they interacted with other courts and sources of authority; none has really addressed the problem of how lords' courts originated. The first scholar to centre a discussion around lords' courts was Sir Frank Stenton, in his 1929 Ford Lectures, published as *The First Century of English Feudalism*.[55] Like Maitland, he did not attempt to explain how lords' courts originated, and simply observed that lords' courts were 'the obscurest institution in Anglo-Norman history'.[56] He began the following discussion of their existence with a reference from the *Leges Henrici Primi*, which noted that lords could summon their dependents to their court. From there, he went on to cite charters from the middle of the twelfth century which showed lords and their dependents transacting business in lords' courts.[57] Stenton

*Domesday Book and Beyond: Three Essays in the Early History of England* (revised edition with an introduction by Edward Miller, London, 1960), 110–14 shows that he saw problems with this view.

54 Frederick Pollock and Frederic Maitland, *The History of English Law Before the Time of Edward I* (second edition, Cambridge, 1898), i. 584–5.

55 Sir Frank Stenton, *The First Century of English Feudalism 1066–1166: The Ford Lectures Delivered in the University of Oxford 1929* (second edition, Oxford, 1961).

56 Sir Frank Stenton, *The First Century of English Feudalism 1066–1166: The Ford Lectures Delivered in the University of Oxford 1929* (second edition, Oxford, 1961), 42.

57 Sir Frank Stenton, *The First Century of English Feudalism 1066–1166: The Ford*

examined the operation of lords' courts, especially honorial courts, during the middle and later twelfth century, but he did not look into their origins at all. There is not even a clear theory about how he thought they might have originated, or when he thought they might have originated, beyond a reference that indicated that he thought they operated during the reigns of the Conqueror and his sons.[58]

Much the same can be said of the other scholar who focussed on the work and significance of lords' courts, S. F. C. Milsom, in his *The Legal Framework of English Feudalism*.[59] This work argues that lords' courts remained of great importance even after Henry II's writs and assizes were devised, and that these developments were designed to support lordly courts, not supplant them. His view was that Henry's legal innovations were designed to deal with procedural problems that arose in lordly courts, especially their difficulties in adjudicating between competing claims to the same piece of land in the aftermath of the peace settlement of 1153–4.[60] Milsom offers a detailed and elaborate model for how lordly courts could have worked in the later twelfth century, but offered no opinion whatsoever about the ways that these courts may have originated. The origin of lords' courts was not central to his arguments, even though it had an obvious relevance, and so as a problem it lay outside the bounds of his book.

Some more recent analysis has gone beyond this inherited incuriousity about the origin of lords' courts. John Hudson recognised that the early history of lords' courts should not be regarded as something that is entirely unknowable, and gathered materials that shed some light on the question in relation to the Anglo-Saxon era. He emphasised the absence of references to lordly courts in the entire body of laws from Anglo-Saxon England, and the lack of mentions of them in the narratives of pleas from the same era.[61] Yet he also noted the slipperiness of some of the evidence, and how it often omitted to classify pleas in terms that would serve the interests of historians. For instance, there was a plea held at Fen Ditton at some point later in the tenth century which did not note what kind of court was involved.[62] These references are essentially unclassifiable; the writer did not note that it was a hundred or a shire meeting, and it is not at all clear what words might have been used to refer to a lordly court. Beyond that, he notes that there were many royal grants to lords, which gave them some control over the dealings of their dependents in hundreds and shires, though these seem to have been

*Lectures Delivered in the University of Oxford 1929* (second edition, Oxford, 1961), 44.

58 Sir Frank Stenton, *The First Century of English Feudalism 1066–1166: The Ford Lectures Delivered in the University of Oxford 1929* (second edition, Oxford, 1961), 45.

59 S. F. C. Milsom, *The Legal Framework of English Feudalism* (Cambridge, 1976).

60 S. F. C. Milsom, *The Legal Framework of English Feudalism* (Cambridge, 1976), chapter 1.

61 Hudson, *Oxford History*, 56.

62 Hudson, *Oxford History*, 57.

exercised within those arenas.[63] Post-Conquest, Hudson sets out the traditional typology of honour courts, manorial courts and franchises, and showed that these could all be traced into the very early twelfth century.[64]

The diffidence of historians in approaching this problem is in many ways understandable; there is no single source that might be used to approach these questions about lords' courts, and sometimes it is not obvious that there are any sources at all. This problem can only be assessed through the use of a wide range of sources, ranging across many different genres; yet the real heart of this study can be found in the charters that are discussed in detail across Chapters 3 to 7 in particular. This enterprise is based on the availability of a range of editions and studies which had not been produced in the times of Maitland, Stenton and even Milsom. As noted above, this study sets out a case that the origins of lordly courts can be traced, and that their origins lay in the way in which lords took over courts, or subtracted business from the communal hundred courts. The origin of these courts, usually called *halimota*, explains much about their roles and competence in the early and middle twelfth century.

## Sources for Law, Assemblies and Courts in England *c.* 1000 to *c.* 1150

The debate over courts and law is inevitably structured by its sources, but these do not concern only matters that could be categorised as criminal or legal. The sources reflect broader changes within society and culture, and mean that some patterns of change tell a story, but not always in relation to the topics covered by this book. Perhaps the biggest single change is about the quantity of sources themselves. Sources from before 1066 are relatively rare, and this has a large effect on how far developments from that era can be traced at all; whereas from the twelfth century sources become much more abundant. Thus, to take only one example, there are just over 1100 surviving royal charters from Anglo-Saxon England in total; this number is easily exceeded by the more than 1500 surviving

63 Hudson, *Oxford History*, 58–62. At p. 60 he states that Edward the Confessor granted eight and a half hundreds in Suffolk to Bury St Edmunds Abbey; Edward actually granted to the abbey soke in the eight and a half hundreds, which is somewhat different. For a fuller discussion of this problem, see Chapter 3 below, which shows that many later franchisal ownership of hundreds originated in similar interests, which were extended and developed over time. Some of this is also covered in John Hudson, *The Formation of the English Common Law: Law and Society in England from King Alfred to Magna Carta* (second edition, Abingdon, 2018), 31–7.

64 Hudson, *Oxford History*, 284–97. There is a shorter version of this in John Hudson, *The Formation of the English Common Law: Law and Society in England from King Alfred to Magna Carta* (second edition, Abingdon, 2018), 31–7.

from the thirty-five years of Henry I's reign, 1100 to 1135.[65] This pattern applies to most of the sources, though details vary considerably. This does not mean that more happened in the few decades of Henry I's reign than in the centuries preceding; it means that documentation was used more widely, that more of it was produced, and that preservation was more likely. This means that there are challenges in working out what apparent change means; something might be well documented from the 1120s and mentioned once only in the 1020s, but this does not necessarily mean that it happened more often. Nor need this be associated with the Normans and the changes they brought with them. It is part of a much broader European development in which schooling and literacy became more common, and in which literate methods of doing business were used more widely.[66] These processes mean that changes in relation to law have to be disentangled from parallel and related, but also distinct, kinds of change in relation to education, literacy and the patterns of documentation related to them.

The pattern of sources does have some marked features of consistency across the period in question. The sources do not reflect all parts of society. Kings in particular are very prominent in the sources, and their authority was invoked widely in all kinds of legal business. Many of these occurrences reflect occasions where kings tried to influence or control events, and did so in accordance with how they perceived their own interests. Yet in some cases the authority of kings is a cloak, used by other participants in pursuit of their own interests. Royal authority was set up through the oaths of loyalty that much of the population had to offer to kings; it was supported also through the validation given by the church and the peculiar religious status of the king as God's anointed. Thus, it was hard to argue against a king or to deny the legitimacy of arrangements that a king had made. This attribute of kingship meant that many participants in the law borrowed royal authority in their own interests.[67] The most blatant demonstrations of this are the numerous forged charters that survive in the names of kings, which far outnumber forged charters in the names of others; there are some in the names of popes, archbishops and bishops,[68] but relatively few in the names of other

65 These numbers are taken from the Electronic Sawyer database of Anglo-Saxon charters (http://www.esawyer.org.uk/about/index.html) and the volumes of *Regesta*: Bates, *Regesta*; *Regesta*, i.–iii.

66 M. T. Clanchy, *From Memory to Written Record: England, 1066–1307* (third edition, Chichester, 2013), chapter 2.

67 For example, note how the monks of Battle argued that their court was actually the king's court, so that they could control an important plea; see Chapter 5 below.

68 Episcopal and archiepiscopal forgeries often have a somewhat different aim; they were prepared by chapters as a means of undermining the position of later bishops. They are essentially internal documents for the micropolitics of great churches. On this see Everett U. Crosby, *Bishop and Chapter in Twelfth-Century England: A Study of the 'Mensa Episcopalis'* (Cambridge, 1994).

individuals. The overall effect is that kings' voices, already loud and prominent, seem amplified by the way that others tried to use the authority of kings.

*Laws and legal texts*

The voice of kings is at its most clear and insistent in the laws.[69] These survive in some quantities from the tenth and eleventh centuries, and they mostly seem to consist of messages sent from kings to their subjects; some are even in the form of a letter. The pattern is not entirely consistent, for one item conventionally included among the royal laws is actually a letter sent from a group of subjects to the king, explaining how they had reacted to the instructions in a letter he had sent to them;[70] others contain little internal evidence that securely links them to particular kings, even though the attribution may be plausible.[71] Some are comprehensive, ambitious works, while others are short and concern a limited range of business.[72] The significance of the laws has been much debated. One compelling argument holds that their importance lies in the act of making them; that law-making was understood as an act of kingship, building on the legislative role of Roman emperors, and so the mere fact of making law was an enhancement and validation of the position of anyone who did so.[73] The implication of this is that the content of the laws is not the most important element, and that they need not be read as responses to specific problems, or as attempts to improve the law; indeed, laws need not, on this reading, have an especially strong link to the actual practice of law. This may be the case for some laws, but many include points which indicate that they were drawn up in response to perceived problems. For instance, the tenth-century code 2 Edmund includes a preface in which the king and his advisers state that he had been concerned at the incidents of violence that had occurred, and that this concern gave rise to the provisions, even though theft was, in the king's understanding, less of a problem at the time.[74] It is entirely plausible that there were feedback loops, that there were mechanisms whereby problems could be reported to the king. The content of the laws, moreover, matches recorded practice rather well; the framework of hundreds was real, and the conduct of pleas was not incompatible with the evidence of the laws. Given the king's theoretical responsibility for

[69] On these see Wormald, *Making of English Law*; Hudson, *Oxford History*, 867–73.

[70] 3 Æthelstan.

[71] For instance, 1 Edgar.

[72] The longest and most wide-ranging is 1–2 Cnut.

[73] Patrick Wormald, '*Lex Scripta* and *Verbum Regis*: Legislation and Germanic Kingship from Euric to Cnut', rpt in his *Legal Culture in the Early Medieval West: Law as Text, Image and Experience* (London, 1999), 1–43; Wormald, *Making of English Law*, chapter 6.

[74] 2 Edmund 1 and 5.

and interest in the management of the law, he would form the obvious target for the expression of concerns and worries. Kings did not act alone in making these laws. Many contain references to the work of advisers and of those who attended the royal court, and it seems that the involvement of others might even have added to the authority of the law when circulated.[75] It might be that the role of advisers was especially important, for they could have been in a position to gather information and take it to the king, if they had lands and other interests that meant that they engaged with the law at a local level. Also, advisers were probably responsible for composing the laws themselves.[76]

Though the laws mostly originated with kings, and may have been written to demonstrate kingship, they did not remain in that setting. They were addressed to the king's subjects, often directly as 'you' when setting out expectations and instructions. Like later proclamations, they were probably circulated to shires and maybe to hundreds, where they could be made known to the leaders of local society. It seems that the texts as transmitted descend from copies which were circulated rather than from any authoritative version kept in a central repository. The writers of laws assumed that locals would have had access to older texts, because some include references to earlier laws.[77] Also, some acquired companion pieces. These survive in some quantity and are hard to date, but they consist of short statements on particular matters, and are often appended to royal laws.[78] They are in Old English rather than Latin, though some were later translated into Latin with the laws to which they were appended. Where royal laws were often cast as first-person commands, these items take a less personal and less authoritative form in most cases. There is very little evidence as to where and by whom many of these were added, but some should be attributed to Archbishop Wulfstan of York.[79] Their relationship to the rest of the laws is uncertain. Often they are concerned with practical matters such as the level at which compensation payments might be set, and none have the range and ambition of the larger legal texts. They do not set out their legal basis. It can be assumed that they might represent custom, and they summarise how business was actually done in local courts; yet, if so, it is not clear why there was any need to write down the information contained in them, if it truly represented any kind of local consensus. The real importance of these anonymous additions to and enhancements of the body of laws is that they show that even at an early date

[75] *The Chronicle of Battle Abbey*, ed. Eleanor Searle (Oxford, 1980), 142–5, states that Henry I made some rules about wreck, but that these died with him because they did not have the wider support of the elite.

[76] Wormald, *Making of English Law*, 449–65.

[77] For instance, 4 Edgar 1.4.

[78] On these see Wormald, *Making of English Law*, 366–97.

[79] Wormald, *Making of English Law*, 389–97.

there was reflection on the texts that were available, and attempts to fill gaps, to clarify, or to provide contextual data.

The production of Anglo-Saxon laws stopped quite suddenly in Cnut's reign. The Norman kings resumed the tradition of royal decrees that were meant to change the way that business was transacted in the law, but did so with short and specific texts that did not range as widely as their Anglo-Saxon predecessors. Even the shortest Anglo-Saxon royal texts rarely match the Norman ones for brevity. What is new from the later eleventh century is that ambitious texts were produced that do not seem to owe much to direct royal authority. These texts are well-known – the *Decem Articuli*, the *Instituta Cnuti*, *Quadripartitus*, the *Leges Henrici Primi*, the *Leges Edwardi Confessoris* – and all built on older texts but adapted them in various ways. Some presented translations of Old English texts into Latin; some enhanced older texts with new material; and some were entirely new productions that set out how the authors understood the law and custom of their own day. All presented law in an historical context, as something that went back to the past and which could best be understood in relation to it.

The laws and other legal texts present various problems of interpretation. The most significant and consistent ones concern the relationship between them and actual legal practice, for this question has been raised repeatedly over recent decades. The debate rests largely on the perception that legal texts are prescriptive, and that their aim was to describe how the writer thought the law should be, not how it actually was. This view of the laws was contrasted with narratives of legal proceedings, which were characterised as descriptive and therefore more true.[80] In this view, laws and legal texts presented an idealised view of the law, in which practices were described in terms that were more rational and consistent than they actually were. Thus, many historians from the 1970s onwards approached laws and legal texts with an attitude of scepticism, and were open to the idea that there was a disjunction between the reality and theory of law.

This is probably not the most helpful framework for approaching these kinds of texts. First, narratives of actual legal cases cannot be assumed to be detached and dispassionate depictions of fact. Written by participants, often the winners, they are usually incomplete and often present aspirations as much as reality, and focus on positives rather than negatives. They are prime instances of describing the world as it should be, not as it was. This is particularly obvious where parallel

[80] For example, Wendy Davies and Paul Fouracre, 'Introduction', in *The Settlement of Disputes in Early Medieval Europe*, ed. Wendy Davies and Paul Fouracre (Cambridge, 1986), 1–5, at 3; see also Patrick Wormald, 'Charters, Law and the Settlement of Disputes in Anglo-Saxon England', rpt in his *Legal Culture in the Early Medieval West: Law as Text, Image and Experience* (London, 1999), 289–311; Patrick Wormald, '*Lex Scripta* and *Verbum Regis*: Legislation and Germanic Kingship from Euric to Cnut', rpt in his *Legal Culture in the Early Medieval West: Law as Text, Image and Experience* (London, 1999), 1–43; Hudson, *Oxford History*, 867–73.

and competing narratives survive from different participants in the same case. For example, the dispute between the monks of Worcester and the monks of Evesham over lands and claims in Worcestershire generated separate accounts which differ substantially, even though the same events were described.[81] They diverge in their accounts of how the dispute started, who all the participants were, and even some of the outcomes. These are not simple factual narratives; they say more about the self-perceptions, jealousies and rivalries of the people who gathered around those two great churches than about the technicalities of pleading these cases. Second, scepticism about the value of laws and other legal texts is sometimes based around a set of priorities as to what a history of the law should be. It tends to emphasise legal strategies and tactics, and how participants in disputes might manoeuvre to gain advantage, because these matters are often recorded quite well in the surviving sources, and because this fits well with common perceptions as to what law is.[82] Yet, this is also quite a limited view of law. Law was not just something done in court by specialists; as noted above, it was a venture that involved the whole of society, and was not just about settling disputes. It was about setting rules for behaviour, and ideas which might shape behaviour, and so reached out into society to include conversations about law, and discussion and debate. These conversations can be seen in occasional references in these legal texts, in places where someone's reputation in law was noted, or where hypothetical cases seem to have been discussed. The legal texts are essential for the study of law conceived in this broader sense. These texts were copied and circulated quite widely, and therefore were presumably read widely as well, so that they had a stronger role than any other texts in forming the ideas that people used about the law, and the words that they chose to use. This is in contrast to the sources for actual disputes, which were usually chronicles or charters and as such essentially private documents, limited in circulation and influence to those directly connected to them. The laws and related legal texts were much more important in forming ideas and approaches, and in reflecting how people might have thought about and engaged with the law.

### *Narratives of legal proceedings*

The numerous narratives of legal activity form perhaps the most vivid of the sources for law between the tenth and twelfth centuries.[83] Though they vary considerably, some are quite detailed and dramatic accounts of what happened in court, and bear the stamp of verisimilitude. They have considerable surface attractions for those who want to find out what actually happened in courts in

[81] Van Caenegem, *Lawsuits*, no. 15.

[82] Massimo Vallerani, *Medieval Public Justice*, translated by Sarah Rubin Blanshei (Washington, 2012), esp. chapter 2.

[83] For an overview see Hudson, *Oxford History*, 877–8.

the central middle ages. Yet, the narratives are not a coherent or consistent body of material. There was no routine recording of cases in any form until the 1190s, and even then the level of recording was limited in scope and detail. This must have a considerable effect on how they should be read. Narratives usually survive embedded in other kinds of source, as part of other works, and though they can and have been excerpted they do not form a single genre, and the intentions behind them are very different.[84] Some are embedded in chronicles and saints' lives, where they have been selected to make a point as part of a bigger and more ambitious work; others are built into charter texts (these will be discussed in the next subsection), where they seem often to be meant as background explanation for the arrangements or dispositions that the charter was meant to put into effect; and, more rarely, they survive as freestanding memoranda, where their purpose seems to be to preserve a record of the legal proceedings themselves. In chronicles and in charters, the material selected for inclusion is that which seemed relevant to the writer or writers as a means of making a bigger point. Court proceedings are often just illustrative examples, and can only be read in relation to the works of which they are a part.

Chronicles and saints' lives provide some of the most detailed and memorable narratives of court cases. They make full use of a range of techniques; reported speech, saintly interventions, dramatic conclusions. Their vividness means that they have been freely used and quoted as illustrative material in modern scholarship. Yet, they present considerable problems as sources, and they cannot be taken as simple descriptions of what actually happened. Many were written as components of chronicles that described the histories of prominent churches, such as the Abingdon or Evesham chronicles. Local interests predominated; the stories as a whole were narrowly focussed, and were concerned principally with the interests of the church in question. These chronicles seem to have been written with the assumption that they would have been read solely or predominantly by individuals who served those churches and were part of their communities, whether monks or canons. They show commitment to and support for the institutional perspectives of their churches. Thus, their causes are always the right ones; their opponents are deluded or evil. The best arguments are always those put up on behalf of the church for which the chronicle was written, and the arguments of their opponents are variously incoherent, deceptive, or merely unconvincing. Saints often act on behalf of the church to defend its interests. Many chronicles were written with a broader focus, but again the aims of the chronicles reflect bigger ideas than the details of the dispute itself. Stories about disputes were meant to reflect the power of kings or the holiness of bishops; these are not simply

[84] For overviews see Patrick Wormald, 'A Handlist of Anglo-Saxon Lawsuits', rpt in his *Legal Culture in the Early Medieval West: Law as Text, Image and Experience* (London, 1999), 253–87 and Van Caenegem, *Lawsuits*.

about law. Many of the narratives of cases in chronicles actually concern land, because that was an important interest of many churches, as well as a vulnerable asset. Where cases based around disputes are covered in these sources, they are usually because they relate to something else; perhaps a saint was thought to have intervened to save someone who had been accused, or the case involved some implication about the claims of the church in question.[85] Overall, such cases are not covered in any great quantity in the chronicles, even if the narratives that are there are some of the more specific and memorable.

Perhaps the simplest narratives are those which were written as narratives of legal work. For instance, there is a much-discussed narrative of legal proceedings at the king's court and at the joint shire courts of Norfolk and Suffolk about 1150, concerning a question about jurisdiction over conspirators.[86] The narrative is a vivid one, and it used reported speech effectively to show how the case proceeded, and how it was resolved. The purpose of this narrative seems to be essentially documentary and legal rather than literary, despite its effectiveness as a piece of writing. It survives in one copy only in Cambridge University Library, ms. Ff. 2. 29, fo. 60r. This is not a chronicle or any single work, but a cartulary of evidences concerning the liberties of the abbey.[87] The narrative is presumably meant as a precedent, as guidance for how such a case might be dealt with in the future, and as a definition of the claims of Bury St Edmunds Abbey itself.

Yet such freestanding narratives were not only produced as internal memoranda. The story of the legal misfortunes of Bricstan of Chatteris,[88] in which he was pursued and imprisoned for concealing treasure, survives through a kind of newsletter which spread the news of his miraculous liberation from imprisonment at the hands of the saints. The explanation of the legal proceedings themselves is clearly meant to convey the sense that Bricstan had been falsely accused and that he had not been able to defend himself effectively, and that he was innocent of the accusation; it seems also meant to emphasise the gravity of his situation, and the extent of the threats that he faced. It may once have been the case that such newsletters about miracles were fairly common; they can be found elsewhere, and sometimes in manuscripts in different places, which might be taken as an indication of circulation.

85 For example, the miracle story in which St Ecgwine was said to have saved a thief apprehended at his shrine; Van Caenegem, *Lawsuits*, no. 14.

86 Van Caenegem, *Lawsuits*, no. 331; H. M. Cam, 'An East Anglian Shire-Moot of Stephen's Reign, 1148–1153', *English Historical Review* 39 (1924), 569–71.

87 Rodney Thomson, *The Archives of the Abbey of Bury St Edmunds*, Suffolk Records Society 21 (1980), 130–1.

88 Van Caenegem, *Lawsuits*, no. 204; full version in Orderic Vitalis, *Historia Ecclesiastica*, ed. Marjorie Chibnall, *The Ecclesiastical History of Orderic Vitalis* (6 volumes, Oxford, 1969–81), iii. 346–60.

### Writs and charters

Charters are among the most cited sources in this book.[89] Charters sometimes include references to and even narratives about actual legal proceedings and disputes,[90] but these are relatively few. In general, charters can be distinguished from other kinds of document because they had elaborate arrangements for authentication. This could involve such matters as the addition of wax seals, rarely metal seals, religious curses on those who defied the provisions made in the document, lists of witnesses who might be called on to vouch for the contents of the document, and marks of approval by the donor, among others. Authentication was necessary because the document itself could be regarded as proof for arrangements that had significant consequences; they could be evidence for interest in land or other matters that were of considerable financial importance. Thus, legal business turns up occasionally in such deeds as explanation for what had happened; that, perhaps, a king had confiscated land from someone because of a deed they had committed, and now chose to regrant it to some other person.[91] In such cases, the narrative explained why older arrangements had been extinguished, and why older claims should be ignored in the future. These stories were context, not the main point of such documents.

Charters are important sources because they were concerned with the documentation of claims, and because many elite persons in medieval England thought about law and courts in terms of claims and ownership. By the twelfth century kings claimed that they had a special right to manage, control and profit from certain kinds of case, known as the king's pleas; many great lords claimed cases that arose on their lands, or concerning the dependents over whom they exercised lordship. How these claims were expressed and organised varied greatly; some tried to gain the fines and compensations that would result from a successful accusation, while others tried to control the whole process by insisting that it must be done through a lord's own court. The form that these took was negotiable in the period under discussion, and there was considerable variation in the way that claims over cases were expressed and managed. In the thirteenth century, there was some measure of standardisation over how comparable claims were managed and described, often using the concept of franchise, but that had not developed fully by the middle of the twelfth century. These were documented using charters.

The commonest form of Anglo-Saxon charter was the diploma or landbook, which went back to the very distant past; yet these generally did not document claims over the management of offences. They were most often concerned with claims over land itself, and while these did include other kinds of claims

89 For an overview see Hudson, *Oxford History*, 873–7.

90 For instance, Van Caenegem, *Lawsuits*, no. 200.

91 For instance, Van Caenegem, *Lawsuits*, no. 317.

over the people on the land, they were often documented less fully.[92] At the end of the tenth century new documentary forms appeared, the writ and writ charter, and these seem to have arisen as a means of managing the relationship between kings and the new grade of officers known as sheriffs, who could act to implement the will of kings locally.[93] These kinds of documents often included references to the management of offences, because kings ordered their servants to, for instance, avoid collecting certain dues from the lands of a favoured landholder. Relatively few such documents survive from before 1066, but they were used in increasing quantities thereafter, partly as an aspect of the general rise in the quantity of documentation seen everywhere from the later eleventh century. Yet writs and writ-charters also became commoner because kings increasingly avoided the diploma form, and came to use writ charters and a new variant, the generally addressed charter, to document claims over land and other matters.[94] Royal documents must usually be handled differently from those of other grantors. They were more numerous, and were produced by professionals, the king's scribes. They were more consistent in form and phrasing than the charters of most other grantors, and paid closer attention to how they related to royal officials. In some cases, they can be read against other sources where they give a consistent impression.

In the thirteenth century, the allocation of such claims was accepted as a matter that was reserved to the discretion and initiative of kings.[95] Yet, this seems not to have been the case earlier. Many of the royal documents from the eleventh century may be recognitions of existing claims by powerful individuals, and were not new grants from kings. The documents instead represent the point at which customary claims, maybe widely accepted ones, were put into written form. The claims themselves were recognised by kings, but did not originate with them, and could still be treated as independent of them. This attitude persisted, and well into the twelfth century such claims could be transferred and traded between individuals, seemingly without any royal input at all.[96] This kind of activity can be seen from the later eleventh century due to the appearance and proliferation of the private deed, which was a variant of the charter that was used by lay individuals of lesser status than kings. In this case, not only do more charters survive, but also a rising proportion of them included grants or recognition of jurisdictional claims, which points to how they were being disseminated more widely.

[92] Alan Cooper, *Bridges, Law and Power in Medieval England, 700–1400* (Woodbridge, 2006), chapter 4.

[93] Molyneaux, *Formation*, 179–82.

[94] Richard Sharpe, 'The Use of Writs in the Eleventh Century', *Anglo-Saxon England* 32 (2003), 247–91.

[95] Donald W. Sutherland, *Quo Warranto Proceedings in the Reign of Edward I, 1278–1294* (Oxford, 1963).

[96] See Chapters 3 and 4 below.

Charters suffer from some of the thematic problems noted above. There is the same difficulty in distinguishing between reality and aspiration in the documents. The arrangements that they describe might look tangible and plausible, but were not necessarily effective. Charters were not always put into force because they might clash with or trample on the interests of others;[97] indeed, contentious claims would be more likely to be expressed in documentation than those that were accepted without objections, because the weakness of the claim made reinforcement attractive. Also, there are very many forged charters. Forged charters, indeed, far outnumber forgeries in other genres of document.[98] The detection of forgery has been a central concern of medievalists for a long time, and there is a considerable commentary on forgeries, and substantial consensus over where they can be identified. Forgeries cannot be discounted as sources because there are important messages contained in them. They show where contention was most likely to arise; they show which claims were seen as valuable enough to be worth defending. They are also important as an index of change, for many forgeries were produced not as shameless and predatory impostures, but as proof of claims that existed but which had been called into contention by changing perceptions of those claims.[99]

*Administrative sources*

Finally, administrative sources are of value.[100] These sources were produced for expediting activities carried out under the aegis of the king, and were often concerned with such matters as finance.[101] Much like the charters, they tend to include information on the management of disputes rather than narratives of pleas in court or how specific cases were handled; where such information does occur – and there are numerous examples in Domesday Book[102] – they are context and background, and explain why arrangements ended up in the form that they were

[97] This is probably the case in relation to the incompatible charters of Geoffrey de Mandeville and the citizens of London; *Regesta*, ii. no. 1645, *Regesta*, iii. nos. 273–7.

[98] For a forged chronicle see David Roffe, 'The Historia Croylandensis: a Plea for Reassessment', *English Historical Review* 110 (1995) 93–108.

[99] Battle Abbey is the clearest example of this; the abbey claimed exemption on the basis of royal grants, but these were indefensible in terms of canon law and papal rights once those were more widely enforced during the twelfth century. On this see *The Chronicle of Battle Abbey*, ed. Eleanor Searle (Oxford, 1980), and Nicholas Vincent, 'King Henry II and the Monks of Battle: The Battle Chronicle Unmasked', in *Belief and Culture in the Middle Ages: Studies Presented to Henry Mayr-Harting*, ed. Richard Gameson and Henrietta Leyser (Oxford, 2001), 264–86.

[100] For an overview see Hudson, *Oxford History*, 878–80.

[101] Some administrative sources were also produced by great churches, but these have not generally been used in this study.

[102] On this see the catalogue of disputes in Fleming, *Domesday Book*.

recorded. The administrative sources are of value because they were produced in response to specific questions and procedures, and because these often differed from the questions that prompted other kinds of sources. Thus, for example, soke is noted in very many charters, but Domesday Book alone includes an estimate of the value of soke in financial terms.[103]

Domesday Book is the most discussed source from the eleventh century, and is rich in evidence for how offences were managed. It records the claims of lords at some length, and can be read against many charters to see what happened on the ground. Domesday Book was planned in relation to a consistent set of questions, yet these were interpreted in rather different ways by different sets of commissioners operating on different circuits, and so Domesday is not uniform in the coverage of and attention given to some matters. Thus, the soke claims of great lords are recorded well in the north-eastern midlands and in Yorkshire, but are rarely given any attention elsewhere.[104] Some places also receive much more detailed treatment than others, and it is not always entirely clear why this should be so. Thus, the description of the bishop of Winchester's great landholding at Taunton in Somerset includes coverage of jurisdictional claims.[105] Domesday Book is thus an essential source, though it is not uniformly useful. Some shires are described in a more summary fashion, with a closer focus on land and geld, and less contextual information.

The sources for this book are thus largely familiar. There is no great new body of sources used here. The significance of the book is more in the way that they have been combined, and how they have been used to answer different questions.

The book is set out in seven chapters. The first describes how lordship worked in England in the decades up to the Norman Conquest, in ways that draw heavily on the existing historiography. The second sets out an interpretation of the aims and priorities of lords, and of how they interacted with their dependents through courts, and of their ambitions in relation to courts. The third builds on that, and shows how lords came to exercise preponderant influence within and then control hundreds in various ways, often without royal authorisation. The fourth shows how lords came to create their own courts for their own men, and how these developed from the hundreds and subtracted functions from them. The fifth starts with the idea that the development of a more complicated pattern of assemblies including lords' courts and ecclesiastical courts meant that there was a need to create a language for jurisdictional debate; this shows how those conversations

[103] Great Domesday Book, fo. 11d: Kent 6.1.

[104] On the making of Domesday Book see Sally Harvey, *Domesday: Book of Judgement* (Oxford, 2014).

[105] Great Domesday Book, fo. 87c: Somerset 2.1–4.

developed and how participants came to win arguments. The sixth looks at how kings dealt with these changes, and how they redefined their claims to maintain influence over the hundreds and their claims within them. The seventh and final chapter looks at how Henry I created justices early in his reign, and how they acted to claim business and penalties so that these were not lost in the new, more complicated landscape of courts.

Overall, these changes amounted to a transformation of the ways in which lordship was organised and managed, and therefore of how lordship worked. The pattern of courts that developed through the later eleventh and earlier twelfth centuries generated new means of doing business, in which lords could manage their dependents without intensive supervision, and without many opportunities for others to interfere. The development of lords' courts was another step in the process of manorialisation, and in redrawing the boundary between free and unfree. Thus, these changes were momentous, and contributed much to the social and political pattern of later medieval England.

# 1

# Lords and their Dependents in Court: The Later Anglo-Saxon Paradigm

This chapter has what is in principle a simple aim: to describe and to review the historiography of recent decades on how lordship was structured in later Anglo-Saxon England, and how this differed from the assumptions and practices about lordship from later eras, especially the twelfth century. The structure and practice of lordship in Anglo-Saxon England are of great importance for understanding how law was carried out and how courts were structured, because lordship was exercised through or in relation to courts, and the claims of lords and their dependents were defined there. Lordship, law and courts acted in concert, where the forms of each had an effect upon the others. Later Anglo-Saxon lordship was complicated, and came in different varieties, in which lordships over any one individual might be owed to different lords. The distinctive quality of later Anglo-Saxon lordship has long been described in the historiography,[1] and that understanding has been expanded in some important and influential studies.[2] Much of that historiography has been based upon the data presented in Domesday Book, and so covers the decades around that work in greatest detail. There have, however, been convincing recent studies that have argued that the tenth and eleventh centuries comprised a period in which the relationships between kings and lords, between royal authority and local power structures, changed markedly, and in which new terms and concepts appeared to describe those relationships.[3] Lordship is thus not a simple matter to describe, for it was a fluid, developing web of relationships. The presentation of thinking of lordship here works backwards. It starts with the reasonably clear pattern that can be detected in Domesday Book, where three distinct kinds of lordship can be discerned. It then moves on to the evidence for lordship that can be seen in the laws, which describe arrangements before those in Domesday Book, and before the posited changes in the relationship between kings and lords of the earlier eleventh century. The laws were not specifically written about lordship,

1 Frederic W. Maitland, *Domesday Book and Beyond: Three Essays in the Early History of England* (revised edition with an introduction by Edward Miller, London, 1960), essay 1, chapter 5; essay 2, chapter 3.

2 Especially Faith, *English Peasantry*, and Baxter, *Earls of Mercia*.

3 Lambert, *Law and Order*, 238–53, 322–42; Molyneaux, *Formation*, 12, 146, 175.

but contain numerous observations, instructions and implications that bear upon it. They contain many points that match the arrangements in Domesday Book, but there are many matters in that later source that are not present in most of the laws, such as soke.

In England before 1066, lordship worked in complex ways, and that complexity was expressed in features that marked off pre-Conquest lordship from that seen in the later twelfth or thirteenth centuries. Most importantly, pre-Conquest lordship was not singular, but multiple; it was broken down into a series of different forms, and so was a distinct experience, for the pattern of bonds between individuals varied considerably. The three kinds of lordship of most importance were commendation, the often strong, personal and fundamental bond between lord and dependent; landlordship, the bond established between lord and dependents over their mutual interest in some parcel of land; and soke, which was a set of claims made by kings from the end of the tenth century, but which some lords kept as a form of exemption or as a specific new grant.[4] Of course, there were other kinds of lordship, such as that exercised by kings, or those claimed by the church, which were usually expressed through obligations to render dues such as churchscot to particular churches or some dues to the king, but for most purposes the three lordships of commendation, landlordship and soke were the most significant in structuring social and economic interactions in England before 1066.

Commendation, landlordship and soke had considerable consequences for the way in which law was managed in pre-Conquest England. To distinguish these from later lordship patterns, they will be referred to here as complex lordship. This formed the social reality and networks within which people lived their lives, and within which they managed their economic activities; and it even helped to structure them. Complex lordship needed careful management, so that its different forms could be kept distinct, and the interests of different lords in the same dependents could be recognised and continued. The importance of lordship meant that the relationship between dependents and their lords was incorporated into legal arrangements; it provided much of the rationale for the allocation of landed and other resources, and it even affected how matters were handled. Disputes could proceed in very different ways depending on how far the lords of those involved might choose to interest themselves in the dispute, or choose to remain outside it. Moreover, lordship is prominent in the legal proclamations of pre-Conquest kings and the descriptions, commentaries and customs that

[4] Lambert, *Law and Order*, 134–5; Faith, *English Peasantry*, esp. chapters. 7, 8 and 10; Baxter, *Earls of Mercia*, 204–15; Stephen Baxter, 'Lordship and Justice in Late Anglo-Saxon England: the Judicial Functions of Soke and Commendation Revisited', in *Early Medieval Studies in Memory of Patrick Wormald*, ed. Stephen Baxter, Catherine Karkov, Janet L. Nelson and David Pelteret (Farnham, 2009), 383–419, at 389–98.

clustered around them, so that it was clearly a topic of considerable concern to those who composed these writings. In any society, legal arrangements were defined by those fundamentals; law had to reflect how societies worked if it had to have credibility and usefulness.

Lordship claims were various and complicated, and seemingly there was a great deal of local variation. Much detail on the exercise of these claims has been lost, and only the most important ones can be seen in the documentation. The Domesday Books, especially Little Domesday Book, include much information about the ways in which lordship worked in 1066 and 1086. The pattern varied greatly in accordance with local politics and property arrangements. In many cases, a lord might exercise all three kinds of lordship in relation to some dependents, but in others lords might have one or two, and so there were individuals who owed obligations of lordship to two or three different lords. Where obligations were owed to two lords of equal status, then presumably both would have been capable of enforcing and defending their claims; but where obligations were owed to lords of markedly different power then it must often have happened that the stronger overrode the weaker, especially where one lord had especially strong influences in local courts.[5]

## Commendation

In principle, much the most visceral form of lordship was commendation.[6] This might be summarised as a kind of personal lordship, based upon a personal submission and oath to the lord from the dependent,[7] and this tied the dependent to the lord as supporter in many important activities. When Byrthnoth's dependents died with him in 991 at Maldon,[8] the ideal of lordship for which they gave their lives was probably commendation, even though some of them

5 Robin Fleming, *Kings and Lords in Conquest England* (Cambridge, 1991), chapter 6; R. P. Abels, 'Sheriffs, Lord-Seeking and the Norman Settlement of the South-East Midlands', *Anglo-Norman Studies* XIX (1997), 19–50; Nicholas Karn, 'Secular Power and its Rewards in Dorset in the Late Eleventh and Early Twelfth Centuries', *Historical Research* 82 (2009), 2–16. For an example, see Van Caenegem, *Lawsuits*, no. 10B, which describes how Abbot Æthelwig of Evesham attracted some of Worcester's dependents to his abbey, and bound them and their lands to it as a prelude to taking over the land; this, however, was Worcester's view of a much-disputed case.

6 Stephen Baxter, 'Lordship and Justice in Late Anglo-Saxon England: the Judicial Functions of Soke and Commendation Revisited', in *Early Medieval Studies in Memory of Patrick Wormald*, ed. Stephen Baxter, Catherine Karkov, Janet L. Nelson and David Pelteret (Farnham, 2009), 383–419, at 391–8.

7 Baxter, *Earls of Mercia*, 204–5.

8 Battle of Maldon, *English Historical Documents,* c. *500–1042*, ed. Dorothy Whitelock (London, 1955), 293–7.

may well have been tied to him by other forms of lordship as well. This form of lordship was so important that betrayal of a lord by commendation was regarded as so grave an act that it was punished by death.[9] Peasants were also caught up in commendation. Little Domesday Book in particular notes that many free peasants or independent farmers in the eastern shires were able to choose their own commendatory relationships, apparently without much limitation. It also shows that many chose to commend themselves to great lords of the region such as Archbishop Stigand.[10] Some significance can be imputed to the way in which the freedom of choice for some was emphasised in Little Domesday; this should probably be taken to indicate that other peasants did not have comparable freedoms, and that their ties were determined by prior arrangements, and even that many were bound to a single lord for all or most of the forms of lordship that bore upon them.

All men were meant to have a lord by commendation.[11] Such men might even offer to undergo ordeals in the place of their lords.[12] In exchange, lords offered their dependents protection, which could be provided within social relations as well as within the courts themselves. As part of the links that bound lords and their dependents together, lords could levy *bot*, one of the kinds of compensation laid down in Anglo-Saxon laws, where men were killed.[13] Lords also had much influence over how their dependents were treated in court. Thus, 1 Æthelred 1.2–12 explains that lords could choose to save their dependents from having to undergo the ordeal, if they stated that the dependent in question had not previously failed in oath or ordeal and provided two supporters of elite status to support this accusation on oath; and it also indicated that lords should advise their dependents, even though it ordained that it was wrong for a lord to advise a dependent to run away. If commendatory lordship was largely a mutual relationship between two individuals, then one of the arenas in which this bond was exercised and made real was that of the public courts, where lordship was often made.[14]

9 Baxter, *Earls of Mercia*, 207; 3 Edgar 7.3, 2 Cnut 57, 64, 77.

10 Fleming, *Domesday Book*, nos. 210, 771, 1208, etc.

11 Various laws indicate that all men should have had a lord: 3 Æthelstan 7, 3 Edgar 6, 4 Edgar 3, 1 Æthelred 1; 2 Æthelstan 2 on special arrangements for the lordless. Most of the laws were prepared before the idea of soke came into common use, and so there are few references to soke within them. The laws refer to lordship and to landlordship, and it seems most probable that lordship refers to the set of ideas later known as commendation. Lambert, *Law and Order*, 273, 321–2.

12 Baxter, *Earls of Mercia*, 207; for some examples see Fleming, *Domesday Book*, nos. 622, 1190, 2164, 2255, 2301, 2326, 2343, 2399, 2403, 2447, 2685, 2723–4.

13 Baxter, *Earls of Mercia*, 208. Stanley Rubin, 'The *Bot*, or Composition in Anglo-Saxon Law: A Reassessment', *The Journal of Legal History* 17 (1996), 144–54.

14 Baxter, *Earls of Mercia*, 205, 2 Æthelstan 2.

## Landlordship

Lordship in later Anglo-Saxon England also arose where someone granted land to a dependent, through the creation of tenurial lordship.[15] This form of lordship was much more akin to the classic theory of the feudal relationship, but differs from that model in that the grant of property was not necessarily assumed to create the kind of intense personal relationship that often arose from commendatory lordship. The relationship could appear to be much more transactional than commendation. It depended, of course, on the grant of property, which could take more than one form. It might be a grant intended for the long term, or it might be for a more restricted term, often a stated number of lifetimes. Usually the relationship was contractual, whereby property was exchanged for a mix of rent and service, which might involve such tasks as delivering messages or helping with the lord's hunt. It involved the acquisition of claims over land without necessarily bringing far-reaching control over the lives of those located upon that land; nonetheless, landlordship and commendation often went together, even though they were conceptually distinct by the later eleventh century.

Landlordship appears in the sources in various forms. There are many grants of land to thegns that established that they could grant out those lands – grants of bookland in particular were a vehicle that could be used to establish networks of landlordship.[16] These often contain little or no specific mention of the people who actually laboured on the land, but their presence should probably be assumed as implicit because, without people, the land would have been of limited utility; and the reference to the abrogation of selected labour services in some cases indicates that some claims over the occupiers of land were implied in the grant itself. The fullest index and description of landlordship is contained in the Domesday Books, which describe this form of lordship more fully than any other. Domesday shows some of the ways in which landlords might use their land as a means of generating income and assets; generally, this shows that landlords were often concerned with generating an inland that they could use for their own direct support.[17]

## Soke

The most difficult of the three kinds of lordship was soke, and it has proven hard to define it. In principle, it meant an obligation to attend, or a claim to manage

15 Baxter, *Earls of Mercia*, 208–10.

16 Frederic W. Maitland, *Domesday Book and Beyond: Three Essays in the Early History of England* (revised edition with an introduction by Edward Miller, London, 1960), 291–306.

17 Faith, *English Peasantry*, 168–79.

and profit from attendance; in essence, what might later be called suit of court.[18] It could also involve a claim to certain kinds of labour service from men within particular areas.[19] In a compelling recent argument, Lambert has set out the idea that soke should best be understood as an historical process, and as something that changed its nature quite markedly over not much more than a century.[20] The term 'soke' first appeared at the end of the tenth century; it did so after kings started introducing sheriffs into localities, for sheriffs demanded that some of the profits of courts should be redirected away from local lordly recipients towards the king.[21] This move was resisted by some lords, and some of those were able to obtain privileges that exempted their dependents and their lands from the demands imposed upon them by these early sheriffs. *Infangthief* probably originated in a similar manner, as a means of giving some exemption to favoured lords from the demands of the king's officers in relation to instances of theft.[22] It is thus rather hard to define exactly what was meant by soke. As a formal grant, it clearly had royal origins, even though it was really a formalisation and recognition of local arrangements that may have been in force for generations.

In principle, soke should have been a universal obligation across England; either it had been allowed to some lord, or it belonged to the king. There seem to have been two areas in which soke could be a cause of ambiguity and problems. The first was simply its content; what actually fell within soke? The laws do not use the language of soke because it was not in place when they were written, or was a novelty; the laws mostly include references to lords, or to landlords, but little on lords who exercised soke alone. So, while it seems that a holder of soke would control the ways in which his dependents would render suit of court, and would receive some at least of the fines and profits that would arise from the activities of his dependents, it is less clear what this involved, especially once

18 Patrick Wormald, 'Law and Justice in the Early English Kingdom: Oswaldslow Revisited', rpt in his *Legal Culture in the Early Medieval West: Law as Text, Image and Experience* (London, 1999), 313–32, at 327. Baxter, *Earls of Mercia*, 210–11. See Alan Cooper, *Bridges, Law and Power in Medieval England, 700–1400* (Woodbridge, 2006), 36–8, who defines the so-called *trimoda necessitas* in terms akin to soke. On suit of court see Hudson, *Oxford History*, 53, 87–8, 554.

19 Baxter, *Earls of Mercia*, 211. Peter Sawyer, 'The Royal *Tun* in Pre-Conquest England', in *Ideal and Reality in Frankish and Anglo-Saxon Society*, ed. Patrick Wormald, Donald Bullough and R. Collins (Oxford, 1983), 273–99, at 280–2; and on the king's reeve see H. Munro Chadwick, *Studies on Anglo-Saxon Institutions* (Cambridge, 1905), 228–39.

20 Lambert, *Law and Order*, 323–5.

21 Soke could be very valuable, according to the only eleventh-century assessment; Great Domesday Book, fo. 11v: Kent 6.1. The entry describing Battle Abbey's manor of Wye includes a statement that the manor would be worth £20 more if the abbot had sake and soke.

22 Lambert, *Law and Order*, 329–32.

kings from Cnut onwards became more assertive in making local claims. At the same time, soke did not limit entirely new claims made by kings from the later tenth century, such as geld. What evidence there is for the specific content of soke is much later, especially from the later twelfth century,[23] and while this was clearly connected to earlier definitions of soke, it could not have been identical. The second was that soke, while clear in principle, could be complicated because the manner in which it was held depended on negotiation and the highly variable claims of individual lords.[24] Perhaps there was no single and simple mode in which soke was exercised in the eleventh century. The difficulty in pinning down how soke should be managed can be seen in the early twelfth century, when the author of the *Leges Henrici Primi* struggled to explain soke.[25] His explanations look very complicated, because there were so many exceptions and variations in terms of how soke was handled. For the anonymous writer of this tract, soke was something that was defined territorially to an extent it may not have been a century earlier, and the territorial dimension was something of a stumbling block, for it meant that soke could be hard to disentangle from claims in land, or the management of soke from the management of land.

It has long been debated whether the soke was equivalent to holding a court.[26] It may have been interpreted to do this at a much later date, but it probably did not do so during the eleventh century. The most substantial problem is that there is no good evidence for lords' courts before 1066 that might have provided a vehicle for the management of soke; and even in the early twelfth century, when lords' courts certainly existed, the author of the *Leges Henrici Primi* could divide soke held by lords into those matters that were dealt with communally – and so presumably in the hundred or the shire courts – and those that were dealt with in

23 The most detailed assessment of soke by the later twelfth century can be seen in the Kalendar of Abbot Samson, in *The Kalendar of Abbot Samson of Bury St Edmunds and Related Documents*, ed. R. H. C. Davis, Camden Third Series 84 (1954). The abbey's claims depended on the grants of soke by Edward the Confessor and his successors; see Richard Sharpe, 'The Use of Writs in the Eleventh Century', *Anglo-Saxon England* 32 (2003), 247–91.

24 *Regesta*, ii. nos. 738 and 739 show how Ramsey had soke over its manor of Lawshall, which lay within that part of Suffolk in which Bury St Edmunds Abbey had soke. The two abbeys were seemingly able to reconcile their claims and did not feel that one excluded the other; see *The Kalendar of Abbot Samson of Bury St Edmunds*, ed. R. H. C. Davis, Camden Third Series 84 (1954), 66.

25 *Leges Henrici Primi*, 20.

26 Frederick Pollock and Frederic W. Maitland, *The History of English Law Before the Time of Edward I* (second edition, Cambridge, 1898), i. 576–9; Frederic W. Maitland, *Domesday Book and Beyond: Three Essays in the Early History of England* (revised edition with an introduction by Edward Miller, London, 1960), 110–39; Lambert, *Law and Order*, 134.

the lords' own courts;[27] the same author also categorised soke not according to a simple distinction between royal and private soke jurisdictions, but into those that could pertain to private courts, those that pertained to the hundred, and those that pertained to the shire.

## Complex Lordship as an Experience in Eleventh-Century England

These three kinds of lordship, of course, overlapped, and any one individual could have owed dues under each to some lord or other. Thus, one dependent might have owed something to three different lords, one for each kind; or, to the same lord for each, or to any combination of them.[28] More complicated possibilities also occurred. One individual could have held lands from two or more lords, and so would have owed dues and services to more than one landlord. Where soke was territorialised it could have involved owing dues derived from soke to more than one lord as well. In some circumstances, an individual could even have more than one lord by commendation.[29] There was great potential for complex permutations, and for circumstances in which individuals owed so many and so varied dues that lordship could be described as confused, even though their meaning might have been readily intelligible to contemporaries. Yet there was scope for confusion also in terms of how others understood these arrangements for lordship, such as arose when the Domesday commissioners tried to describe them and to assimilate them to their rather different ideas about lordship. The model of complex lordship did not entirely correspond to how things were in northern France in the eleventh century, and the behaviour and understanding of immigrant Frenchmen was patterned by their experiences there more than by what they found in England.[30]

The existence of these different types of lordship did much to determine how cases concerning the peasantry and the unprivileged classes were dealt with.

27 *Leges Henrici Primi*, 19.2–20.3.

28 See Baxter, *Earls of Mercia*, 212, for a helpful Venn diagram to illustrate the range of possibilities. See also the comments in Robin Fleming, *Kings and Lords in Conquest England* (Cambridge, 1991), 126–8, where she describes this as serial lordship.

29 Baxter, *Earls of Mercia*, 205–6. The potential for multiple claims and interests was identified by Frederick Pollock and Frederic W. Maitland, *The History of English Law Before the Time of Edward I* (second edition, Cambridge, 1898), i. 107.

30 For example, Robin Fleming, *Kings and Lords in Conquest England* (Cambridge, 1991), chapter 6; R. P. Abels, 'Sheriffs, Lord-Seeking and the Norman Settlement of the South-East Midlands', *Anglo-Norman Studies* XIX (1997), 19–50. See also '*Epistulae Fiscannenses*: lettres d'amitié, de gouvernement et d'affaires', ed. J. Laporte, *Revue Mabillon* 44 (1953), 5–31, and David Bates, *The Normans and Empire: The Ford Lectures delivered in the University of Oxford during Hilary Term 2010* (Oxford, 2013), 115.

Manor courts comparable to those of the later middle ages could not work in this context, because many peasants owed something to more than one lord, and an exclusive forum would not allow for this. There is no indication that any lord ever tried to hold distinct courts for distinct types of lordship, for this would present obvious problems in ensuring attendance, as well as in keeping the types of lordship distinct. Instead, it seems that the claims of multiple lords, and potentially of competing lords, were managed through participation in the public hundred courts, where the claims of lords could be heard and debated alongside each other, and the different claims assessed. Domesday Book shows that hundreds and their attendees had detailed knowledge of local patterns of land tenure and lordship, presumably because the hundreds had some oversight of these matters.

These different kinds of lordship could form a threat to the interests of lords, and their response was to attempt to break down the number of claims that could be made over their dependents. This is especially apparent in the case of soke, for over time it became the norm that soke was contained in grants and confirmations from the king, and that lords were able to discharge much of that business among their own dependents. The general trend was towards the accumulation of as many different kinds of lordship as possible in the hands of landlords, who thus came to exercise exclusive or near-exclusive claims over the dependents on their lands.

Domesday Book offers the most compelling overview of eleventh-century lordship, but there is much to be found in the laws, and the information there is often fuller on some aspects of lordship. The laws give a sense of how kinds of lordship might work as relationships, where much depended on interactions between people, and where individuals were not stuck within inflexible structures, but instead had options open to them, through which they could negotiate and change lordship relationships. The laws also differ from Domesday in that the latter is principally concerned with land, and mostly describes lordship only insofar as it related to land; yet the laws give a wider range of lordship relationships, and address concerns such as public order and social discipline. The laws are also somewhat earlier than Domesday, and reflect earlier stages in development than are reflected there, such as the absence of soke.

Pre-Conquest laws set out a complicated system of compensations, in which actions detrimental to one party could be compensated through the payment of financial dues. This system has usually and rightly been linked with the need to prevent the development of feuds, so that the money was meant to buy off the possibility of further bloodshed.[31] Feud was clearly a concern behind the laws, and also can be seen in contemporary literature, so that it was an important matter,

[31] Paul Hyams, *Rancor and Reconciliation in Medieval England* (Ithaca, 2003), 78–92. For a critique of this see John D. Niles, 'The Myth of the Feud in Anglo-Saxon

especially when feuds among those of very high social status could have such grave consequences. Much of what has been written on compensations focusses on the ways in which families were compensated, on the basis that familial links were most likely to result in the kind of long-term feuds that could have such destabilising effects, and thus *wer* or wergeld is represented most fully in the historiography. Yet, *wer* was only one element of the structure of compensation, and much went to lords.[32] Conceivably, lordship networks were just as effective as family units in waging feuds against each other, and so lords also needed to be placated as a means of avoiding feud.

The three categories of compensation as set out in the laws were *wer*, *bot* and *wite*. *Wer* was a sum that varied in accordance with the status and wealth of an individual. It could be used as the basis for calculating fines, so that in some circumstances an individual might be required to pay his wergild for an offence. If an individual died through another's action, then *wer* was paid to his family. *Bot* was another form of compensation which was linked directly to the person of individuals. If someone was injured, then the person responsible for the injury would pay the *bot* to the injured party; it was calculated on the basis of the injury rather than on the basis of status or wealth.[33] If someone was killed rather than injured, then the *bot* was transferred to the dead dependent's lord instead, as compensation for the way in which the dependent under the lord's protection had been killed. *Wite*, meanwhile, was another form or compensation, in this case calculated on the basis of the nature of the act involved. *Wite* was another due that went to a lord; in most cases, it seems that it went to the lord who had jurisdiction or soke over a dependent, but it might in some cases be destined elsewhere. In the early twelfth century, it could happen that the *wite* went to the landlord in whose territory the action being compensated had taken place;[34] it could also happen that a *wite* for fighting could go with the *bot* to the commendatory lord.[35] In practice the division of compensations could be more complicated than the simple rules of allocation might indicate. There is also much doubt attached to the actual levels of these compensations, for the evidence for them is variable. Information about the levels at which *wer*, *bot* and *wite* should be set can mostly be found in the

England', *The Journal of English and Germanic Philology* 114 (2015), 163–200, though the two positions need not be so far apart as Niles suggests.

32 Domesday Book, fo. 11v: Kent 6.1. The entry describing Battle Abbey's manor of Wye includes a statement that the manor would be worth £20 more if the abbot had sake and soke. This seems to be the only eleventh-century assessment of the financial value of soke.

33 Stanley Rubin, 'The *Bot*, or Composition in Anglo-Saxon Law: A Reassessment', *The Journal of Legal History* 17 (1996), 144–54; 2 Edmund 3, 7.3; 8 Æthelred 3; 1 Cnut 2.5.

34 *Leges Henrici Primi*, 88.18.

35 *Leges Henrici Primi*, 80.6a.

earlier laws, especially those of Æthelberht and Alfred,[36] whereas later laws tend to be more concerned with how the compensation was distributed. The contrast between earlier and later treatments of compensations might be meaningful, and might indicate something about how uncertainty shifted from debate over the appropriate level of payment to the rightful recipients of the dues.

*Wer*, *bot* and *wite* have been described many times, and this summary is not intended to add much to those descriptions. There are a few points about them which indicate something about how the relationships between lords and dependents worked. They show that the relationship was of very great importance. That lords could draw some compensation indicates that they also needed to be bought off from the possibility of carrying out a feud in relation to the death of one of their dependents. These compensations also meant that lords had a substantial financial interest in the proper functioning of this system, and in ensuring that the arrangements set out in the laws were put into effect in full. The practices surrounding judicial fines and other matters could only have operated if those who were liable for paying the fines were accessible to multiple lords through communal institutions.

## Lords and their Dependents in Court

What all this meant can best be understood from an example. In his tract on the miracles attributed to St Swithun, the mid tenth-century writer Lantfred of Winchester included a quite detailed account of one case in which a lord's relationship with a dependent was negotiated in a public forum which included the participation of others apart from the lord himself:

> Thereafter, during these times under discussion, a certain merchant by the name of Flodoald – a dependent who was wise in worldly affairs and very rich – had a slave (*famulum*) whom he loved a good deal. This slave was apprehended by the king's reeve (who was called Eadric of Calne) because of a certain misdeed, and was ordered to be detained by royal thegns until his lord could come and until the slave would carry in his hands, without hesitation, an iron bar made red-hot by coals. And if he were innocent, he would be released without punishment; if he were found to be guilty, he would undergo capital punishment. When his master heard, therefore, that the servant (*servus*) was being detained in chains under cruel custody, he went there as quickly as he could, and implored the king's reeve to waive the ordeal and to keep the aforementioned servant himself under the conditions pertaining to a slave. The king's reeve – not countenancing these promises but exulting overmuch in his

[36] Generally on the compensations and their comparison to Continental laws, see Lisi Oliver, *The Body Legal in Barbarian Law* (Toronto, 2011).

secular authority – ordered the slave to carry a hot mass of iron. As he heard this the owner became extremely anxious about his slave (*servo*) (who was certain to die), and again promised to Eadric the king's reeve that he would give him a pound of pure silver and likewise hand over the slave (*servum*) in question into the reeve's possession, begging only that he drop the unjust charges, since he could not suffer the embarrassment of so great a disgrace, namely, that his slave (*mancipium*) should be executed for a trivial crime and offence.[37]

Lantfred's story is incomplete, of course, and even some matters that might be regarded as of great importance – such as the act that started the series of events – are not explained here. Yet, some important points can be derived from it. Throughout this story, the reeve and Flodoald as lord are always in control. The accused dependent was never even named, and he is denied any sense of agency. Throughout the various stages of debate set out in the story, all the initiatives come from Flodoald or his friends, and there is nothing that indicates that the accused dependent was ever able to present any kind of argument in his own defence. His powerlessness is emphasised by the omission of his name; he is presented almost as though he were a thing, which high-status men could use for their own ends, but which lacked agency of its own. It is not clear exactly what the status of the dependent was, given how many terms were used to describe him. All the negotiations with Eadric of Calne were done by Flodoald or his friends, and even the appeal to St Swithun that produced the miraculous outcome of this story came from Flodoald rather than from the unnamed accused. This is not unusual; it seems that often, where someone of lesser status was involved in a dispute, the transacting of that dispute was in the hands of the lord rather than

[37] *Presignatis denique temporibus, quidam negotiator nomine Flodoaldus – uir in rebus prudens secularibus, plurimis habundans opibus – habebat quendam famulum quem diligebat nimium. Is pro quodam facinore comprehensus a regis preside – qui solito uocabatur Eadric æt Calne – iussus est a regalibus custodiri clientibus donec eius ueniret dominus, et ignitum carbonibus ferrum nudis manibus idem portaret protinus. Et si foret inculpabilis, relinqueretur incolomis; sin culpabilis inueniretur, capite plecteretur. Audiens igitur senior illius quod ipse seruus in uinculis teneretur sub diris custodibus, festinantius quam potuit illo perrexit, exposcens regis praefectum ut dimitteret iudicium et seruili prescriptum condicione famulum possideret illesum. Qui minime fauens eius sponsionibus – ultramodum superbiens pro mundanis fascibus – seruo ferri calidam precepit gerere massam. Dominus autem eius hoc audiens, de seruo perituro nimium condolens, rursus Eadrico preposito spopondit regio dare puri libram argenti et similiter concessit seruum illi possidere prefatum, exorans ut iniquum dimitteret iudicium, quoniam dispendium tanti dedecoris minime quibat perpeti, ut mancipium illius pro uili scelere iugularetur et crimine.* Lantfred of Winchester, 'Miracles of St Swithun', ed. Michael Lapidge, *The Cult of St Swithun*, Winchester Studies 4.1 (Oxford, 2003), 308–11; Patrick Wormald, 'A Handlist of Anglo-Saxon Lawsuits', rpt in his *Legal Culture in the Early Medieval West: Law as Text, Image and Experience* (London, 1999), 253–87, no. 154.

those of the person who lay at the start of the dispute.[38] Indeed, it seems that the case could not even be heard without the participation of the lord.

This dispute, like so many others, was never just a question concerning the individual and his place in society, or even a problem for the relationship between the lord and his dependent, but also brought into question the status of the lord within a broader society. Lantfred tells us that Flodoald was motivated partly by concern for someone to whom he felt attached, but also that Flodoald was concerned about the effects that the death and shaming of his dependent would have upon his relations with others. The term used of Flodoald was *dedecorus*, which might be translated as embarrassment or dishonour. The miracle with which this story ends was mainly a comment on Flodoald rather than his dependent. When a lord's dependent acted, he was not a free agent, in that his actions might also have consequences for the reputation and status of his lord, as well as for the relationships between the lord and his dependent. The laws indicate that lords were meant to act as sureties or guarantors for their dependents, and that the provision of that protection was one of the markers of lordship.[39] Potentially, there might be three kinds of consequences for a lord if one of his dependents were to be convicted and punished in any way: it might involve some direct financial penalty if his formal protection or *borh* were brought into play; it might damage the extent to which the lord's testimony was accepted by others in future transactions; and it might simply dishonour the lord in the eyes of his neighbours and of his other men, and so reduce his effective power.

Finally, none of the discussion reported here was in terms of jurisdiction. There was no debate about which court this case should go to, and no attempt by any of those involved to redirect this matter to some other forum, or even to a private court. Lordship itself was not in question at all, and it apparently had no bearing on where exactly the case might be heard. On the basis of this narrative, there was seemingly no alternative arena in which this case could have been heard. It is not explained in any precise terms where this matter was aired, but the narrative makes clear that it was heard publicly, where many could comment on the question under discussion. The case was ultimately determined by the outcome and interpretation of an ordeal. Ordeals should only have happened as a result of and in conclusion to a public process in which the status of the accused person remained unresolved through less violent or extreme methods.[40]

38 See also Van Caenegem, *Lawsuits*, no. 204, from Orderic Vitalis, *Historia Ecclesiastica*, ed. M. Chibnall, *The Ecclesiastical History of Orderic Vitalis* (6 volumes, Oxford, 1969–81), iii. 346–60. On lords as advisers see 1 Æthelred 1.8, 2 Cnut 30.7, where lords could be fined if dependents fled on their advice; the assumption was clearly that lords controlled the legal behaviour of their dependents.

39 3 Edmund 3, 7; 3 Edgar 6; 1 Æthelred 1–1.2, 1.10; 3 Æthelred 3.4–5; 2 Cnut 30.1.

40 Robert Bartlett, *Trial by Fire and Water: The Medieval Judicial Ordeal* (Oxford, 1986), 25–32, and Paul R. Hyams, 'Trial by Ordeal: The Key to Proof in the Early

The essence of the system of lordship as set out in the laws was that no dependent should stand alone; anyone should be linked to others, who would be counted as sureties or guarantors, and be responsible for the actions of those to whom they were linked. Often, this was expressed through the idea of *borh* or *borg*, that a lord was responsible for the actions of his dependents, which meant that they provided an ultimate source of fines or compensation if a dependent defaulted in some way. Links with lords might arise in one of three ways. First, lords were responsible for the dependents who were in their own households, and were automatically liable for things that they did.[41] There was presumably an element of choice in this, in that lords would select those who served them within their households, and also might choose to exclude individuals whose services were troublesome to them. More was expected of those who served directly in the household, for they might form a posse of supporters for military action or intimidation. Second, lords were responsible for the dependents to whom they had some connection.[42] This applied to those who were in his peace and land; this divides those who held land from a lord from those who were linked in other ways. This might be making a distinction between free and unfree, but noting that the lord was responsible for both. Third, free men were bound to lords, and any who were not bound were required to establish bonds with a lord. The requirement for someone to have a lord was brought up repeatedly in successive laws through the tenth century,[43] so clearly this was seen as a matter of some importance. Where men were without a lord, it was apparently the responsibility of the relatives of someone to fix him in one place and to find him a lord.[44] If there was anyone who still did not have a lord, then such a person was required to go to the triple ordeal – presumably only if he was of such a poor reputation that he was unable to find a lord willing to accept responsibility and liability for his actions.[45]

Such rules about how all men were meant to have lords, and about how the bonds between dependents and their lords were meant to operate, were clearly not observed uniformly and consistently. As well as repeated commands that all men should have lords who were willing to stand surety for them, the laws

Common Law', in *On the Laws and Customs of England: Essays in Honour of Samuel E. Thorne*, ed. Morris S. Arnold, Thomas Andrew Green, S. A. Scully and S. D. White (Chapel Hill, 1981), 90–126. 1 Æthelred 1 shows how the ordeal came at the end of a complex process that had other forms of solution and outcomes.

41 1 Æthelred 1.10.

42 3 Edmund 7.

43 2 Æthelstan 2; 3 Æthelstan 7; 3 Edmund 7; 3 Edgar 6; 1 Æthelred 1; there is curiously no mention in the laws in the name of Cnut. It may have been replaced by the requirement that all be in a tithing (2 Cnut 20). It is possible that tithings were essentially a continuation of *borh* by another means, in which dependents of one lord were put into groups for the purposes of self-discipline and observation.

44 2 Æthelstan 2.

45 3 Edgar 6–7; 4 Edgar 3; 1 Æthelred 1, 4; 2 Cnut 20, 22, 30.

included many instructions that dependents should not change their lords except in closely defined circumstances.[46] That the writers of these laws felt it was necessary to make this point and repeat it many times indicates that transfers between lords were at least a topic of concern, and suggests that it may even have been a common occurrence. The laws are united in presenting the problem of such transfers as being one that arose from the initiative of the men rather than the lords; and there are specific injunctions against the desertion of lords by their dependents.[47] The main concern of these pronouncements against transfer was that dependents should not transfer from one lord to another when they had obligations remaining to their original lord, and that any such obligations should be discharged before the transfer became effective. Despite the many royal instructions for dependents to adhere to lords, clearly in practice lordship was more fluid and less stable than some observers might have wanted.

Once a relationship of lordship was made, there were roles that each side was expected to fulfil towards the other. For the dependent, there was a duty that he support the lord, and avoid kinds of conduct that might damage the lord in any way. Thus, the laws contain a number of instructions that dependents should not plot against their lords,[48] and so forth. Within the topics covered by the laws, it is clear that lords were meant to act as legal protectors towards their dependents, and should take responsibility for managing their appearances in court or in disputes, much as seems to have happened in the story from Lantfred of Winchester discussed above. If someone was accused, the process by which that person was dealt with depended on how the lord chose to participate; indeed, at times the participation of the lord was of influence on the outcome of the case. In some laws from the first half of the tenth century, it seems to have been envisaged that lords would be able to buy back their dependents even after they had taken and failed at the ordeal, simply through providing adequate compensation and fines after the ordeal had taken place.[49] Later in the tenth century, it seems that rules were tightened, for then a dependent under suspicion of theft could be protected to some extent, but not exempted outright, so that there was some possibility that he would still be recognised as a thief:

> If, however, his lord is willing to clear him, along with two good thegns, that he has neither been convicted of theft nor been accused since the assembly was held at *Bromdun*, he shall go to the simple ordeal, or pay threefold.[50]

[46] 2 Edward 7; 2 Æthelstan 22; 3 Æthelstan 4; 4 Æthelstan 4; 5 Æthelstan 1; 3 Edmund 3; 2 Cnut 28.

[47] 2 Cnut 57, 77; 2 Cnut 78 removes the heriot from the heirs of those who fell in battle for their lords.

[48] 2 Æthelstan 4; 2 Cnut 77.

[49] 6 Æthelstan 1.4 and 9.

[50] 3 Æthelred 4.

These statements about procedure make it clear that lords were closely involved in the legal affairs of their dependents, and that they had a claim or duty to step into cases and debates if they felt it in their interests to do so. This might even extend to how the accused was presented in court, for one of Cnut's laws orders that lords should not misrepresent the status of dependents,[51] which rather implies that lords had been in the habit of making claims which others might regard as false, as a means of obtaining some advantage in court. They might indicate that someone was free when that person was not, or vice versa; or it might mean that a recent extension of lordship might have been misrepresented as of long standing. This sense that lords' assertions were assessed by onlookers links to an attribute of the Domesday Books, and especially of Little Domesday Book; the testimony offered by many hundreds there included authoritative statements about the relationships between lords and dependents, and about some individuals' independence from lords.

So, lords had a great deal of power over their dependents in court, and the procedures described in the laws indicate that this was more or less institutionalised. As well as this formal power, lords also might seek to influence the conduct of their dependents through more informal means. To judge from one of the laws of Æthelred, lords were in the habit of advising their dependents in ways that tended to the obstruction of the operation of courts:

> And if the lord is accused of advising the man who had done wrong to escape, he shall choose five thegns, and shall make a sixth, and shall clear himself of the accusation.[52]

The strong influence of lords over their dependents meant that lords were made liable for advice they gave to them. Like most of the other points taken above from the laws, this tends to suggest that disputes and cases were viewed as the business of lords at least as much as that of the dependents involved.

Of course, the laws represent a somewhat idealised view of the relationship between lords and dependents in the tenth century, even before the changes of the eleventh century. They assume an intimacy and knowledge that might have been attainable for a minor thegn who held land in only a limited number of places and dwelt there or nearby. Yet, this was not how lordship was experienced everywhere. Many dependents were linked to great lords, even ealdormen or later earls, who held much land and lordship in many shires, and so could not have attained to close knowledge of all of their dependents, and may have been effective strangers in many of the places where they had claims. In such cases, much must have depended on the local agents and representatives who did much of the practical work of managing the interests of their lords. The role of these representatives

51 2 Cnut 20.1.

52 1 Æthelred 1.8; 2 Cnut 30.7.

might be acknowledged in the laws in the position of the *forspecan*, sometimes translated as advocate, who took on some of the duties normally assigned to the lord in terms of taking responsibility for fines and compensation.[53]

Yet, regardless of how wergild affected lords, and of how *bot* was actually calculated, what is apparent is that lordship had financial implications, and that the ways in which a lord managed his dependents could bring about quite variable results. For some lords, it may have been that the profits of lordship were a considerable and important part of their income, comparable to that from landlordship. The potential financial consequences of a large, disorderly and violent body of dependents must also have been very great. So, both positively and negatively, there were strong reasons for why lords should have supervised and controlled their dependents in courts as closely as they could, and why they should have been inserted into processes so that they could control liabilities and opportunities as far as these arose, even if their interventions might not always be in the interests of the dependents who served them and who must in most cases have started the disputes.

## Hundred Courts and Attendance in Anglo-Saxon England

The discussion hitherto has focussed on the relationships between lords and their dependents. The relationships were important in themselves, and would have been expressed in many places and at many times. Yet lordship was not merely a private matter between the participants in that relationship, for the relationships between individuals had consequences for how those individuals acted in a broader society. These consequences were social, economic and cultural, but were also legal and public, and there was a wider interest in who was bound to whom, and in what kind of relationship. Thus, lordship bonds seem in many cases, perhaps most, to have been made in public, in local assemblies where much of local society was present and could witness the transaction. These bodies, the hundreds, were central to the management of lordship, and were the main place where lordship was made and maintained. According to the laws, the hundreds were meant to take an interest in a wide range of activities and problems, and their operation depended on the participation of substantial numbers of interested and disinterested parties; the hundreds were meant to be the main arena in which disputes and matters of all kinds might be heard.[54] The great men of the

[53] 2 Edmund 7. There were no paid, professional advocates until much later; for accounts of the creation of a legal profession, see Paul Brand, *The Origins of the English Legal Profession* (Oxford, 1992) and Paul Brand, 'The Origins of the English Legal Profession', rpt in his *The Making of the Common Law* (London, 1992), 1–20.

[54] 2 Cnut 17–17.1 is the most specific statement that all should attend the hundred court

hundred attended, but it is less clear how widely the obligation for attendance was enforced.[55] The conclusive demonstration of this is to be found in the Domesday Books, which consist in large part of the testimony offered by hundreds, and show that those who attended the hundreds had comprehensive knowledge of local land tenure and lordship relationships. Indeed, hundreds often drew attention in particular to those places where they could *not* account in full for the origins of particular interests. This knowledge could not have been accumulated instantly; it was probably built up over time as transfers of interests in land and men were notified to or even performed in front of the hundred. There were kinds of knowledge that local elites had to have, such as which men were free, and so potentially liable for kinds of taxation or service; thus, regardless of lords, acts such as freeing or making slaves had to be done in the public arena.[56]

Before 1066, there seems to have been a clear assumption that the hundred was the sole regular arena in which matters should be aired. This idea is based on two items of evidence, one negative and one positive. The negative indication is that there is no clear and precise evidence that lords other than the king held or controlled their own courts before 1066 or how they could have been described; additionally, where the venue of decisions and settlements can be identified, they were always dealt with in shire or hundred or some combination of those. The positive evidence is that the laws make no space for the operation of courts other than the king's, shires, and hundreds, or some combination of those.[57] In

---

and that it was the starting place for all manner of legal business. The status of the hundred as the primary arena for the airing of disputes and others matters is set out in detail across many laws. Thus, 1 Edgar 14 states that all should do justice to each other; 3 Edgar 1.1 that all should have the benefit of the law, and 3 Edgar 5 that all should attend the hundred; 4 Edgar 13–14 that all should be subject to rules for warranty for cattle, and 1 Edgar 4 that this was done in the hundred; 5 Æthelred 1.1 and 6 Æthelred 8.1 that all should have the benefit of the law; 5 Æthelred has many injunctions to all Christian men, which implies that they could hear these messages in a legal setting; and 1 Æthelred 2 and 4 show that the hundred was expected to deal with all men; 2 Cnut 21 that all should take an oath against theft; 2 Cnut 82 that all men should have protection in going to assemblies.

55 The question is raised and discussed in Molyneaux, *Formation*, 144–5.

56 *Leges Henrici Primi*, 78; London version of *Decem Articuli/Willelmi Articuli Retractati*, 15.

57 T. B. Lambert, 'Royal Protections and Private Justice: A Reassessment of Cnut's "Reserved Pleas"', in *English Law before Magna Carta: Felix Liebermann and* Die Gesetze der Angelsachsen, ed. Stefan Jurasinski, Lisi Oliver and Andrew Rabin (Leiden and Boston, 2010), 157–75, at 160. One other instance of possible private jurisdiction has been cited; James Campbell, 'Hundreds and Leets: A Survey with Suggestions', in *Medieval East Anglia*, ed. Christopher Harper-Bill (Woodbridge, 2005), 153–67, at 153, 157. Ely Abbey's claims in its hundreds in Suffolk are a complex problem, and the sources are not consistent. The *Liber Eliensis*, following the *Libellus Æthelwoldi*, states that the abbey had agreed with Æthelwine the ealdorman

the laws the centrality of the hundred is apparent.[58] The laws allow very little beyond the hundred; there were the shire or later county courts, of course, and there were borough courts that were probably analogous to the hundred courts in their operation and remit.[59] It was also possible for hundreds to meet in groups for some kinds of business. The hundred court formed the natural arena in which matters could be dealt with, because it included a large part of the society of each hundred, and so meant that the complex pattern of Anglo-Saxon complex lordship could be managed; because the hundred was not tied to any form of lordship, commendatory lord, soke holder and landlord could all be present and so could assert their respective claims over the person and assets of those who were dealt with through the court. Attendance at the hundred court was also important because it brought financial responsibility with it, such as the hundred pennies that ultimately went to the king.[60] This, of course, applies to the free; it is less clear where matters concerning the unfree might arise.[61]

The laws cannot entirely be taken at face value on this question. They make some notable assumptions about whom it was that was concerned with law and with the hundred. The imagined subject of the laws seems to have been a *ceorl*, a minor freeman with ties to lords, but who also had a measure of free agency. Freemen had much importance within these small societies of the tenth-century hundreds, but could never have amounted to most of it. There were many people who were not free, or who were of lower status within this framework, and their position within it is not always made clear within the laws. Thus, for instance, later Anglo-Saxon England was a slave-owning society. Were slaves and other unfree persons required to attend the hundred? The laws make clear that if slaves and other unfree persons offended against those beyond the circle of dependents

that he would hold three manors from them with the six hundreds that belonged to Sudbourne (*Liber Eliensis*, ii. 41, ed. E. O. Blake, Camden Third Series 92 (1962), 114; *Liber Eliensis: A History of the Isle of Ely from the Seventh Century to the Twelfth*, trans. Janet Fairweather (Woodbridge, 2005), 137). This is based on the wording of a twelfth-century Latin translation made from a lost Anglo-Saxon original, so the original wording is not clear; also, it was common in Domesday Book to indicate that some lands, often former royal ones, might bring with them claims upon the revenue of hundreds, which was not the same as possession; see Helen M. Cam, '*Manerium cum Hundredo*: The Hundred and the Hundredal Manor', rpt in her *Liberties and Communities in Medieval England: Collected Studies in Local Administration and Topography* (Cambridge, 1944), 64–90, at 75–8.

58 1 Edgar 1; 3 Edgar 5.

59 For early mentions of courts for the Parts of Lincolnshire see D. R. Roffe, 'Hundreds and Wapentakes', in *The Lincolnshire Domesday* [introduction and translation] (London, 1992), 32–42, at 33.

60 Great Domesday Book, fo. 87v: Somerset 2.1; also E. B. Demarest, 'The Hundred-Pennies', *English Historical Review* 33 (1918), 62–72.

61 Faith, *English Peasantry*, 118–19, on this.

of their lord and owner, then they might be drawn within the ambit of the hundred court.[62] Members of the households of freemen were certainly regarded as being under the control of the freemen who ruled over them, so that they were for most purposes beyond the control and influence of the hundred court, and their immediate lords were held accountable for them as heads of household.[63] The extent to which women could be involved is also unclear, for their presence and participation in the hundred is not spelled out at all; presumably in many cases they were regarded as being within the control of fathers or husbands, and were accountable for their actions only through their menfolk.

There is much uncertainty as to how matters concerning lower status groups were dealt with before 1066. It has been assumed that manorial courts might have operated before 1066,[64] though this seems to be based on nothing more than that they had a role much later that was not clearly exercised before 1066. The manor court as it existed in the thirteenth century dealt with many different kinds of matters, and some of these could only have arisen later, such as the way that such courts dealt with questions of peasant land tenure. The methods for doing this were modelled on the procedures of the king's courts as they had been developed by about 1200, and need not have been done any earlier.[65] Other matters, such as those concerning agricultural discipline, were later dealt with through those courts, but need not have been, and early tracts on the work of the reeve such as *Rectitudines Singularum Personarum* and *Gerefa* do not indicate that these would need to be dealt with through a court.[66] It is essentially unanswerable how some kinds of business concerning the unfree peasantry were dealt with before 1066. The hundred court was more avowedly concerned with business generated among the free, but was clearly willing to look at some business arising even from slaves, so it might be assumed that even the unfree might be brought to the hundred court if there was business of importance for them there.

The main opening for the possibility of such assemblies might be found in the principle of acquittal. Kings started to demand geld as a uniform imposition upon land from the later tenth century, and so the arrangements for its collection must reflect how matters were commonly run or perceived at that time. Though geld notionally fell upon all who held land, it was often not paid by each

[62] 3 Edmund 4; 1 Æthelred 2; 2 Æthelred 5.1; 7 Æthelred 2.4, 3, 5.1; 8 Æthelred 6; 2 Cnut 20.1, 32, 45.3, 46.2, 68. 1b.

[63] 1 Æthelred 1.10; 7 Æthelred 5; 2 Cnut 31.

[64] Hudson, *Oxford History*, 288.

[65] Zvi Razi and Richard M. Smith, 'The Origins of the English Manorial Court Rolls', in their *Medieval Society and the Manor Court* (Oxford, 1996), 36–68, at 43–6.

[66] *Rectitudines Singularum Personarum*, *Gerefa*; on these see P. D. A. Harvey, 'Rectitudines Singularum Personarum and Gerefa', *English Historical Review* 108 (1993), 1–22, and rpt in his *Manors and Maps in Rural England, from the Tenth Century to the Seventeenth* (Farnham, 2010), no. I.

landowner separately, but rather lesser landholders were added to the responsibilities of local lords, who became liable for the taxation due from those men.[67] The lesser men's liability for geld was subsumed into that of their lords, and they became essentially invisible to those collecting geld; how lords obtained money from these lesser men was a private matter, and something that they or their representatives carried out for themselves. The overall effect was that lords could manage taxation, including (presumably) the ability to judge and compel those who owed them some liability for geld. These kinds of geld liability were reckoned against the lord's hall (or later, manor) and were an important means by which lords increased their power and influence. How this worked in practice at the lowest level is almost entirely lost, but the idea that some had liabilities and had to discharge them at the lord's hall means that they were establishing bonds that prefigured some of those of the manor. They were (presumably) liable for attendance, and had to render dues to the lord; at the same time, their obligations towards the lord were enforceable. Probably, some part of the origins of the later institution of the manor should be sought in the changes to local organisation brought about by the geld system.

Most of the population was not free in the way that thegns or barons were; most were peasants, and were working within a very different environment. They were much poorer, their affairs had much lesser consequences, and were therefore much less likely to be written down. They were also not free, or at least not entirely free, and this meant that they could not and did not act independently in the manner of their superiors. There is still much to debate about how they actually engaged with the law. The later middle ages presents a clear and simple model of how the peasantry engaged with the law, in the form of the manor court.[68] It has been asserted that manor courts existed in the eleventh century, but the evidence for their existence is sparse at best.[69] There is one instance only in Domesday Book, where it was stated that at Acton in Cheshire all cases arising from among the tenants went to the lord's hall: 'this manor has its pleas in the hall of its lord'.[70]

These few words imply quite a lot; most importantly, that the court was one that concerned only this one manor, and so was restricted to those who were within the lordship of William Malbank. This line only occurs in relation to this one manor of Acton, and not to William's numerous other manors in Cheshire; or, at least,

[67] H. R. Loyn, *The Governance of Anglo-Saxon England, 500–1087* (London, 1984), 119–20.

[68] Zvi Razi and Richard M. Smith, 'The Origins of the English Manorial Court Rolls', in their *Medieval Society and the Manor Court* (Oxford, 1996), 36–68, at 43–6; Mark Bailey, *The English Manor,* c. *1200*–c. *1500* (Manchester, 2002), 2–5, 11–16 for definitions.

[69] Hudson, *Oxford History*, 288. Great Domesday Book, fo. 265v: Cheshire 8.16.

[70] Fleming, *Domesday Book*, 120, no. 284.

the existence of similar arrangements for those other manors is not noted. It might be significant that Acton was the only manor for which William's *antecessor* was Earl Morcar. The Domesday reference states that pleas were held there, so that this was a gathering that dealt with disputes or discipline; presumably, these were matters that in other circumstances would have gone elsewhere, perhaps to a hundred court. The broader significance of these few words is harder to place. As has been noted before, the exceptional nature of this reference might mean that the arrangements described and implied were very unusual;[71] alternatively, it might have been merely an oddity, that a common arrangement was noted here because these few words fortuitously escaped deletion during the Domesday editing process; or it might even be that these words were retained because this was the only instance where such arrangements were in place at a manor held by William Malbank. As with so much in Domesday, it is hard to see what significance this might have. Does it mean that manorial courts were so common and had such small implications for taxation that they were not worth recording? Or was the compiler of Great Domesday drawing attention to an anomalous local arrangement? Before Domesday, there is nothing from among the pre-Conquest descriptions of cases that indicates the existence of manor courts,[72] so it is probably safest to regard this as an anomaly. In terms of sources, there is little reason to think that manor courts existed generally in the eleventh century, or that they were an important means by which peasants interacted with law.

## Conclusion

This chapter has set out the historiography and arguments for how lordship worked in the era before the Norman Conquest of England. The patterns of lordship seen then can be understood in greatest detail from the Domesday Books, which show how lordship was a complex and nuanced matter, in which different lords or the same lord could hold or claim different kinds of interest in the same individuals. This pattern meant that lords exercised their claims to lordship in the communal courts, where it would have been possible to claim dues from many, even those who owed dues to other lords. Hundreds in particular thus had a central role in the management of lordship of all kinds, as can be seen in the testimony offered in Domesday Book, where hundreds seemed to have encyclopaedic knowledge of

71 Hudson, *Oxford History*, 288.

72 T. B. Lambert, 'Royal Protections and Private Justice: A Reassessment of Cnut's Reserved Pleas', in *English Law before Magna Carta: Felix Liebermann and* Die Gesetze der Angelsachsen, ed. Stefan Jurasinski, Lisi Oliver and Andrew Rabin (Leiden and Boston, 2010), 157–75, at 160; Hudson, *Oxford History*, 62, 288–9, 561–2.

claims in land and claims to lordship. Hundreds were thus the central mechanism for the administration of lordship in all forms; there is no positive or negative evidence, and there was seemingly no place, for exclusive lordship courts before the Norman Conquest.

The problem of the manor court, its origins and predecessors up to the eleventh century, is not merely resolvable through looking for evidence; it is also a matter of definitions. When the manor court first appears properly in sources at the very end of the twelfth century and into the early thirteenth, it had two main roles: it was a forum in which lords could discipline their peasants, and enforce labour services upon them and manage agricultural duties; but also, it was an arena in which peasants could find some security in tenure of land and air disputes that arose between them, if the parties to that dispute were all under the lordship of the lord who controlled the manor court. The manor court was thus a means for lords to control their tenants and their claims in land, and to prevent them from entering into an arena where another lord might be able to exercise power over them, or even draw revenue from them.[73] The creation of manor courts assumed a particular unitary model of lordship, in which one lord held exclusive jurisdiction over some peasants within a defined area, and no other secular person could claim anything from those peasants, except the limited and specified claims of the king. This model was not a universal one; it was created in a long process through the later eleventh and twelfth centuries, and developed out of the much more complicated Anglo-Saxon system of lordships.

[73] Zvi Razi and Richard M. Smith, 'The Origins of the English Manorial Court Rolls', in their *Medieval Society and the Manor Court* (Oxford, 1996), 36–68, at 37–43.

# 2

# The Aspirations of Lords in Eleventh- and Twelfth-Century England

In one sense, lordship was straightforward; it was a reciprocal relationship between two individuals, where there was a substantial power differential, but where both sides could potentially benefit from the output, protection or cultural capital of the other. Yet lordship was also something rather more than this, in that it was also a matter of aspiration. For lords, lordship was a means for exercising dominance over others, and for creating a miniature society in which they might control those around them and under them.[1] It was a model of interpersonal relationships as much as a legal and economic pattern.

A lot is knowable about how members of the elite conducted themselves in disputes and in court from the tenth to the twelfth centuries, especially in matters linked with land.[2] The implications of cases between powerful and wealthy individuals could be very great, but they were by no means the norm. Those involved in cases over land, whether thegns or barons or knights, were free in law and so could act in accordance with individual or family interests; they were also guided by the expectations that attached to their class, which meant that they acted assertively and in accordance with notions of honour and so forth. Their strategies can therefore look quite modern at times, in that members of this class might act in ways that look individualistic. These kinds of cases and disputes dominate the surviving sources because of their implications and consequences, but they can only have formed a very small part of the total number of disputes that arose in England in the central middle ages.

In some settings, lordship was a powerful ideology that did much to form the conduct of those who were part of lordship relationships. In the poem on the Battle of Maldon, some of Byrhtnoth's men willingly followed their lord to

1 Thomas N. Bisson, *The Crisis of the Twelfth Century: Power, Lordship and the Origins of European Government* (Princeton, 2009); and earlier versions, Thomas N. Bisson, 'The "Feudal Revolution"', *Past and Present* 142 (1994), 6–42; Thomas N. Bisson, 'Medieval Lordship', *Speculum* 70 (1995), 743–59. For another study of how changes in lordship interacted with legal change see Paul Hyams, *Kings, Lords and Peasants in Medieval England: The Common Law of Villeinage in the Twelfth and Thirteenth Centuries* (Oxford, 1980), chapter 13.

2 Hudson, *Oxford History*, chapters 5 and 14.

their deaths, and some tried to avenge him.[3] For such as these, lordship formed a framework that made their lives and deaths meaningful. For these, it could be something that was emotionally satisfying and which made their lives and actions, and ultimately their deaths, intelligible. Yet, while lordship could be an ideal and could form an all-encompassing means of viewing the world, it was always vulnerable to other kinds of claim. Lords might make their claims and some would accept their predominant influence, but others might prefer other kinds of structure and loyalty. There was loyalty to family, which might provide an alternative focus for loyalty. Families could provide the basis for political conduct in the case of feud, and some might have preferred the claims of kin to lords. Arrangements for compensation privileged family above lordship networks in terms of the sums awarded for *wer* as opposed to *bot*. Other focuses of loyalty and identity might be found in locality, in nation, in religion and in the figure of the king. Probably, lords always faced serious competition if they tried to claim that their interests should be the premier ones. In this, kings provided especially keen rivals as their capacities to intervene grew in the tenth century.[4]

The lordship exercised by kings intruded upon the exercise of domination by other lords over their dependents, through imposing obligations upon dependents which might interfere with the demands made by lords. Earlier it was a common ambition among lords that they would be freed from the intrusive claims of kings to the services of bridge work, burh work and military service from their dependents.[5] By the eleventh century, the kinds of demands made by kings were greater than those made earlier in the tenth, for there were local officers in the form of sheriffs who could assert claims on behalf of kings, and there were new claims on resources in the form of the geld. Eleventh-century kings probably looked much more threatening to lords than did many of their predecessors, and therefore the attractiveness of obtaining effective exemption from royal power increased substantially. This could involve written commands from the king to his agents, or it might involve methods for withdrawing a lord's dependents from arenas in which they would be visible and accessible to the king's agents.

## Patterns of Lordly Behaviour

Lordship was always a fluid and flexible matter, but between the tenth and twelfth centuries marked changes can be discerned. These changes affected not just the relationships between lords and their dependents, but also how lords and their

3 Battle of Maldon, *English Historical Documents,* c. *500–1042*, ed. Dorothy Whitelock (London, 1955), 293–7.

4 Molyneaux, *Formation*, 231–49.

5 Alan Cooper, *Bridges, Law and Power in Medieval England, 700–1400* (Woodbridge, 2006), esp. chapter 2.

dependents related to each other as groups, and to local societies in general. They can be described in quite abstract terms, but presumably had effects upon the lives of those who were involved, in that their experience of lordship relationships and their links to other people were altered. The most conspicuous of these changes is what is often called manorialisation, the process by which many lords extended their exercise of lordship through bringing more people under their control, and through intensifying what they could demand from their dependents.[6] There was, however, much else; the same period saw the creation of centralised villages as a means of housing lords' dependants, and even the reorganisation of the local church to reflect lordship units.[7]

Collectively, these changes had huge effects, and these go far beyond the scope of this book. There were, of course, specific legal consequences that arose from many of them, but that is not perhaps their main significance here; their interest is rather that they point to a common methodology, a common approach that many lords used in trying to understand and to manage their relationships with their dependents. This method presumably arose from two main roots. First, tactics and methods could spread through simple imitation, as one lord aimed to match another, and recreate social relationships in a form that enriched or validated that lord. Second, lords' methods looked similar because they worked in what was largely a shared environment within a hierarchical social structure and the ambit of the English kings. Thus, lords had to deal with the ramifications of royal authority itself, with the consequences of the presence, claims and activities of the church, and with patterns of land occupation and jurisdiction.[8]

These matters of local organisation exercised especially great influence. Across much of England in the tenth century, local organisation depended on the ways in which people could interact with central places for small districts. These often and ideally involved the co-location of three key elements; a royal estate centre (sometimes described as a *tun*), a minster church and a hundred court meeting place.[9] Each of these demanded a measure of attention from those within

[6] Faith, *English Peasantry*, esp. chapter 6.

[7] John Blair, 'Introduction: from Minster to Parish Church', in *Minsters and Parish Churches: The Local Church in Transition, 950–1200*, ed. John Blair (Oxford, 1988), 1–19.

[8] Probably the most emphatic demonstration of this can be found in Shropshire, where claims over hundreds were appended to particular manors and are described as such in Domesday Book. The link between tenure of one manor and claims over the surrounding area remained even when the manors had been passed to other lords. See Helen M. Cam, '*Manerium cum Hundredo*: The Hundred and the Hundredal Manor', rpt in her *Liberties and Communities in Medieval England: Collected Studies in Local Administration and Topography* (Cambridge, 1944), 64–90, at 75–83.

[9] On hundred meeting places see Sarah Semple, 'Locations of Assembly in Early Anglo–Saxon England', in *Assembly Places and Practices in Medieval Europe*, ed. Aliki

the boundaries of its jurisdiction, whether this was the hundred or the *hyrnesse/ parochia* of the minster church. This could involve at different times and in different ways some combination of required attendance and financial or agricultural contributions. When lords received land and lordship over the men who farmed it, their influence over those men was qualified and limited by the obligations owed to the hundred, minster and royal estate. This meant that the lord could not dominate them; they were not exclusively the lord's dependents, but also had obligations to the king that limited and interrupted the control of the lord. Lords would regularly see the productivity of their dependents seeping away to others. Those who might have some claim upon a lord's dependents could be many; there might be obligations owed to the king for labour or goods, or obligations for tithes, burial and other dues owed to the clergy of a minster, court attendance enforced by a king's reeve, even personal lordship as distinct from land lordship owed to another lay lord. For many lords, the experience of seeing other lords making demands of their dependents and seeing those fulfilled must have seemed dissonant with the ideal of what lordship should have involved. It seems also that many lords looked upon these multifarious demands as being more or less alike.[10] In these circumstances, it seems to have been a common response that lords tried to monopolise their dependents, and exclude other claimants from access to them.

The presence of different claims and different kinds of lordship over individuals also offered particular threats and opportunities. Powerful lords could try to expand their lordship by clever use of existing claims as a basis for acquiring others. This is especially apparent in the aftermath of Norman Conquest, when lords might, for instance, use claims to soke as a basis for claiming other things from dependents within their soke.[11] This, again, seems to be informed by the aspiration that lordship should be an all-encompassing relationship rather than something merely transactional. Such aggressive use of lordship was doubtless easier during periods of political instability when there

Pantos and Sarah Semple (Dublin, 2004), 135–54, and Aliki Pantos, 'The Location and Form of Anglo-Saxon Assembly-Places: Some 'Moot Points'', in *Assembly Places and Practices in Medieval Europe*, ed. Aliki Pantos and Sarah Semple (Dublin, 2004), 155–80.

10 There is a contemporary description by an outsider from the middle of the twelfth century in the *Epistulae Fiscannenses*, written by an anonymous monk of Fécamp who had been sent to the abbey's manor at Cogges near Witney in Oxfordshire: '*Epistulae Fiscannenses*: lettres d'amitié, de gouvernement et d'affaires', ed. J. Laporte, *Revue Mabillon* 44 (1953), 5–31, at 30. For the development of a new set of demands in the middle of the twelfth century see the comments on *tenserie* in Edmund King, *King Stephen* (New Haven, 2010), 206–10.

11 Robin Fleming, *Kings and Lords in Conquest England* (Cambridge, 1991), chapter 6; R. P. Abels, 'Sheriffs, Lord-Seeking and the Norman Settlement of the South-East Midlands', *Anglo-Norman Studies* XIX (1997), 19–50.

had been widespread expropriation and even destruction; yet, such circumstances were not unique to the years after 1066, and similar aggressions probably occurred during the 1010s as well.[12] Perhaps such things could have happened at any time, especially in districts where there were dominant lords, or where royal supervision was distant and weak.

## Minsters and Parish Churches: A Parallel

Between the tenth and the twelfth centuries many lords were concerned with consolidating lordship, so that claims and potential claims from other territorial lords were excluded, as far as was possible. This meant that they could exercise as strong a lordship over their dependents as possible, with as few potential sources of competition. The assumptions and methods seen here can also be observed in relation to the demands of the church, for the same period in which multiple lordship was consolidated into manorialism also saw a shift from large minster *parochiae* to smaller parishes, which often mapped onto manorial structures.[13] The strategies and assumptions of lords in relation to minsters and parishes closely parallel how they dealt with secular lordship as well.

From earlier Anglo-Saxon times Christianity among the English had been managed through a network of minster churches. These ruled over territories much larger than later parishes, and which included multiple settlements and potentially substantial populations. Minsters were commonly major churches, and in most cases were staffed by groups of clergymen rather than by individual priests; the minsters also had access to considerable resources, in that they could demand all kinds of fees and dues from across the territories they oversaw, and frequently owned land or other resources as well. Compared to the later parish churches, they were powerful and independent organisations, and were competitors with lords in trying to gain parts of the economic output of the peasantry.

The minsters formed a direct ecclesiastical parallel to the secular structures of hundred and royal tun. The two often shared boundaries, especially in the eighth or ninth centuries,[14] and often were sited in close proximity to each other.[15] They

12 Robin Fleming, *Kings and Lords in Conquest England* (Cambridge, 1991), chapters 1–3.

13 John Blair, ed., *Minsters and Parish Churches: The Local Church in Transition, 950–1200* (Oxford, 1988), and especially Blair's own chapter 'Introduction: from Minster to Parish Church', 1–19, are the fundamental statements of this set of ideas.

14 John Blair, 'Parish Churches in the Eleventh Century', in *Domesday Studies*, ed. G. H. Martin, Ann Williams and R. W. H. Erskine (London, 1987), 65–8; also P. H. Hase, 'The Mother Churches of Hampshire', in John Blair, ed., *Minsters and Parish Churches: The Local Church in Transition, 950–1200* (Oxford, 1988), 45–66, at 45–8.

15 Southampton offers a clear instance of this; here, the minster at St Mary's, the royal

also functioned in concert with each other, so that the claims of minster churches to take fees and dues from those under its jurisdiction was enforced through laws and thus presumably through the hundred court;[16] ecclesiastical business was only separated from the hundred court later in the eleventh century,[17] and so, presumably, was ordinarily done there before that. For most purposes, hundred and minster were mutually reinforcing sources of power, which forced those who lived within the territories of each to engage with the kinds of lordship and control that they represented.[18]

From the tenth century onwards, lords created parish churches, which tended to diminish the role of the minsters by diverting some of the traffic and revenues that had hitherto gone to them. This was partly a matter of status; a church was one of the attributes that defined someone as a thegn, and so was of some social importance:

> And if a ceorl throve, so that he had fully five hides of his own land, church and kitchen, bellhouse and burh-gate-seat, and special duty in the king's hall, then was he thenceforth of thegn-right worthy.[19]

Ownership of a church was a potential social benefit for whoever built one, and might have some advantage in religious terms as well. Yet it was a means

tun at Stoneham and the meeting place of Mansbridge hundred at Swaythling all lay in a line, on the west bank of the River Itchen and presumably, before modern development, within sight of each other, approximately in the middle of the hundred and minster *parochia*. See P. H. Hase, 'The Mother Churches of Hampshire', in John Blair, ed., *Minsters and Parish Churches: The Local Church in Transition, 950–1200* (Oxford, 1988), 45–66, at 45; *The Victoria History of the Counties of England: Hampshire*, iii. Ed. William Page (London, 1908), 462 for the Mansbridge hundred moot at the ash tree in Swaythling; the royal tun at Stoneham had been given to the monks of Old Minster, Winchester, in 1045 by Edward the Confessor: http://www.esawyer.org.uk/charter/1012.html.

16 2 Edgar; 5 Æthelred; 6 Æthelred; 7 Æthelred; 8 Æthelred; 9 Æthelred; 10 Æthelred; 1 Cnut.

17 Bates, *Regesta*, no. 128; on this see Colin Morris, 'William I and the Church Courts', *English Historical Review* 82 (1967), 449–63.

18 The minster pattern was often complex, and there were also many cases where hundred and minster did not align clearly. For an illustration of this, see the map in Andrew Reynolds, *Anglo-Saxon Deviant Burial Practices* (Oxford, 2009), 244, which shows that there were hundreds that lacked minsters and royal tuns. There were also differences in northern and eastern England, perhaps related to disruption brought about during the Viking Age invasions; see E. Cambridge and D. Rollason, 'The Pastoral Organization of the Anglo-Saxon Church: A Review of the 'Minster Hypothesis'', *Early Medieval Europe* 4 (1995), 87–104, and the response by D. M. Palliser, 'Review Article: The 'Minster Hypothesis'', *Early Medieval Europe* 5 (1996), 207–14.

19 *Geþyncðo*. Note also Ann Williams, 'A Bell House and a Burh-Geat: Lordly Residences in England before the Norman Conquest', rpt in *Anglo-Norman Castles*, ed. Robert Liddiard (Woodbridge, 2003), 23–40.

of monopolising a lord's dependents, and withdrawing them from the influence of others. A lord, it seems, might demand that their dependents attended his church instead of going to the local minster for many functions. This could have all kinds of practical consequences. It would mean that a lord could direct his dependents to pay their ecclesiastical dues to his own church, and these could involve substantial resources.[20] If some or part of these dues could be redirected from a minster to a lord's own church, then this could increase the lord's influence over his dependents by restricting their capacity to interact with an outside body; it would mean that the resources would be used for supporting an asset that the lord himself controlled and which glorified him and his family; it meant that the lord's patronage might be expanded, if these dues were allocated to the support of a clergyman nominated or controlled by the lord; and it could mean that the lord might abstract some of those resources for himself.

There seems to have been much variation in terms of how this worked in practice. In some cases, lords were able to negotiate with the minster clergy in order to obtain their consent to change. This is attested in the rich but problematic documentation surviving from Christchurch in Hampshire, where it is explained that a church was created at Milford through agreement between the local landowner, one Alvric the Small, and the clergy of Christchurch.[21] Milford church was specifically tied to Alvric's secular claims of lordship, in that the clergy of Christchurch allowed him to have a graveyard, on condition that it was used only by the people from his lands. It was agreed that one of the clergy from Christchurch would continue to serve the church – no provision was made for any separate clergyman – and that some dues would continue to be paid to Christchurch itself. These terms were not that unusual; similar ones were agreed in relation to the nearby church at Boldre. Lords paid the minster in land for these concessions, so that the consent of the Christchurch clergy was bought; a private church was important enough, or profitable enough, that it was worth the loss of land. Christchurch was a more substantial minster than most, and so was able to protect its claims, or at least ensure that some compensation was obtained for the loss of parts of them.

Elsewhere, the creation of new churches and the resulting diminution of others was less consensual. At Swaffham Prior in Cambridgeshire the principal church,

[20] Dues paid to churches could be numerous and various. Tithes, churchscot and fees for burial are the most obvious ones, but there were also local customs such as *scrifcorn* in Herefordshire (see Brian Kemp, 'Some Aspects of the *Parochia* of Leominster in the 12th Century', in John Blair, ed., *Minsters and Parish Churches: The Local Church in Transition, 950–1200* (Oxford, 1988), 83–95, at 87–8).

[21] On this see P. H. Hase, 'The Mother Churches of Hampshire', in John Blair, ed., *Minsters and Parish Churches: The Local Church in Transition, 950–1200* (Oxford, 1988), 45–66, at 55–6.

St Cyricus's, was in the hands of the members of the de Scalers family.[22] In terms of land, Swaffham Prior was a divided village, and various lords had claims there; after the de Scalers, the most important of the lords within the village were the monks of Ely. At some point during or before the early twelfth century, the other lords of Swaffham Prior chose to create a new church, St Mary's, that would free their dependents from the obligation to attend the de Scalers' church of St Cyricus. The relationship between these two churches was complicated by the way that the new church was sited within the same churchyard as the original one. This case was brought to the bishop of Ely's court in the early twelfth century, and he ordered that St Mary's should no longer be a church, that its congregation should instead attend St Cyricus's, and that burials there should be removed. Despite this command, the two churches remained in use, and indeed still stand in the same churchyard.[23]

These are just a couple of isolated instances in a general pattern, that between about 950 and 1200 the pattern of local minsters was mostly replaced by parish churches, and that this was done mostly by and in the interests of local lords. The creation of new parish churches allowed lords to undermine the position of many minster churches, and to restrict the lordship relationships of their dependents to themselves, so monopolising the links of many of them. It was a means of concentrating and strengthening lordship. The creation of parish churches might also involve participation and support from the dependents themselves, who might find a local church more convenient, more accessible or even more satisfying,[24] and these people would have been important in maintaining these churches. The transition from minster to parish church shows an approach very similar to that seen in relation to secular lordships; that lords wanted to extend their control over their dependents, and that this was usually expressed through the tactic of trying to monopolise the relationships of their dependents, at least as far as they could. The extent to which this was possible depended on the level of power and influence that could be used by different lords, which explains the way that not all lords could do this; where a local minster had powerful allies and wealth, as in the case of Leominster, it was possible for such a minster to protect

22 On this see Nicholas Karn, *English Episcopal Acta* 31: *Ely, 1109–1198* (Oxford, 2005), nos. 10 and 30.

23 *The Victoria History of the Counties of England: A History of Cambridgeshire and the Isle of Ely*, ed. L. F. Salzman, J. P. C. Roach, A. W. Mabbs, R. B. Pugh, C. R. Elrington, A. P. M. Wright, J. J. Wilkes, C. P. Lewis and A. F. Wareham (10 vols and index, London and Oxford, 1938–2002), x. 294–5; *Vetus liber archidiaconi Eliensis*, ed. C. L. Feltoe and E. H. Minns, Octavo Publications of the Cambridge Antiquarian Society 48 (1917), 46.

24 Gervase Rosser, 'The Anglo-Saxon Gilds', in John Blair, ed., *Minsters and Parish Churches: The Local Church in Transition, 950–1200* (Oxford, 1988), 31–4, at 31.

and keep many of its claims.[25] Generally, the creation of parish churches was an important step in the concentration of lordship and of manorialisation, and the high quality of ecclesiastical documentation allows some of the methods and aims of lords to be understood better.[26]

## Lordship and Instability

It is possible to distinguish between the varieties of lordship, but conceptual precision offered there does not wholly reflect how lordship might be experienced; it could reflect brute force more than mutual claims. To contemporaries, there was potential for confusion between the different kinds of lordship, and there are clear signs that individual lords might try to exploit the system, and argue that the exercise of one form of lordship implied another. Some of the laws refer to the same kinds of activities,[27] in which lords were not simply passively acquiescent in manifold lordship, but instead tried to exploit it for their own ends and tried to extend their lordship networks for their own benefit. It may be too easy an assumption that the structures of Anglo-Saxon lordship were well-known and respected before the Norman Conquest, only to be disrupted and changed thereafter; lords may well have been trying to use its ambiguities and complexities for their own advantage well before 1066.

Lordship was a fundamental structure, but that does not mean that it was conducive to stability and order. There are reasons for thinking that, in the central middle ages, it was instead a source of instability and disorder. Such has been the argument of recent studies by Thomas Bisson,[28] which have suggested

25 Brian Kemp, 'Some Aspects of the *Parochia* of Leominster in the 12th Century', in John Blair, ed., *Minsters and Parish Churches: The Local Church in Transition, 950–1200* (Oxford, 1988), 83–95.

26 Lay control of churches did not survive long; church dues were defined as something quite distinct from lay lordship through the twelfth century, and changing attitudes towards the clergy and ecclesiastical claims meant that lay possession of them came to be regarded as indecent. Thus, in a distinct process, lay lords were encouraged to transfer many of their claims over parish churches to monasteries during the twelfth century; on this see C. R. Cheney, *From Becket to Langton: English Church Government, 1170–1213* (Manchester, 1956), 155–60. For a local study see R. M. Haines, 'Patronage and Appropriation in Ely Diocese: The Share of the Benedictines', *Revue Bénédictine* 108 (1998), 298–314.

27 2 Cnut 20.1 indicates how lords might choose to represent and misrepresent the position of their dependents according to their advantage.

28 Thomas N. Bisson, *The Crisis of the Twelfth Century: Power, Lordship and the Origins of European Government* (Princeton, 2009); Thomas N. Bisson, 'The "Feudal Revolution"', *Past and Present* 142 (1994), 6–42; Thomas N. Bisson, 'Medieval Lordship', *Speculum* 70 (1995), 743–59.

that a view of lordship as a form of feudal hierarchy is one which misrepresents its true nature, for it overstates the degree to which lords were responsible, and respected the interests of others. Lords tried to assert their own power over dependents, for this brought considerable social, political and economic advantages. Lordship was not infinitely expandable, for it found limits in the size of the population; a lord could only expand his lordship by extending influence and control over those who, perhaps, had not been bound closely into lordship, or through taking dependents from other lords. In either circumstance, lordship was not a matter of simple and passive hierarchy, but rather of undermining other lordships. In practice, the exercise and even preservation of lordship could have been constant struggle.

Lordship was especially unstable in those periods when political power itself was unstable, and throughout the eleventh and twelfth centuries there were, in England, repeated ructions and disruptions which caused realignments in how lordship was distributed and structured. In the eleventh century, there were the major invasions and conquests supervised by Cnut and William the Conqueror, both of which introduced new elite figures who tried to establish new lordships for themselves. For the aftermath of Cnut's conquests, these included new dependents such as Godwine, who established large regional networks of lordship and support.[29] After William the Conqueror's invasion, lordships were created from nothing by French individuals and families who and which acted predatorily against the natives who, largely, were unable to defend themselves because they lacked both the military power and the political influence with the king. The establishment of French dynasties and power structures in England after 1066 is a particularly extreme demonstration of how lordship could be expanded directly against the interests of existing holders of power.[30]

Changing definitions and expectations also tended to alter structures of lordship. In Anglo-Saxon England, there was a fundamental division between inland and warland, which became the basis for how the nature of domination changed over time.[31] The inland was the land owned by the lord, where he exercised various kinds of lordship over the peasants, who were tied to him quite closely; the warland was the land beyond that, where lords exercised some kind of lordship, most often commendation, even where the lord did not actually own the land farmed by those peasants. Independent peasants were pulled into these relationships with lords by various means. It might have arisen because of the ambition of lords to expand their lordship and to draw more men into their ambit;

[29] Robin Fleming, *Kings and Lords in Conquest England* (Cambridge, 1991), chapters 2–3.

[30] Robin Fleming, *Kings and Lords in Conquest England* (Cambridge, 1991), chapters 5–6.

[31] Faith, *English Peasantry*, chapters 2 and 4.

it might have arisen because peasants wanted the protection of a lord against some other threat; or it might have arisen as a result of royal pressure, for laws state that all free men should be able to cite a lord as a pledge, which also might give rise to lordship bonds.[32] These impulses towards the creation of lordship structures were another feature that made the system as a whole dynamic, especially when it was possible for peasants to choose their own lords, and even to change their own lords.

Patterns of lordship did not change only when political disruption provided particularly apt circumstances. Lordship could also alter markedly as social and technological arrangements developed. Military norms changed during the eleventh and twelfth centuries, as the mounted knight came to dominate much military thinking and the practice of warfare. The knight depended on access to metallic arms and armour which were expensive, and which were out of reach for most of the population; these advantages were restricted to a relatively small elite, or to those who had access to them. These developments were the start of the process by which military activity and its ideologies came to be possessions of the elite, so that these ideas came to form the culture and attitudes of the ruling class. These related developments meant that the members of the knightly class came to think of themselves as being part of the elite, and, in this context, they came to aspire towards the kinds of economic and political attributes and status that marked the elite, and which supported their lifestyles, to which they also aspired. In practice, this meant the creation of a fairly large group which aspired to, or even which expected, to be able to exercise lordship and to claim the economic benefits that came from doing so.[33] Thus, through the eleventh and twelfth centuries there arose a group which aspired to lordship, and which possessed the kinds of attitudes and attributes which would allow such lordship to be enforced. Their ambition formed another major cause of instability which, in an English setting, was especially apparent in the period of the so-called 'Anarchy', when lords became expansionist warlords. The ambitions and practices so nakedly apparent then were merely more violent forms of the political activities and aspirations of this group.

Lords and would-be lords had to fight to survive, and had to fight strongly to prosper in any way at all. They might use influence, rewards, protection or even force to try to expand their lordship, and to bring more men into their networks. Inevitably, serious attempts to expand such networks meant attacking someone else, because the expansion of lordship meant attracting dependents from other lords or downgrading the status of free men.

32 3 Edmund 7–7.2; 3 Edgar 6–6.2, 7–7.3; 1 Æthelred 1–1.14, 3, 4–4.3.

33 Thomas N. Bisson, 'Medieval Lordship', *Speculum* 70 (1995), 743–59.

## Soke and the Defence of Lordship

Soke was not an ancient form of lordship, but appeared towards the end of the tenth century.[34] It arose because kings expanded their authority and capacity to intervene, and lords tried to protect their interests from these developments. Kings were willing to allow this protection to some favoured lords; this was soke. It is well evidenced, because it was usually something that was linked to landholding, even though it was not an integral part of landholding itself and only became territorialised over time; it thus appears quite often in the generous documentation for the tenure of land. In the decades before 1066, a soke-holding lord had some control over the ways in which dependents within his soke would be dealt with legally. Soke was a means for protecting the interests and the dependents of lords from the attentions of sheriffs and reeves acting in the interest of the king; it might represent a means of preventing some kinds of change, or it might recognise that some lords could claim more from their dependents to begin with. Practically, it meant that lords could demand some services from those over whom they held soke, and might intervene in or even control how they interacted with others.[35] Soke was thus of central importance in structuring the legal position and behaviour of lords and their dependents. For lords, soke could be very valuable. Domesday Book notes that Battle Abbey's manor at Wye in Kent was worth £100 annually, but that if would be worth £20 more if soke were attached to it.[36] This might be an assessment of what the dues might be in an average year, or what the farm of the soke could be sold for, but either way a considerable sum of money was envisaged.

Soke was held by lords well before the Conquest. There are numerous writs surviving in the name of later Anglo-Saxon kings which convey or confirm to lords that they could hold soke over men, and so attain some measure of control, as well as the financial benefits of this kind of lordship. The writs indicate that there was no single model for how soke should be managed, but rather than there were at least three modes in which they might be exercised. First, it was possible for lords to hold soke over the lands that they owned or over some named part of those lands, which presumably meant that they would be able to exercise soke over the dependents that lived and worked there.[37] This would seem to take the

[34] Baxter, *Earls of Mercia*, 210–11; Lambert, *Law and Order*, 323–5.

[35] The tendency to think of it as a purely royal matter creates problems by themselves; see Lambert, *Law and Order*, 323–5. See Bates, *Regesta*, no. 100 for Chertsey, where soke is defined as a royal claim; this is, however, clearly a later forgery.

[36] Fleming, *Domesday Book*, no. 934.

[37] Harmer, *Writs*, nos. 4 (Abingdon), 12 and 20 (Bury St Edmunds), 34 (Christ Church, Canterbury), 40, 41 and 43 (Chertsey), 57, 59, 60 and 61 (Ramsey), 68, 69 and 72 (Wells), 77, 78, 79, 84, 85, 86, 87, 89, 89, 91, 92, 93, 94, 95, 96, 97, 98, 99, 100, 101, 102, 103 and 104 (Westminster, and all suspect or forged), 109 and 110 (Winchester),

holding of soke closer to a territorialised model of lordship, for in such cases soke was aligned with landlordship. Second, it was possible for lords to hold soke over all their dependents, presumably their commended men, without territorial distinctions being included.[38] Often such concessions were made alongside soke over land. The distinction is presumably meaningful; it might have meant that any lord so affected would hold extraterritorial claims over his dependents, and could claim soke even over (for instance) a commended man who held land from another lord elsewhere. The limits of such claims are never stated; would they apply in the next shire, for instance? And how might this kind of soke intersect with that of other lords? It might be envisaged that a lord who held soke over his dependents could conflict with a lord who held territorial soke if the first lord's dependent killed another on the second lord's lands. Such questions are essentially unanswerable from the surviving evidence, but could have introduced an extra potential source of conflict within an already complex system. Third, there were grants of soke over all dependents of any lords within particular hundreds. These survive only from the archive of Bury St Edmunds Abbey,[39] but the holding of comparable claims elsewhere suggest that there may have been similar ones, though those concern abbeys which have not generally preserved archives of writs.[40] These seem to be the three main variants, it is likely that there were other forms, which point to the complexity and perhaps regional variation in soke. York Minster received a grant of soke over its dependents within the king's soke at York, without any sense that the king's soke was being removed.[41]

Assessments have been made of the extent of lords' holding of soke.[42] These

120 (York); also Bromfield writ, appendix to same volume. Many of these grants also specify that the institution concerned was to receive soke over some new grant of land, perhaps with the implication that such claims were already held over other lands.

38 Harmer, *Writs*, nos. 11, 18 and 24 (Bury St Edmunds, concerning the soke of the eight and half hundreds), 37 and 38 (St Augustine's, Canterbury), 119 (York). One of these writs is the only pre-Conquest writ surviving that deals with soke, no. 11 for Bury St Edmunds. See T. A. M. Bishop and Pierre Chaplais, *Facsimiles of English Royal Writs to AD 1100* (Oxford, 1957), plate 1.

39 Harmer, *Writs*, nos. 9, 10, 18 and 24; on these see Richard Sharpe, 'The Use of Writs in the Eleventh Century', *Anglo-Saxon England* 32 (2003), 247–91.

40 For instance, comparable claims were made by the abbeys of Ely and Peterborough on the basis of assertions about pre-Conquest grants, and for Ely at least it seems that the Conqueror was willing to accept the pre-Conquest origins of Ely's jurisdictional claims; see Bates, *Regesta*, nos. 118, 120, 121, 122, 123 and 124. See also Great Domesday Book, fo. 280v: Nottinghamshire S6; Fleming, *Domesday Book*, nos. 1247, 1250.

41 Harmer, *Writs*, no. 119; repeated in Bates, *Regesta*, no. 351.

42 Stephen Baxter, 'Lordship and Justice in Late Anglo-Saxon England: The Judicial Functions of Soke and Commendation Revisited', in *Early Medieval Studies in Memory of Patrick Wormald*, ed. Stephen Baxter, Catherine Karkov, Janet L. Nelson and David Pelteret (Farnham, 2009), 383–419, at 383–8; T. B. Lambert, 'Royal

are mostly framed within the idea of Anglo-Saxon royal power and 'centralism', so that the granting or recognising of soke is seen as a weakness, and a diminution of royal power, a central concept for Anglo-Saxonists.[43] Thus, the grant of soke has been depicted as a rare and unusual occurrence, something that was only made available to a small number of religious institutions of special importance and good connections. There are grounds for doubting this, however. While the surviving writs that grant soke amount to no more than a few dozen, and concern only a few of the great abbeys or bishops,[44] this is not the best test of the extent of holding of soke in Anglo-Saxon England. Writs only survive through the archives of major ecclesiastical or municipal corporations, and so are not a valid test of how far soke was held by laymen; also, even many major churches have not preserved archives of pre-Conquest writs, so that some very privileged churches (Ely, Glastonbury and St Albans, to pick just three) are not named there. It might be better to observe that, for those archives which preserve substantial numbers of pre-Conquest writs, most of them contain grants of soke. The surviving writs even contain one specific mention of soke belonging to a prominent layperson; one of Queen Edith's writs for the bishop of Wells states that the canons of Wells were to have the land at Mark that she had held, with sake and soke.[45] Collectively, these suggest that even before 1066 there were plenty of instances where kings granted or recognised soke, sometimes to great churches with strong links to the Crown, but often to private landholders who could, for whatever reason, obtain favour or buy it from the king. Even where Domesday includes references to soke, it is likely that it underestimates the number in existence, for the kinds of extraterritorial soke noted above would not fit well into the categories and structures around which Domesday was based.

## The Management of Soke after 1066

The pattern of soke seen after the Conquest displays many of the features seen in the pre-Conquest sources, as might be expected; many of the writs in the name of William I were reissues of those produced by kings before 1066. There are two trends which set apart the post-1066 evidence. First, there is a great deal more of it, and the major pleas of his reign meant that existing claims were debated and

Protection and Private Justice: A Reassessment of Cnut's Reserved Pleas', in *English Law before Magna Carta: Felix Liebermann and* Die Gesetze der Angelsachsen, ed. Stefan Jurasinski, Lisi Oliver and Andrew Rabin (Leiden and Boston, 2010), 157–75, at 172.

43 Lambert, *Law and Order*, 4–6, 147–9.

44 Lambert, *Law and Order*, 172.

45 Harmer, *Writs*, no. 72; but there are concerns over the authenticity of this writ.

recorded in full. Thus, for instance, the Ely pleas show that it was widely thought that Ely Abbey held soke, and the king was willing to recognise that, even though there are no surviving pre-Conquest writs that document Ely's claim;[46] likewise, the writ for Stow orders that the monks there were to hold their lands with the soke once held by Godgifu, the wife of Earl Leofric of Mercia, though her claims are not recorded elsewhere.[47] Pre-Conquest charters and writs from these archives are few or none; any that did exist have long been lost. These extra references expand the known range of pre-Conquest soke holders considerably, and allow such names as Beverley Minster, Regenbald the priest and St Albans Abbey to be added.[48] They also substantiate the idea that ownership of soke by privileged individuals lay and ecclesiastical may once have been more common than the Anglo-Saxon evidence alone would suggest. Second, post-Conquest grants or confirmations of soke tend to focus much more on the association with land.[49] There are still some that concern soke over all of a beneficiary's dependents in any place, such as those for Abbotsbury,[50] but these are cases that refer back to older claims, and do not seem to be new grants. Otherwise, soke is associated with lands, and often with particular parcels of land or new acquisitions, and seems to indicate that soke was coming to be seen more as an additional aspect of landholding rather than as an independent claim itself.

Domesday Book presents a lot of evidence about soke and jurisdiction, but it is often quite hard to interpret. The usual problems attendant upon the use of Domesday data apply here in abundance; features are reported in some shires but not in others, and it is not always clear whether this reflects actual regional differences or merely differences in the ways in which data was gathered or interpreted.[51] Soke is covered in some detail in the three shires that are covered in Little Domesday Book, and so it is possible to see how some could owe soke to lords different from those from whom they held land. Little Domesday Book

46 Bates, *Regesta*, nos. 118, 120, 121, 122, 123 and 124. Ely's jurisdictional claims were then recorded in Domesday Book; Fleming, *Domesday Book*, no. 182.

47 Bates, *Regesta*, no. 276.

48 Bates, *Regesta*, nos. 31, 223 and 224, and 249.

49 Bates, *Regesta*, nos. 2 (Abbotsbury), 12 (Bath), 19.I, 19.II, 20.I, 20.II, 22 (Battle, all forged), 31 (Beverley), 99.I and 100 (Chertsey, both forged), 106 (Crowland), 109, 110, 111, 112, 115, 116 (Durham, all forged), 132 and 133 (Evesham), 152 (Gloucester), 184, 185 and 189 (St Paul's, London), 194 (Malmesbury but forged), 207 (Marmoutier), 216.I and 216.II (Peterborough), 221 (Ramsey), 223 and 224 (Regenbald the priest), 228 (Rochester, but forged), 249 (St Albans), 272 (Selby, but forged), 276 (Stow), 287 (Wells), 293, 294, 298, 299, 301, 302, 306, 307, 312, 316, 317, 318, 319, 320, 321, 322, 323, 331, 332 and 333 (Westminster), 350 (Worcester) and 351 (York).

50 Bates, *Regesta*, no. 1; see also 34 (Bury St Edmunds), 80 (St Augustine's, Canterbury), 98 (Chertsey), 222 (Ramsey), 337 and 338 (Winchester).

51 Sally Harvey, *Domesday: Book of Judgement* (Oxford, 2014), 87–106.

overall shows that lordship could, in practice, be even more complex than the tripartite model would suggest. Thus, commendation could be appended to a manor, so that (presumably) it would be passed from one lord to another if the manor were to change hands. Despite the trauma of the Conquest, there were still many places where dependents owed different kinds of lordship to different lords, and this position was accepted by them, their lords and by the compilers of Domesday. There had been many cases where lords had used the claim they perceived in soke as a means of annexing lands belonging to free peasants,[52] so that in some places the distinction between kinds of lordship was breaking down at the edges, but this was far from universal; overall, Anglo-Saxon practices and structures around lordship still seemed to set the norm in 1086.

Little Domesday Book represents one complete circuit, conventionally labelled as circuit VII, which was surveyed as a unit; the surviving book is an earlier form of the Domesday returns, before they were digested into the more abbreviated form seen in Great Domesday Book.[53] Little Domesday Book thus exposes complexities that are not seen in Great Domesday Book, but the significance of these differences is often hard to pin down. Differences may be due to the ways in which the data was gathered and processed, which would imply that Little Domesday's patterns were present elsewhere, even though they cannot now be observed in the data; or it might indicate that East Anglia was distinctive, and that its organisation differed from that seen elsewhere in England. The theory of East Anglian distinctiveness has much credibility; in the later eleventh century, it was perhaps the richest and most densely populated segment of England, as well as being the most commercialised region; so its distinctive presentation in Little Domesday Book may really reflect those differences from the rest of England.

Soke is not covered in Great Domesday Book to anywhere near the same extent seen in Little Domesday, but again there are some regional exceptions. Consistent attention is paid to soke in the shires covered by circuit VI, for these include a list of the holders of soke in each shire, contained in the opening sections where shire customs are noted. Three such lists are included, one for Yorkshire and one for Lincolnshire, and another within the Nottinghamshire section which covers both Derbyshire and Nottinghamshire.[54] The lists of soke holders are complex and it is not always clear what they mean;[55] that for Yorkshire is clearly labelled as a list

[52] Robin Fleming, *Kings and Lords in Conquest England* (Cambridge, 1991), chapter 6.

[53] For the most recent overview of the process behind the Domesday Books see Sally Harvey, *Domesday: The Book of Judgement* (Oxford, 2014).

[54] Great Domesday Book, fos. 280v: Nottinghamshire S5, 280v: Derbyshire S5, fo. 298v: Yorkshire C36–7, fo. 337r: Lincolnshire T5.

[55] Domesday for these shires, and especially for Nottinghamshire, includes many references to sokelands, which represents another usage of the same term; they denote lands that were associated with a manor, but which did not, for some reason, qualify as berewicks.

of soke holders from the time of King Edward, and the list for Lincolnshire seems to be the same, even though it is not labelled as such, for it includes pre-Conquest landholders only. The joint list for Nottinghamshire and Derbyshire, meanwhile, is a composite one, which includes pre-Conquest landholders alongside the names of lords who held lands in 1086:

> Here are noted those who had sake and soke and toll and team and the king's customary dues of the 2 pennies.[56]
>
> The Archbishop of York over his manors, and Countess Godgifu over Newark Wapentake,[57] and Ulf Fenman over his land; the Abbot of Peterborough over Collingham, and Abbot of Burton; Earl Hugh over Markeaton [Derby]; the Bishop of Chester; Toki; Swein son of Svavi; Siward Barn; Azur son of Svala; Wulfric Cild; Alsige [of] Illing; Leofwine son of Alwine; Countess Ælfgifu; Countess Gode; Alsige son of Karski over Worksop; Henry de Ferrers over Ednaston [Derby] and Doveridge [Derby] and Brailsford [Derby]; Walter d'Aincourt over Granby and Morton [Derby] and Pisley [in North Wingfield, Derby].
>
> None of these could have the earl's third penny except by his grant, and that for as long as he should live, except the Archbishop and Ulf Fenman and Countess Godgifu.
>
> Over the soke which belongs to Clifton [in Nottingham] the earl ought to have the third part of all customary dues and services.[58]

The list emphasises how soke was complex and variable, and that it included claims claims over dependents as well as claims to monetary payments. For

[56] The collection of sake, soke, toll and team was conventional, and can be found in many charters from the later eleventh and twelfth centuries; the addition of the king's two pennies was a more unusual privilege.

[57] Fleming, *Domesday Book*, no. 1250.

[58] *Hic notantur qui habuerunt socam et sacam et thol et thaim et consuetudinem regis ii denariorum.*

*Archiepiscopus Eborac(ensis) super maneria sua, et Godeva comitissa super Neuuercam wapent' et Ulf Fenisc super terram suam; abbas de Burg' super Colingeham; abbas de Bertune; Hugo \comes/ super Marcheton; episcopus de Cestre; Tochi; Suen filius Suaue; Siuuard \Barn/; Azor filius Saleuæ; Ulfric \Cilt/; Elsi Illinge; Leuuin filius Aluuin'; Ælueua comitissa; Goda comitissa; Elsi filius Caschin super Werchessope; Henricus de Ferrar' super Ednodestune et Dubrige et Breilesfordham; Walter de Aincurt super Granebi et Mortune et Pinnesleig.*

*Hoc omnium nemo habere potuit tercium denarium comitis nisi eius concessum, et hoc quamdiu uiueret, preter archiepiscopum et Ulf Fenisc et Godeue comitissam.*

*Super socam quæ iacet ad Cliftune debet habere comes terciam partem omnium consuetudinum et operum.*

Great Domesday Book, fo. 280v: Nottinghamshire S6; Fleming, *Domesday Book*, no. 1247. The translation here is that from the Alecto edition.

some of these, it is simply stated that the person held soke, and this might be taken to mean that the individuals so identified held soke very widely. This might have meant that they held such claims over all of their lands, but perhaps the territorial assumption there is more than the source justifies; it might even mean that they held soke over all of their dependents in the shires in question. For others, it seems that they held soke over named lands only rather than more generally. Thus, the list states that Peterborough Abbey held soke over its lands at Collingham; this should probably be taken to mean that the abbot did not hold soke over the other Nottinghamshire lands of the abbey, at North Muskham.[59] The list also shows how one soke holder, Countess Godgifu, had held soke over all of the hundred of Newark, so that, presumably, she would have been in a position to draw compensations from any lands and any dependents who came within that wapentake, and so draw compensations from the lands or dependents of any lord within that wapentake.[60]

The people named in the list suggest that soke was a complex business, and that the list was not compiled for any one reason. Major churches are well represented in the list, as might be expected given the number of writs which grant soke to these institutions. It is notable that the soke holder for these is listed as the office rather than the occupant.[61] The lay soke holders outnumber the ecclesiastical ones. Some of them were individuals of very high status who presumably would have had easy access to kings so that they could negotiate or demand recognition of such claims; their influence might have been worth buying, or they could have offered substantial resources to purchase such claims. What is not so clear is why only these landholders held soke in Nottinghamshire and Derbyshire, and not the many others comparable to them. The reasons for these are now lost. What can be asserted with confidence is that the granting of soke was essentially an individual matter and presumably reflected negotiations rather than just claims inherent in status.

The lists of soke holders in circuit VI shires are also problematic because they do not explain what they meant chronologically. The Yorkshire list specifies that it was a list of pre-Conquest holders; does this mean that the arrangements in it

59 Great Domesday Book, fo. 284r: Nottinghamshire 8.2. The list of Anglo-Saxon benefactors of Peterborough indicates that these lands were indeed passed to the abbey by different landholders. Muskham was given by Askyl, son of Toke, and Collingham by Turkyl Hoge, brother of Abbot Brand (Susan Kelly, *Anglo-Saxon Charters* 14: *Charters of Peterborough Abbey* (Oxford, 2009), no. 31 (xi) and 31 (xviii). David Roffe, 'From Thegnage to Barony: Sake and Soke, Title and Tenants-in-Chief', *Anglo-Norman Studies* xii (1989), 157–176, at 158 notes later evidence for the claims in Collingham.

60 Fleming, *Domesday Book*, no. 1250.

61 On how grants were made and phrased see Richard Sharpe, 'The Use of Writs in the Eleventh Century', *Anglo-Saxon England* 32 (2003), 247–91.

did not apply in 1086? Or does it indicate that the successors of the pre-Conquest holders continued to hold the soke summarised there? This might be the least unsatisfactory position, for otherwise it would seem that the data in Domesday was out of date, and it would be surprising if out-of-date data survived the winnowing operations of the Domesday surveyors, and then the editing work that reduced the original data into the form in which it survives in Great Domesday Book. Even greater problems are implicit in the joint list for Nottinghamshire and Derbyshire, which is chronologically inconsistent in naming pre-Conquest and post-Conquest landholders as though they were comparable. Do the Normans named in the list represent new grants of soke by the Conqueror? Or do they represent old grants where the names of the soke holders were not known, or were thought too obscure or impolitic to mention? Or might they even represent usurpations by these Norman lords?

Beyond circuits VI and VII, there are occasional hints of how soke was managed, but there is no consistent interest in the ways in which they were held and used. No consistent survey of soke elsewhere is possible from Domesday data. There are, nonetheless, many places where it is noted that claims over a hundred were appended to a manor, and so the lord (sometimes the king) had some financial or other benefits from it.[62]

The existence of soke is therefore clear; what is less clear is how these claims were exercised. There are hints in the evidence noted above; for example, Countess Godgifu's claims in Nottinghamshire were organised in accordance with hundred divisions, in this case over Newark hundred,[63] and so were presumably collected through the hundred court. This probably meant that she would have had agents in the hundred who were responsible for collection. This arrangement can be seen elsewhere. Queen Emma claimed soke in eight and a

62 Fleming, *Domesday Book*, nos. 137 eight hundreds at Stoke Mandeville (Bucks); 182 two hundreds of Ely (Cambridgeshire); 278 Frodsham (Cheshire); 346 Ermington (Devon); Moretonhampstead (Devon); 516 two hundreds at Upper Clopton (Warwickshire); 589 six hundreds at Over Wallop (Hampshire); 597 four hundreds at King's Somborne (Hampshire); 746 two hundreds at Burghill (Shropshire); 749 two hundreds at Much Cowarne (Shropshire); 934 twenty-two hundreds at Wye (Kent); 1250 Newark (Nottinghamshire); 1257 four and a half hundreds at Benson (Oxfordshire); 1259 two hundreds at Headington (Oxfordshire); 1262 two hundreds at Bampton (Oxfordshire); 1300 Blackburnshire (Lancashire); 1301 Salfordshire (Lancashire); 1321 Wrockwardine (Shropshire); 1322 Candover (Shropshire); 1323 Morville (Shropshire); 1324 two hundreds at Corfham (Shropshire); 1354 Taunton (Somerset); 1588 two hundreds at Malmesbury (Wiltshire); 1639, 1643, 1646 1659 Worcester and Oswaldslow; 1672 Pershore (Worcestershire); 1796 Witham (Essex); 1921 Rochford (Essex); 1924 Clavering (Essex); 2188 three hundreds at Yarmouth (Norfolk); 2767 hundred and a half at East Bergholt (Essex).

63 Great Domesday Book, fo. 283v: Nottinghamshire 6.1. Fleming, *Domesday Book*, no. 1250.

half hundreds in western Suffolk, which were later passed to the monks of Bury St Edmunds and still later transformed into Bury's franchise in West Suffolk.[64] One of the writs concerning Bury's soke claims defines them as those that had been collected for Queen Emma by Ælfric, son of Wihtgar.[65] Ælfric is not given any particular title, but he was clearly the queen's agent for collection of her claims, and his role was continued through a successor, Ordgar, who served the abbey.[66] The collection of the proceeds of soke was sufficiently lucrative and important that the queen and the abbey both thought it useful to employ someone, and possibly underlings for that someone, who might enforce the payment of those dues. It might also be conjectured that the activities of these individuals indicates that the collection of these proceeds was not automatic, and depended on the active assertion and enforcement of claims. It might be presumed that the locals, or those who controlled the locals, did not delight in paying these sums, and would neglect that duty if they could.

The duties of such people probably included the collection of small sums of money as hundred pennies, and also all dues arising from pleas and punishments. There is no evidence at all for how other claims, such as carrying services, might have been exploited. Perhaps, on the evidence of these and a few other isolated cases, it might be assumed that soke was usually claimed through the hundred court, for this was the only venue in which all of those who were subject to soke might be expected to be present, especially if those claims went beyond the lands of a lord. Yet, it was noted above that there was a shift during the eleventh century in terms of how soke was described in royal charters and writs. Increasingly, soke was associated with particular lands rather than being held over all dependents of a particular lord anywhere. The territorialisation of soke opened new opportunities for lords, in that they could regard particular territories as theirs; the idea that they might strengthen their lordship through excluding others, especially lords, seems to have been more attractive from the end of the eleventh century onwards. Important early hints can be seen in Domesday Book, and these are discussed below. What should be borne in mind is that what is being described is a set of practices that had no single point of origin; no king set these changes in motion. During the eleventh century there was no single set of terms to describe this, and so quite similar assemblies and courts can be seen under different terms.

64 Harmer, *Writs*, no. 18, and see Chapter 3 below.

65 Harmer, *Writs*, no. 18.

66 Bates, *Regesta*, no. 38; *Regesta*, i, no. 292.

## Conclusion

Complex lordship as it existed in later Anglo-Saxon England was probably always a difficult matter to manage. It meant that different lords could claim different dues from the same person; it meant that individuals could have links to many different lords; and so it meant that both sides had to maintain a lot of relationships. It seems that this system was in some ways unstable. Lords would try to use one kind of lordship to claim another, by browbeating dependents or less powerful lords. Lords might also try to exclude other lords from interference with dependents on their lands. For it seems often that lords tried to make territory the basis of the lordship, and remove others' claims that could intrude onto their lands. It was these impulses that gave rise to soke as a means for protecting the interests of lords and perhaps the interests of their dependents from the potential interference of others. In this, kings were willing to recognise the claims that some lords made to soke, though they were not willing to recognise all. Some favoured individuals, such as earls and bishops, received recognition of such claims automatically. Others might be able to negotiate such recognition, but it seems to have been rather harder for them to do so. There was no simple opposition between kings and their great men, but rather a willingness to co-operate so that the position of each was stabilised. Soke did not result in actual separate courts before 1066, but it did give rise to circumstances that helped their creation; this will be covered in the next chapter. Soke represents overall an ideal of lordship which was intensified and exclusive in managing dependents and their relationships with others.

# 3

# Private Claims and Hundreds in the Later Eleventh and Earlier Twelfth Centuries

The preceding chapters have sketched some of the background to the appearance of private courts. They have suggested that private courts did not exist in Anglo-Saxon England, because there is no concrete evidence for them, and because private courts were not compatible with the forms of lordship that can be seen in England before 1066. So far as can be seen, relationships between lords and dependents were managed in the public assemblies of hundred and shire, though the evidence for this is not uniform; the hundreds included greater lords and lesser lords, and even free peasants, but it is less clear how far they managed the links between lords and the unfree. The laws show, however, that the hundred in the tenth century could claim some powers even over slaves where they were accused of disruption of public order. There are important indicators of change, especially during the earlier eleventh century. The rise of the concept of soke helped to label and formalise some of the claims that lords could exact from their dependents, but also came to be used as a tool against other claims, and as a means for exempting the dependents of a lord from the attentions of the newly created sheriffs. Soke forms a parallel to the way in which lords sometimes used the formation of new churches as a means for hiding their dependents from many of the claims that might be made by minster churches. The drive towards monopolisation was the aspiration that drove the appearance of private courts.

This chapter aims to show how lords were able to take control of hundreds and subordinate them to their own interests. This is one model of change, but not the only one; the following chapter sketches another. Lords' seizure of control over hundreds appears first in this book because it seems to have been the earliest to be put into effect. Other methods, in which lords detached parts of hundreds or created their own courts, accounted for most of the courts that lords controlled by 1150 or so.[1] The appearance of these numerous courts depended on the development of an idea that courts were entities that could be owned, and that idea grew in relation to the hundreds first. The processes described in this chapter thus underpinned the creation of other kinds of court afterwards. So, it shows how lords came to take over hundreds as tools for the management, intensification and

[1] This theme is covered at greater length in Chapter 4.

extension of their lordship. The end result of this process was that some privileged and powerful lords came to, in their eyes and sometimes those of the king, own these entities.[2] Yet, there was no simple process to get to that point. Some prominent examples will be discussed below, but it is notable that the methods varied in detail, and that they progressed by an interplay of local developments and royal recognition and initiative. In a sense, it was a collaborative process. The individual steps were almost certainly undertaken without any clear sense of where the process would end up; ideas of ownership solidified interests and claims that, mostly, were already in place, and then went on to transform them. The cases discussed here generally relate to great churches, because their interests were the ones that were most fully archived, and which have been preserved most completely. One secular case is discussed, that of Arwystli; and it might be suggested that the methods here would have applied elsewhere, and might even explain something of the circumstances behind the status of Cheshire.

Private courts require definition. From the thirteenth century and beyond there were two kinds of private court; there was the model of franchise, whereby claims deemed to pertain to the Crown were transferred to some other individual or corporation so that they could make those claims and hold those courts, under the supervision of the king's officers; and there were courts held as the expression of private claims, where they did not derive from delegated royal claims but rather from individual claims over land and in lordship.[3] This model does not work well for much of the eleventh and twelfth centuries. Kings were less assertive in their claims over local courts than their successors in the thirteenth century, and the idea that courts and jurisdiction could belong to someone appears only uncertainly. Instead, when the idea of private courts is used in relation to the eleventh and earlier twelfth centuries, a much looser and more diverse reality is being described. What all point to is a position whereby individual lords could attain to a position of domination of local courts, where that predominant position was essentially a political rather than a legal reality. Dominance over a court was a means of securing and protecting the interests of a

2 There is a problem around how these relationships to courts should be described. The sources discussed in this chapter show that hundreds could be of someone, in terms that parallel how land could be of someone. These interests will here usually be covered by 'own' and related terms, because this avoids the problematic ideas implicit in possession and seisin. On this see Paul R. Hyams, 'Property Talk in Old English: Did Anglo-Saxon England Know the Concept of Seisin?', forthcoming.

3 Warren Ortman Ault, *Private Jurisdiction in England* (New Haven, 1923), 1–8; also Donald W. Sutherland, *Quo Warranto Proceedings in the Reign of Edward I, 1278–1294* (Oxford, 1963), 1–16. This is also suggested in Hudson, *Oxford History*, and many other places. Note also Patrick Wormald, 'Law and Justice in the Early English Kingdom: Oswaldslow Revisited', rpt in his *Legal Culture in the Early Medieval West: Law as Text, Image and Experience* (London, 1999), 313–32, at 327.

lord, and usually this came through excluding or diminishing interests that might compete with the lord's own.

A court could be regarded as private if it was a means whereby a lord could institutionalise control and influence over his dependents; this need not have involved any specific claim that a lord owned a court, for such claims were not made with much clarity in the eleventh century. What seems to lie behind all this was not the claim to ownership of the court, but rather the claim to regulate, enforce or prevent attendance;[4] also, it is possible that some might have involved the ability to determine what business was transacted, either refusing that which was unwelcome or forwarding that which was desired. This level of control might be attained through a lord's ability to use his own officials to run a court, and so determine how it operated; this would imply influence over both or either the division and allocation of revenues arising from the court, or the ability to determine what business was transacted within the court. It could also be attained through ensuring that a court consisted entirely or overwhelmingly of a lord's own dependents, so that the proceedings of a court reflected the predominant position of a lord, so that a lord could use the influence over his own dependents to ensure chosen outcomes; this could ensure that transactions benefitted the lords whose dependents packed the court, and might even give a strong influence over the dependents of other lords who fell within the remit of such a court. Lords' predominance over courts can be seen in various ways; the presence of an official, the affiliations of those who attended the court, and even the ability to enforce attendance and take penalties from those who failed to attend as they should. The instances discussed below suggest that the origin of private courts should be sought in places where particular lords could establish a predominant claim to influence over courts. There is no single model here; it seems more likely that there were many kinds of lordly influence that could later be developed into a proprietorial interest in a court.

There are no authentic grants of hundreds from before 1066, but often other claims could be extended to generate control over the hundreds in question. For instance, the grant of soke to Bury St Edmunds Abbey in the 1040s formed the basis for its later interest in the hundreds of West Suffolk. Perhaps the experience of Bury's interests in these hundreds did not change much over time, but what did change was how it was described. The idea of ownership of courts was, apparently, not known before 1066; by the early twelfth century and maybe somewhat before that, the idea that a court was an entity that could be owned had been established. There was a process of intellectual change that underlay the rearrangement of lordship in the eleventh century.

4 Lambert, *Law and Order*, 127–8.

## Hundreds with One Lord in the Eleventh Century

There is evidence for private interests in and control of hundred courts in Domesday Book, and this evidence has been known and discussed for an extended period. The heart of this can be found in the much-debated instance of Oswaldslow hundred in Worcestershire:[5]

> The church of St Mary of Worcester has one hundred, which is called Oswaldslow, in which lie 300 hides. By an arrangement of ancient times the bishop of this church has from them all the payments of the jurisdictions, all customary dues there which belong to the supplies of the household, both the king's service and his own, so that no sheriff can have any suit there, neither in any plea nor in any case whatever. The whole county confirms this. The said 300 hides were part of the lordship itself of the church, and if any of them was allotted or leased to any man, in whatever manner, to serve the bishop therefrom, the man who held such land leased to him, could not keep back from it any customary due at all for himself, except through the bishop, nor keep the land except until the completion of the time arranged between them; nor could he ever turn elsewhere with this land.[6]

5 Patrick Wormald, 'Law and Justice in the Early English Kingdom: Oswaldslow Revisited', rpt in his *Legal Culture in the Early Medieval West: Law as Text, Image and Experience* (London, 1999), 313–32. The status of Oswaldslow has been debated over time, and often in relation to two Worcester documents, the charters known as *Altitonantis* (http://www.esawyer.org.uk/charter/731.html) and the *Indiculum* (http://www.esawyer.org.uk/charter/1368.html). If genuine, these would show that Worcester owned the triple hundred in the tenth century. The authenticity of *Altitonantis* was defended in part by Eric John ('An Alleged Worcester Charter of the Reign of Edgar', *Bulletin of the John Rylands Library* 41 (1958), 54–80; *Land Tenure in Early England* (Leicester, 1964), chapters 5–8; 'The Church of Worcester and St Oswald', in *Belief and Culture in the Middle Ages: Studies Presented to Henry Mayr-Harting*, ed. Richard Gameson and Henrietta Leyser (Oxford, 2001), 142–57), who also argued that the interpolations were of the later eleventh century. The problems with the charter are so extensive that this all looks like special pleading, and Julia Barrow has shown that the charter was overwhelmingly forged ('How the Twelfth-Century Monks of Worcester Perceived their Past', in *The Perception of the Past in Twelfth-Century Europe*, ed. Paul Magdalino (London, 1992), 53–74). There has also been much discussion about the extent to which the military commitments in the forged *Altitonantis* and the presence of tenure of land by loan, together with continuity in some holdings on the Worcester lands prefigured 'feudalism' (for a good summary see Christopher Dyer, *Lords and Peasants in a Changing Society: The Estates of the Bishopric of Worcester, 680–1540* (Cambridge, 1980), 35–6, 39–47; and the sceptical comments in C. Warren Hollister, 'The Norman Conquest and the Genesis of English Feudalism', *American Historical Review* 66 (1961), 641–63, at 648–52).

6 *Ecclesia sanctæ Mariæ de Wirecestre habet unum hundret quod uocatur Oswaldeslau in quo iacent ccc hidæ. De quibus episcopus ipsius æcclesiæ a constitutione antiquorum temporum habet omnes redditiones socharum et omnes consuetudines inibi pertinentes*

The passage in Domesday Book is quoted here in full, because discussion has tended to be selective, and to focus on the first part of the passage alone.[7] Much of the debate around private courts has tended to emphasise the relationship between the holder of the court and the king, and to see the private nature of the court as something that was meant to protect the position of the court holder from the intrusions of sheriffs or other royal agents. This is an aspect of the passage above, in that it notes how the sheriff could not transact business through the court of Oswaldslow,[8] and how some of the kinds of service owed to the king belonged to the bishop. Most of the passage does not relate to royal power at all, but instead concerns how the bishop related to other lords, and how effectively the bishop could exploit lands over which he maintained a claim. Thus, the passage notes that the bishop received payments from all jurisdictions, which presumably means that he had a prior and superior claim to all such payments, whether from the lands that he managed himself, or from those of other lords. The king held no particular lands in Oswaldslow hundred, according to Domesday Book, so the claims mentioned here – soke, here translated as jurisdictions – were probably those of the lords who held lands from the church of Worcester. The most detailed points in the passage are those that concern the relationship between the bishop and the lords who held lands from the church. Whoever wrote this passage was concerned with the possibility that the tenants of the church might fail to hand over the customary payments due from the lands of the church,[9] or that those who had leased land might try to convert that temporary interest into a permanent one.

---

*ad dominicum uictum et regis seruitium et suum, ita ut nullus uicecomes ullam ibi habere possit querelam, nec in aliquo placito nec in alia qualibet causa. Hoc attestatur totus comitatus. Hæ predictæ ccc hidæ fuerunt de ipso dominio æcclesiæ et siquid de ipsis cuicunque homini quolibet modo attributum uel prestitum fuisset ad seruiendum inde episcopo, ille qui eam terram prestitam sibi tenebat, nullam omnino consuetudinem sibimet inde retinere poterat nisi per episcopum, neque terram retinere nisi usque ad impletum tempus quod ipsi inter se constituerant, et nusquam cum ea terra se uertere poterat.*

Great Domesday Book, fo. 172v: Worcestershire 2.1. The translation here is that from the Alecto edition.

7 For instance, Patrick Wormald, 'Law and Justice in the Early English Kingdom: Oswaldslow Revisited', rpt in his *Legal Culture in the Early Medieval West: Law as Text, Image and Experience* (London, 1999), 313–32. The main exception is Stephen Baxter, 'The Representation of Lordship and Land Tenure in Domesday Book', in *Domesday Book*, ed. Elizabeth M. Hallam and David Bates (Stroud, 2001), 73–102, 203–8, esp. 85–91, and the points here draw on that analysis.

8 Perhaps this also implied that sheriffs' agents could not exercise control in the hundred.

9 This is also a concern elsewhere in the Domesday Book description of the Worcester interests, where the bishop's claim to some payments was noted in relation to Worcester's holding in Ash hundred; see Great Domesday Book, fo. 174: Worcestershire 2.80.

Much of the modern discussion noted above has tended to see private courts as a response to the potential threats posed by kings, and to see the claims of private-court holders as, essentially, a commentary upon the developing idea of king's pleas, the business claimed by kings as pertaining to themselves. This fits with the broader pattern of the historiography, which depicts the overall development of the law as largely a royal, or at least king-led, story. This was probably not the perspective of those whose views lie behind the Oswaldslow passages in Domesday Book, or those who wrote the other texts that describe the operation and uses of the hundred. For these make it clear that the operation of the hundred was principally meant as a means of ensuring that the primacy of Worcester's interests over its lands was preserved, and that the interests of others were kept under control. Oswaldslow was mostly a weapon for use against Worcester's neighbours, not a shield against the king.

The passage about Oswaldslow needs to be read in relation to the other set of sources that explain what was going on at that time, the various narratives and sources about the disputes between the bishop of Worcester and the abbot of Evesham over lands and dues in Hampton and Bengeworth.[10] These are not unproblematic, for they represent the viewpoints of the two churches involved and not of the other participants, and their interpretation of what happened varied greatly; there is also the likelihood that the representation of what happened was a partial statement intended to inform and condition any future claims made by the two sets of monks. At any rate, the narrative from Worcester seems to reflect many of the assumptions that also underlie the Domesday account of Oswaldslow.[11] Worcester's view on this was that Æthelwig, abbot of Evesham, used his position and kinship networks to attract away some of Worcester's tenants, before depriving them of their lands. This looks like a classic instance whereby a greater lord used a claim to one kind of lordship or domination as a basis for claiming other kinds of lordship or domination. It is notable that Worcester presents the case principally as one between the two great churches, and downplays the involvement of other interested parties. The Worcester narrative indicates that Abbot Æthelwig eventually made some kind of submission and recognition of Worcester's interest in the lands, but that this did not solve the problem for them; after Æthelwig's death, Bishop Odo of Bayeux received from the king all the lands of Æthelwig, and so Worcester lost properties and claims.

Worcester's view was particular to that institution, and Evesham's view differed somewhat.[12] The Evesham chronicle account does not take the same

[10] The sources are set out clearly and usefully in Van Caenegem, *Lawsuits*, no. 10.

[11] The Worcester narrative is Van Caenegem, *Lawsuits*, no. 10B.

[12] Van Caenegem, *Lawsuits*, no. 10A, also Thomas of Marlborough, *History of the Abbey of Evesham*, edited and translated by Jane Sayers and Leslie Watkiss (Oxford, 2003), 177–9.

starting-point as Worcester's, and treats the Worcestershire lands as merely some among a bigger problem, in that Abbot Æthelwig's acquisitions across at least three shires were called into question. Thus, the Evesham narrative does not acknowledge any prior interest or claim from Worcester, presumably because Worcester's claims only affected a small portion of the lands, and any claim by Worcester looked secondary in relation to the attacks of Evesham's tenants and would-be tenants. Evesham attributed the origin of the problem to Abbot Walter, Æthelwig's successor, who tried to remove the occupants of the lands by refusing their homage, and then casts the dispute as one that involved Evesham and its various disappointed tenants; the role of Worcester is entirely omitted. The Evesham story then tells how Evesham's tenants took the case to Odo, bishop of Bayeux, who proceeded to defraud the abbey of twenty-eight out of the thirty-six estates that had been called into question. This ending in loss is what unites the two stories from the two great churches.

The two stories of these complicated legal transactions have a direct bearing upon the aims and interpretation of the Domesday entry for Oswaldslow quoted above. They indicate that both churches were concerned with the possibility that lands and dues might be removed from them, because both had lost lands that each had claimed. In both cases, tenants of the churches had tried to control, define or alter the claims that the churches as their lords had made over their lands; also in both cases, the churches had proven vulnerable to claims from outside, from Bishop Odo as authorised by the king, because some lands were less closely tied to them because others also had interests in them. Evesham was caught out because the new acquisitions of Abbot Æthelwig were not yet so closely linked to the church; Worcester was caught out because parts of its lands were also held by others and it found it harder to assert its exclusive claims.

It might be suggested that the claims over Oswaldslow that Worcester made were meant as a solution to the problems depicted in the narratives surviving from the great churches of Worcestershire. Worcester's claims in Oswaldslow were a means of asserting and protecting that church's claims over its lands. Worcester could already make claims over land, for it could claim to hold much of the land within the hundred, and even many of the parts held by others were in Domesday Book presented as berewicks and Worcester's holdings.[13] Yet Domesday Book for Oswaldslow shows that Worcester had another set of claims. Worcester claimed soke over the whole hundred and all the lands within it, and customary dues from the church's lands and others, and claims to regulate succession to the holders of the lands. Presumably these claims could be enforced through the Oswaldslow hundred court, where Worcester's tenants, agents and representatives formed the judges and oath-helpers who would

[13] Great Domesday Book, fo. 172v–174r: Worcestershire 2.3–5, 7, 16–21, 23–5, 29–30, 32–7, 39–41, 47, 55, 58, 69–71, 73–5 and 78.

determine the outcome of any dispute resolution. The sheriff was excluded according to Domesday Book, and that might imply that his agents were also excluded; though he occupied lands in Oswaldslow, it was as Urse rather than as the sheriff of Worcester. These claims might even have been devised as a response to the actual circumstances of the complicated stories told in the narratives discussed above. It is conspicuous that the aim attributed to Abbot Æthelwig is very close to that envisaged in the Domesday entry for Oswaldslow, for whoever wrote it was concerned by the possibility that the lesser lords who held lands from Worcester as temporary tenants might try to keep the lands beyond the term agreed. This aim is attributed to Abbot Æthelwig, but it is the interpretation of the Worcester writer rather than Æthelwig's own.

The idea that Oswaldslow and comparable cases where great lords claimed a preponderant interest in a hundred had this inspiration can be correlated with another attribute of Oswaldslow and some other hundreds linked with great churches; their shapes. Oswaldslow was not a simple block of territory. There was a coherent zone around the city of Worcester itself, but this amounted to less than half of the surface area of Oswaldslow. The majority of the hundred consisted of fifteen enclaves, some of considerable size, spread out across the southern half of the shire and in exclaves surrounded by Gloucestershire and Warwickshire.[14] The many enclaves consisted of lands that belonged to the church of Worcester, but which were isolated from the main block around the city of Worcester. Oswaldslow's boundaries seem to have been designed to match the pattern of Worcester's lands, and so were probably defined subsequent to the acquisition of those lands. The implication is that they were a secondary development, and that the hundred was formed to support the lands rather than the other way round. Given that there are points in the Domesday description of Oswaldslow that note how the hundred controlled the succession to tenancies on Worcester's lands, it would seem that management of the lands was central to the functions carried out through Oswaldslow. Having so many of Worcester's lands within one hundred meant that the church could use the preponderance of its tenants to control or try to control the ways in which its lands developed and remained.

Oswaldslow has attracted a lot of attention because it is described so fully in Domesday Book. The fullness of the description can be linked to the ways in which Bishop Wulfstan of Worcester was able to subvert the Domesday process to impose his own priorities.[15] Some of Worcester's claims, such as those over the king's customs, may have been specific or even unique to Oswaldslow. Yet

[14] Hundred maps based principally on Domesday data can be found in the Phillimore edition of Domesday Book (*Domesday Book: Text and Translation*, ed. J. Morris (38 vols, Chichester, 1975–86), the Alecto edition of Domesday Book (*Great Domesday Book*, ed. R. W. H. Erskine and G. H. Martin (62 volumes, London, 1987–92).

[15] Stephen Baxter, 'The Representation of Lordship and Land Tenure in Domesday

there were other hundreds that mimicked Oswaldslow's form and structure. Worcestershire offers some of the clearest examples. There was the hundred of Pershore,[16] which matched Oswaldslow in many ways. It included a large area south of Oswaldslow, and seven enclaves spread across the shire, often interleaved with Oswaldslow; the south-western extension of Worcestershire consisted of a patch of Pershore cut off from the rest of Worcestershire by a patch of Oswaldslow, which itself was cut off from the rest of Worcestershire by a patch of Pershore hundred, which itself was cut off from the rest of Worcestershire by a patch of Oswaldslow, which bounded on the southern edge of the main block of Pershore hundred. Enclaves of Pershore hundred made up both the south-western and north-eastern extremities of Worcestershire as a whole. Pershore hundred was more complicated than Oswaldslow because by the time of the making of Domesday Book it did not consist of the lands of one great church, but rather of two: Westminster Abbey and Pershore Abbey. It may have originated as the lands of Pershore Abbey before parts were abstracted and transferred to Westminster Abbey by Edward the Confessor.

The hundred of Fishborough in south-eastern Worcestershire similarly comprised of the lands and interests of Evesham Abbey, which consisted of a block around Evesham itself and two detached segments in northern and central Worcestershire. There are comparable dispersed hundreds in some other shires, such as the hundred of Albanstou or Cashio in Hertfordshire, which corresponded to the lands of St Albans Abbey, the hundred of Wells in Somerset, which corresponded to the interests of the cathedral and collegiate church at Wells; and the hundreds of central Hampshire, based on the lands of the Old Minster, Winchester. The identification of these dispersed, tenurially determined hundreds is not new; they have been discussed at length by F. R. Thorn in relation to Domesday Book, who labelled them as ecclesiastical hundreds, while allowing that there might be some secular ones.[17]

These hundreds stand out because their forms are so distinctive. In many shires, hundreds consisted of regular blocks without numerous enclaves and exclaves.[18] Staffordshire forms perhaps the clearest example of this, for in that

Book', in *Domesday Book*, ed. Elizabeth M. Hallam and David Bates (Stroud, 2001), 73–102, 203–8, at 82–91.

16 Pershore hundred is not named in Domesday Book, though the lands of Pershore and Westminster Abbeys lack rubrics attributing them to particular hundreds; F. R. Thorn, 'Hundreds and Wapentakes', in *The Worcestershire Domesday* [introduction and translation] (London, 1986), 32–7, at 37.

17 F. R. Thorn, 'Hundreds and Wapentakes', in *The Hampshire Domesday* [introduction and translation] (London, 1989), 28–39, at 28, 32.

18 The following discussion is based on the hundred maps in the Phillimore edition of Domesday Book (*Domesday Book: Text and Translation*, ed. J. Morris (38 vols, Chichester, 1975–86), and especially in the Alecto edition of Domesday Book (*Great*

shire there were five hundreds, each of which formed a coherent block. There was only one enclave inside Staffordshire, and that was in the south of the shire where Dudley formed an enclave of Worcestershire. Similar consistent patterns can be seen in Cheshire and in Derbyshire; elsewhere, the territory of Between Ribble and Mersey (otherwise the southern half of the later Lancashire), Nottinghamshire, Leicestershire, Northamptonshire, Warwickshire and elsewhere contain few exclaves and enclaves. In all of these cases, detailed information on hundred boundaries is first presented in Domesday Book, so that hundreds and their boundaries before the later eleventh century are entirely mysterious. It cannot thus be shown what these differences in the patterns of hundreds mean; the neat blocks of Staffordshire might represent hundreds as they had existed in the earlier eleventh century or even into the tenth, but the relationship between the Domesday pattern and its predecessors is essentially unknowable. There are hints in the laws that the assumption of the writers of those sources was that hundreds should be coherent blocks; 1 Edgar 5–5.1 lays down that if one hundred pursued a malefactor into another, then the hundredman of the second hundred should be informed;[19] this does not assume the kind of complicated and intricate hundreds seen in Worcestershire and elsewhere.

Hundreds could be manipulated in many kinds of ways so that they would better reflect the interests and ambitions of lords. Hundreds could end up with baroque and irregular boundaries, so that there is more than a hint of a gerry-mandered district. These were not common, and the clearest examples were in the hands of a few great churches which were particularly favoured by kings. There is no credible documentation that reflects the formation of such hundreds, but it might reasonably be assumed that kings lay behind it and controlled such processes. Presumably, if lords could create such hundreds themselves, then they would do so generally as a means of protecting their dependents from other lords, but most hundreds do not match these patterns; yet hundreds where one lord controlled all or most of landholdings within it were not the norm. In cases such as Oswaldslow, it is not clear when or by whom change occurred, only that some arrangements were in place by 1086. The clearest statement on who was able to change hundreds and their composition is contained in the mid twelfth-century tract known as the *Leges Edwardi Confessoris*, which states this:

> The boundaries of the king's shires properly belong with the judgement of the four royal roads. The boundaries of the hundreds, of the wapentakes, [belong] to the earls and the sheriffs with the judgement of the county.[20]

---

*Domesday Book*, ed. R. W. H. Erskine and G. H. Martin (62 volumes, London, 1987–92).

19 There was an earlier declaration of the same principle in 3 Edmund 6.1, but this survives only in Latin and the unit described was the *villa* rather than the hundred.

20 *Diuisiones syrarum regis proprie cum iudicio iiii cheminorum regalium sunt. Diuisiones*

The general point seems to be that larger-scale arrangements fell to the particular control of kings, and that the boundaries of shires and the four roads were among them. That kings exercised control over the four roads can be substantiated to some extent, as for instance from the way in which Henry I authorised the diversion of the Fosse Way at Newark.[21] It is remarkable that such a local matter was taken to the king for approval, and it seems to imply a recognition that the king had a special interest in matters concerning the Fosse Way. Likewise, there is evidence that the definition of shire boundaries, and also of the division of territories into shires, were carried out with the involvement and approval of kings.[22] So, the assertion of the writer of the *Leges Edwardi Confessoris* can be substantiated to some extent from twelfth-century evidence, at least insofar as it explained what kings had or claimed; and the writer's claim that the alteration of hundreds and their boundaries acquires some credibility from the context in which it was made.

Evidence for small-scale changes to hundreds does not exist in the eleventh century, when there is only a snapshot of the hundreds in the data presented in the Domesday Books. Twelfth-century evidence is somewhat limited, and it is also somewhat ambiguous, for it suggests a more complicated picture than that set out in the *Leges Edwardi Confessoris*. In one well-known case, the determination of the boundaries of a hundred was not done locally by earls, sheriffs and the shire court, but in a royal court in front of the queen while the king was absent in Normandy, when she acted as regent.[23] The document has mostly been noted for its reference to the use of Domesday Book and its data in court, and for the remarkable collection of eminent men and royal functionaries over which Matilda presided. The document is anomalous, for it was unusual to have so many of those who resolved a dispute cited in a royal document of this form; it is hard to

*hundredorum, wapentagiorum, comitibus, uicecomitibus cum iudicio comitatus. Leges Edwardi Confessoris*, 13–13.1.

21 *Regesta*, ii. no. 1660–1.

22 The evidence that the status and boundaries of shires had to be determined through the authority of the king is set out in Richard Sharpe, *Norman Rule in Cumbria, 1092–1136* (Carlisle, 2006). Against this, it might be noted that in the later eleventh century it sometimes happened that lords could transfer particular places between shires, especially where they were or controlled sheriffs, so that kings might not have known. For some examples see Werrington and the boundaries of Devon and Cornwall (H. P. R. Finberg, 'The Early History of Werrington', *English Historical Review* 59 (1944), 237–51) and Halesowen in Worcestershire and Shropshire (F. R. Thorn, 'Hundreds and Wapentakes', *The Worcestershire Domesday* [introduction and translation] (London, 1987), 32–7, at 36; also William Page, ed., *Victoria History of the Counties of England: A History of the County of Worcester*, iii. (London, 1913), 136); W. E. Wightman, 'The Palatine Earldom of William fitz Osbern in Gloucestershire and Worcestershire (1066–1071)', *English Historical Review* 77 (1962), 6–17.

23 *Regesta*, ii. no. 1000; *Abingdon Chronicle*, ii. 170–1.

parallel this document. Nonetheless, its purpose was to show that Matilda's court had heard and determined a case concerning the boundaries of Pyrton hundred in Oxfordshire. The document states that the manor of Lewknor was henceforth to be free of the hundred of Pyrton, and that all of its dues were to be paid in the hundred of Lewknor. It would seem that the point of the proceedings was that some men from Pyrton hundred had tried to assert jurisdiction over the abbey's holding at Lewknor;[24] yet the monks did not approve of this, and used a plea before Queen Matilda to obtain a judgement and an authoritative document to prove that the property in question should lie within Lewknor hundred instead, and that all dues should be paid there. The judgement of Lewknor is hard to parallel elsewhere, for there are no similar royal adjudications of the boundaries and contents of hundreds. The Lewknor case cannot be taken as evidence of a general assertion of royal control over the boundaries of hundreds.[25] More generally, it seems that the management and alteration of the boundaries of hundreds was done at a local level, and that the dominant voice in doing so was that of lords, who used participation in hundreds as an expression of and as a means of maintaining their lordship.

Kings could grant to favoured lords the domination over a whole hundred. There are no clear Anglo-Saxon examples, but some were created after the Norman Conquest. They were often created in regions where there seems to have been some fear of vulnerability, and were sometimes linked to castles. They can be seen in the Welsh borders, in Cornwall, Sussex and Kent, and in Yorkshire. In each of these cases, a lord received lordship over all the lands in a hundred, sometimes excepting lands that belonged to a church, and so obliterated patterns of landholding that had been in place before 1066.[26] Sometimes these grants involved blocks of land that passed beyond the bounds of hundreds, so that the grant of control of all the lands in a hundred seems incidental.[27] It seems that control of the hundred came as a consequence of landed influence over those who held land, and was not the primary purpose of the grant. Some of these developed into private courts, and others did not; this seems largely to reflect how far the lands remained as a coherent block over time, or whether they were broken up. These grants of wide areas of lordship seem often to have been made later in the process of conquest, and probably after 1071.[28]

24 *Abingdon Chronicle*, ii. 168–9.

25 One of the few other cases is *Regesta*, ii. no. 1763 for Bath, but this is a problematic text; it purports to extend the bounds of the bishop's hundred, but the document includes two distinct items of business, which is very rarely seen in authentic original charters.

26 Robin Fleming, *Kings and Lords in Conquest England* (Cambridge, 1991), 145–8, 180–2.

27 Robin Fleming, *Kings and Lords in Conquest England* (Cambridge, 1991), 146, 151.

28 Robin Fleming, *Kings and Lords in Conquest England* (Cambridge, 1991), 161–3.

## Soke over a Whole Hundred

A somewhat different route towards establishing claims over hundreds can be seen in relation to Bury St Edmunds Abbey and its interest in hundreds in West Suffolk, which came to have soke over all the hundreds in question. This interest is the only one that is clearly documented before the Norman Conquest. It was not the same as the dispersed hundreds tied to the lands of one lord that were discussed above. By the thirteenth century, the abbey's interest in the eight and a half hundreds had been assimilated to the model of a franchise, but its origin was not as a franchise at all. The abbey's interest began as a grant of soke over whole hundreds. Soke was usually used as a means of obtaining an exemption, even though in practice it was only an exemption from the perspective of lords; in the Bury charters, soke was a grant over the dependents of other lords. This points to the difficulties in defining soke convincingly. The grant appears in writs in the name of Edward the Confessor, and these show that he assigned to the abbey the soke over eight and a half hundreds in western Suffolk that had been held by his mother, Queen Emma. The writ is datable to 1043–4, so not long after Edward became king, and while Emma was still alive.[29] The eight and a half hundreds probably formed some kind of unit, for they are described in Edward's writ as the hundreds that pertained to Thingoe, a mound near Bury itself.[30]

The grant states simply that the monks were to receive the sokes of the hundreds, and does not spell out its implications. As the grant was of all the sokes of the hundreds, it should probably be read to indicate that this applied to all persons within the hundreds, so that claims were held over men on the lands of Bury St Edmunds Abbey as well as over the lands of other lords. There is a problem here. Before Bury received the grant of the soke of the eight and a half hundreds, it had already been granted sake and soke over its own dependents, which apparently included those within the eight and a half hundreds themselves as well as those outside.[31] It is hard to know how to interpret this. It might be that the soke of a hundred was viewed as distinct from the soke that a lord could hold

George Garnett, *Conquered England: Kingship, Succession and Tenure, 1066–1166* (Oxford, 2007), 27–33, challenges some of the conceptualisation of the process of post-Conquest distribution.

29 Harmer, *Writs*, no. 9. The terms are close to another writ, Harmer, *Writs*, no. 10, which is a clear forgery. See Harmer, *Writs*, introduction pp. 145–6. On this series of writs see Richard Sharpe, 'The Use of Writs in the Eleventh Century', *Anglo-Saxon England* 32 (2003), 247–91, at 262–70, and on the Bury archive generally see Sarah Foot, 'The Abbey's Armoury of Charters', in *Bury St Edmunds and the Norman Conquest*, ed. Tom Licence (Woodbridge, 2014), 31–52.

30 For analysis of these see Helen M. Cam, 'Early Groups of Hundreds', rpt in her *Liberties and Communities in Medieval England* (Cambridge, 1944), 91–106.

31 Harmer, *Writs*, no. 8.

over his own dependents, so that two different kinds of claim were expressed through this, and they were not in conflict with each other. The idea that the two sokes could be distinct is supported by the way in which Edward issued other writs after the grant of the soke of the eight and a half hundreds, which likewise confirmed to the abbey the soke over its own dependents.[32]

On Queen Emma's death, Edward again confirmed the abbey's interest in the soke of the hundreds, and in terms that show something about how soke was managed and exercised.[33] The writ shows that one Ælfric, son of Wihtgar, had acted as custodian for the claims that Emma had in the hundreds, and that he had done so when those claims were in the king's hand – presumably during the gap after he had seized the sokes from his mother, and before he granted them to the abbey. Ælfric, son of Wihtgar, is not immediately traceable elsewhere, but seemingly acted as Emma's agent, who raised her claims within that territory. The presence of such an agent was important; in the same Edwardian writ the king observed that he had not granted away to others any specific claims such as *grithbreach*, and nor had he granted away any penalties. The meaning of this clause is presumably that the abbey was facing some difficulties in enforcing the full collection of these dues. Nonetheless, the mention of Ælfric, son of Wihtgar, shows that these claims involved some measure of change. There was now someone, who might even be called an official, who was engaging with the hundreds to ensure the successful exploitation of a claim. Presumably this involved regular attendance and active participation in the sessions of the hundreds, and collection of fines and dues. Ælfric might also have taken a functional role in the operation of the hundreds, through, for instance, summoning individuals to the courts. The claims managed by Ælfric, son of Wihtgar, were also treated as a clear and identifiable unit in writ-charters of Williams I and II; this document also refers to another person, Ordgar, who had had custody of the same claims in succession to Ælfric, son of Wihtgar.[34]

The eleventh-century documents describe the abbey's claims in the eight and a half hundreds as claims over sokes, but there is a shift in how these claims were presented in the early eleventh century. The development can be seen in how the hundreds were described in documents in the names of William II and Henry I. William described the claims in terms that are a summary of the many writs from the reigns of previous kings; that the abbey's claims consisted of the soke and forfeitures as held by Queen Emma and as managed by Ælfric son of Wihtgar and afterwards by Ordgar.[35] Yet, only a few years later, Henry I thought that the abbey had the hundreds as entities, not merely claims within them. Where William had

32 Harmer, *Writs*, nos. 11 and 12.
33 Harmer, *Writs*, no. 18; the same terms are repeated in no. 24.
34 Bates, *Regesta*, no. 38; *Regesta*, i. no. 292.
35 *Regesta*, i. no. 292.

written that claims in the hundreds pertained or belonged to the abbey, Henry used the verb *habere* to redefine the relationship between the two:

> I will and firmly command that St Edmund and Abbot Robert have (*habeant*) the eight and a half hundreds as well and as honourably as Abbot Baldwin ever held it. And I command that all who hold within the said hundreds should attend hundreds and pleas as they are required by the justice of the abbot. And the abbot should implead those who will not, so that they attend. I command also that the servants of the abbot in the same hundreds should collect my gelds and taxes, and carry them to my treasury as they were accustomed to do in the time of Abbot Baldwin, because I do not want that he (i.e. the abbot) should lose the customs he had in the time of my father.[36]

It also sets out something of what it meant for the abbey to have this level of interest in a hundred. The terms in which it is written are fairly specific, and it might be most plausible to regard them as a response to local circumstances; that the abbey was having difficulties in maintaining its interests in the hundreds, and so the monks obtained from the king a clarification of what they could claim, and of what others owed to them. Thus, those who should attend the hundred were ordered that they should do so, and as they were required by the abbot; those who did not were ordered to explain themselves to the abbot. This makes clear that the management and enforcement of attendance at the hundreds was something that pertained to and was organised by the abbey. Henry also ordered that the abbey's officials should be responsible for the collection of financial dues, and for their onward transmission to the king's treasury. The point behind the latter might be that other officers had been intervening in the abbey's hundreds, and that the abbot wished to ensure their exclusion. Overall, it is clear from this source that the abbot and his officials were very closely involved in the management and running of the hundreds, and that some of the mechanisms for self-government within the hundred envisaged in the Anglo-Saxon laws – such as the collective management of attendance and non-attendance – had fallen into the hands of the abbot and his officials.

36 *Volo et firmiter precipio ut sanctus Ædmundus et Robertus abbas ita bene et honorifice habeant viii[to] hundretos suos et dimidium sicut Baldewinus abbas melius habuit. Et precipio ut omnes qui tenent infra predictos hundretos requirant hundretos et placita per iusticiam abbatis sicut requirere habent. Et qui noluerint iustificet eos abbas ut ueniant. Precipio etiam ut ministri abbatis in eisdem hundretis colligant geldos et scottos meos et portent usque ad thesaurum meum sicut solebant facere in tempore Baldewini abbatis quia nolo ut perdat consuetudines quas habuit in tempore patris mei. Regesta*, ii. no. 777; *Feudal Documents from the Abbey of Bury St Edmunds*, ed. D. C. Douglas (London, 1932), 67, no. 32. Contrast Henry I's *Regesta*, ii. nos. 644 and 656, which repeat terms taken from the eleventh-century writs in describing the abbey's interests as sokes. The terms of *Regesta*, ii. no. 777 were repeated in *Regesta*, ii. nos. 1227, 1605 and 1642.

The above source does not present itself as something that set out to transform the ways in which the abbey and the locals thought about the relationship between the two. Yet, it should be read in such radical terms. Hitherto, the abbey's interest in the hundreds had been presented as claims to financial dues and the ability to control proceedings through an official, things which were within the framework of the hundred. Now, the abbey's interest was recast as something that applied to the hundred as an entity, and the abbey became in some sense the proprietor of the hundred. The abbey now 'had' the hundred, using the verb *habere*, which was one of the terms used to describe claims in land (it was rare that it was used by itself in relation to land).[37] The case of Bury St Edmunds and its hundreds is not the earliest one, but the transition from interest to proprietorship is more fully documented here than anywhere else. It is a landmark in the development of ideas of claim and jurisdiction that a hundred could be something that might belong to someone. The way in which the hundreds could be thought of as an interest comparable to other items of abbey property can be seen in another Henry I document in favour of the abbey, where interests in lands and in hundreds were exactly equated:

> I command that Anselm, abbot of St Edmund should hold (*teneat*) his abbey and hundreds and lands and men and all customs pertaining to the same abbey with soke and sake and *warpeni* just as I conceded to him by my charter and just as the charter of King Edward and my father show.[38]

Just as the abbey's relationship with the hundreds changed, so seemingly did the relationship with the king where that concerned the hundreds. Many of the earlier documents, including the first of the writ-charters in the name of Henry I quoted above, indicate that the abbey's interests in the hundreds were ones of management. The abbey's representatives collected dues from the hundreds and then forwarded them to the king's treasury. The point, presumably, was that the abbey could keep any income that exceeded its obligations towards the treasury. Yet the transmission of the revenues of these hundreds to the king's treasury does not appear as a separate item on the Pipe Rolls, so it seems that they were not made in 1129–30 at least. Perhaps the monks had been released from the obligation to pay, or maybe the payments are hidden within the revenues accounted for by the sheriff. Some revenues that probably arose from the eight and a half hundreds

37 There are many examples where *habere* is used to describe the tenure of land; for instance, *Volo et precipio ut ecclesia sancte Marie de Abbendona habeat et teneat terram suam de Winicfelda*, from *Regesta*, ii. no. 736; *Abingdon Chronicle*, ii. 128–9.

38 *Precipio quod Anselmus abbas de sancto Eadmundo teneat abbaciam suam et hundreda et terras et homines et omnes consuetudines eidem abbacie pertinentibus [sic] cum soka et saka et warpeni sicut ei concessi per cartam meam et sicut carta regis Eadwardi et patris mei testantur. Regesta*, ii. no. 1597; *Feudal Documents from the Abbey of Bury St Edmunds*, ed. D. C. Douglas (London, 1932), 77, no. 52.

were later accounted for on the Pipe Rolls, such as the 40s. 3d. assize from the lordship of Bury St Edmunds that appears on the roll for 2 Henry II.[39]

The abbey's administration of its interests in its hundreds can be studied in some depth from a source made in the later twelfth century. This, known and published as the Kalendar of Abbot Samson,[40] was made in the 1180s and earlier 1190s, and covers Blackbourn double hundred, Thedwestrey hundred, Thingoe hundred, Cosford half hundred, and Babergh double hundred; the sole surviving manuscript does not include surveys of Risbridge hundred and Lackford hundred. The Kalendar is mentioned in Jocelin of Brakelond's chronicle,[41] and there the making of the Kalendar is attributed to the agency of Abbot Samson, who was led by concern that the abbey was not exploiting its interests to the fullest, and that the practice of outsourcing the management of the hundreds to farmers meant that the abbot did not exactly know what belonged to the abbey. The Kalendar thus presents a snapshot of the abbey's interests towards the end of the twelfth century, and there are obvious problems in treating a source from such a late date as a straightforward depiction of the abbey's interests in the hundreds in the eleventh or earlier twelfth centuries. Some of the categories named in the charters of William the Conqueror are not named in the Kalendar, for instance, as though they were no longer significant for the monks or were no longer productive of income. Some of the arrangements in the Kalendar were also created in the very early twelfth century, and so have no more extended history;[42] it is possible that some of the arrangements may be of later creation.

The Kalendar covers in some detail how the abbey collected and managed the customs it could claim from the hundreds. This included such dues as hidage, sheriff's aid, foddercorn, *warpeni* and *summa avene*. These were the labour services that originally formed a large part of the content of soke, and which by the later twelfth century had generally been commuted into monetary payments, which were explained in some detail in the Kalendar. The other claim that the Kalendar covers is that of suit of court. This was an obligation that the abbey could police in its own interests, and demand amercements from those who failed to carry it out. Suit of court meant that an obligation was laid upon some persons through their tenure of certain named holdings, which meant that they were

39 *The Great Rolls of the Pipe for the Second, Third, and Fourth Years of the Reign of King Henry II, AD 1155, 1156, 1157, 1158*, ed. Joseph Hunter (London, 1844), 9.

40 *The Kalendar of Abbot Samson of Bury St Edmunds and Related Documents*, ed. R. H. C. Davis, Camden Third Series 84 (1954).

41 *The Kalendar of Abbot Samson of Bury St Edmunds and Related Documents*, ed. R. H. C. Davis, Camden Third Series 84 (1954), xi–xii; Jocelin of Brakelond, *Chronicle*, ed. H. E. Butler (Edinburgh, 1949), 29.

42 This is probable because Ramsey Abbey's soke over its lands at Lawshall was first documented and perhaps granted in the early twelfth century; see *Regesta*, ii. nos. 738 and 739.

obliged to attend the regular hundred courts.[43] There is no mention of suits of court in the Anglo-Saxon laws, and it would seem reasonable to see the practice as a later one. The idea in the laws that all should attend the hundred court is based on an idea of what the hundred should be that is antithetical to what was represented by suit of court. The point of suit of court was that it was a mechanism by which a lord or community could diminish their interactions with a hundred court and transact business within their own territory. The earliest occurrence of suit appears to be in Domesday Book, where it is noted in relation to Robert Malet's holding in Dunwich, Suffolk, that two or three were obliged to attend the hundred if warned, and that the king could fine them for non-attendance if they did not do so.[44] These two or three could only have been a small fraction of the population of Malet's holdings there, so the question arises where the rest of his tenants were. It might be that here the obligations of the other tenants were being discharged by representatives – it is hard to see what else might be meant here by the role of the two or three – and that Malet held a court for his own tenants, separate from the hundred. Regardless of the origins of suit of court, the Kalendar lays out in some detail how many suits were owed, from which fees, and so forth, so it would seem that policing attendance was an important element of the work of the abbey's officials.

It is probable that there were other courts operating within the territory composed by the eight and a half hundreds. Manorial courts also operated there from the twelfth century, and other lords had claims which overlapped or complemented those of Bury St Edmunds Abbey. The identities of these other lords is set out in the Kalendar, but in a few cases the claims and activities of those lords can be seen because their own records survive as well as those from Bury. This is especially true for the ecclesiastical lordships within the eight and a half hundreds. Ramsey Abbey had a manor at Lawshall, south of Bury St Edmunds, which had been presented by Leofsige the deacon, and was mentioned in the 1062 diploma in the name of Edward the Confessor.[45] The terms on which the manor was held are not fully described until early in Henry I's reign, when Ramsey Abbey obtained two writs from the king which regulated its tenure of this holding.[46] From these, it can be seen that the abbey held Lawshall with sake and soke, toll and team and *infangthief*, and that this was not seen as incompatible with Bury St Edmunds Abbey's claims over soke in the eight and a half

[43] Robert C. Palmer, *The County Courts of Medieval England, 1150–1350* (Princeton, 1983), chapter 3, for a clear overview of suit of court and its operation.

[44] Fleming, *Domesday Book*, no. 2836.

[45] http://www.esawyer.org.uk/charter/1030.html.

[46] There was a third later one, *Regesta*, ii. no. 1067, which granted to Ramsey warren in Lawshall.

hundreds.[47] The two writs were probably written on the same occasion, but one was addressed to Roger Bigod as sheriff of Norfolk and Suffolk, while the other went to the abbot of Bury. Both stressed that the abbot of Ramsey was to have his claims as in the time of William I, but the one to the sheriff contained an extra injunction, that Ramsey's manor was to be free of shires and hundreds and all pleas except murder and theft.[48] Despite the apparently generous claims allowed to Ramsey in the king's writs, the competing claims of Bury St Edmunds were not excluded. According to the Kalendar, Bury still claimed from Lawshall 5d. in *warpeni* and 4s. in suits to its hundred.[49] Bury acknowledged its special status, and the Kalendar contained a note that Lawshall did not give sheriff's aid, but that from ancient custom it gave 4s. for obtaining the goodwill of the reeves.[50] This might be the same 4s. that elsewhere in the Kalendar are described as suit of the hundred. Lawshall's exemption from attendance at shires and hundreds ultimately gave rise to a lordship court held in the name of Ramsey Abbey; some court rolls survive from the fourteenth and fifteenth centuries to show that these could operate successfully within the framework of Bury's claims.[51] Lawshall is a useful case in that the manor belonged to a major ecclesiastical corporation which was a careful guardian of its own claims. This meant that it had the contacts and resources to obtain such writs, and that it had the institutional stability and archival mentality to preserve the texts of those documents. The Kalendar shows that other lords made claims, and that the position of Bury St Edmunds Abbey in relation to the various vills and manors varied considerably. Its general claims over the soke of the eight and a half hundreds broke down into very many detailed, local arrangements where the abbey's interests intersected with or overlapped the interests of other parties.

The manorial courts in Lawshall were not the only ones operating within and alongside Bury's claims. The Kalendar is not consistent in reporting them, but a few are mentioned in passing. The Kalendar includes an observation in relation to Blackbourn hundred, that apart from the obliged suitors all others were instead required to attend pleas in the halls of the lords who held them, and were required to render the hundred customs there to the lords, who would then transmit that collection to the abbot as the abbot's customs.[52] These seem to be references to

47 *Regesta*, ii. no. 738 and 739.

48 *Regesta*, ii. no. 738.

49 *The Kalendar of Abbot Samson of Bury St Edmunds and Related Documents*, ed. R. H. C. Davis, Camden Third Series 84 (1954), 63, 65, 69, 70.

50 *The Kalendar of Abbot Samson of Bury St Edmunds and Related Documents*, ed. R. H. C. Davis, Camden Third Series 84 (1954), 66.

51 London, National Archives, SC 2/203/96 (1364–8); London, British Library, Additional Roll 34933 (1466); London, National Archives, SC 2/203/97 (1484–9), SC 2/203/97 (1498–9).

52 *The Kalendar of Abbot Samson of Bury St Edmunds and Related Documents*, ed. R. H.

courts held on the basis of lords' lands for those on their lands; these are early kinds of manorial courts. From the later middle ages, manor court rolls survive in sufficient quantity to suggest that such courts were not less common within the territory of the eight and a half hundreds. Probably, most of the lords whose interests are noted in the Kalendar would have held manorial courts by the later twelfth century when the Kalendar was made.

The Kalendar shows much about the existence of another kind of sub-hundredal organisation. Each hundred was divided into into smaller units, called leets (in Thedwestrey, Thingoe, Blackbourn and Cosford hundreds) and ferderings in Babergh hundred (for convenience this distinction will not be observed here, and these units will all be called leets). These leets were principally fiscal rather than judicial units, and were the basis for the collection of the dues laid out in the Kalendar. Liabilities are expressed in terms of the leets rather than the hundreds themselves. The leets do not reflect the landscape of lordship in any way. The later courts leet followed the landscape of lordship very closely, whereas the leets of the Kalendar did not; most of the Kalendar leets included the lands of more than one lord, and, moreover, there is no specific evidence in the Kalendar that there were meetings for the Kalendar leets.[53] Meanwhile, the Kalendar makes it probable that lords held courts for their own dependents only as hallmoots, which were distinct from the leets.

## Ownership of a Hundred

Bury St Edmunds is important because it shows how the relationship between a great church and courts could develop, but it is not the earliest case in which a great church could be said to own a hundred. The idea that a hundred court could be owned is contained in Domesday Book, for a number of hundreds are said to be the hundred of some person or church. Thus, as has been noted in many places, Worcestershire Domesday states that *Ecclesia sancte Marie de Wirecestre habet unum hundret quod uocatur Oswaldeslau*.[54] Elsewhere, the disputed claim to the hundred or cantref of Arwystli in central Wales is noted, for Robert of Rhuddlan and Roger de Montgomery both raised claims over the hundreds: *Isdem Robertus calumniatur unum hundredum, Arvester quod ten' Rogerius \comes/. Walenses testificantur istud hundredum esse de his Nortwalis*.[55] The assumptions behind this statement are worth emphasising; Robert claimed the hundred, not just some claims within it, and in terms that paralleled claims that might be raised over land;

C. Davis, Camden Third Series 84 (1954), 38–9; also 66.

53 Against this, it could be objected that the obligation for suit of court was expressed in terms of leets.

54 Great Domesday Book, fo. 172v: Worcestershire 2.1.

55 Great Domesday Book, fo. 269r: Cheshire G2.

meanwhile, Roger held the hundred, just as he might hold land or other claims.[56] Arwystli, of course, was something of an exceptional case. It was marginal to the English kingdom, and it was populated with Welsh people, whose identity is noted in the Domesday discussion of the claims over the hundred. It might thus be regarded as somewhat outside the English norm. Yet Earl Roger was a very wealthy and privileged English landholder as well as the holder of Arwystli. The attitudes towards hundreds that are seen here would not have been restricted to one side of a border. It is possible that this instance shows something of how Roger understood his own position as a great lord with extensive, quasi-proprietorial claims over much of Shropshire.

In Cambridgeshire, a heading within the holdings of the abbey of Ely states 'In the two hundreds of Ely which meet at Witchford'.[57] The hundreds were later usually called the two hundreds of Witchford, or North and South Witchford; what is not clear about the intention behind these few words in Domesday is what is denoted by stating that these hundreds were 'of Ely'. Later, the hundreds of the Isle of Ely were held as private hundreds by the bishops of Ely as the successors of the abbots, and they held them free from normal administrative input from the king's officers.[58]

In Somerset, meanwhile, the manor of Taunton belonged to the bishop of Winchester, and the claims pertaining to it are described in unusual detail. It is not clear what the detailed description of Taunton means, and whether Taunton was exceptional, or merely recorded with unusual fullness. Probably the recent nature of the concession to the bishop of Winchester at Taunton was the cause for the detail given in Domesday Book:

> These customs belong to Taunton: borough-right; thieves; breach of the peace; house-breaking; hundred pence[59] and St Peter's pence; church-scot; thrice in the year the bishop's pleas to be held without summons; setting out on military service with the bishop's men.
>
> ...

[56] On Robert and Roger and their setting see J. F. A. Mason, 'Roger de Montgomery and His Sons (1067–1102)', *Transactions of the Royal Historical Society* fifth series 13 (1963), 1–28 at 12–13; Robert Bartlett, *The Making of Europe: Conquest, Colonization and Cultural Change, 950–1350* (London, 1993), 29, 32; J. F. A. Mason, 'Montgomery, Roger de, First Earl of Shrewsbury (d. 1094)', *ODNB*; C. P. Lewis, 'Avranches, Hugh d', First Earl of Chester (d. 1101)', *ODNB*.

[57] *In duobus hundredis de Ely qui conveniunt apud Wiceforde*: Great Domesday Book, fo. 191v; Cambridgeshire 5.43.

[58] Edward Miller, *The Abbey and Bishopric of Ely: The Social History of an Ecclesiastical Estate from the Tenth Century to the Early Fourteenth Century* (Cambridge, 1951), chapter 7.

[59] E. B. Demarest, 'The Hundred-Pennies', *English Historical Review* 33 (1918), 62–72.

From these lands those who have to make oath or undergo the ordeal come to Taunton. When the lords of these lands die, they are buried at Taunton.

…

The customary dues and service from these lands always belonged to Taunton; and King William granted these lands for St Peter and Bishop Walkelin to have, as he himself recognised at Salisbury in the hearing of the Bishop of Durham, whom he commanded to write this grant in the returns.[60]

All this was presented as something that belonged to the manor of Taunton as a holding of the bishop of Winchester. As Domesday observes, the dues and service had always been paid to Taunton, and thus were held to have belonged to Taunton; what seems to have happened is that the dues which had once been paid to Taunton and divided thence – including elements paid to the church, other lords and the king and maybe even others – were to be transferred to the bishop of Winchester. This even included some claims over thieves and house-breaking in Taunton hundred, which must have meant that dues from these matters were taken by the bishop of Winchester. These dues would have been taken from the lands and dependents of the bishop of Winchester, for the hundred of Taunton was overwhelmingly under Winchester's control. Yet it also included lands that were held by subtenants of the church of Winchester,[61] and the claims in Domesday Book would have been levied over those lands as well.

It was possible for soke over a hundred to amount to a generous measure of control. Bury St Edmunds Abbey could use its representatives to claim dues and services from the people of the hundreds, and in practice controlled much about the operation of those assemblies. Yet, it was only into the twelfth century that

60 *Istæ consuetudines pertinent ad Tantone: burgheristh, latrones, pacis infractio, hainfare, denarii de hundret et denarii sancti Petri, circieti, ter in anno teneri placita episcopi sine ammonitione, profectio in exercitum cum hominibus episcopi.*

…

*De his omnibus terris facturi sacramentum uel iudicium portaturi ad Tantone ueniunt. Cum domini de his terris moriuntur, in Tantone sepeliuntur.*

…

*De his terris semper iacuerunt consuetudines et seruitium in Tantone, et rex W. concessit istas terras habendas sancto Petro et Walchelino episcopo, sicut ipse recognouit apud Sarisberiam audiente episcopo Dunelmensi cui precepit ut hanc ipsam concessionem suam in breuibus scriberet.*

Great Domesday Book, fo. 87v: Somerset 2.1. The translation here is that from the Alecto edition. J. C. Holt, '1086', *Domesday Studies*, ed. J. C. Holt (Woodbridge, 1987), 41–64, at 44, on the occasion mentioned; also Pierre Chaplais, 'William of Saint-Calais and the Domesday Survey', *Domesday Studies*, ed. J. C. Holt (Woodbridge, 1987), 65–77, at 75.

61 Great Domesday Book, fo. 87v: Somerset 2.5–9, 19.40.

the abbey started to describe its influence over its hundreds as something akin to ownership, as though the hundred was something that could be possessed and owned. Before the Conquest, there are no indications that hundreds could be thought of thus, and so there is some diversity in how relationships between privileged churches and hundreds were described. In Domesday Book, for instance, there is no consistent terminology to describe this, as can be seen from the examples noted above.

The idea that a hundred could be owned, and that it could belong to individuals or institutions, seems to have spread quite widely during the early twelfth century. As noted above, documents concerning Bury St Edmunds Abbey first refer to its claims in the hundreds in Suffolk in such terms in the early twelfth century, and similar transitions in how hundredal claims were conceived can be seen in other archives. Abingdon Abbey offers an excellent example, in relation to the hundred of Hormer in Berkshire, where the abbey held landlordship over all the hundred. The claims as landlord are noted in Domesday Book, but significantly there is nothing about claims over the hundred as a unit. Abingdon's claims first appear in written form in a writ of Edward the Confessor, which granted to the abbey soke and other claims over its own lands.[62] There is no qualification as to where exactly these claims could be exercised, and presumably they could have applied to all of Abingdon's lands, including those that fell outside the hundred of Hormer. There is another writ in the name of Edward the Confessor which grants to the abbey the hundred of Hormer, but this is a clear forgery from the twelfth century which represents an attempt to backdate the control of Hormer.[63] The earliest authentic act in which the abbey's claims were localised at Hormer is one of William II, in which a general writ ordering that Abingdon's claims be observed was amplified through the addition of a codicil which likewise ordered that the hundred of Hormer should remain with the abbey.[64] The unusual structure of the writ points to how the idea was developing at this time, for it was necessarily produced during the later 1080s or 1090s. Writs tended not to include instructions relating to very different kinds of business,[65] so that the inclusion of the clause about Hormer indicates that it was seen as related to the earlier command that soke should be respected, even that it was seen as a specific

[62] Harmer, *Writs*, no. 4.

[63] Harmer, *Writs*, no. 5; on this see Harmer, *Writs*, pp. 125–8 and 429. Susan Kelly, *Anglo-Saxon Charters 7–8: The Charters of Abingdon Abbey* (two volumes, Oxford, 2000–1), 572–5, nos. 148–9, suggests that Harmer, *Writs*, no. 4; Kelly 148 is genuine, while Harmer, *Writs*, no. 5; Kelly 149 is probably interpolated.

[64] *Et hundredum de Hornimere, sicut tunc temporis habuit, testibus predictis*: *Regesta*, i. no. 289; *Abingdon Chronicle*, ii. 20–1. There are other writs with additional clauses added after the witnesses, such as *Regesta*, ii. no. 399 and 499a.

[65] This is the general point of Richard Sharpe, 'The Use of Writs in the Eleventh Century', *Anglo-Saxon England* 32 (2003), 247–91.

application of the general principle stated earlier. After all, much of Abingdon's lands lay within Hormer hundred, so it would inevitably be linked closely to the exercise of the abbey's jurisdictional claims. Moreover, the relationship between the abbey and the hundred is characterised using the verb *habere*, which indicates that soke could, for a landholder with as predominant a position in a hundred as Abingdon had, result in an interest in the hundred itself. Abingdon obtained more writs concerning Hormer from Henry I, and these represent a major change in that they are unambiguous in regarding the hundred as something that could be owned by the abbey. This is clear from how the abbey's interest in the hundred was confirmed to it in a writ that was probably prepared soon after the appointment of Faritius as abbot in 1100.[66] This is not a unique item; another writ repeated this message with the instruction that the abbot should be allowed to have the plea concerning a horse.[67]

Though there is much variation, the basic pattern is fairly clear. There was a move away from describing claims within a hundred towards allowing for the idea that hundreds had become an entity that could belong to a lord. In this, the phrases used approximated towards those which were used for land and related matters. Most commonly, a lord was said to 'have a hundred', using the verb *habere*, more rarely *tenere*, though other terms were used as well. This is not far from the way in which tenure of land was described, which was most often *habeat et teneat* or variants thereof. Ideas about the relationship between lords and their lands were themselves developing in this era. Later conceptions, such as possession and seisin, were not yet in use consistently.[68] Tenure must be viewed as, in part, a political matter.[69] In this context, where tenure was conditional and negotiable, the relatively loose drafting does not look anomalous. Hundreds could even be held in free alms, a form of ecclesiastical tenure,[70] or in fee and in chief from the king.[71] This is not the whole picture, for royal acta could also depict hundreds in very different terms, as external impositions upon property, when

66 *Regesta*, ii. no. 728; *Abingdon Chronicle*, ii. 168–9, confirmed by Henry II in similar terms, *Abingdon Chronicle*, ii. 216–17 and 220–1.

67 *Regesta*, ii. no. 1111; *Abingdon Chronicle*, ii. 168–9, which depends on a forgery in the name of William II; *Regesta*, ii. no. 1477; *Abingdon Chronicle*, ii. 230–3.

68 On all this see Hudson, *Oxford History*, 337, and especially Paul R. Hyams, 'Property Talk in Old English: Did Anglo-Saxon England Know the Concept of Seisin?', forthcoming, and John Hudson, *Land, Law and Lordship in Anglo-Norman England* (Oxford, 1994), especially chapter 2.

69 J. C. Holt, 'Politics and Property in Early Medieval England', *Past and Present* 57 (1972), 3–52.

70 *Regesta*, iii. nos. 34, 35, 36 (all for Barking), 204 (Cluny), 402 (St Benet Hulme), 592 (Montacute, forged), 758, 759 (both Bury St Edmunds), 845, 846 (both Templars, though both annexed to property).

71 *Regesta*, iii. no. 34; see also no. 4.

hundreds were included in lists of exemptions alongside pleas, shires, *warpeni* and such like.[72] So, hundreds were not entirely assimilated to the category of property. There is also a clear structure to royal grants of hundredal claims. There are few positive grants from Henry I's reign, and most of those are forgeries,[73] but there are many more, including probably authentic ones, from Stephen's reign.[74] This may well represent an actual increase in control of hundreds by lords.

The partial assimilation of the control of hundreds to the conventions of property means that much about the nature of tenure of hundreds is hidden. If a lord was granted a hundred by a king in the early twelfth century, what did that actually mean? Royal acta usually do not state whether a grant should be taken as including the ability to exclude royal officials, and yet these questions were of importance to holders. Stephen made a generous grant of hundredal claims to the church of Barking,[75] but subsequently an enhanced version was produced which set out the exclusions that the nuns wanted. In the following extract, the main additions are italicised:

> Wherefore I will and firmly command that the said church and abbess and said nuns hold and *in perpetuity* possess (*possideant*) the said hundred *with all things pertaining to it in lands and tolls and aids and all customs, so that neither any justice nor sheriff nor any other servant of mine should intrude themselves against the abbess or her servants introduce any plea or any other thing which pertain to the said hundred, but they [i.e. the abbess and nuns] should have it* well and in peace and freely and honourably and quietly *with sake and soke and toll and team and infangthief and with all other liberties which belong to it, that is, in a plea, warpeni and with the collection of murdrum and danegeld and all pleas and other things*, just as St Edmund and the church of St Etheldreda of

72 For instance, *Regesta*, ii. no. 1453: *Precipio quod A(gnes) abbatissa Berchingie teneat totam terram et homines suos bene et in pace quietos de placitis et querelis et sciris et hundredis et warpeni et omnibus aliis rebus excepto murdro et latrocinio.*

73 From Henry I's time there are *Regesta*, ii. no. 774 for Chertsey Abbey, probably forged; *Regesta*, ii. no. 831 for Evesham Abbey, clearly forged; one for Romsey Abbey, not in *Regesta* but noted in Stephen's confirmation of Wherwellsdown hundred (*Regesta*, iii. no. 722). The clearest example is *Regesta*, ii. no. 911 for William d'Aubigny pincerna, a grant of the manor of Snettisham *cum duobus hundredis et dimidio*, the hundreds of Smithdon and Freebridge. Grants of exemption from another hundred are excluded from this list.

74 For grants of hundreds see *Regesta*, iii. nos. 4 (Abingdon Abbey); 34, 35, 36 (Barking Abbey); 178 (Ranulf, earl of Chester); 183 (Chichester Cathedral); 204 (Cluny Abbey); 402 (St Benet Hulme); 592 (Montacute Priory, forged); 640 (Oxford, St Frideswide's); 669 (Ramsey Abbey); 758 (Bury St Edmunds Abbey); 758, 759 (Bury St Edmunds Abbey); 761 (Bury St Edmunds Abbey); 784 (Salisbury Cathedral); 817 (Selby Abbey); 845, 846 (Templars); 846 (Templars); 949 (Winchester Cathedral); 964 (Worcester Cathedral, suspect); 975 (York Minster, suspect).

75 *Regesta*, iii. no. 35.

> Ely hold and have their hundreds, saving those pleas of my crown which ought to be pleaded by my justice.[76]

The italicised additions are important in that they indicate what the nuns most wanted from Becontree hundred, and what formed the largest threat to their achievement of this aim. The added clauses specifically command that sheriffs, justices and other royal officials should not intrude themselves into the abbey's hundred, and that they should not interfere in pleas or any other business being held there. The function of this grant for the nuns of Barking was that it would have allowed them to exercise a large measure of control over the district in question – which in this case included much owned by the abbey anyway – and to claim whatever fees and proceeds might arise from running the court. The latter function might involve claiming fees or fines from the dependents of other lords who happened to have interests within the bounds of the hundred in question.[77] These dual aims of protecting the abbey's lordship and generating direct profits might be affected by the intrusion of such functionaries. The addition of these clauses also indicates that the real meaning of a grant of a hundred was still unsettled; it implies that, even though local officials recognised the king's grant, nonetheless they insisted on continuing to exercise some of their functions. In this case, the specific exclusion of sheriff and justice might be taken as a counter to the holder of both of those offices in the early 1140s, Geoffrey de Mandeville, who had likewise been given those jurisdictions by King Stephen and the Empress Matilda;[78] though, obviously, Stephen's reign cannot be taken as a norm. Much rarer was exemption for a hundred from the demands of forest law; this seems to occur only for the double hundred of Tendring in Essex, where both St Paul's, London,[79] and St John's, Colchester,[80] obtained documentation of the removal of this source of interference.

[76] Quare uolo et firmiter precipio quod ecclesia predicta et abbatissa et moniales *memorate* teneant *et in perpetuum* possideant hundredum prenominatum *cum omnibus ei pertinentibus in terris et theloneis et auxiliis et omnibus consuetudinibus, ita scilicet quod neque iustitia aliqua neque uicecomes neque aliquis minister meus super abbatissam uel ministros suos se inde intromittat de placito aliquo uel de aliqua re que ad hundredum predictum pertineat, set* habeant *illam* bene et in pace et libere et honorifice et quiete *cum saca et socna et toll et theam et infangenetheof et cum omnibus aliis libertatibus que ad illud pertinent, scilicet in placito, warpeni, et cum collecta murdri et danegelde et omnibus placitis et aliis rebus,* sicut ecclesia Sancti Edmundi et ecclesia Sancte Atheldrithe de Ely tenent et habent hundreda sua, saluis *tantum placitis corone mee que per iustitiam meam debent placitari. Regesta*, iii. no. 36.

[77] This seems to have been the intention in *Regesta*, iii. no. 285, where Stephen granted to Exeter Cathedral land in Colyton with the hundred of Colyton. See also *Regesta*, iii. no. 402 for St Benet Hulme.

[78] *Regesta*, iii. nos. 273–6.

[79] *Regesta*, iii. no. 566.

[80] *Regesta*, iii. nos. 239 and 239a.

The grant of a hundred to an individual or institution was not always accepted in simple terms, because it meant a rearrangement of the organisation of local lordship. It often meant that a lord who had been one among equals could now interfere in and demand money from the dependents of the other lords, and so acquire greater local control and power. In the later 1140s Stephen granted to St Benet Hulme abbey the two hundreds of Flegg and Happing in Norfolk,[81] which brought the abbot control over dependents of the earl Warenne. Some local dispute arose from this, which ultimately prompted a writ from Stephen which ordered that the abbot should hold his hundreds without injury:

> Stephen, king of the English, to William, bishop of Norwich, and Reginald de Warenne and William of Norwich and all his sworn men and the servants of Earl Warenne, greeting! I command that Abbot William of St Benedict of Hulme and his church hold the two hundreds of Flegg and Happing well and in peace and quietly just as I conceded them to the same church and confirmed by my charter, lest injury or ill treatment happen to them about this. Witness, Hugh of the assarts. At Dunstable.[82]

Presumably either the earl had withdrawn his dependents from the hundred, or he or his officials had prevented the abbot from controlling the hundred at all. Even in cases where hundreds had been granted years before, some holders of jurisdiction still felt a need to get royal writs which ordered those within the area of the hundred to attend the courts, as in the case of a writ of Stephen for Ramsey abbey concerning the hundred of Clackclose in Norfolk.[83]

Alongside the specific grants of hundreds, there are also many instances in which Stephen granted to an individual or institution the ability to exempt its dependents from a hundred.[84] Much as with the examples from Henry I's reign

81 *Regesta*, iii. no. 402.

82 *S(tephanus) rex Anglorum W(illelmo) episcopo Norwycensi et Rainaldo de Warenne et Willelmo de Norwyco et omnibus fidelibus suis et ministris comitis Warenn(e) salutem. Precipio quod Willelmus abbas Sancti Benedicti de Hulma et ecclesia sua teneant duo hundreda de Fleg et Happinge bene et in pace et quiete sicut illa concessi eidem ecclesie et carta mea confirmaui, ne super hoc fiat eis iniuria uel contumelia. Teste Hugone de Essartis. Apud Dunestaplum. Regesta*, iii. no. 403. For a similar pair showing a grant and then concern over its continuation see *Regesta*, iii. nos. 722 and 723, both for Romsey.

83 *Regesta*, iii. no. 668. *Regesta*, ii. nos. 1411 and 1585 are suspicious; See also *Regesta*, iii. nos. 753 for Bury St Edmunds and 2 for Abingdon.

84 *Regesta*, iii. nos. 104 (Biddlesden Abbey); 207 (Coggeshall Abbey); 278 (Évreux Cathedral); 449 (Lewes Priory); 547 (London, St. Martin le Grand); 576 (Marcigny Priory); 658 (Peterborough Abbey); 675 (Reading Abbey); 677 (Reading Abbey); 687 (Reading Abbey); 770 (Bury St Edmunds Abbey); 791 (Salisbury Cathedral); 852 (Templars); 866 (Templars); 901 (Tockenham, Roger de); 915 (Waltham); 916 (Waltham); 918 (Waltham); 928 (Westminster Abbey, forged); 929 (Westminster Abbey, forged); 937 (Westminster Abbey); 961 (Woburn Abbey, forged).

discussed above, this meant that the lord was able to transfer matters which had once been part of the hundred's remit into the lord's own court, and so protect the lord's dependents from outside interference. Some of these grants were quite limited, and concerned the dependents of a particular lord in a particular place or district;[85] in others, the exemption granted was a blanket one, which freed all the dependents of a given lord from any external hundredal jurisdiction in any place.[86] There are even some instances in which a grant of a manor specified that hundredal claims were not included in the grant, as though the association between the two had become so natural that the one might be taken as implicating the other.[87]

## Other Models of Control over Hundreds

The two sections above addressed two models for how great lords, whether lay or ecclesiastical, might come to control a hundred, through holding claims over the people within the hundred, or through, in some sense, owning the hundred itself. Yet there were other ways in which an interest in a hundred could be acquired. William II granted the hundred of Normancross in Huntingdonshire to Thorney Abbey, so that it would be held in fee farm for a rent of 100s. each year:

> William, king of the English, to all his sheriffs and barons of Huntingdonshire, greeting! Know that I have conceded to the abbot and monks of Thorney the hundred of Normancross in annual fee farm of 100s. which I will that they turn over to my sheriff of Huntingdon. And I prohibit that any of my ministers do injury or ill treatment to them on this.[88]

The meaning of this was presumably that Thorney Abbey could administer the hundred. From the revenues that were produced, 100s. had to go to the king, but any sums beyond that could be kept by the abbey for its own purposes. Yet the abbot of Thorney did not claim the hundred outright, merely the ability to

85 *Regesta*, iii. no. 105 for Binham, though this may be as much about poor observation of an existing claim; *Regesta*, iii. nos. 297 for Eynsham; 370 for Godstow; 427 for Kirkstead.

86 *Regesta*, iii. nos. 31, for Barking when in custody of queen (and therefore time-limited); 75a for Bec; 93 for Bermondsey, which specifies that that monks were to have their own court; 295 for Eynsham; 371 for Godstow; 399 and 400 for St Benet Hulme.

87 *Regesta*, iii. nos. 174, 175.

88 *Willelmus rex Anglorum omnibus uicecomitibus et baronibus suis de Huntend' scire salutem. Sciatis me concessisse abbati et monachis de Thorneia hundredum de Normancros in feudofirmam annuatim pro c solidis quos uolo ut reddat uicecomiti meo Huntend'. Et prohibeo ne aliquis ministrorum <meorum> inde eis iniuriam uel contumeliam faciat. Regesta*, i, no. 453; *Regesta*, i. p. 139, Appendix no. LXXXI; the same text was reissued in almost exactly the same words by Henry I in *Regesta*, ii. no. 1028.

administer, and throughout the twelfth century and beyond the abbey's tenure of the hundred remained in this form. This case was not unique; an exact parallel can be seen nearby in the Huntingdonshire hundred of Hurstingstone, which was held by Ramsey Abbey for a fee farm of four marks a year.[89]

In practice, in terms of how the hundred operated and how it was experienced by those who had to take part in it, this might not have looked very different from the kind of arrangements discussed above in relation to western Suffolk and Hormer in Berkshire. In both cases, a major local religious house used the revenues of the hundred as an extra form of income, and intruded itself into the management of the hundred in different ways; partly through the need to manage the sending of the rent to the king, and partly through the way in which in all of these cases the holder of hundredal claims was also a major landholder within the hundred in question.

There were also cases in which an institution was given a partial interest in the revenues of a hundred. These often took the form of a grant of a fixed financial interest in the revenues of the hundred, such as the two marks each year given to the nuns of Redlingfield by Henry I,[90] or the hundred shillings each year from the hundreds of Walsham and Blofield given to Bishop Everard of Norwich, also by Henry I.[91] In each of these cases, it seems that the receipt of a financial interest did not mean that the recipients were able to put their own official into the hundred to run it, and so were unable to turn this interest into a proprietorial interest in the hundred.

## Conclusion

This chapter has aimed to show how some favoured lords developed claims over and interests in hundreds across the eleventh and earlier twelfth centuries. By the middle of the twelfth century, it was possible for a lord to own a hundred, and to be granted one by the king. Yet, this idea did not appear suddenly; it developed over time, and it formalised interests that had often existed for some time. Lords had been able to intrude their interests into hundreds, by inserting agents to manage them, or by gaining soke over all who were within the hundred, or by restricting hundreds to their own dependents. There was no single method where these interests began, but most of them lead to the same conclusion in terms of ownership of hundreds. The story here is not simply one about claims and control, but also about intellectual change, and how ideas about ownership came to be spread more widely over time.

89 *Regesta*, ii. no. 1632. This survives as an original.

90 *Regesta*, ii. no. 1866.

91 *Regesta*, ii. no. 1854.

# 4

# The Division of Hundreds and the Proliferation of Courts

The previous chapter has set out how lords could come into positions of control and influence over hundreds, and how these kinds of interests could be turned into claims. That story is an important one for how jurisdiction developed in the eleventh and twelfth centuries, but it is not the only one. Lords also came to preside over large numbers of courts which had more restricted scope and jurisdiction. These ultimately came to be predecessors of the omnipresent lordship and manorial courts of later medieval England, and of others such as courts leet. These early lordship courts are not well attested in the sources, and theories about their origins often have the quality of a conjecture. Much the most cited theory is that of Frederic Maitland, who suggested that these lesser courts began with their lords and the lands they allowed to their dependents, and so had a distinct point of origin from the hundred and shire; the two kinds of court had separate moments of genesis. Their later history was driven by the need to refine divisions of jurisdiction between lords' courts and the others. From this starting place with lords, courts proliferated under the influence of kings and their agents, who defined franchise over time and so drove lords to reflect those definitions in the structures of their courts.[1]

This chapter will offer a slightly different model. It will suggest that lords' courts originated because lords broke parts off from the functions of hundreds. The evidence for this will be set out below, but largely it depends on two kinds of behaviour that can be seen in the eleventh and twelfth centuries. First, there was a trend towards the use of units beneath and within the hundreds. The eleventh-century hundred is an an obscure entity whose history has not yet been written,[2] especially when compared to the vision of the tenth-century hundred that can be reconstructed from the laws. What indications there are suggest that in many parts of England after 1000 the hundred was run in ways not anticipated in the tenth century. In the eleventh century, many hundreds had been divided into lesser units that seem to have been the basis for the functions of the hundred in

1 F. W. Maitland, *Select Pleas in Manorial and Other Seignorial Courts: Volume 1, Reigns of Henry III and Edward I*, Selden Society 2 (1889), xvi–xxvii.

2 The most coherent study is still H. R. Loyn, 'The Hundred in England in the Tenth and Early Eleventh Centuries', in *British Government and Administration: Studies Presented to S. B. Chrimes*, ed. H. Hearder and H. R. Loyn (Cardiff, 1974), 1–15.

taxation and other matters. These units are not covered in the laws and seem to have been highly variable in function and form; there is no sense as there is with the hundreds that these were created through the imposition of a single model. The lesser units were called by many different names – ferderings, hundreds (confusingly), leets, and so forth – and can be traced in many, but not all, parts of England. Some at least of these subhundredal units had courts of their own in the twelfth century, and in the case of some of the East Anglian leets they could be held jointly between multiple lords. These units were not lords' courts so far as can be seen, but they are important for the story of lords' courts because they show how some hundreds at least were used to breaking up functions and working with smaller units. Second, by the early twelfth century there were courts controlled by lords which carried out parts of the business of hundreds, and which were often coincident with the limits of the lands of those lords. They were often a means by which a lord could subtract his dependents from the hundred for many functions and manage them through his own assembly, and they were often called *halimota*. The ability to subtract dependents from a hundred seems often to have been linked to holding soke, and represented a new turn in definitions of that term. These kinds of courts had a wide competence; they could deal with matters such as disputes and offences, as well as business arising from the exercise of lordship itself. It is probable that this model was highly influential, and that lords who did not hold soke also came to hold *halimota*, even if these only dealt with business arising from lordship, or which concerned matters among the peasantry of one lord.[3]

## The Division of Hundreds[4]

The most cited and compelling description of the hundred is that contained in the mid tenth-century Hundred Ordinance, sometimes known as 1 Edgar, and this depicts the hundred as a unity. It has set the tone for discussion, which has

3 There is one other place where courts seem to have divided in the eleventh century; London. There, the court of husting developed alongside the *burhgemot*, and is attested in the eleventh century, and maybe in the tenth. On this see Pamela Nightingale, 'The Origin of the Court of Husting and Danish Influence on London's Development into a Capital City', *English Historical Review* 102 (1987), 559–78. Some of the points made there are criticised in M. K. Lawson, *Cnut, England's Viking King, 1016–35* (second edition, Stroud, 2011), 187–8, who points out that the term husting need not have a Scandinavian origin. Regardless of its provenance, the existence of the court seems settled, though its functions and procedure are not.

4 On these in general see James Campbell, 'Hundreds and Leets: A Survey with Suggestions', in *Medieval East Anglia*, ed. Christopher Harper-Bill (Woodbridge, 2005), 153–67; also D. C. Douglas, *The Social Structure of Medieval East Anglia*, Oxford Studies in Social and Legal History 9 (Oxford, 1927), 191–204; C. R. Hart, *The Danelaw* (London, 1992), 83–93.

tended to see the hundred as a singular entity, and as one where the fundamentals were relatively unchanging.[5] There are, though, indications that the pattern depicted in the Hundred Ordinance was not universal and did not persist, and that the operation of the hundred was different by at least the middle of the eleventh century. There is very strong evidence that from that point hundreds tended to take account of subhundredal units. These were not envisaged in the arrangements set out in the Hundred Ordinance or any of the other tenth-century laws. Their existence is clear, and it is apparent that they had some fiscal, administrative and legal functions, but what is probably more important is that their existence implies that the methods of operating the hundreds had changed from the principles set out in the Hundred Ordinance. They suggest that decisions and assessments of all kinds were being made, or at least managed or implemented, at a lower level, and that many hundreds worked in more complicated ways by the later eleventh century.

The existence of such units can be seen across many, but not all, parts of England. Across much of the East Midlands, there were units called hundreds that existed at a level beneath the wapentakes that were the local equivalents of hundreds in other parts of England.[6] These are known from the Domesday Book coverage of Derbyshire, Leicestershire, Lincolnshire, Nottinghamshire and Rutland where their existence is noted in passing;[7] there is also some twelfth-century evidence for these lesser hundreds.[8] The function of these units is rather obscure, but the detailed evidence of the Leicestershire Survey shows that they were larger than most manors and represented a grouping of vills; it seems unlikely that any one of these small hundreds corresponded to the holdings of any one landholder. The Nottinghamshire Domesday indicates that these small hundreds were used as the

5 H. R. Loyn, 'The Hundred in England in the Tenth and Early Eleventh Centuries', in *British Government and Administration: Studies Presented to S. B. Chrimes*, ed. H. Hearder and H. R. Loyn (Cardiff, 1974), 1–15.

6 Hudson, *Oxford History*, 283, 386, 409.

7 D. C. Douglas, *The Social Structure of Medieval East Anglia*, Oxford Studies in Social and Legal History 9 (Oxford, 1927), 191; F. R. Thorn, 'Hundreds and Wapentakes', *The Northamptonshire and Rutland Domesday* [introduction and translation] (London, 1987), 35–39, at 39; F. R. Thorn, 'Hundreds and Wapentakes', *The Nottinghamshire Domesday* [introduction and translation] (London, 1990), 32–43, at 34, and at 41 for Rutland; D. R. Roffe, 'Introduction to the Nottinghamshire Domesday', *The Nottinghamshire Domesday* [introduction and translation] (London, 1990), 1–31, at 8–9; F. R. Thorn, 'Hundreds and Wapentakes', *The Leicestershire Domesday* [introduction and translation] (London, 1990), 22–30, at 24, with a note on Derbyshire; D. R. Roffe, 'Hundreds and Wapentakes', in *The Lincolnshire Domesday* [introduction and translation] (London, 1992), 32–42, at 32, 33.

8 *The Leicestershire Survey* c. *AD 1130*, ed. C. F. Slade (Leicester, 1956), 68–82; J. H. Round, *Feudal England: Historical Studies on the Eleventh and Twelfth Centuries* (reset edition, London, 1964), 160–74, esp. 166.

basis for collecting financial penalties in some circumstances;[9] meanwhile, the *Leges Edwardi Confessoris* show that they bore some liability for the allocation and levying of the *murdrum* fine.[10] Other subhundredal units can be seen in Little Domesday Book for Norfolk. They are mentioned in the rubrics concerning the hundreds of South Greenhoe, which had fourteen leets,[11] and the hundred and a half of Clackclose, which had ten leets.[12] In Clackclose, the number of leets did not match the number of vills or the number of landholders who held land within the hundred, so, just as in the east-midland hundreds discussed above, these leets must have cut across and combined different vills and different landed interests;[13] nor do they obviously correspond to the soke interests of particular lords.

In west Suffolk eight-and-a-half hundreds came to be controlled by Bury St Edmunds Abbey, as was discussed in the previous chapter, and the abbey's later twelfth-century records show that most of those hundreds were likewise divided into smaller units, which were called leets or ferderings.[14] There were leets within the city of Norwich, which operated for many purposes as though they were miniature hundreds, with jurors and presentments.[15] Some phenomena elsewhere

[9] Hudson, *Oxford History*, 283, 386, 409; Great Domesday Book, fo. 280v: Nottinghamshire S1; fo. 298v: Yorkshire C38; fo. 336v: Lincolnshire C32.

[10] *Leges Edwardi Confessoris*, 27, 33.

[11] Little Domesday Book fo. 119v: Norfolk 1.71. On this and the next instance see J. H. Round, *Feudal England: Historical Studies on the Eleventh and Twelfth Centuries* (reset edition, London, 1964), 90; James Campbell, 'Hundreds and Leets: A Survey with Suggestions', in *Medieval East Anglia*, ed. Christopher Harper-Bill (Woodbridge, 2005), 153–67; and on the word see F. W. Maitland, *Select Pleas in Manorial and Other Seignorial Courts: Volume 1, Reigns of Henry III and Edward I*, Selden Society 2 (1889), lxxiii–lxxvi.

[12] Little Domesday Book fo. 212v: Norfolk 15.1.

[13] The number of leets cannot be matched to the number of lords; see Little Domesday Book fo. 149r: Norfolk 4.43, shows that Count Alan held sixty acres; fos. 159v–160r: Norfolk 8.15–20, that William de Warenne held lands in seven vills; fo. 190r–v: Norfolk 9.230–2, that Roger Bigod held lands in two vills; fos. 205v–206v: Norfolk 13.1–11, that Hermer held lands in twelve vills; fo. 209r: Norfolk 14.1–3, that Bury St Edmunds Abbey held lands in three vills; fos. 212v–213r: Norfolk 15.1–3, that Ely Abbey held lands in five vills; fo. 215r–v: Norfolk 16.1–2, Ramsey Abbey held lands in four vills; fos. 230r–231v: Norfolk 21.1–8, that Reginald fitz Ivo held lands in ten vills; fo. 236r: Norfolk 22.14, that Ralph de Tosny held lands in two vills; fo. 238r: Norfolk 23.9, that Hugh de Montfort held lands in one vill; fos. 250v–251r: Norfolk 31.20–30, that Ralph Baynard held lands in nine vills; fo. 263r: Norfolk 42.1, that Gilbert fitz Richard held lands in one vill; and fos. 273v–274v: Norfolk 66.1–16, that Hermer de Ferrers had appropriated lands in nine vills. On the arrangements involved see J. H. Round, *Feudal England: Historical Studies on the Eleventh and Twelfth Centuries* (reset edition, London, 1964), 89–90, who also notes parallels in Cambridgeshire.

[14] *The Kalendar of Abbot Samson of Bury St Edmunds and Related Documents*, ed. R. H. C. Davis, Camden Third Series 84 (1954).

[15] *Leet Jurisdiction in the City of Norwich during the XIIIth and XIVth Centuries*, ed.

also point to the existence of comparable units. For instance, at Sherborne in Dorset, a charter of Earl William and Countess Mabel of Gloucester of the later 1140s returned to the bishop of Salisbury various claims including the tithings, which in south-western England were usually territorial rather than personal;[16] later lists indicate that there were subdivisions of the hundred of Sherborne that were named tithings, and that these ran across the considerable landed interests of the bishop as well as those of other landholders.[17]

Subhundredal units can be shown quite widely in the eleventh and twelfth centuries. They cannot be shown in all parts of the country, but they were widespread, and it is notable that where they appear corresponds to documentary structures. Thus, the area of the midlands where small hundreds can be seen corresponds to most of Domesday circuit VI; it is possible that the appearance of the small hundreds in the Great Domesday Book is more about the ways in which those responsible for circuit VI interpreted their instructions, and how it differed from the choices made in other circuits. Much the most detailed depictions of the operation of subhundredal units comes from the records of Bury St Edmunds Abbey; no other abbey had claims and privileges of quite this scale and nature, and there are no registers elsewhere that are like the Kalendar of Abbot Samson. If the surviving references to subhundredal units do actually reflect the pattern of sources rather than the underlying pattern of the units themselves, then it is possible that such units might have been found quite widely across many parts of England. The variation in words used to describe them – leets, hundreds, tithings, ferderings – suggests that these units were not created as part of a single campaign to achieve a uniform result, but rather that their origins were multiple, local and variable.

It is also not clear whether these units all had courts as a means of transacting business, nor when such courts might have appeared. Courts for the Norfolk leets were clearly in place by the early thirteenth century, from when there survive charters reflect the activity of such courts.[18] Some of these courts were dominated

---

William Hudson, Selden Society 5 (1892).

16 *Earldom of Gloucester Charters: The Charters and Scribes of the Earls and Countesses of Gloucester to AD 1217*, ed. Robert B. Patterson (Oxford, 1973), no. 171. On territorial tithings see F. W. Maitland, 'Leet and Tourn', rpt in *Selected Historical Essays of F. W. Maitland, Chosen and Introduced by Helen M. Cam* (Cambridge, 1957), 41–51; F. W. Maitland, *Select Pleas in Manorial and Other Seignorial Courts: Volume 1, Reigns of Henry III and Edward I*, Selden Society 2 (1889), xxvii–xxxviii.

17 John Hutchins, *The History and Antiquities of the County of Dorset ... with a Copy of Domesday Book and the Inquisitio Gheldi for the County*, third edition ed. William Shipp and James Whitworth Hodson (London, 1861–70), iv. 119.

18 Cited in D. C. Douglas, *The Social Structure of Medieval East Anglia*, Oxford Studies in Social and Legal History 9 (Oxford, 1927), 195–8. For another, even bigger, example see Nicholas Karn, *English Episcopal Acta* 42: *Ely, 1198–1256* (Oxford, 2013), no. 91.

by individual lords, but in some cases that domination was held by a few lords jointly, who used these leets to manage shared interests in the fens of western Norfolk. They were thus somewhat outside the pattern seen elsewhere, where one lord owned one court for that lord's own dependents. Other evidence that these early leets had courts is much less abundant. There is a clear reference in the early twelfth-century foundation charter of Wymondham Priory, but that source should not be taken as wholly convincing in its authenticity.[19]

It should be noted that these early leets were not the same as the courts leet that were later common across England. Early courts leet were subdivisions of the hundred which often reached beyond the bounds of any particular estate, and so their operation did not entirely reflect the structures and priorities of landlordship, though they might have reflected co-operation between lords. Later courts leet or views of frankpledge were more clearly franchisal, and represented the concession of some parts of the hundred's activities to a lord, who could manage them within his own lands, or within defined bounds.[20] Early leets are much less well understood and much less well documented than later ones, but it is apparent that they were generally much larger and less the creation of lords.

The significance of these units is that they point to how the operation of the hundred had developed since the Hundred Ordinance in the tenth century. They suggest that there was subdivision of the responsibilities, duties and liabilities of the hundred, and which, presumably, aided their implementation. The existence of these units implies that the procedures followed in the hundreds had evolved markedly from their origins in the tenth century, and that the hundred was a fissiparous entity. It is not clear if these units were new ones of the eleventh century or if they represent the reuse of older ones, but their integration into the structure of hundreds is first seen clearly in the eleventh century. Their integration meant that parts of the business of hundreds was done in smaller units in ways that were not envisaged in the laws.

## The *Halimota*

There is evidence from the early twelfth century for courts that existed alongside the hundreds, and were in some sense a substitute for them. Soon after 1100, a term that occurs regularly is *halimota* or *halimotum*.[21] There is some diversity

[19] D. C. Douglas, *The Social Structure of Medieval East Anglia*, Oxford Studies in Social and Legal History 9 (Oxford, 1927), 194, and references therein.

[20] For definitions of leets see F. J. C. Hearnshaw, *Leet Jurisdiction in England, especially as Illustrated by the Records of the Court Leet of Southampton* (Southampton, 1908), esp. chapter 1; F. W. Maitland, 'Leet and Tourn', rpt in *Selected Historical Essays of F. W. Maitland, Chosen and Introduced by Helen M. Cam* (Cambridge, 1957), 41–51; Mark Bailey, *The English Manor,* c. *1200*–c. *1500* (Manchester, 2002), 178–9.

[21] The spelling varies a great deal; *halmota*, *hallemota* and other similar forms also

of opinion as to what exactly this term might mean. It has been suggested that it might be regarded as meaning holy moot,[22] perhaps indicating that such courts originated as courts held by great churches in the names of their saints.[23] Alternatively, it has been suggested that the term means hallmoot, and that it was used to indicate a court that was held as a meeting in the lord's hall. On the basis that the term used is most often in English – *halimota* rather than *aula* – it has been suggested that these courts might have been in existence before 1066,[24] though there is no specific evidence for this. Indeed, there seem to be no genuine uses of this term before 1100, let alone 1066, so the argument from language is speculative at best.[25] The appearance of these courts is of great importance; they are the earliest unambiguous cases where courts were clearly controlled by lords, were operated separately from the courts of shire and hundred (if in relationship to them), and were recognised as legitimate and valid by those who held them as well as by kings, bishops and others.

The references to *halimotas* are often rather vague, and in many cases amount to no more than that the existence of the court is acknowledged, or perhaps that its testimony is noted. Thus in this discussion some of the most important references are given as full quotations, so that the limitations of the evidence are made apparent. The most precise statements about *halimotas* are those in the *Leges Henrici Primi*, and these define the *halimotas* of the early twelfth century as being somewhere between a court of lordship and a court that expressed claims normally managed through the hundred. The *Leges* notes that *halimotas* were one of the few places in which pleas could be held:

---

appear, but presumably all refer to the same kind of entity. Similar variations occur in relation to spelling of the hundred, such as *hundret, hundreta, hundredum.*

22 F. W. Maitland, *Select Pleas in Manorial and Other Seignorial Courts: Volume 1, Reigns of Henry III and Edward I*, Selden Society 2 (1889), lxxvi–lxxvii.

23 The use of the term *Haliwerfolc* to describe the Durham region offers an analogy. Alternatively, the moots might have been holy in the sense that holy relics or holy books were present, and that religious acts in the form of oaths and blessings were undertaken there as part of doing business. The term *hallemote* appears for secular courts quite commonly by the thirteenth century; for many instances, see *The Court Rolls of the Honor of Clitheroe in the County of Lancaster*, ed. William Farrer (three volumes, Manchester, 1897–1912).

24 Frederick Pollock and Frederic W. Maitland, *The History of English Law Before the Time of Edward I* (second edition, Cambridge, 1898), i. 38; followed by many later commentators; Stephen Baxter, 'Lordship and Justice in Late Anglo-Saxon England: the Judicial Functions of Soke and Commendation Revisited', in *Early Medieval Studies in Memory of Patrick Wormald*, ed. Stephen Baxter, Catherine Karkov, Janet L. Nelson and David Pelteret (Farnham, 2009), 383–419, at 387.

25 There is a possibility of an earlier parallel in Domesday Book, where occasionally tenure of land is said to be *in dominio aule*; for instance, Great Domesday Book, fo. 283r: Nottinghamshire 5.4.

> And every matter shall be settled either in the hundred or the county or the *halimota* of those who have soke or the courts of lords or the boundaries of equals or known places for doing business ...[26]

So, *halimotas* of those who held soke were legitimate places for the hearings of pleas if they were the *halimotas* of holders of soke. This should probably be taken as an indication that there were two kinds of *halimotas* that the author of the *Leges Henrici Primi* recognised; those that pertained to holders of soke, and those that did not, and the latter were not entitled to hear pleas. It is not clear what *halimotas* without soke did; perhaps their function lay in matters that did not overlap with the powers of hundreds, such as in enforcing agricultural discipline upon the dependent peasantry.[27]

The link between soke and the *halimotas* is made apparent in another passage in the *Leges Henrici Primi*, where it is explained that soke was managed through three forms of custody, and again some kinds of cases were allocated to the *halimotas*:

> All soke is simple or complex for those possessing it, for it is divided principally into three forms; under the reeves of estates in matters belonging to the *halimotas*; under the leaders of the hundreds and the boroughs; and under the sheriffs.[28]

This short passage makes two important points. First, it shows that writer of the *Leges Henrici Primi* expected that the *halimotas* would be under the authority of the reeves of the manor,[29] who were presumably named as the representative of the lord who owned the soke; nowhere is it claimed that soke could belong to the *halimotas* without the lord.[30] Second, it shows that there was a limitation on

26 *Et omnis causa terminetur uel hundreto uel comitatu uel halimoto socam habentium uel dominorum curiis uel diuisis parium uel certis agendorum locis adiacens ... Leges Henrici Primi*, 9.4. The *halimota* is also noted in *Leges Henrici Primi*, 57.8, where it appears among a list of courts in which it was stated that it might be expected that a lord would support his dependent in different courts, including *diuisis uel [m]erchimotis, aliquando super ipsam terram uicine, aliquando in curia domini, aliquando in hundreto uel hundretis, aliquando in comitatu uel burgimoto uel hallimoto*.

27 David Roffe, 'From Thegnage to Barony: Sake and Soke, Title and Tenants-in-Chief', *Anglo-Norman Studies* XII (1989), 157–76, suggests that the later courts leet originated in earlier grants of soke.

28 *Omnis autem socna simplex est habentibus aut coniuncta, in custodia uero trina principaliter distincta: sub prepositis maneriorum in causis adiacentibus halimotis; sub prelatis hundretorum et burgorum; sub uicecomitibus. Leges Henrici Primi*, 20, 1a

29 Note the emphasis on the co-ordinating role of the reeve in *The Kalendar of Abbot Samson of Bury St Edmunds and Related Documents*, ed. R. H. C. Davis, Camden Third Series 84 (1954), 44, from the later twelfth century.

30 On reeves generally see P. D. A. Harvey, 'The Manorial Reeve in Twelfth-Century England', rpt in his *Manors and Maps in Rural England, from the Tenth Century to the*

what the *halimotas* could do. Whereas no limits are laid on what could be heard under the leaders of the hundred or under the sheriff, the *halimotas* could only hear under its reeve those matters that pertained to the *halimotas*. This is not a clear or full statement, but it might be linked with the way in which many royal writs grant soke but reserve certain matters to the communal courts, especially *murdrum* and theft.

Something of the same idea, that there were kinds of cases that might pass to the *halimotas* while others were kept in the hands of the hundred, is indicated also in the following passage from the *Leges Henrici Primi*:

> Archbishops, bishops, earls and other great powers in the lands of their particular power[31] have sake and soke, toll and team and *infangthief* (in other possessions they might have sake and soke by purchase, by exchange or by other method, in shared matters and in those belong to *halimotas*) over their own men and in their own possessions, and sometimes over the men of other [lords], especially if they are taken or held in a forfeiture, and they have full compensation.[32]

According to this, sake and soke and other claims were held by some high-status persons, but that there were differences in how they exercised those claims. Some of those soke holders could make agreements to hold sake and soke in pleas, presumably those that were managed through the communal courts of

*Seventeenth* (Farnham, 2010) chapter II. There are no specific mentions of the manor court by that name in the *Leges Henrici Primi*, and looser references could as easily apply to the *halimotas* themselves, such as *Leges Henrici Primi*, 34.1a; 56.1 notes the need for settlement with the manor (translated as manor court by Downer, though the word *curia* is not used in the text); *Leges Henrici Primi*, 56.4 also instructs that, and states that a claimant should be heard in the manor or in the court of the lord. Forms of words suggestive of the manor court are vanishingly rare in twelfth-century sources, and often do not mean anything akin to the later manor court. For example, the Battle Abbey Chronicle includes a reference to a case *in eiusdem manerii curiam* (*The Chronicle of Battle Abbey*, ed. Eleanor Searle (Oxford, 1980), 108), but this cannot refer to a manorial court as defined later because the shire nobles of Kent were among those who attended. It is more likely that the hundred court of Wye was meant, because its court was appended to the abbey's manor of Wye. That such a form of words could be used (probably) of a hundred court suggests that there was little general recognition of the manorial court as a distinctive and separate category of assembly.

31 The meaning of this is presumably that, say, a bishop would have sake and soke over the episcopal lands by virtue of his office, but that this would not automatically apply to any lands held privately.

32 *Archiepiscopi, episcopi, comites et alie potestates in terris proprii potentatus sui sacam et socnam habent, tol et theam et infongenþeaf (in ceteris uero per emptionem uel cambitionem uel quoquo modo perquisitis, socam et sacam habent in causis communibus et halimotis pertinentibus) super suos et in suo et aliquando super alterius homines presertim si in forisfaciendo retenti uel grauati fuerint, et illic competentem emendationem habeant. Leges Henrici Primi*, 20.2.

shire and hundred, as well as those that pertained to the *halimotas*. Again, this might be linked to the ways in which certain kinds of plea were reserved to the king's soke, notably those concerning *murdrum* and theft.

The final point about the *halimotas* that can be deduced from the *Leges Henrici Primi* is that it was a place where changes of lordship and status could be managed:

> If anyone becomes a slave, according to who the owner is, it should be done in the *halimota* or the hundred or in the locality before witnesses, he should pay toll so that he cannot deny it afterwards.[33]

Transition in status from free man (presumably) to slave had to be done publicly, before witnesses. That *halimotas* could do this indicates that they had something of the same quality as the hundreds, and that their testimony could be regarded as equal in weight to that of the hundred. This can be compared to some instances from the later twelfth century, where the testimony of a *halimota* could be accepted as evidence even by the king.[34] The recognition whether someone was of free or unfree status was a public matter, with consequences for their liability for taxation, for labour services, for military duties and so forth. Thus, though it could be primarily something that was between two persons, it had public consequences that had to be shown. If it were restricted to lords' courts, then such a lord would control the freedom or unfreedom of his dependents.

The idea that *halimotas* could be equivalent to or even a form or subset of the hundred court is not restricted to the *Leges Henrici Primi*. It can also be seen in charters from the period, such as in the following example concerning the village of Boraston in Shropshire. The first is a grant by Hugh son of Osbern, which confirmed and augmented the grant of his father. Hugh licensed the monks of Worcester to create a *halimota* for their own dependents, and so divide them from the hundred of Burford. Boraston was not freed entirely from the hundred, for in matters concerning theft and robbery cases would still go to the hundred court at Burford, but the profits of justice would be passed back to the monks of Worcester:

> I Hugh son of Osbern add to the alms of my father at Boraston which he gave to God and to the holy mother of God Mary in Worcester this liberty for my soul and those of my ancestors. In the first place, I release them from the king's geld from the other hide in perpetuity, so that they should not pay geld except on one hide. Then, I give in perpetuity to the prior and monks of Worcester for the redemption of my soul all my customs and services which arise from

33 *Si quis in seruum transeat, sicut possessor est, in halimoto uel hundreto uel uicinio coram testibus agatur, eum extol[n]eet ut nec ille deinceps abneget. Leges Henrici Primi*, 78.2.

34 Van Caenegem, *Lawsuits*, nos. 369, 372.

> that vill to Burford and to the hundred and *halimota* there. So, if it should ever happen because of a complaint by someone from another district, so that it is necessary to plead in the *halimota* of Burford about robbery or pillaging, and a man of Boraston falls into forfeiture, the prior himself should have that forfeiture which I ought to have there, by my gift and in perpetuity, and so that I might enclose the often-named vill of Boraston, I give to the prior and monks of Worcester all things, so free and quit from all exactions, just as I hold it from my lord, King Henry, with sake and soke and toll and team and all things pertaining to me. I, Hugh, confirm my generosity with my seal and with the sign of the cross. And these are the witnesses, etc.[35]

These arrangements represented a considerable intrusion into the operation of the hundred of Burford, and reveal how complicated the actual operation of such a hundred could be in the very early twelfth century. The changes were made in relation to an existing arrangement where there was a hundred and a *halimota*. This might mean that there was a *halimota* already ruling over a portion of the hundred, or conceivably the term *halimota* was being used in relation to the hundred court. The main point of Hugh's grant was that all that he could claim from the operation of that hundred and *halimota* was resigned to the monks, with the reservation that matters concerning theft and pillage should be heard in the *halimota* of Burford. Afterwards, the king's confirmation even expanded on the terms of Hugh son of Osbern's grant, for it specified that the sheriff of Shropshire was not to attach the land or its dependents in his courts; this would imply that the

[35] *Ego Hugo filius Osberni adicio ad elemosinam patris mei de Burestune quam dedit deo et sancte dei genetrici Marie in Wirecestre hanc libertatem pro anima mea et parentum meorum. In primis pardono geldum regis de altera hida perpetualiter ita ne amplius geldant nisi pro una hyda. Deinde omnes consuetudines meas et seruitia que de illa uilla de Bureford pertinebant et hundredum et hallimot deinceps in perpetuum dono priori et monachis de Wirecestre pro redemptione anime mee. Ita tamen ut si etiam propter querelam alicuius extranee prouincie hominis, necesse fuerit in halimote de Bureford' placitare de latrocinio aut rapina, et homo de Burestune cadit in forisfacturam, habeat prior ipsam forisfacturam quam ego ibi debebam habere meo dono deinceps inperpetuum, et ut breuiter omnia concludam ipsam sepe nominatam uillam Burestunam do priori et monachis de Wirecestre ita liberam et quietam ab omnibus exactionibus sicut ego de domino meo rege Henrico eam teneo cum saca et soca et toll et team et omnibus ad me pertinentibus. Ego Hugo hanc meam munificentiam meo sigillo et cum signo crucis corroboro. Et hii sunt testes, etc. The Cartulary of Worcester Cathedral Priory (Register I)*, ed. R. R. Darlington, Pipe Roll Society 76, new series 38 (1968), 82, no. 146. Also in *Registrum sive Liber Irrotularius et Consuetudinarius Prioratus Beatæ Mariæ Wigorniensis*, ed. William Hale Hale, [*sic*] Camden Society 91 (1865), 9a–9b. The charter is not dated, but must precede the confirmation by Bishop Sampson of Worcester, who died in 1112 (*The Cartulary of Worcester Cathedral Priory (Register I)*, ed. R. R. Darlington, Pipe Roll Society 76, new series 38 (1968), 82–3, no. 147; *English Episcopal Acta* 33: *Worcester, 1062–1185*, ed. Mary Cheney, David Smith, Christopher Brooke and Philippa M. Hoskin (Oxford, 2007), no. 24.

*halimota* of Boraston did not include only the unfree dependents of the monks, but also free men, to judge from the references to attachment:

> Henry, king of the English, to Payn fitz John and his servants of Shropshire and of Herefordshire, greeting! I command that the church of St Mary and the monks of Worcester hold their land of Boraston so well and in peace and quietly just as Osbert son of Richard and Hugh his son and Osbert son of the same Hugh gave and conceded it to them, and so that no injury or ill treatment happens to them. And neither that land nor their men should be attached for any forfeiture or debt unless for their own. And they should not follow any hundred except the *halimota* of Burford, and they ought to do that justly. Witness, etc.[36]

The link between *halimotas* and hundreds can also be seen in the middle of the twelfth century. Two charters of Henry II show that recognitions could be made through a *halimota* and a hundred or wapentake in concert, as though the two were linked:

> Henry, king of the English and duke of the Normans and Aquitanians and count of Anjou, to his justices and sheriffs of Nottinghamshire and Derbyshire, greeting! I command that the church of Chesterfield has and holds all liberties and all customs and all its holdings in meadows and pastures and in woods and in all things, so well and in peace and freely and quietly and justly and honourably and fully, just as well and freely as it held in the time of King Henry my grandfather and as was established by the legal men of the *halimota* and of the wapentake, and beyond this it should hold all lands and incomes which the parishioners gave to the same church after the death of King Henry my grandfather, just as the charter of Roger, bishop of Chester, witnesses, and I prohibit that anyone forfeit from the same church or from the goods pertaining to it in any way. Witness, Nigel de Broc. At Nottingham.[37]

[36] *H[enricus] rex Angl' Pagano filio Johannis et ministris suis de Salopescir' et de Herefordescir' salutem. Precipio quod ecclesia sancte Marie et monachi de Wirecestr' ita bene et in pace et quiete teneant terram suam de Burestona sicut Osbertus filius Ricardi et Hugo filius eius et Osbertus filius ipsius Hugonis eis eam dederunt et concesserunt, et ita ne eis inde iniuria uel contumelia fiat. Et non esnamietur ipsa terra uel homines eorum pro alicuius forisfacturo uel debito nisi pro suo proprio. Et non sequantur aliquod hundredum nisi hallimotum de Bureford', et sicut iuste sequi debent illud. T', etc. The Cartulary of Worcester Cathedral Priory (Register I)*, ed. R. R. Darlington, Pipe Roll Society 76, new series 38 (1968), 84–5, no. 153. This document was omitted from the *Regesta*. On Payn fitz John as sheriff see Judith A. Green, *English Sheriffs to 1154* (London, 1990), 72.

[37] *H. rex Anglie, dux Normannie et Aquitannie, comes Andegauie iusticiariis et uicecomiti suis de Nothingham syra et de Derbi syra salutem. Precipio quod ecclesia de Cestresfelda teneat et habeat omnes libertates et omnes consuetudines et omnia tenementa sua in pratis et pascuis et nemoribus et in omnibus rebus ita bene et in pace, libere et quiete et iuste et honorifice et integre sicut melius et liberius tenuit tempore regis H. aui mei et sicut recognitum est per legales homines de halimato et de wapintac.*

The writ is not entirely clear on the process involved. The church of Chesterfield was to have its claims as in the time of Henry I, and these were to be defined by the *legales homines* of the *halimota* and of the hundred. The *legales homines* were those men who had sworn oaths and who were of sufficient and free status that they could offer testimony under oath; it is significant that here the *halimota* had *legales homines* in the same way that the hundred did, for this indicates that it was more than just an assembly of the dependent and unfree peasants of a particular place, and that its testimony could be equivalent to that of the hundred itself.

> Henry, king of the English and duke of the Normans and Aquitanians and count of Anjou to Geoffrey d'Iwoi, greeting! I command that the abbot of Osney and the canons serving God there hold the land of Holcombe which was released to them by the men of the *halimota* of Benson and by trusted men (*per probos homines*) of the hundred in exchange for my alms of Benson which they were accustomed to have in pennies from the alms of the ancient kings of the English, and I prohibit that no man take nor admit anything from my alms, because I will and firmly command that they hold well and in peace and justly and honourably so that I do not hear any more about it. Witness, Thomas the chancellor. At Westminster.[38]

This writ again indicates that the hundred and the *halimota* were comparable, but that the participants in each were described in different terms. The men of the *halimota* were *homines*, while the men of the hundred were *probi homines*. Nonetheless, the testimony of each was sought as though they were comparable to each other. The two writs of Henry II are of much importance in defining the nature of *halimota*, for they indicate that the king did not see them as being fundamentally distinct, as something that was antithetical to royal institutions. *Halimotas* were not simply private courts, but were integrated into systems of royal government, and could be of equal status in offering testimony. They were

---

*Et preter hec teneat omnes terras et redditus quos parrochiani post mortem regis H. aui mei eidem ecclesie dederunt, sicut carta Rogeri episcopi Cestr(ensis) testatur. Et prohibeo ne quis eidem ecclesie uel rebus ad eandem pertinentibus in aliquot forisfaciat. Teste, Nigello de Broch. Apud Nothingham.* Van Caenegem, *Lawsuits*, no. 369, of 1155 x August 1158.

38 *Henricus, rex Anglie et dux Norm' et Aquitanie et comes Andegauie, Gaufrido de Iuoi salutem. Precipio quod abbas de Oseneya et canonici ibidem Deo seruientes teneant terram de Holecumba que liberata eis fuit per homines de halimoto de Bensintone et per probos homines de hundreto pro elemosina mea de Bensintone quam solebant habere in denariis de antiquis elemosinis regum Anglie. Et prohibeo quod nemo de elemosinis meis quicquam capiat nec intromittat quia uolo et firmiter precipio quod bene et in pace et iuste et honorifice teneant, ne inde amplius clamorem audiam. Teste, Thoma cancellario. Apud West'.* Van Caenegem, *Lawsuits*, no. 372; of 1155 x August 1158.

not merely manorial courts catering for the unfree, but as in the first of the Henry II documents quoted above, were also places where free men, *legales homines*, might be found. These courts of the middle of the twelfth century do not really match the later pattern of courts, but might parallel some of the later composite courts such as that of Clitheroe, where franchisal and lordly business were dealt with in the same assembly.[39]

There is a distinct pattern to royal engagement with the *halimotas*. It appears in a few acta from the time of Henry I, such as that for Worcester quoted above, and two others concerning a grant to the canons of Sées. These granted to the canons Brighthampton (Oxfordshire), which was a member of the royal manor of Bampton; as part of the grant, it was stated that:

> And I will and firmly command that they hold well, honourably, and in peace and freely and quietly, always and in perpetuity [free] from hidages and gelds and danegelds and aids and labour services, with soke and sake and toll and team and infangthief and all customs and liberties and pleas and complaints and all things which I held when it was in my lordship, in lands and waters and meadows and pastures and mills and woods and in the open and in all places, and their men shall plead in their *halimota* (*hallimoto suo*) of Brighthampton at the summons of the canons of Sées or their servants.[40]

This seems to confirm the idea that a *halimota* was a portion withdrawn from a larger whole, for Henry I's charters indicate that he considered that Brighthampton was a member of the manor of Bampton, which was, of course, also head of the hundred of Bampton.[41] So, a *halimota* could be established through a grant by the king by dividing a unit from the hundred in which it lay.

*Halimotas* are entirely absent from royal documents in the time of King Stephen, though a private deed from that reign mentions how a dispute was settled in a *halimota* in Oxfordshire.[42] There are more mentions from the very

39 Warren Ortman Ault, *Private Jurisdiction in England* (New Haven, 1923), 267–300.

40 *Et uolo et firmiter precipio ut bene, honorifice, et in pace et libere et quiete teneant semper et in perpetuum de hidagiis et geldis et danegeldis et auxiliis et operationibus, cum socha et sacha et toll et theam et infangeteof et omnibus consuetudinibus et libertatibus et placitis et querelis et omnibus rebus cum quibus ego tenebam dum esset in meo dominio, in terris et aquis et pratis et pascuis et molendinis et nemoribus et in plano et in omnibus locis, et homines sui placitent in hallimoto suo de Bristelmetona in submonicione canonicorum Sagii uel ministrorum suorum. Regesta*, ii. no. 1711; Charles Homer Haskins, *Norman Institutions* (Cambridge, 1918), 302–3, Appendix F; compare also *Regesta*, ii. no. 1698. On Brighthampton see Stephen Baxter and John Blair, 'Land Tenure and Royal Patronage in the Early English Kingdom: A Model and a Case Study', *Anglo-Norman Studies* XXVIII (2006), 19–46, at 37.

41 Helen Cam, '*Manerium cum Hundredo*: The Hundred and the Hundredal Manor', in her *Liberties and Communities in Medieval England* (Cambridge, 1944), 64–90, at 76.

42 Van Caenegem, *Lawsuits*, no. 332.

early years of Henry II's reign, including the two items quoted above and a handful of others.[43] Thereafter, there is no real evidence for royal engagement with the *halimotas*. There are references to *halimotas* as venues in which pleas were debated, but without the direct input or authorisation of the king.[44] It might be suggested that *halimotas* were henceforth rejected and avoided by the king's scribes and officers. The Assize of Clarendon of 1166 contains detailed instructions for how inquests into robbers, murderers and thieves were to be held in each hundred, and through four men from each vill.[45] There is no recognition here of the role of *halimotas*; no suggestion that men might be empanelled for each *halimota*, for instance. A choice has been made to emphasise the category of hundred over that of *halimota* for this process. If kings no longer sent writs to *halimotas* after 1166, then they no longer engaged with those who attended those courts. This is surely a step on the path towards unfree status, in which the unfree could not engage with or use the king's courts.

What, therefore, can be safely assumed about the nature of *halimotas*? The historiography on this question is neither extensive nor consistent. Much the commonest approach has been to assume that the *halimota* was a precursor of the later manor court, and that it was therefore a court that expressed lordship rather than soke.[46] One writer suggested that the *halimota* could be an expression of soke rather than lordship, though did so on the basis of the *Leges Henrici Primi*

43 Van Caenegem, *Lawsuits*, no. 349: *Precipio et concedo quod Walterus episcopus de Couentr' habeat omnes libertates et consuetudines suas in bosco et plano, in pratis et pascuis, in aquis et molendinis, infra burgum et extra et in omnibus locis, et socam et sacam et tol et theam et infangenetheof et hallemotum suum in omnibus terris suis*. Also *Calendar of the Charter Rolls Preserved in the Public Record Office*, ed. The Deputy Keeper of the Records (6 vols, London, 1903–27), *1300–26*, 414, no. 2; *H(enricus) rex Angl(orum) et dux Norm(annorum) et Aquit(anorum) et comes Andeg(auorum) toti halimoto de Lectona et halimoto de Breholla salutem. Precipio quod fratres de hospitali de Sanctingefelda iuxta Witsandam teneant terram suam totam quam eis dedi in elemos(inam) ita bene et in pace et iuste et libere sicut carta mea eis testatur, et prohibeo ne quis eis iniuriam vel contumeliam faciat. T(este) Thom(a) canc(ellario) apud Sanctum Audemar'*.

44 Van Caenegem, *Lawsuits*, nos. 379, 466, 488, 498, 625–6, 650. It is not really clear why many of these cases were included in this book.

45 Assize of Clarendon, ed. Nicholas Vincent, http://www.earlyenglishlaws.ac.uk/laws/texts/ass-clar/view/#edition,1/apparatus,1_0_c_1.

46 On this see Frank Stenton, *The First Century of English Feudalism, 1066–1166* (second edition, Oxford, 1961), 43; and followed by Hudson, *Oxford History*, 62, 284, 289, 291; also Warren Ortman Ault, *Private Jurisdiction in England* (New Haven, 1923), 8; F. W. Maitland, *Select Pleas in Manorial and Other Seignorial Courts: Volume 1, Reigns of Henry III and Edward I*, Selden Society 2 (1889), lxxiii–lxxvi; Frederick Pollock and Frederic W. Maitland, *The History of English Law Before the Time of Edward I* (second edition, Cambridge, 1898), i. 421; L. J. Downer, in notes to *Leges Henrici Primi* (Oxford, 1972), 319.

alone.[47] The few sources noted and quoted above indicate that could it be either or both, and that the single term *halimota* comprises kinds of meeting and business that would in the thirteenth century and beyond be transacted by different courts. The *Leges Henrici Primi* seems to assume that *halimotas* were common in the early twelfth century, and that those held by lords who held soke might deal with kinds of business more usually done in the hundred court. This leaves the problem of what *halimotas* on manors held by lords who did not have soke might have done; perhaps they merely dealt with matters such as agricultural discipline that were later managed through the manor courts, if they existed. *Halimotas* for privileged soke-holding lords would presumably deal with both, and as such seem to prefigure both the later manor courts as well as the later courts that represented franchises, such as courts leet and views of frankpledge. In some places, the word *halimota* survived into later centuries, and this happened most often in places where lords had extensive privileges; within major franchises, where soke (or, later, royal pleas) were held privately, manorial courts operated as *halimotas*.[48]

There is also the problem of whether these *halimotas* can justly be regarded as private courts. There were aspects of their courts that look rather like private courts. They were clearly related to landholding, and it seems that some at least were composed solely of the dependents of one lord. This must have meant that the lords had a very strong voice in these courts, for all the dependents would have owed rents and other dues to the lord, and would have been within his power; this must have meant that lords could influence these courts directly or indirectly.[49] These features make the *halimotas* of the twelfth century look like

[47] This was pointed out by Julius Goebel, *Felony and Misdemeanor: A Study in the History of Criminal Law* (New York, 1937), 398 note; also in David Roffe, 'From Thegnage to Barony: Sake and Soke, Title and Tenants-in-Chief', *Anglo-Norman Studies* XII (1989), 157–76.

[48] Frederick Pollock and Frederic W. Maitland, *The History of English Law Before the Time of Edward I* (second edition, Cambridge, 1898), i. 586. For Durham see *Halmota Prioratus Dunelmensis, Containing Extracts from the Halmote Court or Manor Rolls of the Prior and Convent of Durham, AD 1296–AD 1384*, edited by W. H. D. Longstaffe and John Booth, Surtees Society 82 (1889); on some of the later rolls see Peter L. Larson, 'Village Voice or Village Oligarchy? The Jurors of the Durham Halmote Court, 1349–1424', *Law and History Review* 28 (2010), 675–709; for Chester see *Accounts of the Manor and Hundred of Macclesfield, Cheshire, Michaelmas 1361 to Michaelmas 1362*, edited by P. H. W. Booth, The Record Society of Lancashire and Cheshire 138 (2003), xix; for St Albans see Ada Levett, *Studies in Manorial History*, edited by H. M. Cam, M. Coate and L. S. Sutherland (Oxford, 1938), 111–12, 134–47; for Peterborough see *Peterborough Medieval Court Rolls*, translated by Margaret Briston with an introduction by Nicholas Karn, Northamptonshire Record Society 48 (2015), xx, and references noted at 34; and many others.

[49] Though Van Caenegem, *Lawsuits*, no. 332, shows a *halimota* recommending the return of property that a lord had occupied.

private courts. What is not clear is whether the *halimotas* could exclude others; this is an important later feature of many private courts. Whether sheriffs or hundred bailiffs or others could intrude into them is entirely unclear from the limited sources that reflect them, so any answer to this question cannot now be attempted. Thus it would be rash to describe them as private courts for the evidence is not full enough to determine the question.

The importance of the appearance of *halimotas* was that they showed transformation in the ways in which lords thought about and managed their interests in their dependents. Under the later Anglo-Saxon model, dependents might owe dues to different lords, and these would be settled through testimony as to the nature of the relationship between those dependents. This debate was made possible because all dependents and lords from a particular territory would be likely to be present in the same hundred court. The appearance of *halimotas* changed this dynamic entirely. Now, it was necessary to find some means of adjudicating not within one court but between them; this often meant that it was necessary to bring in outside authority. A dispute between the abbeys of Peterborough and Thorney in 1120 illustrates this nicely; four fishermen owed dues to both abbeys, and, so the Thorney narrative indicates, had been accustomed to attend the Thorney *halimota* until the abbot of Peterborough attempted to divert their loyalties and attendance.[50] The discussion was no longer within one arena about lordship and relationship, but rather was about jurisdiction, and the ability to compel the attendance of men.[51]

## Lordship through Private Agreement

Changes in lordship need not rely upon the action of kings, for lords could do much to alter the ways in which lordship worked through action and agreements among themselves. These changes might come to be confirmed by kings afterwards, but this need not always happen; many seem to have been made by private agreements between lords of different kinds, and it is not obvious in most of these cases how these clarifications, reshapings and consolidations of lordship were done and managed. Presumably one or other lord initiated the deal; yet the documentation does not usually record exactly who and when was responsible. These kinds of transactions tend to underline the point that *halimotas* should not be regarded as essentially franchisal.

Grants by lords other than the king are particularly important because they expose two attributes that are not always apparent in the charters made by kings. First, they show how much of the initiative for consolidating lordship came from

[50] Van Caenegem, *Lawsuits*, no. 219.

[51] This theme is explored more fully in Chapter 5 below.

lords themselves, and that these changes to lordship could have taken place even without the contribution of kings. Second, the charters by great lords other than the king are not bound by the ambiguous conventions that ruled the products of the king's scribes, and so the charters of these lords are often much more specific about what was actually involved in the transaction. They did not merely include stock phrases of debatable meaning, such as the cliché of sake and soke, toll and team, and the private charters sometimes explain what a grant actually meant. Charters written for great secular lords were not bound by the same narrow conventions as those in the names of kings. This often meant that private charters explain what a recipient of a grant needed to do, or did not need to do, and so they are often much more specific about the consequences and possibilities of holding a *halimota* or leet court.

The abbots and later the bishops of Ely held soke over the hundreds of northern Cambridgeshire that later comprised the Isle of Ely. It seems that originally this meant that the abbots and bishops claimed soke over all men within that district, regardless of who the lord of those men might have been. In Domesday Book, the two hundreds of Witchford were the vehicle through which Ely controlled the district, and were described as belonging to Ely. Yet, in 1127 the first bishop of Ely, Hervey, granted that the abbey of Thorney should obtain some part of Ely's claims over its own land and dependents. For, Thorney lay in the far north-west of Cambridgeshire, within the district over which Ely held claims. This is apparent from Domesday Book, where it is stated that *Hoc manerium iacuit et iacet in dominio ecclesie de Torny, sed socam habet abbas de Ely*, and that the manor was *In duobus hundredis de Ely*.[52] This seems an arrangement of divided Domesday lordship of the kind familiar from other places, but which here persisted into the 1120s. Hervey granted his claims to the monks in the following terms:

> May it be known to all whether present or future that I, Hervey, by the grace of God first bishop of Ely, have conceded and given in alms to the church of Thorney all those customs and secular causes that the church of Ely had in its hundreds of Witchford from the land and from the men of the church of Thorney from Whittlesey, excepting the royal customs which are levied upon that land.[53] I have made this donation on the day of the dedication of the church of Thorney with the consent of the whole convent of the church of Ely.

[52] Great Domesday Book, fo. 192d: Cambridgeshire 8.1; *Inquisitio Eliensis*, ed. N. E. S. A. Hamilton, *Inquisitio Comitatus Cantabrigiensis* (London, 1876), 97–195, at 115.

[53] Some manuscripts change this line somewhat, so that it is more specific in its preservation of royal claims, in these terms: *exceptis* propriis *regalibus consuetudinibus que super terram illam evenerint* que nec ad me nec ad ecclesiam nostram pertinent. This can be found in The National Archives, C66/224 (Patent Roll 22 Edward III), m. 24, CUL ms. Additional 3020 (Red Book of Thorney; s.xiv ex. general cartulary), fo. 166r, and other copies listed in the notes to Nicholas Karn, *English Episcopal Acta* 31: *Ely, 1109–1197* (Oxford, 2005), no. 11.

> With these witnesses: Gilbert, bishop of London, John, bishop of Rochester, Waltheof, abbot of Crowland, Henry, archdeacon of Huntingdon, Hugh de Scalers, etc.[54]

The charter shows that different kinds of claims were involved. There were two kinds of customs involved. One set of customs belonged to the king, and another belonged to the bishop in his role as lord; the latter were presumably identical with the soke noted in Domesday Book. Exactly what customs were involved and how they were divided is not stated, but presumably these included such matters as soke, hundredpenny and so forth, so that what was essentially being debated here was the allocation of financial dues of one kind or another. As well as these, the charter transferred to Thorney claims over the *causas seculares* from the dependents and land of Thorney; this presumably meant any claims or disputes from among the abbot's dependents or from his lands, without any apparent definition apart from the reservation of royal customs. Thus the bishop reserved to himself the ecclesiastical causes which would by this date have been managed through the bishop's own ecclesiastical courts. Hervey's charter does not really explain how these claims were to be exercised, whether Thorney could have its own court, or whether it merely claimed dues through the bishop of Ely's court.[55] Later the claims that Thorney held over its lands in north-western Cambridgeshire were expressed through a hundred or leet court that ruled over the abbey's dependents separate from the hundreds of the bishops of Ely. Thus, at some point the grant here was taken to mean that the abbot of Thorney could withdraw the attendance of his dependents for most matters from the hundreds of the bishops of Ely.

54 *Notum sit omnibus tam presentibus quam futuris me Herveum Dei gratia Eliensem episcopum primum concessisse et in elemosinam dedisse Thornensi ecclesie omnes illas consuetudines et causas seculares quas habebat Eliensis ecclesia in hundredis suis de Wicheford' de terra et de hominibus Thornensis ecclesie de Witleseya, exceptis regalibus consuetudinibus que super terram illam evenerint. Hanc autem donationem feci in die dedicationis Thornensis ecclesie concessu totius conventus Elyensis ecclesie. Hiis testibus: Gilberto London' episcopo, Iohanne Rofensi episcopo, Walthefo abbate Croyland', Henrico Huntend' archidiacono, Hugo [sic] de Scalariis, etc.* CUL ms. Additional 3020 (Red Book of Thorney, s.xiv ex.), fo. 166v, and many other copies listed in Nicholas Karn, *English Episcopal Acta* 31: *Ely, 1109–1197* (Oxford, 2005), no. 11. The dedication of Thorney abbey church can be dated from other sources to 1127; see Nicholas Karn, *English Episcopal Acta* 31: *Ely, 1109–1197* (Oxford, 2005), no. 11 note.

55 The confirmations of this charter repeat the terms of Hervey's charter without further detail. *Regesta*, ii. no. 1798; Avrom Saltman, *Theobald, Archbishop of Canterbury* (London, 1956), 525–7, no. 300; Nicholas Karn, *English Episcopal Acta* 31: *Ely, 1109–1197* (Oxford, 2005), no. 85; and a confirmation by the prior of Ely, in note to Nicholas Karn, *English Episcopal Acta* 31: *Ely, 1109–1197* (Oxford, 2005), no. 11. *Ibid*, no. 10, covers a case in the bishop's court.

Much the most specific explanation of how a grant of claims might work comes from another charter where a favoured lord made a grant to a monastery. Much like the Isle of Ely, the Isle of Wight was an area dominated by one lord, who had claims over the hundreds within the island.[56] This was not an ecclesiastical potentate, but rather a series of great secular lords, for lordship passed through the hands of members of the de Redvers family and their descendants.[57] The holder of claims over the Island in the second quarter of the twelfth century was Baldwin de Redvers, earl of Exeter, and over a few years in the later 1130s and 1140s he chose to create a new monastic foundation within his lordship, in the form of the Savigniac house at Quarr. His foundation charter names various grants to the monastery by himself and his dependents, and also granted to the monks various jurisdictional claims:

> Also I concede this liberty to the men residing in the alms of the said church,[58] that they should go to no hundred except to the hundred of theft (*latrocinii*), and if it happens that they fall into any forfeiture, the justice thence is mine and the compensation and fine belong to the abbot and monks.[59]

[56] Robert Bearman, *Charters of the Redvers Family and the Earldom of Devon, 1090–1217*, Devon and Cornwall Record Society, new series 37 (1994), 18.

[57] Robert Bearman, *Charters of the Redvers Family and the Earldom of Devon, 1090–1217*, Devon and Cornwall Record Society, new series 37 (1994), 18–26; on some of the descendants of the Redvers family see N. Denholm-Young, *Seignorial Administration in England* (London, 1937), esp. 99–107.

[58] This presumably means that the grant was made to those men who lived on those lands that the abbey held in free alms tenure.

[59] *Item hominibus in elemosina predicte ecclesie manentibus talem libertatem concedo, ut ad nullum hundredum eant nisi ad hundredum latrocinii et si contigerit eos cadere in aliquod forisfactum, iusticia inde sit mea et emendatio et catelum sit abbatis et monachorum*: Robert Bearman, *Charters of the Redvers Family and the Earldom of Devon, 1090–1217*, Devon and Cornwall Record Society, new series 37 (1994), 68, no. 17 extract; phrase shown in frontispiece plate; translation in S. F. Hockey, *Quarr Abbey and its Lands, 1132–1631* (Leicester, 1970), 6–8 and in Latin at 257–8 appendix A; calendared in S. F. Hockey, *The Charters of Quarr Abbey*, Isle of Wight Records Series 3 (1991), 1, no. 1; and facsimile in V. H. Galbraith, 'Monastic Foundation Charters of the Eleventh Centuries', *Cambridge Historical Journal* 4 (1934), 205–22, with facsimile facing p. 222, and discussion at 215–18. On the abbey and its history see S. F. Hockey, *Quarr Abbey and its Lands, 1132–1631* (Leicester, 1970). For another instance in similar terms, see the slightly later charter of Reginald, earl of Cornwall: *Et concessi eis quod non placitent in hundredis nec in comitatibus nec pro aliqua summonicione eant ad placitandum alicubi extra villam de Triueru et quod quieti sint de tolneo dando per totam Cornubiam in feriis et in foris et ubicumque emerint vel vendiderint et quod de pecunia eorum acredita et non reddita namium capiant in villa sua de debitoribus suis* (Charles Henderson, 'Records of the Borough of Truro before AD 1300', *Journal of the Royal Institution of Cornwall* 23 (1929), 103–36, at 121).

Baldwin's grant is much the most specific concession from this period. It contains a number of important messages about how jurisdiction was managed in the first half of the twelfth century. First, the grant here is not formally to the monks at all, but rather to their dependents; they were granted the liberty that they need not attend the hundred. Of course, this should not be taken as a special concern for Quarr Abbey's peasants, for they were being freed within the context of a grant to the abbey, and so presumably they would have remained subject to whatever courts the abbey itself operated as a means of managing those dependents. Second, the nature of the liberty granted to them is described as the freedom that they need not attend the hundred. The link between attendance and obligation is implicit in the idea of soke, that it represented an obligation to seek the court or lordship of the superior; it might have been that the obligation to attend was what was felt particularly burdensome by the peasants to whom this concession was formally granted. Third, the grant shows that the cycle of meetings of the hundred was structured. Some were more important than others, and those designated as hundreds where cases involving robbery were dealt with were not readily dispensed with.[60] Perhaps these might have been sessions at which investigations were made into cases of theft and robbery within the locality;[61] or perhaps these were the sessions at which the oath against theft was administered.[62] Perhaps the two functions were carried out alongside each other at the same hundred sessions. From the later twelfth century, it was a general practice that there were special sessions of the hundred, which were then known as the view of frankpledge, when the sheriff appeared to investigate the maintenance of the frankpledge tithings. Originally these views of frankpledge were limited to two such sessions a year, but this was reduced to one a year; nonetheless, those hundreds and leets that had obtained exemption from shrieval visits continued to hold two views a year.[63] In their liberty of the Isle of Wight, the de Redvers had their own private sheriff,[64] who could well have carried out such functions. Fourth, Baldwin felt capable of freeing the peasants of Quarr Abbey from obligations to attend the other sessions of the hundred apart from the *hundredum latrocinii*; presumably, any cases about matters other than theft had therefore passed away from the hundred court towards some other assembly, presumably manorial courts held by the abbey over its own dependents. Fifth, Baldwin makes provision for the

60 The possibility of separate hundred meetings concerning theft might also be implicit in the Domesday Book entry for Taunton: Great Domesday Book, fo. 87v: Somerset 2.1.

61 This might be seen as a continuity of the special sessions of the hundred on theft ordered in 3 Æthelred 3.1–4.2.

62 On this see William Alfred Morris, *The Frankpledge System* (New York, 1910).

63 Nicholas Karn, introduction to *Peterborough Medieval Court Rolls*, translated by Margaret Briston, Northamptonshire Record Society 48 (2015), xiii.

64 Robert Bearman, *Charters of the Redvers Family and the Earldom of Devon, 1090–1217*, Devon and Cornwall Record Society, new series 37 (1994), 27–31.

allocation of forfeitures, presumably those arising from the *hundredum latrocinii*. At least on the Isle of Wight, theft remained the dominant matter that was dealt with through the hundred court well into the twelfth century, and something of the priorities established in the later Anglo-Saxon legislation continued to mould the operation of courts. Baldwin makes a distinction which has been much debated in relation to English courts in the central middle ages, but which is very rarely seen in the sources themselves.[65] He grants that, even in those cases which still came before the protected jurisdiction of the *hundredum latrocinii*, he divided the claim to oversee the case from the destination of the profits. Thus, he reserves to himself the *iustitia* over any such case. *Iustitia* is a word that becomes much more prominent in legal texts during the early twelfth century, and it does not mean the same as the modern 'justice', but rather signifies 'right' or even 'jurisdiction'. In using this term, Baldwin is clearly asserting that he should continue to have claims over the hearing of the case, which took place in courts over which he had some measure of control and power, and perhaps over the handling of those who were convicted in this setting. Thus, Baldwin and his representatives could keep some control over the management of these categories of business. Yet, at the same time any forfeitures would go to the monks of Quarr. As lord of the Isle of Wight, Baldwin was the custodian and repository of the claims normally held by the king and his representatives, and so this grant would mean that any of the penalties normally claimed by the king would go to the monks.

Earl Baldwin's charter is unusually clear but far from unique; many lords produced charters that conveyed soke, and even claims over pleas involving theft. The implication of these is that these were not viewed as special claims, ones which especially belonged to the king. Instead, they could be granted and traded in ways akin to how land itself could be bought, sold and transferred. The pattern of survival of these charters may be somewhat misleading. Charters conveying or recognising soke were almost exclusively in the name of kings before 1066; the only clearly genuine exception is the writ of Queen Edith which conveyed soke at Mark in Somerset to the church of Wells.[66] This is related to the surviving pattern of charters from later Anglo-Saxon England, for there are very few charters in the name of individuals other than the king. Charters in the name of lords other than the king survive in much greater numbers from after 1066, and especially from after 1100, and so the transfer of these claims can be seen much more fully. It is possible that lords before 1066 were similarly willing to trade and convey these claims, but that their dispositions were either made orally, or through kinds of documentation that have not survived.

The increasing quantity of charters from lords from the later eleventh century means that these transfers of soke can be seen in many places. Even soon after

65 Lambert, *Law and Order*, chapter 7.
66 Harmer, *Writs*, no. 72.

1066, French lords familiarised themselves with the importance of these claims, and their documents included these grants:

> Earl Ralph to E. the priest and all the barons of the hundred, greeting! Know that I have given to Grim my chaplain the homage of Askitel and whatever he holds in Walsham with sake and soke and all custom and *ingang* and *utgang* for the work of the church of St Benet of Hulme, just as well as I had it. Goodbye.[67]

Ralph was earl of East Anglia, and thus the probable holder of soke across the region; his grant of sake and soke is thus unproblematic here. It left the grantee, Grim the chaplain, holding quite privileged status over Askitel; Grim received Askitel's personal oath of commendatory lordship, lordship over Askitel's land, and then the soke as well.

Other earls were generous grantors of soke. The earls of Chester and their relatives, to take the most prominent example, frequently gave soke and other matters linked to courts to their men and to others. Their grants seem to show that their holding of soke was not in relation to the earldom as such, but rather in relation to their honour, for they gave soke across the whole span of their lands, including places far beyond the bounds of Cheshire,[68] as well as places within.[69] The pattern becomes yet more complicated when other comital honours

[67] *Radulphus comes E. presbitero et omnibus baronibus de hundredo salutem. Sciatis me dedisse Grim capellano meo manredam Askitelis et quicquid tenet in Walsham cum sache et sokne et omni consuetudine et ingang et utgang ad opus ecclesie sancti Benedicti de Hulmo sicut egomet melius habui. Valete.* F. M. Stenton, 'St Benet of Hulme and the Norman Conquest', *English Historical Review* 37 (1922), 225–35, at 230; also in *St Benet of Holme, 1020-1210: The Eleventh and Twelfth Century Sections of Cotton MS Galba E. ii.: The Register of the Abbey of St Benet of Holme*, ed. J. R. West, Norfolk Record Society 2–3 (1934), i. 32, no. 58. It must have been before Ralph's disgrace in 1075. For another instance of hundred witnesses called barons see Van Caenegem, *Lawsuits*, no. 254.

[68] Charter of Countess Lucy, granting sake and soke and toll and team in Spalding, Lincolnshire, *c.* 1135, *The Charters of the Anglo-Norman Earls of Chester, c. 1071–1237*, ed. Geoffrey Barraclough, Record Society of Lancashire and Cheshire 126 (1988), no. 16; Earl Ranulf, grant to Geoffrey Ridel, sake, soke, toll, team and *infangthief* in Drayton Basset, Staffordshire, *c.* 1150, *ibid*, no. 40; Earl Ranulf, grant to William the falconer of Weekley (Northants) with sake, soke, toll, team and *infangthief*, 1141 x 1143, *ibid*, no. 56; Earl Ranulf, grant to Hugh Bardulf in Waddington (Lincolnshire), with sake, soke, toll, team and *infangthief* 1142 x 1146, *ibid*, no. 66; and others.

[69] Charter of Earl Ranulf establishing the court of Basingwerk abbey, 1135 x 1140, *The Charters of the Anglo-Norman Earls of Chester, c. 1071–1237*, ed. Geoffrey Barraclough, Record Society of Lancashire and Cheshire 126 (1988), no. 37; Earl Ranulf, grant to Hugh son of Bigod of Gawsworth (Chester), toll and team and own court, need not respond to reeves of Macclesfield, 1136 x 1154, *ibid*, no. 43; Earl Ranulf, grant to Alured de Combray of claims in Whitley in Haltonshire 1143 x 1144, *ibid*, no. 67; and others. On some of this see Paul Dalton, 'Ranulf II and Lincolnshire',

are considered; the Warennes, the earls of Surrey, produced numerous surviving charters, but did not explicitly grant soke within them. It is not really clear what this means. Some contain phrases indicating that the grantee was to have all the claims that the Warenne earls had over their lands,[70] which might be thought to include soke, but it is curious that soke is not explicitly named. Is it possible that the Warennes did not hold soke so fully? Or merely that charters from their honour were used and drafted in different ways?

Soke was not only granted by earls. Lords of lesser status but still great wealth also had soke and granted them freely. Thus, for instance, members of the d'Aubigny family held sake and soke across many of their lands,[71] and granted it to others, including secular and ecclesiastical grantees across Yorkshire.[72] Their ownership of soke cannot be linked to an earldom, but rather (presumably) to the favour that Nigel d'Aubigny received from Henry I; this might be an example of how kings could grant soke to favoured lords.[73]

It is possible to find very many instances where it seems that lords agreed among themselves to manage these claims, or that one lord granted claims to another. Sometimes, one lord merely took such claims, and lords had to struggle over whose will would prevail. This need not have involved the invocation of royal authority, but was managed locally:

> In the year of the Lord 1187, I Oliver de Laumvelay lord of Kingstone have recognised in the presence of Prior Jocelin of Montacute at Tintinhull in full hundred held there on Sunday in the octave of St Michael, that I Oliver and my men of the vill of Kingstone ought to come thrice in the year to the said hundred of Tintinhull just as other suitors and tithings of the said hundred come and ought to come to the same, that is, in the octave of St Michael, in the octave of the Epiphany and in the octave of *la hokkedaye*; and that my said men in the same [i.e. the hundred] shall present all those things which [pertain to] the view of frankpledge ...[74]

---

in *The Earldom of Chester and its Charters: A Tribute to Geoffrey Barraclough*, ed. A. T. Thacker, *Journal of the Chester Archaeological Society* 71 (Chester, 1991), 109–34, at 111–13.

70 *Early Yorkshire Charters*: VIII, *The Honour of Warenne*, edited by Charles Travis Clay, Yorkshire Archaeological Society, Extra Series 6 (1949), 101, no. 54, a grant by Earl Hamelin, 1164 x 1179, granting all that the earl had, and *si homines sancti Pancratii commiserate contra me vel meos unde emendacionem vel forisfacturam habere debeam, prior sancti Pancratii eam pro me accipiat et habeat.*

71 *Charters of the Honour of Mowbray, 1107–1191*, edited by D. E. Greenway, Records of Social and Economic History, new series 1 (1972), lviii–lxix.

72 *Charters of the Honour of Mowbray, 1107–1191*, edited by D. E. Greenway, Records of Social and Economic History, new series 1 (1972), 5, no. 1; 16, no. 13; 220–1, no. 343, etc.

73 *Leges Henrici Primi*, 19.2.

74 *Anno domini millesimo centesimo octuagesimo [sic] septimo ego Oliverus de Laumuelay*

The clear implication of this document is that Oliver de Laumvelay had tried to stop his dependents from Kingstone from attending the hundred court at Tintinhull. Kingstone was a detached portion of the hundred, and was some nine kilometres south-west of its south-western extremity. His decision to try to remove his dependents was challenged by the holder of the hundred, the prior of Montacute, and Oliver was somehow cajoled into making this recognition of his and his dependents' obligation to attend the hundred three times a year and to carry out the view of frankpledge there. This might be taken as an indication that he and his dependents had carried out the view of frankpledge separately in Kingstone, which would imply that he was able to obtain the approval and participation of the sheriff to carry out this process. Presumably he held a court for his dependents in Kingstone anyway, so that withdrawing his dependents from Tintinhull and adding some business to his court at Kingstone might not have involved very radical change anyway. Examples such as Kingstone suggest that the experience of hundreds could be changeable.

## Conclusion

This chapter has set out an argument about how courts functioned and were experienced between about 1000 and 1130. During those decades, the roles and functions of the hundred changed considerably, and its roles diminished. The tenth-century laws, especially the Hundred Ordinance, depict the hundred as central to the functioning of society, and dealing with a mass of business linked to social order and trade; they also drew in large parts of the societies over which they ruled, and were essential in disseminating the ideologies of kingship.[75] Maybe the ambitions set out for the hundred in the tenth century were never

---

*dominus de Kynggeston' recognoui in presencia Iocelini prioris de Monte Acuto apud Tyntehull in pleno hundr' ibidem tento die sabbati in octab' sancti Michaelis quod ego Oliverus et homines mei de uilla de Kynggeston' uenire debemus ter in anno ad dictum hundredum de Tyntehull sicut ceteri sectatores et decenne dicti hundredi ueniunt et uenire debent ad idem, uidelicet in octab' sancti Michaelis in octab' epiphanie et in octab' de la hokkedaye; et quod homines mei antedicti in eodem presentabunt omnia que ad uisum franci* ... Oxford, Bodleian Library, ms. Trinity College 85, fo. 58v (once fo 37v), calendared in *Two Cartularies of the Augustinian Priory of Bruton and the Cluniac Priory of Montacute*, ed. Members of the Council, Somerset Record Society 8 (1894), 146, no. 58. The next quire of ten folios is missing from the manuscript, and so the rest of the document is lost.

75 Hundred Ordinance; for instance, H. R. Loyn, 'The Hundred in England in the Tenth and Early Eleventh Centuries', in *British Government and Administration: Studies Presented to S. B. Chrimes*, ed. H. Hearder and H. R. Loyn (Cardiff, 1974), 1–15; Patrick Wormald, '*Engla Lond*: the Making of an Allegiance', in his *Legal Culture in the Early Medieval West: Law as Text, Image and Experience* (London, 1999), 359–82.

achieved in full, but its centrality is inescapable in the sources from that century. Yet, by 1100 the hundred had been substantially weakened. This weakening was not a result of leadership from kings, but rather was due to the work of mostly French lords, who chose to withdraw their dependents from it. In this, they were basing their actions on the way in which lords' claim to soke was granted or recognised by kings, and expressing these claims through the creation of sub-hundredal units. These appear in increasing quantities from the later eleventh century onwards, and appear under many different names; leets and *halimotas* at first, and later (confusingly) hundreds, tourns, views of frankpledge and so forth. They probably helped to consolidate lords' control over the freer peasants on the warland, and may form the model and precedent on which manor courts were later formed. The rise of these new kinds of court meant that a writer in the early twelfth century thought about the English administrative landscape in terms that would not have been recognisable to many of his predecessors.

These developments meant that the central position of hundreds in their localities was being challenged. A lot of business was withdrawn, and the dependents of many lords were simply not turning up for meetings of the hundred. In this setting, the role of the hundred in vouching to warranty and in dealing with minor matters was substantially weakened. Domesday Book shows that hundreds then bore testimony about the landholdings of many lesser and greater men. Even peasants, it would seem, could get recognition of their claims from the hundreds. Once *halimotas* came into being, peasants no longer received this public recognition, but had to rely on the goodwill of their lords. This altered the balance of power radically, and must have been a key step in the process of manorialisation, and in lordly takeover of peasant holdings.

The hundred still dealt with business and still met, but the nature of its discussions and debates had to alter; much more debate was about jurisdiction, and which court had the ability to deal with a case. Charters that were concerned with jurisdiction became increasingly complex as a means of managing these problems. There were many effects of these changes in terms of how law was actually done. Kings tried to turn back the clock, apparently with limited success; later, new administrative structures were created by lords and by kings to try to control their claims in this multitude of courts; new legal texts were written to try to bring some order to the mass of courts and jurisdiction; and new vocabulary developed to define the roles of individuals within these courts, and the relationships between them.

# 5

# From Debate Within Courts to Debate Between Courts: The Origins of Jurisdictional Debate

In 1000, business was transacted overwhelmingly through the hundred court, and to some extent the shire court, which required the attendance of many people from across the districts they covered, and which were neutral ground in which the complicated patterns of later Anglo-Saxon multiple lordship could be defined and managed. There are some indications that hundreds might try to protect their territories from interventions from other hundreds,[1] but otherwise there is little evidence for jurisdictional debate, that is, discussions that assumed that it was of great importance *where* a dispute was heard, or where participants assumed that someone could hear a case. It is hard to see how cases were allocated to one assembly or to another. *Bocland* was associated with kings, but they did not claim to hear cases arising about *bocland* exclusively, so that some were heard before kings but others in shires; there is no clear principle behind the choices made.[2] More than one king stated that none should approach the king for justice unless he had been denied it in the hundred.[3] There are clearly cases heard by kings before 1066, but those seem to have been few.[4] The laws indicate that the hundred was the primary venue for hearing disputes, but the relationships between the various assemblies are far from clear.[5]

Long before 1200, the role of the hundred had been considerably diminished. Lords formed units and courts below or within the hundred, which were termed *halimota*, and which meant that much business could now be transacted within the bounds of one lordship. This reduced the scope for others to interfere with the interests of the lords who held these *halimota*, and also allowed the holder of these courts to monopolise, or at least take much of, the dues and proceeds that

1 For instance, 1 Edgar 5.

2 A. G. Kennedy, 'Disputes about *Bocland*: The Forum for their Adjudication', *Anglo-Saxon England* 14 (1985), 175–95.

3 3 Edgar 2; 2 Cnut 17.

4 For instance, the events analysed in Nicholas P. Brooks, 'The Fonthill Letter, Ealdorman Ordlaf and Anglo-Saxon Law in Practice', in *Early Medieval Studies in Memory of Patrick Wormald*, ed. Stephen Baxter, Catherine Karkov, Janet L. Nelson and David Pelteret (Farnham, 2009), 301–17.

5 Hudson, *Oxford History*, 43–65.

arose from the meeting of the court. These changes were in the interests of lords, and were more or less driven by them; the preceding chapter set out evidence for how lords created these courts themselves. Perhaps the creation of these smaller units was in the interests of others too – those attending the court had shorter distances to travel – but the principal role in making these units lay with the lords behind their creation.

The appearance of lords' courts meant that, in many cases, there was henceforth a choice over where individual pleas might be aired and settled. In many cases, it might be assumed, there was not really a problem, if all participants could agree on one court as the most suitable venue for a plea, or if inequalities in power meant that only one view determined the outcome. Yet, in some cases there were problems in determining the most suitable venue, and markedly different views about which was most appropriate. These views might originate among the participants in the dispute, or among the lords who controlled the courts themselves. Participants in pleas might feel that they would receive a more favourable hearing in one court rather than another, especially if there were more members of kin or friendship networks in one court than other; or, conversely, if one court were packed with the adherents of an opponent, there would be a strong incentive to avoid pleading there. Lords, meanwhile, might want to ensure that their dependents' pleas were heard in their own courts, so that they could make sure that the outcome was favourable to their own interests, or to make sure that they could control the consequences of the plea in terms of penalties or the reallocation of property.

It took a long time for the implications of this new situation to be thought through. Various parties might *want* a case to be heard in one court rather than another, but it took a while to sort out how such wishes could be expressed publicly, through conventions for asserting that a particular plea should rightly be heard in one court rather than another. There was nothing in the Anglo-Saxon legal materials that helped with such questions,[6] for these problems about competing claims between different courts and litigants did not arise in the same way then, and so ideas had to be adapted in the later eleventh and earlier twelfth centuries. The sources from that period show how conventions were generated gradually over time that allowed such claims about the claims and status of courts – essentially, jurisdictional claims – to be made and settled.

The development of something approximating to jurisdictional debate in Anglo-Norman England does not seem to have been something that was closely managed by kings. William I made a proclamation that set out how some ecclesiastical pleas were to be handled,[7] and Henry I made another that set out principles

6 Hudson, *Oxford History*, 64–5.

7 Bates, *Regesta*, no. 128.

for deciding how to allocate pleas between lords' courts in some circumstances.[8] Of course, there may have been other royal proclamations that have since been lost, and which helped to shape thinking on these matters, but there is no evidence for this, or compelling reason for assuming that such ever existed. Rather than being legislated legal change, it looks much more like cultural change, as words and arguments attained to widespread acceptance and usage through convention rather than through authority.[9] This, of course, fits well with the reality of how law was managed in the eleventh and twelfth centuries, for there were no professional lawyers who might create a specialised vocabulary and norms of argumentation; instead, law was more open, and was a concern for any who held land or influence. In such circumstances, ideas might spread most effectively by imitation and through conversation.

Participants in pleas from the last decades of the eleventh century tended to assume that their links of lordship should determine the way in which pleas should be handled, and the places and assemblies in which those pleas should be held, should be determined in accordance with those ties.[10] Lords in many cases worked towards achieving this. These kinds of assumptions were commonly expressed through descriptions of the relationships between the individuals involved. Elsewhere, the relationships desired were described in terms of jurisdiction, as though lordship brought with it a say in how lords and their dependents should behave, or should not behave, in courts.

The earlier chapters in this book set out an analysis which showed how it happened that courts were diversified and proliferated, especially from about 1100. In some places, lords were able to assert claims of interest and finally claims of ownership over hundred courts. At the same time, lords were able to create their own courts as *halimota*. The appearance of these changed the terms of debate fundamentally. In the Anglo-Saxon model, the rival claims of lords would be aired in the shire or hundred as venues that represented, in a sense, neutral ground. Once lords' courts were in place, that was no longer possible, and competing claims of lords had to be resolved outside those courts, before the plea had actually been heard or during its progress. These kinds of debates are highlighted by Henry I's proclamation on the shire and hundred courts, which set out some basic regulations for how these debates might be conducted.[11] This often

8 *Regesta*, ii. no. 892. This charter is discussed in detail in Chapter 6 below.

9 John Hudson, 'Court Cases and Legal Arguments in England, *c.* 1066–1166', *Transactions of the Royal Historical Society* sixth series 10 (2000), 91–115, esp. 91–3, sets out a model for how ideas and ideals lay behind legal actions and decisions.

10 John Hudson, 'The Fate of Earl Waltheof and the Idea of Personal Law in England after 1066', in *Normandy and its Neighbours, 900–1250: Essays for David Bates*, ed. David Crouch and Kathleen Thompson (Turnhout, 2011), 223–35, disposes of the idea that personal law was important in Anglo-Norman England.

11 *Regesta*, ii. no. 892 and Chapter 6 below.

meant that the decision over *where* a plea should be heard had to be conducted outside the courts themselves. There was no real precedent for this before 1066; the story of this chapter is how lords, their agents and others gradually felt their way forward towards conventions for these kinds of conversations.

In those cases for which evidence survives, it often happened that the dispute over where cases should be held could only be decided through the invocation of royal authority, for the basic idea that kings could exercise some form of oversight over the administration of law in general was widely accepted. Thus, the development of lords' courts and the consequences that came from that were one of the causes of the expansion of royal involvement in this period; royal interest in the law did not grow because kings had a grand plan to expand their authority, but rather because lords and others brought kings into local disputes increasingly often because they saw kings as the solution to some of their own problems. The issues at debate were about the nature, scope and powers of courts. Of course, the courts were in most cases expressions of the lordship and power of the lords who controlled them, but these debates were most often phrased in terms of who had the power to deal with particular matters. These kinds of debates cannot be seen before 1066, and their sudden appearance is not only a significant change in itself, but also an index of the way that the patterns of courts were changing in these decades.

The earliest case of all is a secular one discussed below, but many of the early ones have a substantial ecclesiastical component. This means that many have senior churchmen as participants, or are disputes between senior churchmen, or were disputes where exclusive claims were raised for the church. This is probably very important. Though canon law had been known and studied before 1066,[12] and had been an influence upon the royal laws,[13] interest in it differed substantially after 1066. A new and influential collection of canon law was introduced into England, seemingly by Archbishop Lanfranc,[14] and it had been disseminated

[12] For instance, J. E. Cross and Andrew Hamer, *Wulfstan's Canon Law Collection* (Woodbridge, 1999); R. H. Helmholz, *The Oxford History of the Laws of England*: 1, *The Canon Law and Ecclesiastical Jurisdiction from 597 to the 1640s* (Oxford, 2004), chapter 1.

[13] 1 Cnut in particular embodies extensive regulation of the clergy and the religious which parallels canon law.

[14] On this see, among much else, Martin Brett, 'The *Collectio Lanfranci* and its Competitors', in *Intellectual Life in the Middle Ages: Essays Presented to Margaret Gibson*, ed. Lesley Smith and Benedicta Ward (1992), 157–71; R. H. Helmholz, *The Oxford History of the Laws of England*: 1, *The Canon Law and Ecclesiastical Jurisdiction from 597 to the 1640s* (Oxford, 2004), 73–4; Nicolás Alvarez de las Asturias, 'The Use of the *Collectio Lanfranci*: The Evidence of the Manuscripts', in *Bishops, Texts and the Use of Canon Law around 1100: Essays in Honour of Martin Brett*, ed. Bruce C. Brasington, and Kathleen G. Cushing (Aldershot, 2008), 121–7; Michael Gullick, 'Lanfranc and the Oldest Manuscript of the *Collectio Lanfranci*',

quite widely among senior churchmen and great churches.[15] Perhaps inspired by this, there were attempts at defining the boundaries between secular and canon law. The most important of these was the decree of William the Conqueror which ordered that pleas concerning episcopal laws should no longer be held by bishops or archdeacons in the hundred court.[16] This decree was one of the first explicit recognitions of the idea that canon law and secular law (described here as the law of the hundred) might be separate spheres in some matters; it also includes the idea that it was important who heard the case, in that it states that certain kinds of cases should not be heard by laymen. It thus assumed that difference in kinds of law should bring with it institutional expression of that difference. It also assumed that such a division was unproblematic; there is no mechanism for allocating pleas to the hundred court or not to the hundred court.

There are a few early cases that show concern for the jurisdictions of canon law.[17] They will not be discussed in detail here because this study is principally concerned with the secular law, and in any case they have received more attention and discussion than most of the other cases analysed here. There are some features of these cases which are worth noting. The best known of these is the plea against William of Saint-Calais, bishop of Durham, where he was accused by William II after being implicated in the 1088 rebellion, and which is known from the tract *De iniusta uexacione Willelmi episcopi primi*.[18] The plea acquired a jurisdictional element through the agency of the bishop, not the king. Saint-Calais argued that

in *Bishops, Texts and the Use of Canon Law around 1100: Essays in Honour of Martin Brett*, ed. Bruce C. Brasington, and Kathleen G. Cushing (Aldershot, 2008), 79–89; Nicolás Alvarez de las Asturias, 'Lanfranc of Bec's Version of Decretals in a Canonistic Context', *Catholic Historical Review* 98 (2012), 649–78.

15 The fundamental work on this remains Z. N. Brooke, *The English Church and the Papacy from the Conquest to the Reign of John* (Cambridge, 1931); for a case study see Mark Philpott, 'The *De iniusta uexacione Willelmi episcopi primi* and Canon Law in Anglo-Norman Durham', in *Anglo-Norman Durham, 1093–1193*, ed. David Rollason, Margaret Harvey and Michael Prestwich (Woodbridge, 1994), 125–37.

16 Bates, *Regesta*, no. 128. On this see Colin Morris, 'William I and the Church Courts', *English Historical Review* 82 (1967), 449–63, which cautions against ambitious readings of the significance of the document.

17 The best known is the trial of Odo, bishop of Bayeux: Van Caenegem, *Lawsuits*, no. 11; and on the case see David R. Bates, 'The Character and Career of Odo, Bishop of Bayeux (1049/50–1097', *Speculum* 50 (1975), 1–20, at 15–18.

18 Van Caenegem, *Lawsuits*, no. 134; *De iniusta uexacione Willelmi episcopi primi per Willelmum regem filium Willelmi magni regis*, ed. H. S. Offler, A. J. Piper and A. I. Doyle, *Camden Miscellany* xxxiv: *Chronology, Conquest and Conflict in Medieval Britain*, Camden fifth series 10 (Cambridge, 1997), 49–104; on him see W. M. Aird, 'An Absent Friend: The Career of Bishop William of St Calais', in *Anglo-Norman Durham, 1093–1193*, ed. David Rollason, Margaret Harvey and Michael Prestwich (Woodbridge, 1994), 283–97, and Frank Barlow, 'St Calais [St Carilef], William de (*c.* 1030–1096), *ODNB*. On the rebellion in which Saint-Calais was implicated see

as he was a bishop his case should not be heard in the king's court before barons and secular men, but before ecclesiastics, who alone should be his judges because they were his equals. Presumably he hoped for a more sympathetic hearing among his own kind, or that the jurisdictional arguments would prevent the hearing of the plea before the king and his court; the latter is, mostly, what happened. The Saint-Calais plea is important for jurisdictional debate among the elite. It shows that there were many who could take part in that debate with apparent knowledge of the meaning and implications of their choices, including the bishop of Durham, Archbishop Lanfranc, the king and even some of the barons – or, at least that the writer of the tract thought that it was plausible that such people might know of these matters. It shows that litigants could compare the content and procedures of different laws and choose which one they thought they might profit from most, and jurisdictional debate was not merely something that arose from the holders of courts, but also from those implicated in them.[19]

Canon law was probably a key influence on the creation of jurisdictional debate, but there are important differences between debates involving canon law and debates involving other kinds of claim. Most obviously, there was a clear and general recognition that canon law was a different system that operated on its own basis with its own authorities and texts. In contrast, the creation of separate courts did not generate any claims that these courts should use or devise their own distinct laws. Some sources reflecting English secular law are rather conspicuous for their attempts to integrate all kinds of law, including canon law.[20] Likewise, other courts differed from ecclesiastical ones in that they did not express the power and status of the clergy as a distinct estate. Instead, beyond canon law and its courts, the more usual pattern is that jurisdictional debate took on a proprietary character. Claims were based upon ideas akin to those of ownership and possession, and in terms of the claims that lords held over their dependents and land. Rather than claiming an entirely separate origin in ecclesiastical law, such courts were integrated within existing structures of secular authority through ideas about land tenure and lordship.

---

Richard Sharpe, '1088 – William II and the Rebels', *Anglo-Norman Studies* XXVI (2004), 139–58.

19 For another case that shows elements of jurisdictional thinking see Van Caenegem, *Lawsuits*, no. 138, of 1093–4. In this, Archbishop Thomas claimed that the parts of the diocese of Lincoln and province of Canterbury rightly belonged to the see of York, and seems to have regarded diocesan jurisdiction as something that could be owned; this seems to be the first time that diocesan territory, as opposed to a diocesan see, was presented in this way.

20 The *Leges Henrici Primi* includes quotations from or references to sources including Isidore of Seville, *Etymologiae*, Ivo of Chartres, *Panormia*, the Salic law and so forth.

## Jurisdictional Debate in Secular Courts: Some Seminal Cases from the Later Eleventh Century

To begin with, it is worth emphasising that these changes are not in origin exclusively legal ones, for they began with ideas and aspirations about the relationships between lords and their dependents. The idea that the presence of lordship bonds meant that outsiders should be excluded from the potential for interference cut across existing arrangements. One of the earliest echoes of this attitude can be seen in relation to the great rebellion of 1075. Roger, earl of Hereford, and Ralph, earl of East Anglia, chose to rebel against the king, in some association with Earl Waltheof. The exact causes of their rebellion are not entirely clear, but seem to arise from the idea that they had been denied their rightful status and assets;[21] the most specific evidence on their reasons can be found in letters sent to Earl Roger by Lanfranc, archbishop of Canterbury, which seem to respond to points that Roger had made to him either in a lost letter or via a messenger. Lanfranc indicates that expectations about the handling of pleas were among the causes of Roger's rebellion:

> On another point, the king has ordered his sheriffs not to hold any pleas[22] within your lands until he himself returns to England and can hear personally the matters in dispute between you and those sheriffs.[23]

The implications of this short clause in a letter are considerable, even though it lacks much in the way of specific details. The issue seems to have been that sheriffs had been holding pleas in Roger's lands (*in uestris terris*). The plural was used, so more than one sheriff was involved. Various sheriffs might claim some interest in Roger's lands. In Herefordshire, Roger's position as earl meant that the sheriff was probably under his control or influence, as has been suggested in relation to Roger's father, William fitz Osbern.[24] Presumably Roger was not complaining about the activities of someone bound to him. The sheriffs who had irritated Roger might therefore be found elsewhere, in shires where he held lands but did not hold comital power. This view is also directly in accord with Lanfranc's words; he wrote that the problem was in Roger's lands, and did not

[21] On the setting of this see David Bates, *William the Conqueror* (New Haven, 2016), 378–88.

[22] The text reads *placita*; the Clover-Gibson translation uses *courts*.

[23] *Item mandauit rex ne sui uicecomites aliqua placita in uestris terris teneant quoadusque ipse mare transeat, et inter uos et ipsos uicecomites per semetipsum causas uestras audiat.* Lanfranc, *ep.* 31, ed. Helen Clover and Margaret Gibson, *The Letters of Lanfranc, Archbishop of Canterbury* (Oxford, 1979), 118–21.

[24] W. E. Wightman, 'The Palatine Earldom of William fitz Osbern in Gloucestershire and Worcestershire (1066–1071)', *English Historical Review* 77 (1962), 6–17; Chris Lewis, 'Herefordshire under William I', *Anglo-Norman Studies* VII (1985), 195–213, at 207–8; Judith Green, *English Sheriffs to 1154* (London, 1990), 45.

mention Roger's shire. So, the problem was that sheriffs were holding pleas relating to Roger's lands outside his area of particular control in Herefordshire, in the other shires where he held lands. If this reasoning is correct, it seems that Roger was objecting to the work of sheriffs where they were carrying out their roles in leading or participating in pleas within their areas of jurisdiction. It is possible that there was some specific initiative to which he was objecting, whereby sheriffs were enquiring into or dealing with some perceived problem; but it would be more economical to assume that Roger was objecting to their ordinary activities, for that means there is no need to invent otherwise undocumented royal initiatives that affected multiple sheriffs. The business against which Roger objected is not specified here, but it might be suggested that these were not land pleas; Lanfranc acknowledged that the pleas were *in uestris terris*, so he was quite happy to reckon the lands as in Roger's ownership and not as being in doubt. Something more can be inferred from the solution that Lanfranc mentioned; clearly, it was not just the suspension of one objectionable plea that Roger sought, but rather the cessation or suspension of activity by sheriffs in his lands. A moratorium on sheriffs in Roger's lands was seen as a means that might help to divert the earl from outright rebellion.

Roger's objection to the work of sheriffs was, so far as can be seen, unprecedented. When sheriffs had been introduced in the later tenth century, they altered local power relationships substantially, and it seems that some lords had tried to protect their interests against the potential intrusions of sheriffs through obtaining grants of sake and soke, which minimised how far sheriffs could demand financial dues from their dependents.[25] In many cases, such grants were more like formal recognition of claims that had been exercised informally and locally from an earlier date. These grants of sake and soke were mostly about protecting the financial interests of lords, and need not have implied that the dependents over which these claims were made had been withdrawn from attendance at and participation in the usual shire and hundred courts. In these, they would presumably on occasion have been subject to pleading or other activity by sheriffs, and indeed by many others, given the ways in which these assemblies worked as gatherings of local elites and their functionaries. The concession to Roger, that all pleas by sheriffs within his lands should be halted, seems to have meant that all this activity was stopped, and the usual local supervision through shire and hundred at least temporarily ceased. Much of this is inferential because Roger wrote no manifesto for his rebellion, but the idea underlying this aspect of his revolt seems to be that he expected and demanded that his lordship over his lands and the tenants on them should be sufficiently strong that he wanted to exclude the involvement or interference of the sheriffs as agents and representatives of the king. His conception of lordship was a powerful one, and one which

[25] Molyneaux, *Formation*, 168–9; Lambert, *Law and Order*, 309, 323–5.

undermined many of the legal arrangements that had hitherto obtained. Roger's desire was not really a legal one, for it disregarded and overturned functional legal arrangements, but instead was an attempt to reshape legal practices to reflect his own notions of lordship over his own lands and dependents. His sense of the importance of lordship can also be seen in how a permanent future resolution was postponed to a future meeting between Roger and his own lord, King William.

The ideal of lordship implicit in Lanfranc's letter to Earl Roger was not simply a device of imperious earls, but seemingly offered something to those of lesser status. The story of the re-establishment of monasticism in the north is well known,[26] and one of its lesser-known sources is the narrative by Stephen of Whitby, first abbot of St Mary's, York, concerning the movements of the group of monks he led, and the ultimate foundation of St Mary's. His narrative describes the misadventures of the monks in the later 1070s and 1080s before they settled in York, and the persecutions against them carried out by William I de Percy, and the damage done by raiders, probably Vikings. As abbot, Stephen attempted to protect his monks, but his strategies against William de Percy in particular passed by the usual legal arenas and methods, and involved direct appeals to the king, on the grounds that the king had a special interest in, and protection over, monks:

> Scared to death by this, we wanted to escape the threatening danger by any means, and so we decided to tell the king about those things that were a nuisance to us. He, sufficient in goodness as he was, sympathised with our needs on account of God, and mercifully showed himself ready and willing to help us. For there was not far from Whitby in the lordship of the king himself a certain place that was called Lastingham, then indeed empty but once outstanding for the multitude and religion of the monks living in it.[27] So, little by little, we began to restore this place given to us by the king, and to build those things that were necessary for monastic habitation. Then William de Percy, on whose estate we remained, or others subordinate to him, presumed to bring various adversities against us, for they knew that we had a refuge, suitable for our profession, under the hand and authority of the king himself.
>
> And so after this came a suitable time for me to take the imposition of the pontifical hand and the blessing of an abbot, and it entered my mind that it

26 Symeon of Durham, *Libellus de exordio atque procursu istius, hoc est Dunhelmensis, ecclesie/Tract on the origins and progress of this the Church of Durham*, ed. David Rollason (Oxford, 2000), 200–7; Janet Burton, 'The Monastic Revival in Yorkshire: Whitby and St Mary's, York', in *Anglo-Norman Durham, 1093–1193*, ed. David Rollason, Margaret Harvey and Michael Prestwich (Woodbridge, 1994), 41–51; J. Burton, *The Monastic Order in Yorkshire, 1069–1215* (Cambridge, 1999), 31–42.

27 Bede, *Historia ecclesiastica*, iii. 23 (ed. B. Colgrave and R. A. B. Mynors (Oxford, 1969), 287–8), on its establishment; also iv. 3 (*ibid*, 336–8). On the choice of this as a former Northumbrian monastery see R. H. C. Davis, 'Bede after Bede', in *Studies in Medieval History Presented to R. Allen Brown*, ed. C. Harper-Bill, C. J. Holdsworth and J. L. Nelson (Woodbridge, 1989), 103–16, at 109.

should be at Lastingham, because, as a professed monk was under the sole power of the king, so I ought to be consecrated abbot of that place. This idea seemed good and sensible to our congregation and to the king and our lord Archbishop Thomas besides others whose advice I sought. And so at last by the influence of God and with those persons willing it came to happen. But William de Percy after this remained an annoyance as he had been before and violently opposed us; and, as was said, he worked by all means to expel our little convent from his estate in which it lived. Upset by such trouble, I was often forced to go to the justiciars of this kingdom,[28] to tell our misery and ruin to the ears of many, and to demand help against those overthrowing us. But, gaining not at all by this, at last I crossed to Normandy, where the king was then staying, by chance together with William de Percy,[29] and I tried by prayers and whatever means I could to ensure that we could have our things in peace as before. And so at last, having made peace by a chirograph,[30] I returned to our possessions, but only obtained peace for us and our possessions for a short time. For after that the mind and anger of William burnt more fiercely against us, and he did not allow us to have lasting peace and quiet until he had completely expelled us from Whitby. What more? At last, for these pressing reasons, that is, both worn down by the long annoyance of assailing oppressions, and also constrained by the frequent, unavoidable violence of the said William, now Whitby itself was publicly and unjustly taken from us,[31] we migrated at the king's command to the said place which is called Lastingham, wanting somehow to remain there.[32]

28 The justiciars are not readily identifiable. This is an unusually early use of the word, but its authenticity is made more likely by the use of the plural (for another early use see Anselm, *ep.* 461, ed. F. S. Schmitt, *Sancti Anselmi Cantuariensis Archiepiscopi Opera Omnia* (6 vols, Edinburgh, 1946–61); trans. W. Fröhlich, *The Letters of Saint Anselm of Canterbury*, Cistercian Series 96–7, 142 (3 vols, Kalamazoo, 1990–4), a letter of Henry I, where the justiciars are instructed to follow Anselm's direction during the king's absence). On this see F. West, *The Justiciarship in England, 1066–1232* (Cambridge, 1966), and D. Bates, 'The Origins of the Justiciarship', *Anglo-Norman Studies* IV (1981), 1–12, 167–71, where it is argued that institutions of regency formed the basis for the early justiciarship. On justices and justiciars see Chapter 7 below.

29 It is not clear which of the king's visits to Normandy was meant. Between 1078, when Stephen became abbot, and the king's death in 1087, the Conqueror was in Normandy to mid or late 1080, from autumn 1081 to autumn 1082, from early 1083 to 1085, and from late summer 1086 to his death (Bates, *Regesta*, pp. 80–2). William de Percy only once attests for the king, and that, unhelpfully, at *Lachoche*, perhaps Lacock (Wiltshire) and certainly in England due to the witnesses (Bates, *Regesta*, no. 146).

30 This agreement between the monks and William de Percy does not survive.

31 However, by 1086 it was recorded that the abbot of York held two ploughs in Whitby (Great Domesday Book, fo. 305a: Yorkshire 4N1), so that either some of the property had been recovered, or the claim of the abbot alone was being registered.

32 *Ob quam rem usque ad mortem contristati, imminens periculum aliquo modo uitare cupientes, quecumque nobis molesta erant regi intimare decreuimus. Qui, benigno satis ut erat, miserationis affectu necessitatibus nostris propter deum compatiens, promptum se ac uoluntarium nobis ad subueniendum exhibuit. Erat uero non longe a*

There are hints here of formal legal process, such as when Stephen referred to how Whitby had been taken publicly and unjustly from the monks, but overall this story does not give much scope for the usual arenas in which pleas were settled. Stephen does not mention that he tried to justify his landholdings through pleading in shire or hundred courts, which would be the more usual venues

---

*Witebeia in ipsius regis dominio locus quidam qui uocatur Lestingeham, tum nimirum uacuus sed olim monachorum in eo habitantium frequentia et religione egregius. Hunc ergo locum a rege nobis datum paulatim restaurare, et que habitationi monachice erant necessaria cepimus edificare, quatinus scilicet predictus Willelmus de Percei in cuius predio morabamur uel alii eo minus nobis aduersa aliqua inferre presumerent, quo nos refugium aliquod professioni nostre congruum sub ipsius regis manu et ditione habere agnouissent.*

*[8] Cumque post hec oportunitatis tempus adesset quo manus pontificalis impositionem et abbatis benedictionem (fol. 31v) suscipere deberem subiit animo ut ad Lestingeham quia sub sola regis potestate erat monachus professus eiusdem quoque loci abbas consecrarer. Que res pariter etiam congregationi nostre et ipsi regi domnoque Thome archiepiscopo nostro necnon et omnibus quorum inde consilium querebam bona et utilis uisa est, ac tandem auctore deo illisque uolentibus usque ad actum perducta. At uero sepefatus Will(el)mus sicut antea consueuerat et postea quoque molestus nobis et aduersus uehementer existebat, atque, ut dictum est, de predio suo in quo adhuc conuenticulum nostrum degebat modis omnibus expellere laborabat. Unde ego nimio dolore perculsus, iusticiarios regni huius frequenter adire, miseriam nostram et oppressionem multorum auribus insinuare et auxilium aduersum opprimentes nos flagitare compulsus sum. Sed neque ita quicquam proficiens, tandem usque in Normannia(m) in qua rex simul et Will(el)mus de Percei tunc forte morabantur transfretare; et qualiter nostra in pace ulterius haberemus precibus apud regem et modis quibus poteram satagere curaui. Et ita demum accepto pacis cirographo ad propria reuersus non longo tempore cum nostris et de nostris pacem obtinui. Exarsit quippe ex eo tempore multo uehementius aduersum nos animus et ira Will(elm)i et quoad usque penitus nos de Withebeia effugasset pacem diuturnam uel quietem habere non permisit. Quid multa? His namque exigentibus causis postremo tam ingruen-(fol. 32r)-tium pressurarum longa molestia attriti quam ineuitabili totiens memorati Will(elm)i uiolentia coacti iam quidem publice et iniuste ablata nobis Withebeia ad predictum locum qui dicitur Lestingeham ibi saltem manere cupientes per iussionem regis transmigrauimus.*

There are two twelfth-century manuscripts, London, British Library, ms. Additional 38816, fos. 29v–34v (from St Mary's Abbey itself, which is the manuscript used here) and Cambridge, Corpus Christi College, ms. 139, fos. 152r–154r (probably from Sawley Abbey). The two texts are identical except in matters such as the spelling of places names, and the translation here is based on both. There are two later manuscripts, Bodleian ms. Bodley 39, fos. 92r–97r of the later thirteenth century and from St Mary's, and Bodleian ms. Dodsworth 63, fos. 1r–5v, a seventeenth-century transcript by Roger Dodsworth from an unknown source, which differs from the other three manuscripts. It was edited from the thirteenth-century manuscript in Roger Dodsworth and William Dugdale, *Monasticon Anglicanum, sive Pandectae coenobiorum* (3 vols, London, 1655–73), i. 383–6, and thence in W. Dugdale and R. Dodsworth, *Monasticon Anglicanum*, ed. and revised J. Caley, H. Ellis and B. Bandinel (6 vols in 8 parts, London, 1817–30, reprinted 1846), iii. 544–6.

where such disputes were aired. Perhaps he feared that William de Percy's local political influence meant that any claim that he brought would not be heard fairly; yet, given his liking for listing persecutions against himself and his monks, it might be assumed that any such occurrence would have been described in some detail. Putting on one side what the narrative does not include, what it does say is that Stephen tried to defend his interests and those of his monks through using his status, and the assumed claim that it brought upon the king; he clearly thought that the king's duties as lord and protector of monks meant that Stephen could draw upon royal authority and power as a means of propping up his position; he tried to assert that the king had a personal jurisdiction and responsibility towards him and his monks. Seemingly, this was done before there was much engagement with the more usual mechanisms for dispute resolution that would have been open to him. The trust in that individual jurisdictional link to the king underpinned Stephen's position, and shaped how the dispute with William de Percy was conducted; effectively, Stephen did not contest William's attacks, but instead fled from one property to the next as he sought somewhere that offered less problematic neighbours. Never did Stephen confront William directly, at least so far as his narrative tells; instead, he approached William as supplicant, asking for toleration and support, rather than as a divinely inspired pleader, as churchmen elsewhere sometimes presented themselves.[33] The importance of Stephen's narrative is that he put so much faith in the personal link to the king, and in the protective lordship over monks that he imputed to the monarch. In so doing, he avoided the mechanisms of debate, testimony and compromise that can be seen in many legal disputes, and almost abandoned the monks' troubles as a legal matter in favour of patronage and lordship. The basis for this can be found in his perceptions of the nature of the king's role and the ways in which he chose to interact with it.

Lanfranc's letter and Stephen of Whitby's narrative both suggest that, in the later eleventh century, there were some who assigned a very high value to lordship, and sought to recast, or avoid, established structures of shire and hundred so that they could carry on disputes in accordance with their preferences for strong bonds with particular lords rather than engagement with the elites of localities and the resulting cacophony of claims and interests. In both those cases, these ambitions took the form of an attempt to avoid other sources

[33] This is a common trope in accounts where bishops pleaded in court; for instance, Archbishop Lanfranc at the Penenden Heath plea (Van Caenegem, *Lawsuits*, no. 5). On the Penenden Heath plea see W. Levison, 'A Report on the Penenden Trial', *English Historical Review* 27 (1912), 717–20; John Le Patourel, 'The Date of the Trial on Penenden Heath', *English Historical Review* 61 (1946), 378–88; Alan Cooper, 'Extraordinary Privilege: The Trial of Penenden Heath and the Domesday Inquest', *English Historical Review* (2001), 1167–92.

of authority, through exclusion of some participants or through special appeal to others. In both these aims, the formulators of these strategies were trying to change how they interacted with law, and do things in ways that circumvented established structures through personalising the issues at hand. The language is purely one of lordship; but, in the hands of other writers, these impulses to cleave towards a particular and special lordship relationship could be expressed as a clash of views over *where* a plea should be heard, and might use jurisdictional terms. Using such language was a means of turning claims into lordship, and formalising the relationship of lordship. It meant that the claims of a lord could be characterised as a recognisable claim, rather than being a vaguer claim to influence. The rise of such language depended on one prior development, which can also be seen in the later eleventh century; the appearance of a choice of assemblies in which disputes could be dealt with.

Among the earliest occurrences of jurisdictional language and thinking is the following plea, for it presents courts and potentates in competition for hearing a plea. It does not concern the communal courts of shire and hundred, but rather an ecclesiastical dispute, in which the tenure of the abbacies of Athelney and Muchelney was debated. The narrative must concern events between Thurstan's appointment as abbot of Glastonbury in 1077 and the death of Bishop Giso of Wells in 1088:[34]

> For when archbishop Lanfranc stingingly attacked them at a general council of England, as a result of a false accusation by Giso, bishop of Wells, the abbot of Muchelney, who was more practised in secular affairs, replied that he would make a response in the chapter of Glastonbury, when commanded by that place and its abbot, but that he did not fear such extraordinary accusations. But the abbot of Athelney jocularly dodged the inquiry by the archbishop, who was threatening to take his staff away from him, saying, 'I do not care because I have a better one; but just the same I am not handing this one over to you'. Then abbot Thurstan, who was ordered to undertake the case if he knew that it was appropriate for him to do so, rose in that place where judgements are given and pleaded with great and flowing eloquence, repeating from memory the privileges of kings from Centwine and Ine to Edward, by which, he affirmed, no-one except that abbot of Glastonbury had any jurisdiction (*iurisdictionem*) over those abbots, so that no abbot ought to enter those churches unless he were chosen by the convent of Glastonbury. The archbishop turned to the king and said that he did not want to undermine the nurse-maid of the blessed Dunstan[35] and the king replied that he did not wish to sadden the mother of God but

34 D. Knowles, C. N. L. Brooke and V. London, *The Heads of Religious Houses I: England and Wales, 940–1216* (second edition, Cambridge, 2001), 51, 250; D. E. Greenway, *Fasti ecclesiae Anglicanae, 1066–1300*: vii, *Bath and Wells* (London, 2001), 1.

35 Dunstan had been a monk at Glastonbury; his nurse-maid was thus Glastonbury Abbey.

> that, to protect posterity, the bishop of Wells ought to determine the matter in the chapter of Glastonbury. The abbot then resumed his speech, saying that his church's privileges were authentic, that no person of whatever rank ought to come to Glastonbury, since all jurisdiction there, both in ecclesiastical and secular affairs, was his, that it could easily be that the victorious king and the holy archbishop were being impelled by ever-present ill-will to make a new arrangement, but that what his predecessors had maintained inviolate he, who defended his church's dignity with the same vigilant spirit, would by no means neglect. Wherefore the bishop of Wells, if he had any allegations to make, should come to Glastonbury at his command, not that of the king or the archbishop. Need I say more? The abbot won his case and the bishop did indeed come to the chapter, but he had to depart ingloriously because victory escaped him when the abbots justified themselves.[36]

There are some obvious concerns that must be applied to this source. It comes from William of Malmesbury's tract on the antiquity of Glastonbury Abbey, which was written in the later 1120s, long after the events described. William's sources for this story are unknown, but he had access to the archives at Glastonbury, and might be assumed to have drawn on materials that he found there. It survives only in later and interpolated manuscripts, so that it cannot be stated with certainty that this narrative is what William intended, even though there are good indications

[36] *Nam cum eos falsa delacione Gisonis Wellensis episcopi Lanfrancus archiepiscopus in generali concilio Anglie mordaciter impeteret, Muchaniensis, qui exercitacior esset in seculi rebus, respondit se in capitulo Glastonie iussu eiusdem loci et abbatis sui responsurum, ceterum extraordinarias accusaciones non timere, Ethelingensis autem iocclariter eludens questionem minanti archiepiscopo baculum ei auferendum: 'Non curo' inquit, 'quia meliorem habeo, nec tamen istum tibi trado.' Tum iussus abbas Turstinus, ut si sibi competere sciret causam ageret, surrexit loco sentencie dicende egitque multa et constanti facundia, memoriter retexens priuilegia regum a Kentuino et Ina regibus usque ad Eduuardum, quibus allegauit in eos abbates nullam iurisdictionem aliquem nisi Glastoniensem abbatem habere adeo ut in predictas ecclesias nullus debeat abbas intrare nisi fuerit electus a conuentu Glastonie. Tum cum archiepiscopus in regem conuersus dixisset se beati Dunstani nutriculam nolle minuere illeque retulisset nec se uelle matrem Domini contristare sed pro caucione futurorum episcopum Wellensem debere in Glastonie capitulo rem diffinere, resumpsit abbas sermonem, (dicens) priuilegia ecclesie sue autentica esse, nullam cuiuslibet dignitatis personam causa iudicii Glastoniam debere uenire, sua ibi esse omnia et in ecclesiasticis et in secularibus rebus iudicia, facile fore ut inuictus princeps et sanctus archiepiscopus in re noua constituenda perpetua pulsarentur inuidia; ceterum quod antecessores sui habuissent integrum, se, qui in defensenda dignitate ecclesie eodem uigilaret spiritu, nequaquam omissurum. Quocirca episcopus Wellensis, si quid allegandum putaret, suo non regis uel archiepiscopi iussu Glastoniam ueniret. Quid plura? Optinuit causam abbas et quidem episcopus in capitulum uenit, sed purgantibus se abbatibus uictoria excidit et inglorius discessit.* William of Malmesbury, *De Antiquitate Glastonie ecclesie*, ed. John Scott (Woodbridge, 1981), 155–7.

that it might be.[37] William's authorship also raises some doubts; he was a serious classicist, and had read much more than most of his contemporaries in ancient texts. He had certainly read Roman law,[38] and this might account for the choices of words in this passage. *Iurisdictio* is not a common word in accounts of pleas from the later eleventh and earlier twelfth centuries, and it might be that this reflects William's reading; nonetheless, his inclusion of this term indicates that he must have expected that it would be recognised by at least some of the readership that he assumed.

The narrative is notable because it describes a debate about choice, in which some of the participants asserted that there was a choice as to where the plea might be heard. In this case, the plea began in a council that reflected the English church as a whole. Elsewhere, councils certainly dealt with comparable business, where the tenure of particular abbots was questioned, so this would seem an appropriate forum. In this case, the council did not deal with the plea, because a claim was raised that it should be dealt with in the chapter at Glastonbury. It is not entirely clear what this assembly was; it could have been the monks who formed the chapter at Glastonbury who would have determined the plea, or it could have been some other collection of persons who assembled within the chapter house at Glastonbury. The point of the assembly was that it policed the exclusive claims that in this narrative were asserted by Abbot Thurstan, and that it symbolised and preserved the position of pre-eminence that the abbot claimed. At least according to the narrative, Thurstan was successful in convincing Archbishop Lanfranc and King William that his claim should be allowed, on the grounds that Glastonbury's ancient charters supported the claim – even though the surviving charters do not include specific mentions – and through respect for St Dunstan. Regardless of these details about how a decision might have been made, and of other problems such as the lack of corroborative evidence for this incident, the importance of this story is that it shows that some legal participants thought that lordship and pre-eminence should be expressed institutionally through the provision of separate assemblies in which the dominance of the lord was expressed through the exclusion of other potentates, and through the attendance of the men upon their lord.

The Glastonbury plea showed how jurisdictional language could be used by individuals to maintain their links and to exclude those who tried to intervene into that relationship. In that case, the two were united in trying to keep out the

[37] Other abbeys might claim to head families of monasteries; see Susan Kelly, *Anglo-Saxon Charters* 14: *Charters of Peterborough Abbey* (Oxford, 2009), 67–78; and presumably Cluny was the inspiration behind this.

[38] R. M. Thomson, *William of Malmesbury* (revised edition, Woodbridge, 2003), 110, 205–6. His copy of the Breviary of Alaric survives in Oxford, Bodleian Library, ms. Arch. Seld. B 16.

potential negative influence of the bishop. Yet, this story of unity against a threat was not the only end for which jurisdictional language might be used. Where there was a choice about where a plea could be heard, then participants could try to use the decision to obtain some advantage for themselves in the form of a favourable hearing.

The sense of all these early disputes is that it was hard for participants to devise plausible arguments to win their cases. Earl Roger seems to have found it problematic that outsiders could interfere with the dependents on his lands, which seems to involve not much more than the usual chains of lordship that bound people together in the eleventh century; meanwhile Abbot Stephen tried to get the king to take an interest by arguing that there was a special bond that meant the king should look after him; and Abbot Thurstan argued on a basis of old charters and precedent or tradition. There is no particular unity here; it seems that different litigants were using various ideas, and experimenting to see which worked, and which seemed to have greater traction with those who were listening. The most rigorous jurisdictional arguments from later eleventh-century England were those used by Bishop William of Durham in his attempt to get the case against him moved from the king's court with its barons to an exclusively ecclesiastical assembly. He had advantages in doing so, in that canon law could be presented as a distinct system and an embodiment of the privileges of the clergy. The other litigants discussed in this section had a less clear-cut mission, in that they were not trying to place themselves outside English law, but simply obtain some particular advantage within it.

## Jurisdictional Debate in Secular Courts: Some Seminal Cases from the Twelfth Century

If the eleventh-century pleas involving jurisdictional debate show signs of variation and experimentation, then from the early twelfth century there are signs that litigants, or at least some kinds of litigants, had devised strategies that they found effective in enforcing and managing their claims. The argument that litigants seemed to find effective, and which was used in courts in many of the recorded cases, was that which aligned royal authority with that of the litigant, and used respect for kingship to win a case. This could happen in more than one way. Sometimes, litigants claimed that their authority was based upon a grant from a king, or that they in some way represented royal authority, which meant that their claim had precedence over claims raised by others. On other occasions, those who wanted to claim authority could, if they had the necessary connections and wealth, obtain from the king a specific grant which recognised the claim that they made and ordered that it be carried out. It is perhaps meaningful that such specific grants survive through the archives of major religious houses, which would have had the wealth and networks to allow the gaining of such a writ, though of course so much of the evidence comes from such collections that the pattern is perhaps not wholly significant.

Battle Abbey in Sussex had been founded by William the Conqueror as a monument to his victory at Hastings, and was liberally provided with privileges by that king and his successors.[39] These privileges were not uncontroversial, and were challenged by others, especially by the bishops of Chichester. In these arguments, the monks consistently stressed their fidelity and closeness to kings, and how their abbey was akin to a chapel royal or private church of the kings, and that therefore an attack on them was also an attack on the kings themselves. The assumptions behind this were used by the monks in a plea of 1102[40] from the Battle Abbey Chronicle in which they used their closeness to kings to argue for the precedence of the claims of their own court over another:

> When he visited the church's principal manor, Wye, which a servant of the late abbot, one Robert, surnamed 'de Chilton', had charge of, he found it entirely fragmented. He began to question this manager as to the reasons, and to demand an accounting of his management. The man retorted that he had satisfied his lord, now dead, and would not agree to summoning witnesses therefore. At last the procurator charged him in the court of the manor[41] as one manifestly guilty. However, the manager was there backed by the force of the shire nobles whom he had brought with him, and he totally refused to come to an equitable agreement. Therefore the procurator of the church summoned him in the king's name, along with his supporters who were present, to appear at the court of Battle on a named day. After much dispute they made no positive reply, and they parted on this note.
>
> ...
>
> Thus after lavish hospitality, the court was constituted and with the brothers seated around him Geoffrey addressed the men he had summoned, 'My very dear lords, since you have presented yourselves to this court in response to a summons, I ask whether you have come for the purpose of pursuing and accepting justice here.' They urged that they were bound to be subject to all justice done in their own shire court, but not here. After much argument, Dom Geoffrey put it to them, 'If therefore, as you assert, you are not bound by pleas of justice except in your own shire, would you not resist the settlement of your complaint, supposing you were brought before the royal court?'
>
> 'Not at all', they replied.

39 On Battle Abbey see Eleanor Searle, *Lordship and Community: Battle Abbey and its Banlieu, 1066–1538* (Toronto, 1974), especially chapter 1.

40 *The Chronicle of Battle Abbey*, ed. Eleanor Searle (Oxford, 1981), 108–9; also in Van Caenegem, *Lawsuits*, no. 174.

41 *In eiusdem manerii curiam.*

> 'Well then', he said, 'you cannot on that ground resist this court, for it is the king's.'
>
> But they trusted to the reasoning of force and attempted to resist by actually walking out, and so he instantly commanded that the doors of the church be locked, vowing that each of them would be reported to the king if they would not subject themselves to the claims of a royal court. When they had thought over the courage of this man and the fairness of the royal distraint, finally the timid bullies subsided and declared that they would both do and receive justice there.[42]

The Battle Abbey chronicle was written some decades after the events described, but there are indications that it may reflect early priorities. The relationship between courts and even their natures are relatively undefined, which points to an early date. This is a difficult case, and it involved a number of complex problems. Estate managers were often not the dependents of the

[42] *Cumque precipuum ecclesie manerum Wi adisset quod quidam abbatis defuncti seruiens procurauerat Robertus cognomento de Ciltuna inuenissetque illud undique distractum, cepit causas ab ipso preposito rationemque requirere uillicationis. Qui cum domino suo iam defuncto se inde satisfecisse referret, nec sic ille adquiescens testes exigeret, tandem conuictum in eiusdem manerii curiam compulit. Cumque ui nobilium prouincie quos sibi asciuerat equitati parere penitus detrectasset, eum suosque presentes ex regis nomine die denominato precipiendo apud Belli curiam adesse isdem ecclesie procurator summonuit. Quibus nec post multam conflictationem quicquam certi respondentibus in his disceditur.*

...

*Itaque post opulentam hospitalitatem curia statuta, circumassidentibus sibi fratribus, summonitos Gausfridus affatur, 'Quoniam, mi seniores carissimi, presenti uos premoniti intulistis curie, utrum rectitudinis hinc exequende et recipiende causa adueneritis sciscitor.' Illi uero cum non ibi sed in suo comitatu omnem rectitudinem se exequi debere insisterent, post plurimam dominus Gausfridus controuersiam intulit, 'Si ergo ut asseritis non nisi in uestro comitatu iustitie subdimini causis, nunquid non regie asciti curie conquesta definiri uetaretis?'*

*'Nequaquam', inquiunt.*

*'Ergo presenti', inquit, 'curie que regis extat hac ratione contraire nequibitis.'*

*Qui cum ui ratiocinatione freti renitentes demum erumpere conarentur, protinus basilice ualuas iussit obserari, obtestans singulos regie maiestati exponendos si non regie exequerentur iura curie. Cumque uiri animositatem regieque districtionis recogitassent equitatem, tandem pauidi cessere tiranni et se illic rectitudinem facere et recipere uelle profitentur.*

*The Chronicle of Battle Abbey*, ed. and trans. Eleanor Searle (Oxford, 1980), 109–13. On this see Nicholas Vincent, 'King Henry II and the Monks of Battle: The Battle Chronicle Unmasked', in *Belief and Culture in the Middle Ages: Studies Presented to Henry Mayr-Harting*, ed. Richard Gameson and Henrietta Leyser (Oxford, 2001), 264–86.

lords they served; they need not hold any property or assets from the lord, and so were not within his lordship. The management of claims by lords against former estate managers was a difficult business, because they did not fit into many of the categories that formed the jurisdictions claimed by lords.[43] Here, Robert de Chilton claimed that he need not answer the claim, because he had been linked to the former abbot, not to the present administrator of Battle Abbey. The core of the plea became about which court should rightly hear the case. Battle Abbey's representative brought the case *in eiusdem manerii curiam*. This has been translated as manor court, though it is a remarkably early occurrence for a manor court, and the phrase is misleading, if the later meaning of this term is assumed. The Battle Chronicle describes the abbey's interests in Wye as a *manerium*, including the soke and other claims that came with the abbey's tenure of the hundred of Wye, for this was treated as an appendage of the manor, *manerium cum hundredo*.[44] This story indicates that the court in which Robert de Chilton's case was heard included not just the abbey's peasants from Wye itself, but some of the barons of Kent. If this were a manor court as understood later, then their presence would be hugely problematical, for the manor court was meant to be an exclusive assembly for those within the abbey's lordship. It would therefore be safer if it were assumed that this assembly was not a manorial court, but rather a hundred court appurtenant to the hundredal manor, which might perhaps have dealt with business that, later, would have been dealt with by a manorial court. Such undifferentiated courts existed elsewhere,[45] and it would be more economical to assume that that was what was meant here, for otherwise there is no good evidence this early for specialised manorial courts.

The first hearing in the (probable) hundred court at Wye was not a success for the abbey. Robert de Chilton was able to arrange that some of the great men of Kent were present, and they supported his unwillingness to come to an agreement. Little is known about Robert de Chilton beyond his roles in the Battle Chronicle, so it is not clear how he might have been able to muster the support of these locally distinguished men. Clearly their presence was a decisive influence on this part of the plea, for under the traditional procedure followed in hundred courts the voices of the more esteemed were deemed of greater value. Their presence and influence should be regarded as a main reason for the abbey's strategy in the next stage of the dispute. The monks' representative was unwilling that the plea should be pursued further in the court of Wye, for against such opposition there

[43] On this see John Sabapathy, *Officers and Accountability in Medieval England,* c. *1170–1300* (Oxford, 2014), 26–9.

[44] On this conjunction see Helen M. Cam, '*Manerium cum Hundredo*: The Hundred and the Hundredal Manor', in her *Liberties and Communities in Medieval England: Collected Studies in Local Administration and Topography* (Cambridge, 1944), 64–90.

[45] Warren Ortman Ault, *Private Jurisdiction in England* (New Haven, 1923), 267–300.

was little chance that they would be able to force a favourable outcome. Thus, the next step was to try to obtain an advantage by moving the plea to their own court; this was done in the court at Wye, and might have been a tactic to prevent the court of Wye from finalising a decision.

On the appearance of Robert and his supporters in the court of Battle, there proceeded a jurisdictional dispute over competence to hear the plea. According to the Chronicle, Robert and his supporters argued that the proper arena for hearing the plea was the shire court of Kent; presumably this was because the plea concerned lands in Kent, and had already been aired within (probably) a hundred at Wye, which was a component of Kent. It would clearly have been to Robert's advantage if the case were heard in Kent, for he had the support of some of the leading men of Kent, and so could presumably have counted on their support in a hearing in the shire court there. The claim that the plea should be heard in the shire court of Kent was not really dealt with; rather, the monks of Battle advanced claims that their court was a royal court and so Robert and his supporters were bound to plead there. The argument is an unusual one, but it parallels points made by the monks elsewhere, that they identified themselves with royal interests very strongly, as in the pleas over the jurisdiction of the bishops of Chichester.[46] Robert and his supporters seemingly had no response to this – they did not point out that the shire court of Kent could also be a venue for the application of royal justice[47] – and so acknowledged that the plea should have been determined in the court of Battle. Seemingly, the Battle monks did not need any specific interventions from the king in order to obtain this.

In other cases, litigants who wanted to claim jurisdiction did go directly to kings to get documents which ordered that pleas should be heard by them or in their courts. These are especially common in the archive of documents surviving from Abingdon Abbey in Berkshire. It is hard to know how significant this might be. It could be that Abingdon found it particularly difficult to enforce its claims, and so the monks were obliged to contact the king regularly for assistance in doing so. Alternatively, Abingdon has preserved an unusually large collection of royal documents through its chronicles, and so it may be that this abbey preserved documents of short-term importance that were not copied elsewhere, even if parallels once existed.

One of these must date from early in Henry I's reign, for it was written before the death of Roger Bigod, who witnessed it:

> Henry, king of the English, to Hugh of Buckland and Aubrey and all barons, French and English, greetings! Know that I have conceded to Faritius, abbot of St Mary of Abingdon, that he should make his *iusticiam* concerning the

[46] *The Chronicle of Battle Abbey*, ed. Eleanor Searle (Oxford, 1981), 146–208.

[47] On this question see Chapter 6 below.

> thieving priest, who is in his custody in Abingdon. And concerning his other thieves, let him make his *iusticiam* in the same way, in the sight of the shire. Witness, Roger Bigod, through Walter Hosatus. At Brill.[48]

It says that the abbey was to have a case concerning a priest who was also a thief; and also that the abbey was to have jurisdiction over other unspecified thieves. It is probably significant that the writ was addressed to the sheriff of Berkshire and the barons, evidently those of Berkshire, and that the king ordered that the pleas concerning the other thieves should be heard in the sight of the shire. These points might indicate that the sheriff and shire had been trespassing on the claims of the abbot, and that they were now ordered not to interfere, and to bear witness to the abbot's exercising of his claims. Kings had long claimed particular interest in theft, and so it might be that the sheriff and shire had been claiming this in the king's name, or attempting to do so, and that the king now ordered that such cases should be heard in the abbot's court. It might even be that the clerical status of one of the thieves generated doubt as to the correct method for dealing with such a plea. At any rate, the document was deemed of sufficient interest that it was copied into the abbey's chronicles from later in the twelfth century, and so it might be assumed that the instructions contained in it were implemented. As the sheriff operated in the name of the king, it would be hard for him to reject outright an instruction directly from the king, and authoritatively expressed in writing and presumably supported by a royal seal. An order from the king would thus be a means for putting Abingdon's claim to jurisdiction over these thieves beyond any other claims from the sheriff or the shire.

A similar pattern can be seen in another writ of Henry I which started with a general acknowledgement of the abbey's claims in Hormer hundred, before proceeding to specifics about how one particular plea should be discharged:

> Henry, king of the English, to Hugh of Buckland and his justiciars and all his barons, French and English, of Berkshire, greetings! I command that the abbot of Abingdon has his hundred of Hormer well and in peace and honourably, just as well as his predecessors had in the time of my father and my brother and of myself. And especially the plea concerning a horse, concerning which Osbert was accused. Witness, the chancellor. At Winchester.[49]

48 *Henricus rex Anglorum Hugoni de Bochelanda, et Albrico, et omnibus baronibus, Francis et Anglis, de Berchesira salutem. Sciatis me concessisse Faritio, abbati sancte Marie de Abbendona, ut ipse faciat iusticiam suam de presbitero latrone, qui in captione sua in Abbendona est. Et de aliis latronibus suis, faciat iusticiam suam similiter, uidente comitatu. Teste Rogero Bigod, per Walterum Hosatum. Apud Bruhellam. Regesta*, ii. no. 695; *Abingdon Chronicle*, ii. 132–3; Van Caenegem, *Lawsuits*, no. 169.

49 *Henricus rex Anglorum Hugoni de Bochelanda, et iusticiariis suis, et omnibus baronibus suis, Francis et Anglis, de Berchescira, salutem. Precipio quod abbas de*

Once again, the chronicle does not provide anything in terms of context for the specific plea mentioned here. Thus, it is not clear why a horse was involved in a plea, whose horse it might have been, or what the real issue was. Once again the writ was addressed to the sheriff of Berkshire – indeed, to the same sheriff of Berkshire – and to the shire, so that it would seem that the question of the relationship between the abbey's claims and the shire's jurisdictions were in some sense in contest here.

Finally, the abbey used the same strategy of invoking the king's authority to deal with an instance where the abbey's claims had been questioned in part. According to the abbey's chronicle, the men of the hundred of Pyrton had tried to bring part of the abbey's holding at Lewknor within their hundred,[50] but Abbot Faritius took the dispute to Queen Matilda:

> Matilda, queen of the English, to Robert, bishop of Lincoln and Thomas de St John and all barons, French and English, of Oxfordshire, greetings! Know that Faritius, abbot of Abingdon, in the court of my lord and myself, at Winchester in the treasury, before Roger, bishop of Salisbury, and Robert, bishop of Lincoln, and Richard, bishop of London, and William de Courcy, and Adam de Port, and Thurstan the chaplain, and Walter of Gloucester, and Herbert the chamberlain, and William d'Oilly, and Geoffrey son of Herbert, and William de Enesi, and Ralph Basset, and Geoffrey de Mandeville, and Geoffrey Ridel, and Walter, archdeacon of Oxford, and through the book of the treasury, has proven that his manor of Lewknor never owed anything in the hundred of Pyrton. But all those things which it ought to make, it ought to make in the hundred of Lewknor, in which hundred the church of Abingdon has seventeen hides. Witness, Roger, bishop of Salisbury, and William de Courcy, and Adam de Port. At Winchester.[51]

---

*Abbendona habeat hundredum suum de Hornimera bene et in pace et honorifice, sicut unquam antecessores sui melius habuerunt tempore patris mei et fratris mei, et meo. Et nominatim placitum de equa, unde Osbertus calumpniatus fuit. Teste cancellario. Apud Wintoniam. Regesta*, ii. no. 1111; *Abingdon Chronicle*, ii. 168–9; Van Caenegem, *Lawsuits*, no. 199.

50 *Abingdon Chronicle*, ii. 168–9.

51 *Mathildis Anglorum regina Roberto episcopo Lincoln', et Thome de Sancto Iohanne, et omnibus baronibus, Francis et Anglis, de Oxenefordscira, salutem. Sciatis quod Faritius abbas de Abbendona, in curia domini mei et mea, apud Wintoniam in thesauro, ante Rogerum episcopum Salesbiriensem, et Robertum episcopum Lincolniensem, et Ricardum episcopum Lundoniensem, et Will' de Curceio, et Adam de Portu, et Turstino capellano, et Waltero de Gloecestria, et Herebertum camerarium, et Willelmum de Oileio, et Gosfr' filium Herberti, et Will' de Enesi, et Radulfo Basset, et Goisfr' de Magnauilla, et Goisfr' Ridel, et Waltero archidiacono de Oxeneford, et per Librum de Thesauro disratiocinauit quod Leuecanora manerium suum nichil omnino debet in hundredo de Peritona facere. Sed omnia que debet facere, tantummodo in hundredo de Leuecanora facere debet, in quo hundredo habet ecclesia de Abbendona decem et septem hidas. Testibus Rogero episcopo Salesb', et Willelmo de Curci, et Adam de*

It is fairly obvious why the abbot chose to take the case to the queen; if it had been judged within Pyrton hundred, the case would have been heard by his opponents in this case, and they would also have been present in the shire court of Oxford as well. Taking the case to the queen as regent was thus a means for avoiding his opponents in an arena where their power would have been greatest. The document is very full on the authorities behind the judgement; it was enacted in a case that represented not only the queen's authority but also the king's, as well as that of many of the leading men of the kingdom and even of Great Domesday Book. The judgement expressed in this document put the case beyond the capacity of the men of Pyrton hundred to question it, for it invoked kinds of authority that they must have recognised and which they could not readily avoid. This seems to be the common idea behind all the royal writs which ordered that Abingdon Abbey's jurisdictions and pleas should be respected and should remain in the hands of the abbey.

The role of the king as the ultimate determiner of cases concerning jurisdiction can be seen elsewhere, in a plea between the abbots of Thorney and Peterborough.[52] Here, some fishermen belonged to the abbot of Peterborough, but also owed dues to the abbot of Thorney, and attended his *halimota* at Farcet. The abbot of Peterborough withdrew the men without the consent of the abbot of Thorney, but, after much debate in the hundred and attention from the sheriff and others, it was terminated before the king on terms that were mostly favourable to Thorney. From the narratives in the Thorney cartulary, it seems that it was the evidence produced by a panel of eighteen men in the hundred that determined the outcome of the case, but it was the engagement of royal authority to validate and confirm it that settled the dispute and confirmed the victory of the abbot of Thorney. The implication, presumably, is that earlier stages within Huntingdonshire itself had not been sufficient to dissuade the abbot of Peterborough from further pursuit of the plea.

Invocation of the king, or engagement with the king, was the most common strategy for dealing with jurisdictional problems, at least if the pattern in the surviving sources is taken as representative of contemporary trends. Participants did not necessarily want kings to hear the disputes themselves, merely to settle the question of venue in their favour, and allow the case to proceed there. The involvement of royal authority need only have been indirect, but its importance was that it allowed others to make decisive judgements that affected the interests of many but which might not have been so acceptable if the king's authority was not seen as standing behind that judgement. This can be seen in the previous plea, where the decision of the hundred was what was actually decisive, but it

*Portu. Apud Wincestram. Regesta*, ii. no. 1000; *Abingdon Chronicle*, ii. 170–1; Van Caenegem, *Lawsuits*, no. 189.

52 Van Caenegem, *Lawsuits*, no. 219.

was strengthened through recognition by the king, and the sense that the makers of that decision were acting in the king's name. This could even be used by confident litigants as a means of obtaining their own desired outcome against kings, as in the well-known plea of 1150 where the liberties of the abbey of Bury St Edmunds were at stake. The case had arisen because one of the abbey's knights had been accused of treason against the king, and so was claimed both by the abbey, which wanted to try its own dependent (and presumably therefore control any forfeitures that might arise from a conviction), and by the king. Stephen handed over the matter to the joint shire court of Norfolk and Suffolk for determination, and so resigned it into an assembly where the abbey's wealth and power made it particularly influential. Thus, the matter was settled through the charismatic intervention of one of the abbey's tenants.[53] The arguments used were about custom, that Hervey de Glanville had seen and heard the privileges in court over decades; but his comments counted because the monks had already obtained from King Stephen the ability to have their plea heard in the shire court of Norfolk and Suffolk. Ensuring that the plea was heard in the right place was critical to the way in which the abbey's claims were asserted, because knowledge of the custom claimed by the abbey could not have been assumed among the barons of the king's court.

## Conclusion

Collectively, these pleas contain an important message about how law was being carried out in England in the later eleventh and twelfth centuries. They show that attitudes and practices had both changed from how they had been before 1066, and that these changes tended to undermine earlier assumptions about how law should be done and experienced. First, it seems that individuals thought about lordship in different ways, and that they expected that the conduct of pleas should follow categories of lordship. Thus, some of the individuals noted above either objected to the interference of others in lord–dependent relationships, or thought that pleas should be pursued in attendance upon lords. This is a marked transformation from pre-Conquest habits, where pleas were almost always handled in the communal courts of shire and hundred, where lords could make claims but could not exclude other lords and outsiders from involvement in pleas including their dependents. Second, these ideas about lordship as an active and influential element in pleas came to be expressed through terms which conflated expectations about lordship with ideas about jurisdiction. Such claims cut across former practices of shire and hundred, and could result in complex and difficult debates. Pre-Conquest legislation set out no framework for adjudicating claims

[53] Van Caenegem, *Lawsuits*, no. 331.

on jurisdiction, because this was not an important part of debate; and so participants in legal cases had to find their own way, for there were no clear rules for argument, or for making decisions. The rise of jurisdictional thinking and arguing was almost inevitable once lords started holding courts separate from those of shire and hundred, for some means of allocating cases to one or another was necessary. In pleas such as these ones, the basis for thinking about and making those allocations was trialled and tested, and so the ground was prepared for royal attempts to manage the system more consistently.

The desire to engage royal authority arose among those who wished to claim jurisdictions. Royal authority offered a means of terminating disputes, for all of those involved recognised the role of the king, and it was therefore relatively difficult to deny the authority of the king – except during much of Stephen's reign. So far as can be seen from the surviving narratives and other documents, kings did not go looking for this role, or encourage it; their involvement arose from requests from others. These involvements have a broader significance which has, perhaps, been underappreciated. The requests for involvement from many elite litigants meant that kings were being drawn into the administration of pleas at a local level to an extent that had not been seen before; prior to 1066, there were occasional instances where royal representatives were active in pleas locally, but these were rare. Regular involvement in the administration of the law at the level of the hundred cannot be seen earlier than this. These interventions therefore represent an extension of royal power, even if that extension did not really start with kings themselves, but rather with those who wished to invoke royal authority.

# 6

# Courts, Pleas and Kings in the Early Twelfth Century

Chapters 1–4 have set out a model for how change happened in the eleventh and earlier twelfth centuries. According to this, lords took business away from the communal courts of shire and especially of hundred. They did so either by taking control of hundred courts by various means, or by creating courts that were purely for their own dependents, and which did not match existing hundreds. The latter were mostly created through subtracting business from the hundred courts, which meant a rearrangement of power relationships between lords and their dependents. If someone's tenure of land was witnessed through a lord's court, then that tenure relied on the link to the lord. The creation of new courts had many consequences for the process of manorialisation, but had others for the hundreds themselves. Business had been taken away to other fora; attendees at the hundred no longer made their way there as often as they once had. If these processes had been pushed further, it was possible that shire and hundred might have petered out in England as fully as the *mallus* had in France. If so, this would have had substantial consequences for royal authority, for the hundred was a principal vehicle for the implementation and recognition of royal commands and authority. Without the hundred, kings would have had to work through the lords who controlled their courts to gain access to their dependents, or make claims over them. The point of lords' courts, after all, was to prevent others gaining access to them.

Yet this did not happen. Hundreds survived, and continued to meet and operate. That they did so depended on some decisions made early in Henry I's reign, and on some ideas which allowed for the diversifying landscape of courts to be organised in the king's interest. First, kings asserted that the hundreds belonged to them. It is probable that earlier kings had regarded hundreds as in some sense theirs, for hundreds carried out their commands; but they did not state this explicitly, and hundreds had not been run by any royal reeve or representative.[1] The royal

[1] Lambert, *Law and Order*, 250. Contrast Patrick Wormald's view in his 'Charters, Law and the Settlement of Disputes in Anglo-Saxon England', rpt in his *Legal Culture in the Early Medieval West: Law as Text, Image and Experience* (London, 1999), 289–311, at 304–6.

claim over the hundreds subverted their communal nature, and turned them into a lordship court, in which they were run in the interests of the kings as lords. In this way, kings used the idea that lords had developed, that it was possible to own a court and use it as a vehicle for enforcing and representing their lordship. Kings also created new mechanisms for protecting their interests in hundreds, especially for claiming business that may have gone elsewhere. Second, there appeared a distinction which allowed for the continuation of their claims. In the last decades of the eleventh century, various words were in use to describe courts, and there seems to have been no particular pattern to their use. Royal charters from the start of the twelfth century brought some organisation to usage. Some words that were used then passed out of legal use entirely, but two were chosen and became fundamental to how legal business was described and categorised. Where *curia* and *placitum* once seem to have been equivalents, from the early twelfth century the one was used more consistently for the assembly, while the other was used for business conducted within an assembly. This distinction opened up various possibilities; it meant that the ability to have a court could be described as such and separated from the ability to hold a plea, so that one was not conceived as a denial of the other. Without such a distinction it would have been hard to set out clearly what it meant to own a court, and how this intersected with other kinds of interest. It also meant that kings could classify their claims as pleas, and so as an interest that did not threaten or rival lords' courts. Kings could thus insist on the observation of the king's pleas without undermining lords' courts. The distinction between the two first appeared in royal charters in the time of Henry I, and it was so central to how Henry and later kings interacted with the law that it might be assumed that it was devised by someone or some people close to Henry I.

## Legal Texts and the Norman Kings

The Anglo-Saxon legal tradition is well known, and it ends with the great law known as 1–2 Cnut.[2] There are no documents of comparable ambition surviving in the names of the last few Anglo-Saxon kings, and nor is there anything of that nature surviving in the names of any of the Anglo-Norman kings. There are a few proclamations on specific matters, but they lack the scope and range of their Anglo-Saxon predecessors; instead, they mostly deal with only one set of political and legal problems at a time, and do not address great swathes of human activity in the manner of the larger Anglo-Saxon ones. This change in the pattern of the sources is surely significant, but it is not entirely clear why it is so.

It is possible that the pattern described above is not a product of royal decisions and actions, but rather is a consequence of the ways in which legal

2 Wormald, *Making of English Law*, 398.

texts were handled in the generations after they were written. All legal texts survive only in later copies, and often those copies are substantially later than the time of the composition of the laws themselves. What happened between their composition and the creation of the surviving copies is almost entirely obscure, but surely there were processes that had a substantial effect on the pattern of surviving texts. Some texts were lost during this transmission process;[3] others acquired supplementary glosses, or were bundled together with other texts.[4] How all this happened is essentially mysterious; the identity of those who carried out these tasks is not known, and their interests and intentions can only be understood from the evidence of the surviving texts, copies and manuscripts. It is possible and maybe likely that there were principles and ideas that informed the choice of texts for particular manuscripts, and which have determined the shape of the evidence base as it survives. Thus, for instance, the great law 1–2 Cnut survives more often than any other text; it is included in almost every manuscript that contains multiple legal texts; and it was adapted, imitated and translated more often than any other Anglo-Saxon legal text.[5] These patterns probably indicate that 1–2 Cnut was seen as the most useful and most valuable legal text – it is certainly the most wide-ranging – and that it possessed some kind of special status within legal discourse in the eleventh and earlier twelfth century. It is even possible that its status meant that it was seen as the culmination of earlier laws and the conclusion of legal collections, and that any texts circulated in the names of subsequent Anglo-Saxon kings were merely allowed to disappear. Thus, the mysterious processes of selection, copying, deletion and transmission that underpin the surviving pattern of legal texts might structure them in ways that cannot now be fully recovered, and might mean that any post-Cnut laws were considerably less likely to survive than those written before that king's reign; it is possible that there were once many more legal texts in the name of Anglo-Norman kings than now survive, for the pattern of survival is so haphazard.[6]

The older laws and their patterns of circulation provided the context against which the new legal texts of the later eleventh and earlier twelfth centuries must be read. Because they were not integrated into the canon of texts transmitted via manuscripts principally containing laws, there is no simple list of legislation in the names of the Norman kings. Many of the proprietorial claims conveyed by charter to specific individuals or corporations could be read as in some sense legislative, for they set up new legal arrangements which had effects beyond the

3 For instance, the reference to the lost *Bromdun* code in 1 Æthelred 1.2.

4 Wormald, *Making of English Law*, 366–97.

5 Wormald, *Making of English Law*, 345–66; Bruce O'Brien, 'The Instituta Cnuti and the Translation of English Law', *Anglo-Norman Studies* XXV (2003), 177–97.

6 See the *Decem articuli*; it is possible that these all go back to lost texts. See Wormald, *Making of English Law*, 402–6.

particular bounds of the lands of the beneficiaries. Thus, for instance, William I's renewal of laws for the borough of London and Henry I's grant of liberties to the same have both commonly been included among lists of legislation of the Norman kings, even though they created private privileges and claims – albeit ones with substantial implications beyond London.[7] Yet these are probably not the most effective instances of decrees that developed the law, when compared to those that had a more general application.[8]

Post-Conquest texts contrast with the older ones in two essential attributes. First is their method of authentication and dissemination. They are almost all cast as letters, with royal title, address clause (sometimes to specific local recipients, which implies that multiple copies were sent out) and with the implication that they were once authenticated by the royal seal. In these details of format, they are essentially royal charters. Yet many of the Anglo-Saxon laws are framed instead as statements, without the opening protocols that came with the letter form. These older texts were often described as the product of extensive consultations orchestrated by the king, rather than as simple expressions of royal will and authority. Even where a Norman-era text is attributed to the agency of others, such as William I's decree on the management of church pleas and the hundred court, the decree itself is authorised by royal power alone.[9] Second, the decrees in the names of the Norman kings often concern one issue only.[10] They seem to have a specific function within the law; to lay down some new provision, or to convey orders about how something was to be done. None seems to be meant as a recognition of custom. Thus, William I's decree on ecclesiastical pleas in the hundred courts states that it was prompted by a concern that pleas were not being carried out properly;[11] his decree on exculpation lays down how pleas were to be managed if they involved individuals who claimed to follow either English or Norman customs, and was probably prompted by the appearance of such pleas in the years after 1066, and a lack of earlier guidance on how such pleas were to be handled;[12] Henry I's decree on the hundred and shire courts orders that past practice is to be observed (so implying that it was not) and lays down some principles for allocating cases to courts;[13] and Stephen's 1136 charter for the church promises to end royal interference in some aspects of the administrative

7 Bates, *Regesta*, no. 180; *Regesta*, ii. no. 1645.

8 Bates, *Regesta*, nos. 128, 130; *Regesta*, ii. nos. 488, 501, 531, 892, 1476; *Regesta*, iii. no. 271.

9 Bates, *Regesta*, no. 128.

10 This applies even if the *Decem articuli* is taken into account, for those are single-issue statements, and quite possibly a compilation of other lost decrees of William.

11 Bates, *Regesta*, no. 128.

12 Bates, *Regesta*, no. 130.

13 *Regesta*, ii. no. 892.

work of the church.[14] None of these ranges across numerous topics or contains any general statement of the ideals of Christian kingship. The only decree from this era that does range widely is Henry I's coronation charter,[15] which contains lots of promises about future good government, and its role was more political than legislative. Its role in supporting Henry I's occupation of the role perhaps makes it closest to the Anglo-Saxon model in which laws and especially their promulgation were constitutive of kingship itself.

The key point about the post-Cnut legislation is that it is different in aim from what came before. Where the earlier laws often included substantial and ambitious messages about the nature of society, the role of religion and so forth, those after Cnut seem much less ambitious. Most were concerned with quite practical matters, and as much with the implementation and administration of law as with changes to its substance. They show that there was a feedback loop, that there were mechanisms which allowed ideas about the shortcomings of the law to be sent to kings, and that they were sufficiently interested in the law to act upon those where it was seen to be useful and appropriate. This shows that Norman kings maintained the idea that they had some responsibility for and oversight of the law in their kingdom. Yet there is no sense at all that kings tried to assert control over the law in general through legislation, for they never tried to either recast the law inherited from the past, or even to repeat its promulgation.

## The Decrees of 1108

In 1106, Henry I successfully fought the Battle of Tinchebray, captured his brother Robert and brought Normandy under his rule. He spent some months in pacifying and organising Normandy before his return to England in 1107. It is very likely that, during that period of pacification in Normandy, he considered the claims that past dukes had made; and it is likely that he considered the list of claims in relation to the *Consuetudines et iustitie*, which had been prepared by his two brothers.[16] After his return to England, Henry issued a series of decrees which defined royal claims in England in relation to the law and other matters, and regularised some of the ways in which kings interacted with the law.[17]

Henry did not circulate some great law which covered all of these points, but addressed them through a series of decrees during the spring of 1108. They

14 *Regesta*, iii. no. 271.

15 *Regesta*, ii. no. 488.

16 On this see Mark Hagger, *Norman Rule in Normandy, 911–1144* (Woodbridge, 2017), 441–61.

17 For the context of all of this see Judith A. Green, *Henry I, King of England and Duke of Normandy* (Cambridge, 2006), 96–117.

did not present grand ideas that impacted on all of society, but rather concerned specific themes, and they were presented in different ways. Four were in the king's name, while the fifth concerned the clergy and was presented as the canons of an ecclesiastical council in which the king and his barons had been participants. This was a very different method of proceeding from that seen in the pre-Conquest laws. There were at least five of these documents, and maybe more. They do not survive as a group, but as a mix of references in chronicles, copies surviving through registers, and so forth. They have not been brought together historiographically before. Two now survive, but three others are known from references to them in chronicles and other sources. The five are:

*Decree on reform of the king's court*[18]

No written text survives for this decree, but it is reported quite fully in two chronicles. It is described in most detail in Eadmer of Canterbury's *Historia Nouorum*.[19] Eadmer states that the people of the king's court had engaged in plundering the localities through which they passed. This is attributed to the time of William II, but with the implication that it was ongoing. Depredations included seizure of property, illegal sale of property, destruction of property, and personal violence. Henry stopped this and imposed a penalty of blinding and castration; Eadmer indicates that these penalties were imposed on some individuals, though he names no names. Eadmer places this after the death of Bishop Gundulf of Rochester on 7 March 1108,[20] and before the ecclesiastical council of late May in the same year.[21]

The same decree is mentioned by William of Malmesbury in his *Gesta Regum*.[22] William repeats many of the details provided by Eadmer about the scope of the decree in terms of problems and punishments. He called the decree an *edicto*, which tends to support the idea that it took a written form, and

18 On this see Judith A. Green, *Henry I, King of England and Duke of Normandy* (Cambridge, 2006), 110–12.

19 Eadmer of Canterbury, *Historia Nouorum in Anglia*, ed. Martin Rule (London, 1884), 192–3; trans. Geoffrey Bosanquet (London, 1964), 205–6.

20 *Fasti ecclesiae Anglicanae, 1066–1300*, ii: D. E. Greenway, *Monastic Cathedrals: Northern and Southern Provinces* (London, 1971), 75.

21 Eadmer of Canterbury, *Historia Nouorum in Anglia*, ed. Martin Rule (London, 1884), 192–3; trans. Geoffrey Bosanquet (London, 1964), 205–8; John of Worcester, *Chronicle*, ed. R. R. Darlington and P. McGurk (two volumes of three published, Oxford, 1995–8), iii. 112–17; *Councils and Synods with other Documents relating to the English Church: Part 1, AD 871–1204*, ed. D. Whitelock, M. Brett and C. N. L. Brooke (2 vols, Oxford, 1981), ii. 694–704.

22 William of Malmesbury, *Gesta Regum Anglorum/The History of the English Kings*, ed. and trans. R. A. B. Mynors, R. M. Thomson and M. Winterbottom (two vols, Oxford, 1998–9), i. 724–5.

indicated that William I had similarly circulated regulations about the conduct of the court, which Henry took as the basis for his decree.

A decree on the conduct and discipline of the king's court, in which the king himself took the lead in defining conduct, emphasised the point that the king's court was under the particular jurisdiction of the king and that he alone could regulate it. Apart from dealing with abuses, the decree might have been meant to assert the king's claims over his court and the people of the court. The abuses described by Eadmer suggest that it was not possible or not practical for those who had suffered from the depredations of the people of the court to pursue claims through local courts, and of course the people of the king's court would mostly have been outsiders to those assemblies in any case.

*Decree on the coinage and moneyers*[23]

Like the decree on the king's court, this does not survive as a written text, but is widely reported by the chroniclers. William of Malmesbury described it in simple terms; moneyers had been producing forged coins, and so those responsible for this were mutilated by losing a hand.[24] Eadmer reported it in slightly different and fuller terms;[25] he stated that disorderly moneyers were punished by blinding and castration, and that as a result of these concerns about the coinage all coins should be perfect, except that they should bear an indentation. Eadmer's description was repeated by John of Worcester.[26] Both William of Malmesbury and Eadmer place this decree after the one on the regulation of the king's court, and John of Worcester places it before the ecclesiastical council.[27]

The royal interest in the coinage is obvious. It was circulated in the name of the king, and carried the king's image on it. John of Worcester implies that the

[23] Judith A. Green, *Henry I, King of England and Duke of Normandy* (Cambridge, 2006), 112.

[24] William of Malmesbury, *Gesta Regum Anglorum/The History of the English Kings*, ed. and trans. R. A. B. Mynors, R. M. Thomson and M. Winterbottom (two volumes, Oxford, 1998–9), i. 724–5; *Councils and Synods with other Documents relating to the English Church: Part 1, AD 871–1204*, ed. D. Whitelock, M. Brett and C. N. L. Brooke (2 vols, Oxford, 1981), ii. 694–704.

[25] Eadmer of Canterbury, *Historia Nouorum in Anglia*, ed. Martin Rule (London, 1884), 193; trans. Geoffrey Bosanquet (London, 1964), 206.

[26] John of Worcester, *Chronicle*, ed. R. R. Darlington and P. McGurk (two volumes of three published, Oxford, 1995–8), iii. 112–13

[27] Eadmer of Canterbury, *Historia Nouorum in Anglia*, ed. Martin Rule (London, 1884), 192–3; trans. Geoffrey Bosanquet (London, 1964), 205–8; John of Worcester, *Chronicle*, ed. R. R. Darlington and P. McGurk (two volumes of three published, Oxford, 1995–8), iii. 112–17; *Councils and Synods with other Documents relating to the English Church: Part 1, AD 871–1204*, ed. D. Whitelock, M. Brett and C. N. L. Brooke (2 vols, Oxford, 1981), ii. 694–704.

decree was used in 1108, for he says it was of great benefit to the kingdom.[28] In 1125 some moneyers were punished in terms that match those specified by the chroniclers, and this was done at Winchester before Bishop Roger of Salisbury, not locally in shire and hundred courts.[29] The assertion of royal jurisdiction was thus seemingly effective.

### *Decree on theft and judgements*[30]

Like the two preceding decrees, this does not survive as a written text. It is noted by John of Worcester, who stated that Henry legislated in 1108 that anyone who was found in theft or robbery should be hanged.[31] John links this to the decree against false moneying noted above. The two linked decrees are also noted in a writ in favour of Gerard, archbishop of York:

> Henry by the grace of God king of the English to Osbert the sheriff and Richard son of Gero,[32] greeting! I will and command that Gerard, archbishop of York, in the lands of his churches and in all lands of the archbishopric of York, has his pleas in his court about his moneyers and about robbers and about all others; and he has all his laws and customs and [those] of all his churches concerning all things and just as well as Archbishop Thomas had in the time of my father and brother. And he shall carry out my new establishments (*statuta*) concerning judgements or concerning the pleas of thieves and false moneyers, and he shall do this through his own justices in his court. Nor should he or his church lose anything on account of my new establishments (*statutis*), but, as I have said, he should do this in his court through his own justice according to my establishments (*statuta*). Witness, Robert, bishop of Chester. At Winchester at Easter.[33]

[28] John of Worcester, *Chronicle*, ed. R. R. Darlington and P. McGurk (two volumes of three published, Oxford, 1995–8), iii. 112–15.

[29] *The Anglo-Saxon Chronicle: A Revised Translation*, ed. Dorothy Whitelock with David C. Douglas and Susie I. Tucker (London, 1961), 191.

[30] William Stubbs, *Select Charters and Other Illustrations of English Constitutional History*, ed. H. W. C. Davis (ninth edition, Oxford, 1913), 114.

[31] John of Worcester, *Chronicle*, ed. R. R. Darlington and P. McGurk (two volumes of three published, Oxford, 1995–8), iii. 112–13.

[32] The Patent Roll text has Gero; the slightly garbled versions in the York registers have Gozo.

[33] *Henricus dei gratia rex Anglorum O(sberto) uicecomiti et R(icardo) filio Geronis salutem. Volo et precipio ut Gerardus Eboracensis archiepiscopus in terris ecclesiarum suarum et in omnibus terris Eboracensis archiepiscopatus placita sua in curia sua habeat de monetariis suis et de latronibus et de omnibus aliis; et omnes leges et consuetudines suas et omnium ecclesiarum suarum de omnibus habeat sicut et Thomas archiepiscopus melius habuit tempore patris uel fratris mei. Et noua statuta mea de iudiciis siue de placitis latronum et falsorum monetariorum exequatur et faciat per suam propriam iusticiam in curia sua. Nec ipse aliquid perdat uel ecclesia sua pro nouis statutis meis, set sicut dixi in curia sua faciat per propriam iusticiam suam secundum statuta mea. Teste R(oberto) Cestrensi episcopo. Apud Wynt(oniam)*

To judge from the reports by the chroniclers, the decrees on false moneyers and on theft were uncompromising in their application; Eadmer even specified that the decree on moneyers disallowed any monetary penalty in place of mutilation.[34] Yet such decrees must have raised questions about how far they intersected with specific local privileges on particular matters. In this case, the archbishop of York's privilege was confirmed, so that its terms overrode the king's new decree.

There are some concerns about the dating of this document. The editors of *Regesta* dated it early, on the grounds that the sheriff was Richard, son of Gotse, who they thought could not have been sheriff of Nottingham (which is presumably why he was addressed alongside the sheriff of Yorkshire) later than 1105.[35] The succession to the post of sheriff of Nottingham is not that clear in this period, and there are considerable gaps and potential overlaps in terms of office,[36] so that the 1105 terminal date cannot be relied upon. The *Regesta* editors connected this writ with an earlier decree on the coinage,[37] which must be dated to Christmas 1100 because it has an internal date of Christmas, but by Christmas 1101 William Giffard, who witnessed it as chancellor, was no longer in that office. Yet this charter for York is based not just on a decree on moneyers, but also on one about theft and judgements; there is no evidence for the latter in 1100, whereas there are other sources noted in this chapter which show that there were linked and contemporaneous decrees on theft and on moneyers in 1108. Acceptance of the suggested 1100 date for the York writ means that it would be necessary to assume extra royal decrees on the law which have no other evidentiary basis. Assuming the attribution to 1108, it must have been before Archbishop Gerard died on 21 May 1108.[38]

Moreover, to judge from the description in the chronicles, the 1108 decree on moneyers may have been somewhat different from that of 1100. The 1100 text ordered that all townsmen should swear to observe the king's legitimate coinage, so that it involved a lot more people than the 1108 decree. The 1100 decree states that any found with false coin should belong to the king's *iustitia* or claim to punish, while the 1108 decree restricts this to those who made false

*in paschis*. *Regesta*, ii. no. 518. This is from the copy in *Calendar of the Patent Rolls Preserved in the Public Record Office*, ed. Deputy Keeper of the Records (75 vols, London, 1901–86), *1338–40*, 166. For an earlier discussion of this document see James W. Alexander, 'The Alleged Palatinates of Norman England', *Speculum* 56 (1981), 17–27, at 20.

34 Eadmer of Canterbury, *Historia Nouorum in Anglia*, ed. Martin Rule (London, 1884), 193; trans. Geoffrey Bosanquet (London, 1964), 206.

35 *Regesta*, ii. no. 518 notes.

36 Judith Green, *English Sheriffs to 1154* (London, 1990), 67.

37 *Regesta*, ii. no. 501.

38 *Fasti Ecclesiae Anglicanae, 1066–1300*: vi, *York*, ed. Diana E. Greenway (London, 1996), 2.

coin.[39] The penalties described in the 1100 decree are a blend of those set out by William of Malmesbury and Eadmer. What they had in common, and what may have prompted the document for the archbishop of York, was that both claimed that the king had exclusive claims over matters linked to false coin. This claim for exclusivity would have interfered with the specific local claims claimed by the archbishop of York, and probably would have overridden the claims of others as well. The archbishop claimed to have a private moneyer at York,[40] and so a claim by the king to exclusive jurisdiction over all moneyers would infringe upon the archbishop's position. Thus, this writ ordered that pleas concerning false moneyers in the archbishop's lands should be deemed as the archbishop's own pleas and should be dealt with in his court.[41]

Much the same point can be made in relation to theft. The king ordered that the archbishop should have pleas concerning theft that arose from his lands as his pleas in his own court. Even the provisions of the new *statutum* should be done by the archbishop's own official in his court. Presumably, therefore, the lost decree on theft ordered that the opposite should take place where there was no privileged lord to obtain a local exemption. If this inference is true, it would mean that the lost decree stated that the king claimed that theft should be regarded as a plea that belonged to the king; that it should be dealt with in the king's own court; that it should be done by the king's representative, not the representative of the lord. The king did state that the archbishop's representative was to deal with matters of theft in accordance with the king's *statutum*, which indicates that the lost decree made some provisions for procedure, and how theft cases were to be dealt with. The range of themes covered in the references to this lost decree suggests that it may have paralleled the coverage of theft in the Assize of Clarendon.

*Decree on the shire and hundred courts*

This is the best known of the 1108 decrees because a text survives, and it has been discussed by many scholars. Its terms can thus be studied in some detail:

> Henry king of the English to Bishop Samson and Urse d'Abetot and to all his barons French and English of Worcestershire greeting! Know that I grant and command that hereafter my shires and hundreds shall sit in the same places and at the same terms as they sat in King Edward's time and not otherwise. And I will that my sheriff shall not cause them to sit otherwise for any need of his own, for only I shall cause them to be summoned when I will for my

39 John of Worcester, *Chronicle*, ed. R. R. Darlington and P. McGurk (two volumes of three published, Oxford, 1995–8), iii. 112–13.

40 *Calendar of the Patent Rolls Preserved in the Public Record Office*, ed. Deputy Keeper of the Records (75 vols, London, 1901–86), *1338–40*, 166.

41 Van Caenegem, *Lawsuits*, no. 172.

> lordly needs at my pleasure. And if hereafter a plea shall arise concerning the boundary of lands or concerning encroachment, if it is between my demesne barons, the plea shall be dealt with in my court. If it is between vavasors of one lord of my own honour, the plea shall be dealt with in the court of their lord. And if it is between vavasors of two lords, it shall be dealt with in the shire court. And this shall be done by duel unless it be stayed between them (that is, to come to a composition). And I will and command that all of the shire shall go to the shires and hundreds just as they did in King Edward's time, and there shall be no stay on account of any peace or quiet of mine but that they shall do suit at my pleas and my judgements as they did at that time. Witness, Bishop Richard of London and Bishop Roger and Ranulf the chancellor and Count Robert of Meulan. At Reading.[42]

This decree did something that had never appeared in any of the Anglo-Saxon laws; it set out a clear framework for allocating cases to different courts. It stated that in certain kinds of cases the allocation of business to one court or another was to be done in accordance with tenure, and who was the superior lord of the participants in the dispute. Thus, cases between the tenants-in-chief of the king were to be dealt with in the king's court, and cases involving tenants of the same lord in their own court; cases involving tenants of different lords were then to be held in the shire court. Whether the same structure was meant to apply to other areas is neither stated nor implied. The significance of all this is considerable. It shows that the king was willing to recognise and legitimise the courts of any lords, which had not really been done before, and set out some rules for their relationships to other courts. Henry could conceive of these courts as part of the same pattern.

[42] *Henricus dei gratia rex Anglorum Samsoni episcopo et Vrsoni de Abetot et omnibus baronibus suis francis et anglis de Wirecestrescira salutem. Sciatis quod concedo et precipio ut amodo comitatus mei et hundreta in illis locis et eisdem terminis sedeant, sicut sederunt in tempore regis Eadwardi, et non aliter. Et nolo ut uicecomes meus propter aliquod necessarium suum quod sibi pertineat faciat ea sedere aliter. Ego enim quando uoluero faciam ea satis summonere propter mea dominica necessaria ad uoluntatem meam. Et si amodo exurgat placitum de diuisione terrarum uel de preoccupatione, si est inter dominicos barones meis, tractetur placitum in curia mea. Et si est inter uauasores duorum dominorum, tractetur in comitatu. Et hoc duello fiat, nisi in eis remanserit. Et uolo et precipio ut omnes de comitatu eant ad comitatus et hundreta, sicut fecerunt in tempore regis Eadwardi, et non remaneat propter aliquam pacem meam uel quietudinem, quin sequantur placita mea et iudicia mea, sicut tunc temporis fecissent. Testibus R(icardo) episcopo Lundonie et Rogero episcopo et Ranulfo cancellario et R(odberto) comite de Mellent. Apud Rading'. Regesta*, ii. no. 892; Liebermann, *Gesetze*, i. 524; here from the version at https://actswilliam2henry1.files.wordpress.com/2013/10/h1-a-liberties-2013-1.pdf. It survives through various routes; through copies addressed to Worcestershire copied into exchequer registers in the thirteenth century, through *Quadripartitus* and through the latter's extended version in the London *Leges Anglorum*.

Yet, while recognising the courts held by lords, he also insisted on the continuation of the shire and hundred courts. The command that they should sit as they had in Edward the Confessor's time and that sheriffs should not make them sit elsewhere probably indicates that the regularity of these courts had been disrupted recently;[43] it is hard to see other evidence for this, though. The decree also commands that suitors should attend these courts as they (or, more likely, their predecessors) had in the time of King Edward.[44] This implies that there were concerns about non-attendance, and this concern is apparent from other documents of similar date. Seemingly, it was hard to get people to attend these courts in the early twelfth century. Where there were hundreds in the hands of lords, some obtained orders from the king to their tenants instructing that they should attend.[45] It is not clear who was meant to act upon these commands. It might be that other lords interfered with tenants to prevent their attendance, or it might have been the tenants themselves who tried to escape their obligations.[46] They might have been motivated by laziness or boredom – the hundred may well have been a particularly irksome committee – or they might have been discouraged from attendance by their lords.

Chapters 1–4 of this book showed how during the eleventh century lords aspired to exercise control over their dependents through interactions within, and even through control of, the communal courts, and the creation of other courts that reflected patterns of lordship. The methods by which this was achieved were various, but involved the development and assertion of the idea that courts could be owned. So far as can be seen, this idea developed among lords and their agents, but spread outwards from that point of origin. Kings came to grant courts, especially hundred courts, as things that could be owned. Such grants contained the implication that such courts were in some sense owned by the king to begin with. This represented something of a development, for there seems to have been no clear position on this in documentation from the Anglo-Saxon era. Courts were viewed within a more open framework, where they might be seen as arenas for the management of royal claims as well as those of lords; and they represented customary understandings of law and communal, shared local power rather than a singular royal authority.[47] Yet, in this decree Henry boldly claimed that they were 'my shires and hundreds'.

43 *Leges Henrici Primi*, 7.1, suggests that sheriffs had summoned courts too often.

44 William I may have issued a decree which ordered people to attend courts as in former times; *Decem Articuli*, 8a.1.

45 *Regesta*, ii. nos. 1503, 1771, 1865, *The Cartulary of Worcester Cathedral Priory (Register I)*, ed. R. R. Darlington, Pipe Roll Society 76, new series 38 (1968), 27, no. 42; *Regesta*, iii. no. 753.

46 *Regesta*, ii. no. 1503 for Ely implies this.

47 Lambert, *Law and Order*, 148.

Earlier kings had not been so assertive or so precise in claiming that shires and hundreds belonged to them. The hundred had been set up as an assembly of local society, and did not have a royal representative as its driving force, unlike the sheriff in the shires court.[48] Yet now Henry I specifically identified shires and hundreds as his. It is not entirely clear what he meant by this statement. When Henry referred to 'my shires and hundreds' he might have meant all of those contained within his kingdom, which could in some sense be described as his. Or, he might have been making a distinction between those hundreds and shires which had been granted to, or recognised in the control of, other lords.[49] It is hard to see whether this would have been perceived as a novelty, or as an assertion of an existing situation. When in dispute with their former reeve of Wye in 1102, the monks of Battle used the argument that the abbey's court had been authorised by kings and as such represented royal authority; the abbey's court was thus a royal court, in contrast to the hundred of Wye, which was not.[50] For those observers at least, a hundred court was not seen as an expression of royal authority, but instead as a vehicle for the power of local elites.

By the earlier twelfth century, many lords had claims over hundred courts, or claimed the ability to compel the attendance of their tenants. In this context, royal claims to own shires and hundreds can be seen as a response to those developments. Control of some hundreds begged the question of who owned the rest; also, royal claims to ownership were a means of pre-empting the claims of others, if it was seen as worthwhile to do so. It would be going beyond the evidence to assume that kings viewed the interest or control or other lords in hundreds as something that detracted from their own dignity. It is entirely plausible that they viewed it in neutral terms, as something akin to the possession of land by others; this did not detract from kings, but instead enhanced their reputation through creating dignified and wealthy dependents who might be ornaments to their court.

This decree must be dated after Richard de Belmeis was nominated as bishop of London on 24 May 1108,[51] and before the king departed for Normandy in July 1108.[52]

48 Lambert, *Law and Order*, 250. Contrast Patrick Wormald's view in his 'Charters, Law and the Settlement of Disputes in Anglo-Saxon England', rpt in his *Legal Culture in the Early Medieval West: Law as Text, Image and Experience* (London, 1999), 289–311, at 304–6. He argued that hundreds should be regarded as royal because they received the king's commands and did his business. Yet, Anglo-Saxon kings did not state the hundreds belonged to them.

49 See Chapter 3 for grants of hundreds to others.

50 *The Chronicle of Battle Abbey*, ed. Eleanor Searle (Oxford, 1981), 108–9, and discussion above in Chapter 5; Van Caenegem, *Lawsuits*, no. 174.

51 *Fasti Ecclesiae Anglicanae, 1066–1300*: i, *St Paul's, London*, ed. Diana E. Greenway (London, 1968), 1.

52 https://actswilliam2henry1.files.wordpress.com/2013/10/h1-a-liberties-2013-1.pdf.

*Statutes of the ecclesiastical council about the clergy*[53]

This decree repeated instructions about how the clergy should maintain celibacy, and added some procedures for identifying and dealing with clergy who were not compliant with those requirements.[54] It was published in the name of the two archbishops and the bishops, so that this was ecclesiastical legislation rather than royal, secular legislation, but nonetheless it involved the king; the statutes state that they were made in the presence of the king, and with the assent of his barons. In that way the ecclesiastical statutes fitted into the pattern of sustained royal legislative activity during 1108. While there was royal input, the form of the statutes was ecclesiastical, and there is an obvious contrast with earlier practice; Anglo-Saxon kings had not hesitated to lay down requirements or advice for the clergy, and did so within laws which often addressed a wide range of business.

The decrees of 1108 represented an attempt by Henry I to set out a specific role for the king which recognised and responded to recent change in relation to courts and the law. Henry claimed that, in the fluid and changeable pattern of courts of the early twelfth century, some matters belonged especially to kings. He did not try to claim that all business was the king's, but instead allowed that some matters properly belonged to lords. It might well be that some kind of bargain lay behind this, in which the king claimed some matters for himself and with the consent of the elite, in return for allowing that other kinds of business pertained to others.

*The 1108 decrees as a group*

It is a little hard to know how to read these decrees overall. There are points in them that seem new, at least in how they were expressed, such as the notion of the king's pleas and the king's ownership of hundreds, but it seems that contemporaries may not have read it that way. It could be that the decrees represented a recognition of arrangements that had been in place on the ground for some time, or even that they restated points from lost, older decrees. Yet there was a response written soon after these decrees, and which acclaims the decrees as reassertions of past situations. The *Leges Henrici Primi* comments thus: 'Just as it was framed by ancient ordinance, it is lately, by the king's healthful command, reaffirmed by true

53 *Councils and Synods with other Documents relating to the English Church: Part 1, AD 871–1204*, ed. D. Whitelock, M. Brett and C. N. L. Brooke (2 vols, Oxford, 1981), ii. 694–704.

54 John of Worcester, *Chronicle*, ed. R. R. Darlington and P. McGurk (two volumes of three published, Oxford, 1995–8), iii. 114–17; *Councils and Synods with other Documents relating to the English Church: Part 1, AD 871–1204*, ed. D. Whitelock, M. Brett and C. N. L. Brooke (2 vols, Oxford, 1981), ii. 694–702.

restatement …'.[55] This introduces a summary of and commentary on the decree on the courts, which is described as recent.[56]

Ambiguity here is perhaps the best approach. Henry I's 1108 decrees were not great reformist gestures that reshaped the pattern of courts and laws, but rather conservative documents. They affirmed features and processes that had been in place for a long time, and restated priorities inherited from the past, such as the emphasis on theft. Yet, while responding to these longstanding concerns, they introduced processes that may have been new (as that seems to be the implication of the York exemption from the theft decree) and subtly reshaped legal activity through the introductions of new ideas and distinctions, such as the king's pleas and the distinction between courts and pleas.[57] Overall, the idea that the king had specific claims in the law was sharpened and clarified, and the ability of the king to use those claims was strengthened.

## *Curia* and *Placitum*

If the royal claim over the hundreds was asserted more clearly by Henry I, the same king's reign also saw the development of classifications that governed how private courts were viewed. In the later eleventh century it seems that there were a few words that could be used for courts, and they seem to have been used interchangeably and indifferently. Thus, in sources from the later eleventh century, the terms *curia*, *placitum*, *comitium*, *mallus* and *gemotum* can all be found, and it seems that they were not used in any technical sense. Any of these could be used for an assembly that had some kind of legal function, and there was much inconsistency in how they were used. Thus, for instance, *placitum* seems to have been used both for a legal assembly, and also for business transacted within that assembly. In such circumstances, it would have been difficult to articulate claims over kinds of business without also making an indirect claim to hold a court as well. The vagueness of classifications meant that it must have been hard to articulate exactly what was meant or claimed in jurisdictional terms.

*Curia* was the most common Latin term for denoting a court in post-Conquest England. It can cover a range of meanings that make it a close parallel to the modern English term court, in that it could signify a law court, a monarchical court in its social and political dimensions, or a courtyard or precinct. This means

55 https://actswilliam2henry1.files.wordpress.com/2013/10/h1-a-liberties-2013-1.pdf.

56 Nicholas Karn, 'Rethinking the *Leges Henrici Primi*', in *English Law before Magna Carta: Felix Liebermann and* Die Gesetze der Angelsachsen, ed. Stefan Jurasinski, Lisi Oliver and Andrew Rabin (Leiden and Boston, 2010), 199–220, at 216; https://actswilliam2henry1.files.wordpress.com/2013/10/h1-a-liberties-2013-1.pdf.

57 Hudson, *Oxford History*, 384.

that any occurrence of the term *curia* must be examined in its context to see which of these was meant; fortunately, it is usually clear from the context. The spread of the use of *curia* for describing legal assemblies established a category that could be wide-ranging, and which stressed what lords' courts had in common with other assemblies, such as the king's court. The term *curia* was used in such a way that any assembly designated using this term was based around a person. For *curia* could not be used by itself; a *curia* could not be a free-standing item. A *curia* was something based around paying court to someone whether as an individual, as an office holder, or as the embodiment of an office. Thus the royal court was based around the king; writers could refer to the heavenly court, which was based around God.[58] It is perhaps significant that the assemblies of hundred and shire were not usually described using the term *curia* in this period, because they did not express the dominance of an individual, but instead were meetings of local elites.[59] The Old English term *mot* was used for shire and hundred before the Conquest, because it expressed the idea that the assembly was a meeting based on those territories, which were essentially impersonal; a Latin equivalent such as *conventus* was not used instead of *mot*, because a lord's court did not express any category separate from the person of the lord. *Curia*, meanwhile, recognised and legitimated the authority of the lord who held the court, and drew attention to how that lord's authority paralleled that of the king.

The sense of *curia* as a law court is very rare in documents originating in Anglo-Saxon England, or from before the end of the eleventh century. Something close to it appears a couple of times in glossaries, where it was used to describe the building in which judgements or advice were given;[60] and it appears a few times in places where it must describe an assembly of dignitaries accompanying the king, in other words, the royal court.[61] These often were used where the court appears in its political or social aspect rather than its judicial one. The term does not appear in pre-Conquest writs,[62] and nor does it appear in clearly authentic diplomas from before the Conquest.[63] It was not used to translate the Old English *mot*, and indeed sources from the eleventh century show considerable uncertainty about how *mot* should be translated. This can

58 *Regesta*, ii. nos. 1241 and 1312, both forgeries from Nostell Priory.

59 See Chapter 8 below for this.

60 *Dictionary of Medieval Latin from British Sources*, 537, *sub verbo curia*, sense 1.

61 *Dictionary of Medieval Latin from British Sources*, 537, *sub verbo curia*, sense 3b.

62 Harmer, *Writs*, has been checked.

63 Anglo-Saxon Charters indexes checked via http://www.esawyer.org.uk/. For a post-Conquest forgery from the later eleventh century that includes *curia* see the charter in the name of Harthacnut for Bury St Edmunds Abbey; http://www.esawyer.org.uk/charter/995.html. On this see Sarah Foot, 'The Abbey's Armoury of Charters', in *Bury St Edmunds and the Norman Conquest*, ed. Tom Licence (Woodbridge, 2014), 31–52, at 48–9.

be seen very clearly in *Quadripartitus*, the translations of pre-conquest laws produced in the 1090s,[64] where there is no consistency at all. Just to pick on one example, within a few lines within its translation of 2 Æthelstan there is considerable variation in terminology:

2 Æthelstan 20.

De his qui ad gemotum (some mss. mallum) uenire supersederint. Si quis gemotum (id est placitum/some mss. publicum comitium) adire supersedeat …

2 Æthelstan 20.1.

… seniores homines qui ad eam curiam (OE *byrig*) obedient.

Thus, variants of *mot* could be translated into Latin using the term *mallus*,[65] more generally used in the early middle ages and on the Continent for courts, or using the bizarre and archaic *comitium*,[66] or *placitum*,[67] which alone of these terms appears regularly in writings from eleventh- and twelfth-century England. Perhaps even more odd is that the writer of *Quadripartitus* could in the 1090s use *curia* to signify (apparently) a town. Maybe the idea here comes from the notion that a courtyard was an enclosure, for *curia* can be found in this sense in Great Domesday Book.[68] The evidence of *Quadripartitus* and its variable translations suggests that there was, by the 1090s, no consensus as to the vocabulary by which courts could readily be described.

The term *curia* appears commonly in the acta in the name of William I, but there is a catch; most of the examples in which *curia* appears in a place where it must refer to a judicial assembly are forgeries. There are a number of grants in William's name which purport to convey to an institution the ability to hold a court, and these were usually produced for churches that have since acquired a certain notoriety as forgers. Thus, William I was ventriloquised to grant the ability to hold courts to Battle Abbey,[69] Chertsey Abbey,[70] Durham Cathedral,[71]

64 On this see Richard Sharpe, 'The Dating of Quadripartitus Again', *English Law before Magna Carta: Felix Liebermann and* Die Gesetze der Angelsachsen, ed. Stefan Jurasinski, Lisi Oliver and Andrew Rabin (Leiden and Boston, 2010), 81–93, esp. 91.

65 *Dictionary of Medieval Latin from British Sources*, 1696, *sub verbo mallus*. The word *mallus* also occurs in *Leges Henrici Primi* 89.3, but in a passage borrowed from the additions to the Salic law.

66 *Dictionary of Medieval Latin from British Sources*, 390, *sub verbo comitium*. There are a few other instances of its use, mostly in the eleventh and twelfth centuries.

67 *Dictionary of Medieval Latin from British Sources*, 2301–2, *sub verbo placitum*.

68 For instance, Great Domesday Book, fo. 154v: Oxfordshire 1.13.

69 Bates, *Regesta*, no. 22.

70 Bates, *Regesta*, no. 99.ii.

71 Bates, *Regesta*, nos. 109, 111, 111 ×2.

Selby Abbey[72] and Westminster Abbey;[73] most are of the twelfth century. That so many of these well-known forgers wanted charters of William I that included the grant or recognition of a *curia* suggests that they did not have any authentic ones, but nonetheless the grant or recognition of a *curia* was seen to be of sufficient important to justify the forgery. The other uses of *curia* within William I's acta either referred to the king's court in its social and political aspect,[74] or to the settlement of a dispute in the king's court in its judicial aspect.[75] It is conspicuous that uses of the word in England are outweighed by those from Normandy.[76] The pattern is much the same in the acta of William II, where the grants to hold a *curia* are forged,[77] and where mentions of the word *curia* either refer to the ducal or royal court,[78] or are Norman.[79]

A similar lack of definition can be seen in relation to *placitum* and *placitare*. These terms are likewise rare in sources from before the Conquest, but appear uncertainly in the early eleventh century. It might be used to describe a series of meetings of a court to deal with a series of problems, as in the Penenden Heath pleas, where the various disputes were all said to have been resolved *in eodem placito*, where a singular form covered what seems to have protracted proceedings.[80] Something similar can be seen in relation to the use of the term in the Ely land pleas.[81] In the Worcester pleas, the *placitum* was something that was held by Geoffrey, bishop of Coutances, as the king's representative, which emphasises his role as the convenor of the session rather than that of the participants who pleaded within it.[82] If many of the uses in William I's acta seem to use *placitum* to identify the meeting or the court, there are a few which align with later usage to denote an item of business. Thus, the decree on separating ecclesiastical pleas from the hundred court observes that *in hundret placita teneant*,[83] while a plea held before King William himself was introduced with the phrase *Willelmo rege tenente curiam et placitum*.[84] Overall, it is clear that the term *placitum* did not yet,

72 Bates, *Regesta*, no. 272 ×2.
73 Bates, *Regesta*, nos. 290 ×2, 316, 324.
74 This is the case in Bates, *Regesta*, no. 15 ×4, which is itself probably another one of the Battle forgeries.
75 Bates, *Regesta*, no. 39, for Bury St Edmunds Abbey; also no. 146, for Fécamp Abbey, but concerning the abbey's holding at Steyning in Sussex.
76 Bates, *Regesta*, nos. 201, 205.i ×2, 204.ii ×2, 214, 230, 235 ×3, 259, 267.i, 267.ii ×6.
77 *Regesta*, i. nos. 307, 366 and 367.
78 *Regesta*, i. nos. 186, 338, 378, 416, 423, 429 and 478. Some of these are clear forgeries.
79 Most notably, *Regesta*, i. no. 316, which includes many mentions of the Norman ducal court.
80 Bates, *Regesta*, no. 69.
81 Bates, *Regesta*, nos. 117, 119, 120, 122, 125.
82 Bates, *Regesta*, no. 350; see also no. 349.
83 Bates, *Regesta*, no. 128.
84 Bates, *Regesta*, no. 146.

by the later eleventh century, have the more distinct and precise meaning that it had by the later twelfth century. The conceptual distinctions that underpinned that usage had not yet emerged.[85]

The loose and relaxed usage of these words changed very soon after 1100. From that point, *curia* appears regularly in English royal documents. That these writs must refer to courts held by individuals beyond the structures of hundred and shire can be seen by an example, in this case a writ of Henry I for Abingdon Abbey:

> Henry king of the English to Ralf Basset, greeting! I command that you shall cause Vincent abbot of Abingdon to have his court (*curiam suam*) at Oxford as well and fully as ever the church of Abingdon or any of his predecessors well and fully and honourably had it. And his men shall not plead (*non placitent*) outside his court (*curiam suam*), unless the abbot shall have first failed to do justice in his own court (*curia sua*). And just as you will be able to discover from the lawful men of Oxford that he ought to have his own court (*curiam suam*). Witness the chancellor. At Woodstock.[86]

From this, it is clear that the court mentioned was something that pertained to the abbot of Abingdon, because it is consistently called *his* court. The king also recognised that the abbot's court was not merely a courtyard, for it was a place in which pleading might take place; pleading is a term that always carried a legal meaning, for it was used when some litigants made a submission or argument. The king also stated that the abbot had to do justice to his dependents in the court; this again proves that the abbot's court had a judicial aspect to its activities. Thus, it is beyond doubt that the term *curia* in royal acta must in many cases refer to courts that were held by lords and which had kinds of judicial functions. This is but one example. Many acta mentioned the king's court and its judicial

[85] Among William I's acta, *placitum* also appears in the forged Bates, *Regesta*, nos. 14.ii, 19.i, 20.ii, 22 (all for Battle Abbey), 99 (for Chertsey Abbey), 105 (for Coventry Abbey), 194 (for Malmesbury Abbey), 220 (for Ramsey Abbey), 290, 305, 318, 319, 320, 324, 328 (for Westminster Abbey). Most of these are in exemption clauses, which purport to convey exemption from pleas.

[86] *Henricus rex Anglorum Radulfo Basset, salutem. Precipio quod facias habere Vincentio abbati Abbendone curiam suam in Oxeneford, ita bene et plenarie sicut unquam ipsa ecclesia Abbendonensis uel aliquis antecessorum suorum melius et plenarius et honorificentius habuit. Et homines sui non placitent extra curiam suam, nisi abbas prius defecerit de recto in curia sua. Et sicut poteris inquirere per legales homines de Oxeneford, quod habere debeat curiam suam. Teste cancellario. Apud Wdestoca. Regesta*, ii. no. 1516; *Abingdon Chronicle*, ii. 232–5.

functions,[87] and a few used *curia* to designate courtyards or other enclosures,[88] but there were numerous ones that acknowledged or permitted a court belonging to a beneficiary.[89] It is also notable that this document uses the term *placitent*, pleading, to denote the activity that could take place in courts.

The idea that *curia* referred to the assembly and *placitum* to business transacted within the assembly was thereafter enforced consistently in royal acta, and this seems to have established norms about usage that were widely accepted. The words occur alongside each other in clearly distinct senses in two of the documents discussed above, Henry I's decree on the shire and hundred courts, and his grant of exemption to the archbishop of York from his decree on theft and judgements;[90] and the same can be found in many others, both genuine[91] and forged.[92] Setting up distinct categories allowed interests in law to be defined more precisely than they had been before, and allowed for other kinds of interest to operate alongside a lord's control of a court.

The pattern in the royal acta can be paralleled elsewhere. Much the same can be seen in texts that presented legal authority, or which tried to depict legal processes. It has already been noted that the *Quadripartitus* translation of the 1090s was variable and inconsistent in its terms for legal gatherings, and used a range of words without much sense that there was an agreed and settled

87 *Regesta*, ii. nos. 683, 961, 1000, 1037 (all for Abingdon Abbey); 1898 (for Bayeux Cathedral); 875 (for Binham Priory); 766 (for Burton Abbey); 871, 944, 1283 (for Canterbury Cathedral); 1096 (for St John's Colchester); 660 (for Durham Cathedral); 684 (for Ely Abbey); 1579 (for Fécamp Abbey); 934 (for Ghent Abbey); 1266 (for Glastonbury Abbey, forged); 1485 (for Gloucester Abbey); 1014 (for Goldcliff Priory, forged); 809 (for Longueville Priory); 1952 (for Montebourg Abbey); 762, 876 (for Norwich Cathedral); 1947 (for Odoin de Malpalu); 1451 (for Ramsey Abbey); 1898 (for Reginald); 1094 (for St Benet Hulme); 1019 (for Saint-Evroul); 1200 (for Troarn Abbey); 1178 (for Westminster Abbey); 1070 (for Winchester Cathedral).

88 *Regesta*, ii. nos. 939 (for Barnwell Priory); 1703 (for Canterbury Cathedral); 1704 (for St Augustine's Canterbury); 1618 (for Cluny Abbey); 819 (for Godfrey); 1414 (for Thorney Abbey).

89 *Regesta*, ii. nos. 654, 1516 (both for Abingdon Abbey); 529 (forged), 530, 1313, 1394 (all for Battle Abbey); 962 (for Bermondsey Priory); 1073 (for Burton Abbey); 1314 (for St Augustine's Canterbury); 768, 778, 1574 (for Durham Cathedral, mostly forged); 510 (for Lewes Priory, forged); 581, 582, 587, 1066, 1751 (for Ramsey Abbey); 495 (for Selby Abbey, maybe forged); 1869 (for Shrewsbury Abbey); 1536 (for Thetford Priory); 975 (for Thorney Abbey); 913, 914, 1323 (for Tynemouth Priory, some doubts); 1174, 1252 (for Westminster Abbey); 1482 (for Wymondham Priory); 518 (for York Minster); 1276 (for York, St Mary).

90 *Regesta*, ii. nos. 892 and 518.

91 *Regesta*, ii. nos. 525, 766, 898, 962, 973, 1094, 1283, 1485, 1516, 1536, 1579, 1618, 1869, 1956, and *The Early Charters of Waltham Abbey, 1062–1230*, ed. Rosalind Ransford (Woodbridge, 1989), 5, no. 4.

92 *Regesta*, ii. nos. 429, 510, 529, 530, 1313, 1394, 1574.

vocabulary for how they should be described. Yet, legal works written after 1100 are prolific in their use of the term *curia*. The term occurs more than forty times in the *Leges Henrici Primi* of 1108,[93] and many of those occurrences must refer to lordly courts rather than to the king's court or to courtyards and enclosures. The term also occurs a number of times in the shorter *Leges Edwardi Confessoris* of the 1140s, where the occurrences refer to ecclesiastical courts and baronial courts as varieties of the same kind of entity.[94] Not much later, *curia* appears in the *Libertas Londoniensis* tract where it explicitly refers to baronial and royal courts as equivalents.[95] Moreover, *curia* appears regularly in charters by individuals other than the king throughout the early twelfth century, as lords made arrangements concerning courts among themselves, or made arrangements concerning the management of disputes or potential disputes.[96]

## Conclusion

The processes that allowed lords to assert control over hundreds, and to create new courts for their dependents on their lands, seem to have originated among the lords themselves, and to have reflected their ambitions and aspirations. Kings sometimes had a role in recognising and validating those actions, but the inspiration seems to have arisen from among the lords themselves. Their actions had considerable consequences for kings, in that lordly control over courts would have made it harder for kings to interact with their subjects directly. Clearly there was debate over how to deal with this. Largely, the solutions adopted accepted the aims which underpinned the moves to create lords' courts, and involved royal recognition of the reality and legitimacy of the courts controlled by lords. Thus, Henry I acknowledged that lords had jurisdiction over their dependents, and simply tried to regulate competing claims to jurisdiction in some circumstances; he tacitly accepted the enterprise of lords' courts. Yet

93 *Leges Henrici Primi*, 8.1b; 9.4; 9.10a; 16; 25.1; 25.2; 26.1; and many others. For an instance which shows that lordly courts in their judicial aspect were signified by many of these occurrences, see *Leges Henrici Primi*, 25.1: 'tractetur placitum in curia domini sui'.

94 *Leges Edwardi Confessoris*, 9.1: 'Barones autem, qui curias suas habent de hominibus suis …'.

95 *Libertas Londoniensis*, 2: ed. Felix Liebermann, *Die Gesetze der Angelsachsen* (three volumes, Halle, 1898–1916), i. 673.

96 For example, among the charters of the earls of Gloucester up to approximately 1150 the following examples include the word *curia*: Robert B. Patterson, *Earldom of Gloucester Charters: The Charters and Scribes of the Earls and Countesses of Gloucester to AD 1217* (Oxford, 1973), nos. 44, 95, 106, 109, 151, 177, 286, 287. Examples could be proliferated from other collections of charters.

Henry's acceptance of the idea that courts and jurisdiction could be owned went beyond that; he applied those same ideas to himself. Thus, from early in his reign he claimed that the hundreds belonged to him, much as other courts belonged to lords. Earlier kings had not done this in these terms,[97] but instead the hundreds were understood as having a communal and local basis, not as being vehicles of royal authority alone. This claim may well have been understood at the time not as an innovation but as a reassertion of an assumed past position. This development meant that kings had a vehicle for their authority in the localities, and could use the enforcement of attendance as a means of interacting with their subjects, with lords and with their courts. Henry's decision ensured that the hundred did not go the way of the *mallus*.

Henry also, through his charters and decrees, brought about a crucial distinction that allowed for the successful operation and control of courts in this system. In the later eleventh century there was no technical vocabulary to describe courts or the activities that went on within them. Many words were in use, but they were not deployed consistently in the eleventh century, so there was no agreement about what an assembly convened for the purposes of lordly functions and the adjudication of disputes should be called. This may not have had a great effect upon the actual operations of these assemblies, for they depended on the differential power relationships between lords and their dependents, for which assemblies were in many ways a demonstration and actualisation. Yet, it mattered much more how these assemblies were described when their legitimacy, status and interrelationships were being debated and decided. Consensus over how these assemblies were to be described allowed them to be claimed and to be compared. As in so many settings, naming is claiming, and allowed the parameters of these assemblies to be defined. Here, again, the key decisions seem to have been made by those close to Henry I, and were disseminated through consistent choices about words in his acta. His decrees made a distinction between two central concepts; *curia* (court) and *placitum* (plea). The two were often used interchangeably before,[98] but they came to describe different matters, and that distinction seems first to be made in these decrees. A court was an assembly of people who could transact business; a plea was an item of business done within a court. Separating and defining these concepts meant that it could now be possible that (for example) someone representing the king could make a plea in a lord's court, and that this did not imply the takeover of that court.

Linked to this, Henry I through his charters and decrees claimed that some kinds of business, categorised as *placita* (pleas), belonged to the king. These were in areas where kings had long carried out work in their own interests, but

97 Lambert, *Law and Order*, 243–50.

98 *Dictionary of Medieval Latin from British Sources*, 537–8, *sub verbo curia*; 2301–2, *sub verbo placitum*.

in each case an argument was made that flagrant abuse meant that kings should act in the public interest to solve a problem by claiming exclusive claims over it. In each case, these were accompanied by a marked increase in the level of punishment. Thus, for instance, Henry ordered that all thieves should be hanged; this was much harsher than the provisions in the Anglo-Saxon laws, which set out that lords could intervene to protect their dependents when they were accused of theft. The concept of the king's pleas was a novelty, but it encapsulated older ideas and allowed for their continued enforcement. The king also claimed that some kinds of business should be dealt with in particular courts. The exemptions granted to the archbishop of York indicate that the theft and counterfeiting were allocated to the king's own courts rather than to others. The same source also indicates that the presence of particular officers, and the use of certain procedures, were defined as essential for carrying out some kinds of business. The decree on the shires and hundreds likewise laid down that certain kinds of business should properly go to certain courts.

# 7

# Pleas and Justices in the Early Twelfth Century

The previous chapter set out how the distinction between *curia* and *placitum* appeared, and how it was important for the definition of what lords and others claimed. From the early twelfth century the distinction was fundamental to how claims in kinds of legal business were described. Among the most significant applications of these categories was their use in relation to the idea of the pleas of the crown. This was one of the key claims used by kings to project their authority out into the shires, and it has been prominent in the historiography.[1] It has tended to be understood in terms of how royal claims developed over time and the strength of kingship, from the statements about the king's interests in 2 Cnut to the more comprehensive coverage in the Assize of Clarendon and even in Glanvill.[2] There has been much debate over what the changing lists of royal interests meant, and what those changes indicate about the developing strength and authority of kings.[3] The list of royal interests went through distinct phases in how it was described and categorised, and it is likely that these changes indicate something about how these interests were managed over time. In the law 2 Cnut 12, there is a list of the king's interests which described them quite vaguely as rights or *gerihta* (or as *iura* in the *Quadripartitus* translation); it is only in the continuation of this passage in 2 Cnut 15 that a *wite* or financial penalty is noted, which indicates that the king could draw some financial benefit from these matters. By the later eleventh century, the interest of the king in some of these

1 The literature on the king's rights and pleas is large, and tends to divide into two trends; one is concerned with the power of the later Anglo-Saxon state, and the other with the model of administrative kingship. On the former see T. B. Lambert, 'Royal Protections and Private Justice: A Reassessment of Cnut's "Reserved Pleas"', in *English Law before Magna Carta: Felix Liebermann and* Die Gesetze der Angelsachsen, ed. Stefan Jurasinski, Lisi Oliver and Andrew Rabin (Leiden and Boston, 2010), 157–75, and the literature cited therein. On the latter see Judith A. Green, *The Government of England under Henry I* (Cambridge, 1986), chapter 5.

2 2 Cnut 12–15; *Leges Henrici Primi*, 10–13; *The Treatise on the Laws and Customs of the Realm of England Commonly Called Glanvill*, 1.2, ed. G. D. G. Hall and M. T. Clanchy (Oxford, 1993), 3.

3 T. B. Lambert, 'Royal Protections and Private Justice: A Reassessment of Cnut's "Reserved Pleas"', in *English Law before Magna Carta: Felix Liebermann and* Die Gesetze der Angelsachsen, ed. Stefan Jurasinski, Lisi Oliver and Andrew Rabin (Leiden and Boston, 2010), 157–75, and the literature cited therein.

matters could be described as a *forisfactura* or forfeiture,[4] which again draws attention to the financial aspect of the king's involvement in these matters. Much of the historiography on crown pleas and their antecedents has focussed on the content of the claims that kings would raise, and has taken the number of themes that kings called their own as an index of the strength of kingship. This approach regards rights, forfeitures and pleas as essentially synonyms. Yet, these changing patterns in the meanings of words are probably meaningful, and say something about the ways in which kings could interact with localities, and how they could claim and demand their dues. It may be that *how* kings enforced their claims was just as important as *what* comprised those claims.

In Cnut's time, the claiming of the king's *gerihta* or *iura* was probably straightforward. Disputes and claims of all kinds were held in the hundred court and the shire court. These could arise in many ways, whether from individual accusations and appeals or from the activity of panels of twelve thegns, as prescribed in 3 Æthelred 3.[5] They would have been heard before the assembly as a whole, and determined in quite traditional ways, through bringing together sufficient numbers of oath-helpers, through the ordeal, or through agreement of one kind or another. These hearings would have been public, and it would have been possible for any of those present to raise their own claims to some parts of the proceedings or outcome. In many of these, there would have been a king's representative who would have been able to step in and claim something on the king's behalf, even if the claim or dispute had originated somewhere else. The sheriff was an important element in the shire court from an early date, and was probably involved in some hundreds as well; also, there were many royal reeves on royal estates or in towns, and they could also have claimed dues and forfeitures for kings.[6] This assumes a rather administrative model in which dues had to be claimed by specific officers; it might be assumed that the prestige and ideological power of kingship meant that some dues and forfeitures might merely be handed over to the king's representatives. The ways in which the communal hundreds and shires operated meant that they could have been efficient in ensuring that all kinds of business that could be of interest to kings was heard before them. This

4 Great Domesday Book, fo. 1r–v: Kent, D1–10 and C11–25; fo. 56v: Berkshire, B10–11; fo. 172r: Worcestershire, C4–5; fo. 179r: Herefordshire, C1–15; fo. 252r: Shropshire, C1–14; fo. 262v: Cheshire, C1–25; fo. 280v: Nottinghamshire, S1–6; fo. 298v: Yorkshire, C37–40; fo. 376v: Lincolnshire, C32–3; Frederick Pollock and Frederic Maitland, *The History of English Law Before the Time of Edward I* (second edition, Cambridge, 1898), i. 454.

5 Raoul C. Van Caenegem, 'Public Prosecution of Crime in Twelfth-Century England', in *Church and Government in the Middle Ages: Essays Presented to C. R. Cheney on his Seventieth Birthday*, ed. C. N. L. Brooke, D. E. Luscombe, G. H. Martin and D. Owen (Cambridge, 1976), 41–76, at 41–7.

6 For an example of this see Great Domesday Book, fo. 1r : Kent D13.

assumption that claiming the king's dues was relatively unproblematic seems to underlie the laws, which set out no administrative mechanism for collecting dues or for transmitting them to the king.

Yet, this straightforward pattern was disrupted by the processes and developments set out in Chapters 3, 4 and 5 of this book. Some privileged lords came to control hundreds, which meant that they acquired a strong influence over the dealings of those who engaged with that hundred. Sometimes, this seems to have involved the exclusion of royal officers such as sheriffs, as in the case of the bishop of Worcester's hundred of Oswaldslow.[7] More commonly, the business done in hundreds broke up into lesser units. The small, private courts created by lords as *halimota* were meant to allow them to control many of the kinds of business that arose on their lands and among their dependents, and to do so without the oversight or interference of others. The appearance of these lesser courts meant that much business about the tenure of those who worked the land, about disputes internal to the estate, about agricultural discipline and so forth was now dealt with at this level, rather than within the hundred. Yet the creation of these courts was through a largely informal process, and there was no comprehensive division of duties between the hundreds and the *halimota*. In these circumstances, what was to stop a lord dealing with a case of theft, perhaps one involving people solely on his own lands and in his lordship, in his own court? If it were dealt with in such an assembly, then news of it would not necessarily reach up to the hundred. In such circumstances, the idea of the king's rights became problematic, and the ability of kings to rely on their future enforcement might have faded. The problems in enforcing the king's claims in new circumstances would have brought about many kinds of perhaps unwelcome change; it would have meant that kings could no longer carry out their fundamental obligations to preserve order and prevent sin, and they would have lost revenue arising from forfeitures in relation to these claims. The problems would thus have been both ideological and practical.

The continuation of the king's rights and forfeitures was accomplished by a set of developments seen early in Henry I's reign. Some have already been described and analysed above in Chapter 6; Henry and subsequent kings claimed that hundreds were their courts, even though their predecessors had not done so in those terms, so that they could claim that the hundred and attendance at it was a vehicle for their lordship as other lords used their courts; and from Henry's time the king's clerks imposed a sharp and consistent distinction between *curia* and *placitum*, so that one meant a court and one meant business transacted within a court – hitherto the words had often been used interchangeably – and which allowed clear categorisation of the kinds of dues that kings and others claimed

7 Great Domesday Book, fo. 172v: Worcestershire 2.1. On this see Chapter 3 above.

in courts and pleas through imposing consistent categories. These were largely structural changes that set a framework for the continuation of royal enforcement of claims. There were other changes that came beyond that. First, the phrases 'king's pleas' or 'royal pleas' came into regular use. What set this development apart from older ideas of the king's rights was much more than a small terminological change. *Placitum*, a plea, was linked to the verb *placitare*, to plead; it was a term than implied activity. From the early twelfth century, the king's pleas were matters where someone actively pursued cases in the king's interest, summoning participants into the king's hundreds and bringing accusations against them. The shift in vocabulary thus marked a different approach to the enforcement and maintenance of the king's claims. Second, again from early in Henry I's reign, there appeared a new class of royal functionaries who carried out the work of managing pleas in the king's hundreds: the justices. The appearance of the king's pleas marked a moment when kings began to pursue their claims much more aggressively than hitherto, precisely because the proliferation of courts meant that they had to devise new means to protect their position.

## The King's Rights and the King's Pleas

Kings claimed many kinds of business and activity, and these claims have formed much of the basis for discussion of kings' legal impact on their subjects and kingdom. There was clearly a perception that these claims were important, for lists of them were included in various sources, and they differ substantially. There is one in the law 2 Cnut,[8] and there are many in the individual shire sections of Domesday Book,[9] though these often concern local claims rather than ones of general applicability; there is a particularly extensive list from the early twelfth century in the *Leges Henrici Primi*, chapters 10 and 11, and potentially through to chapter 13, and there is even another list from later in the twelfth century in Glanvill.[10] It is tempting to think of these as a set, and that the king's pleas represented some kind of fundamental set of royal claims that linked the Anglo-Saxon kings to the Angevins and beyond, but that is probably not what the idea of the king's pleas originally signified. The idea of the king's pleas was in origin about how they were collected and managed, not about their attachment to the king.

8 2 Cnut 12–15.

9 Great Domesday Book, fo. 1r–v: Kent, D1–10 and C11–25; fo. 56v: Berkshire, B10–11; fo. 172r: Worcestershire, C4–5; fo. 179r: Herefordshire, C1–15; fo. 252r: Shropshire, C1–14; fo. 262v: Cheshire, C1–25; fo. 280v: Nottinghamshire, S1–6; fo. 298v: Yorkshire, C37–40; fo. 376v: Lincolnshire, C32–3.

10 *The Treatise on the Laws and Customs of the Realm of England Commonly Called Glanvill*, 1.2, ed. G. D. G. Hall and M. T. Clanchy (Oxford, 1993), 3.

The phrase 'king's pleas' or 'crown pleas' first appears regularly in the early twelfth century, in the reign of Henry I. There is nothing on this idea in the Anglo-Saxon laws, for the phrase does not precisely match any in Old English, and the first commentary on its meaning can be found in the *Leges Henrici Primi*, which must be dated with the rest of the text to 1108–9.[11] The passage is a complex one. It starts off in ways that point towards the Anglo-Saxon past. It begins with the claims of the king, described here as *iura*, the same term used in the *Quadripartitus* translation of 2 Cnut 12. The list of claims that follows contains many that appear before 1066, but which became less important as part of the king's claims during the twelfth century, such as *flemenefyrmth*,[12] and there is quite a lot of Old English vocabulary there as well. Overall, this appears as a rather conservative assessment of the king's claims, which owes much to the Anglo-Saxon laws. Yet there are also some items that cannot owe much to the Anglo-Saxon past. *Castellatio trium scannorum* has no precedent from pre-Conquest England, and indeed its meaning is not clear at all; it might represent an adaptation of Norman customs rather than English, and so point to kinds of change in the decades before 1108.[13] Others seem more novel; there are pleas (*placitum* in the source) about the neglect of royal writs, slander against the king, and so forth. Perhaps the most striking statement in that list comes at the end. There, all these claims are described as *placita regis*, in contrast to their designation as *iura* at the start of the list, and the real significance of the list is explained; these are claims that belonged to the king directly, and were not part of the shire farms of the sheriffs and their underlings. The significance of this list is that all these claims were dealt with in a particular way.

The following chapters in the *Leges Henrici Primi* give other lists of kinds of business that were dealt with in distinctive manners. Thus, chapter 11 covers ecclesiastical pleas in which the king had a stake, and which would presumably have been carried out in a different way from other pleas, either through the close involvement of the clergy or even through the developing ecclesiastical courts, though there is no specific comment on how these claims were managed and enforced. Chapter 12 has a list of matters which would generate *wer* and *wite* (in other words, they would have been dealt with under the principles set out in the Anglo-Saxon laws), and where presumably the pleas would be composite in nature, in that families, lords and the king would all have some claims, and those

11 Nicholas Karn, 'Rethinking the *Leges Henrici Primi*', in *English Law before Magna Carta: Felix Liebermann and* Die Gesetze der Angelsachsen, ed. Stefan Jurasinski, Lisi Oliver and Andrew Rabin (Leiden and Boston, 2010), 199–220, at 216–17.

12 On this see Florence E. Harmer, *Anglo-Saxon Writs* (second edition, Stamford, 1989), 81–2.

13 Richard Eales, 'Royal Power and Castles in Norman England', rpt in *Anglo-Norman Castles*, ed. Robert Liddiard (Woodbridge, 2003), 41–67, at 62–3.

would need to proceed by negotiation. Chapter 13, meanwhile, gives a list of matters which would put a man into the king's mercy. It overlaps substantially with chapter 10, though chapter 13 does not give indications for how these matters should have been handled. The following chapters then cover other matters that belonged to kings but which were managed in different ways, including reliefs, Danegeld and the forest pleas.[14] The aim of these sections overall is not to convey messages about how much control kings could have over legal matters, but rather to explain difference, and how it was that royal claims were divided into different categories which were handled in distinct manners. The king's pleas of the early twelfth century were far from the totality of the king's claims.

The *Leges Henrici Primi* thus shows that by the early twelfth century there were some kinds of royal claims which were classified as the king's pleas, and that, unless particular arrangements had been made, they did not belong to the sheriffs or to other royal officers such as reeves, and were not included within the shire farms. This might be interpreted in more than one way. It might mean that sheriffs and reeves had no part in the management of this segment of the king's claims, or it might refer simply to financial arrangements, in which these matters were pursued by the usual network of sheriffs and reeves, but the proceeds of that activity were accounted for through different channels. The former option does not mean that sheriffs and others were excluded from the management of the king's claims, for the lists of claims in these chapters of the *Leges Henrici Primi* do not include many direct references to the king's claims over his own estates, or to customary dues, labour services and so forth. Yet questions must arise about the practicality of excluding the king's pleas from the shire farms. Sheriffs were not salaried, and their incentive for working came in the form of any surplus they might collect in excess of the sum they had to render each year to the king's treasury. If sums of money arising from the claims listed in chapter 10 of the *Leges Henrici Primi* were not included within the shire farms, then it is not at all clear that sheriffs could have some hope of drawing profit from their enforcement. In such circumstances, then there was no clear reward for sheriffs and others in pursuing instances of theft and so forth.

The solution to this conundrum is contained in other points made in the *Leges Henrici Primi*. There is little in this source on the legal role of sheriffs, or of the reeves of royal estates. Instead, the *Leges Henrici Primi* includes a lot of references to the role and functions of the justice (*iustitia* in Latin), and these references make it clear that the justice was responsible to the king and his authority, and that the justice had a considerable role in transacting legal business, including accusation, summoning and so forth. The functions allocated to justices in the *Leges Henrici Primi* were not judicial ones – they did not form

[14] *Leges Henrici Primi*, 14–19.

judgements – , but rather were concerned with the bringing of pleas of all kinds. It is notable that the role of justice was a novelty in 1108–9 when the writer of the *Leges Henrici Primi* was at work.[15] The reasons for dating the appearance of justices to the very early 1100s will be discussed further below, but such a date would indicate that the arrangements described in the *Leges Henrici Primi* reflected current practice closely, and could not simply represent an adaptation of older materials – after all, the older materials contained no references to justices or to pleas, because those terms had not been in common use earlier, where they occur frequently in the *Leges Henrici Primi*. It is possible, perhaps likely, that the arrangements described in there were not ones that went back to the Anglo-Saxon laws – most of what is in the *Leges Henrici Primi* cannot be paralleled in the older texts – and it need not be assumed that any arrangements there were old, unless there are specific sources that indicate that.[16] In the case of the classification of royal pleas in chapters 10 to 13, it might be suggested that these arrangements were new, and that they represented an alteration in how the king's claims were enforced.

## King's Justices in the Early Twelfth Century

The *Leges Henrici Primi* includes the term *iustitia* very frequently; there are almost eighty occurrences of the word therein. Some of these must mean justice in the sense of right, but most attribute functions and actions to the term, and

15 *Leges Henrici Primi*, 6.4 refers to a new method of impleading, which should probably be linked with this; and on this Raoul C. Van Caenegem, 'Public Prosecution of Crime in Twelfth-Century England', in *Church and Government in the Middle Ages: Essays Presented to C. R. Cheney on his Seventieth Birthday*, ed. C. N. L. Brooke, D. E. Luscombe, G. H. Martin and D. Owen (Cambridge, 1976), 41–76, at 53.

16 There is some evidence that king's reeves could have a role in managing pleas before 1066. Great Domesday Book, fo. 1r: Kent D13 shows that they might claim forfeitures. Also, Robert Malarteis, discussed below as a royal official who claimed pleas for the king in Henry I's time, held lands in Huntingdonshire and Bedfordshire (*The Great Roll of the Pipe for the Thirty First Year of the Reign of King Henry I, Michaelmas 1130*, ed. Judith A. Green, Pipe Roll Society 95, new series 57 (2012), 38. 83). Probable descendants of his held lands at Washingley in Huntingdonshire (*The Great Roll of the Pipe for the Thirteenth Year of the Reign of King Henry II, AD 1166–1167*, Pipe Roll Society 11 (1889), 166), which was probably land that in 1066 and 1086 had belonged to a king's thegn (Great Domesday Book, fo. 207v: Huntingdonshire 29.1), and other that may have belonged to another one (Great Domesday Book, fo. 206r: Huntingdonshire 19.3). On this see H. G. Richardson and G. O. Sayles, *The Governance of Medieval England from the Conquest to Magna Carta* (Edinburgh, 1963), 174–7, and Doris M. Stenton, *English Justice between the Norman Conquest and the Great Charter, 1066–1215* (London, 1965), 61. It is possible though wholly unprovable that there was some continuity in function to match that in tenure.

so can only be taken as references to justices as functionaries. This, of course, fits well with the way in which individuals are identified as justices in narratives of pleas, in charters, and so forth. Yet the *Leges Henrici Primi* offers the most detailed and the most coherent account of justices, for most of the other sources for these individuals are not much more than mentions, and older texts do not mention justices at all.[17] The account in the *Leges Henrici Primi* is thus of particular importance. So far as can be seen, it is original and does not draw on older sources, and it reflects a wider range of activity than can be seen in any other one source.

The *Leges Henrici Primi* shows that justices in the early twelfth century were responsible for pleading and managing pleas in the interest of the king, and that their pleading activities took precedence over the work of others in the courts. The *Leges Henrici Primi* explains how a plea should be handled if someone had been impleaded by a justice.[18] The term translated as 'impleaded' is *inplacitatus* or variants thereof; an act of impleading someone meant the initiation of a plea by accusation or other means, not that the justice was involved in the decision-making process.[19] The statements about impleading by justices in the *Leges Henrici Primi* show that justices were able to insist that cases where they had impleaded someone and where the plea involved the king's claims should be dealt with first.[20] This meant that they had a prior claim on those who were impleaded, comparable to that held by lords over their dependents.[21] The *Leges Henrici*

17 Justices do not appear in the Anglo-Saxon laws; they first appear in the *Leges Henrici Primi* of 1108–9, and are covered also in the so-called *Leges Edwardi Confessoris*, written during Stephen's reign.

18 *Leges Henrici Primi*, 43.1, 48.1a, 52.1, 63.1, 66.8–9.

19 Raoul C. Van Caenegem, 'Public Prosecution of Crime in Twelfth-Century England', in *Church and Government in the Middle Ages: Essays Presented to C. R. Cheney on his Seventieth Birthday*, ed. C. N. L. Brooke, D. E. Luscombe, G. H. Martin and D. Owen (Cambridge, 1976), 41–76, at 53.

20 The use of the term *placitare* in the early twelfth century can be understood most fully from the *Leges Henrici Primi*. Pleading was something done in court by those involved in it; thus, *Leges Henrici Primi* 49.1 states that there were some matters in which it was necessary to respond, but not to plead at once (*Quedam cause sunt de quibus statim respondere, sicut dictum est, set non statim placitare necesse est* …). Pleading in this sense must have been something done by the participants in the case, as a means of making a denial and defence. It cannot refer to the holding of a court (though this is suggested by R. E. Latham, *Revised Medieval Latin Word-List from British and Irish Sources* (Oxford, 1965), 354), because that idea of convening and holding rights in a court is described in the *Leges Henrici Primi* 27.1 as the holding of courts, not as pleading (*Habeant autem uauasores qui liberas terras tenent placita* …). Where pleading is mentioned in the *Leges Henrici Primi*, it is as a stage in a process in court (49.2a; 50.1; 57.5; 61.5; 61.13b; 61.16; 61.17).

21 For instance, *Leges Henrici Primi*, 51.5, 55, 58, etc. On many of these references see Raoul C. Van Caenegem, 'Public Prosecution of Crime in Twelfth-Century England',

*Primi* comments on how justices could summon people to court;[22] how they took charge of *murdrum* cases;[23] how they could set the day for a plea;[24] how, if a justice summoned someone to the shire court, a failure to attend was regarded as an infraction of royal claims and was fined as such;[25] how justices could distrain people just as a lord might;[26] and so on and so forth. Overall, the *Leges Henrici Primi* repeatedly draws attention to how justices could plead against someone, presumably referring to advocacy undertaken by them. These references do not give specific details about how proceedings would develop, but show that the writer conceived that justices were enmeshed in pleas with other litigants. For instance, it was regarded as a failure punishable by a monetary fine if a litigant who had been impleaded by a royal justice left on advice and did not respond to the *inculpatio*, which presumably means a statement of the claim against him.[27] Elsewhere, the text lays stress on how a refusal to engage with or respond directly to a claim made by a justice was a serious matter.[28] Among these references is one which distinguishes between the role of the justice in initiating a plea, and the role of judges in determining it.[29]

The *Leges Henrici Primi* is not the only source which describes justices in these terms. A similar impression is conveyed in the *Leges Edwardi Confessoris*, which probably reflects legal behaviour in the 1130s and 1140s. This shows the variety in the uses of the term, for there could be justiciars of hundreds and even of tithings.[30] Justices were responsible for managing *murdrum* cases, which presumably meant that they oversaw the presentments needed as part of it, and would pursue financial penalties;[31] they were involved in summoning people to

in *Church and Government in the Middle Ages: Essays Presented to C. R. Cheney on his Seventieth Birthday*, ed. C. N. L. Brooke, D. E. Luscombe, G. H. Martin and D. Owen (Cambridge, 1976), 41–76, at 53–4.

22 *Leges Henrici Primi*, 42.2.

23 *Leges Henrici Primi*, 92.3.

24 *Leges Henrici Primi*, 60. That justices might initiate pleas and order that judgements be made is implied in David M. Smith, *English Episcopal Acta* 1: *Lincoln, 1076–1185* (Oxford, 1980), no. 185, printed in F. M. Stenton, 'Acta Episcoporum', *The Cambridge Historical Journal* 3 (1929), 1–14, at 12, where Robert de Chesney, bishop of Lincoln, ordered the justice and others that henceforth judgements, which in this letter probably means ordeals, should only be done in St Peter's church in Northampton, not elsewhere in the town.

25 *Leges Henrici Primi*, 53.1.

26 *Leges Henrici Primi*, 51.5.

27 *Leges Henrici Primi*, 48.1a.

28 *Leges Henrici Primi*, 34.5; 52.1.

29 *Leges Henrici Primi*, 34.5.

30 *Leges Edwardi Confessoris*, 28. For another occurrence see *Regesta*, iii. no. 105.

31 *Leges Edwardi Confessoris*, 15. Compare *Leges Henrici Primi*, 92.3.

court, and could make attachments as a means of ensuring their attendance;[32] and they could initiate the process of ordeal.[33] The overall impression given is very much like that in the *Leges Henrici Primi*.

Narratives of disputes from Henry I's reign support the same point, that there were royal functionaries who concerned themselves with accusing individuals of having done things that were implicated in some of the king's claims. Much the clearest example of this is the narrative written by Hervey, bishop of Ely, concerning the misadventures of a man named Bricstan, and which concluded with a miracle story. Hervey's letter has been preserved through its inclusion in Orderic Vitalis's great history. It describes how a man named Robert *Malarteis* pursued a would-be monk of Ely in the interest of the king and with his authority:

> When his action was generally known, for although he was not a man of the first rank he was nevertheless of some repute, a certain minister of King Henry, who was more particularly a servant of the devil with wolf-like fangs, appeared on the scene.
>
> Now indeed, so that you may know who and what manner of man he was, I will digress a little. His name was Robert and he was nicknamed *Malarteis*, from the Latin meaning 'ill-doer'. The name was deserved. For he seemed to have no function except to catch men out. All men, I repeat; monks and clerks, knights and peasants, men of every order, whether living under a religious vow or otherwise; but, lest I be accused of lying, this was his constant practice wherever he could exercise his malice. He accused all equally whenever he could, striving with all his might to harm everyone. When he injured one or more men he was numbered among those of whom it is said, 'They rejoice to do evil, and delight in evil and subversive acts'. If he could find no valid reason for condemning him, he became an inventor of falsehood and father of lies through the devil who spoke in him. But since no one, not even one who had been his constant companion since childhood, could relate, let alone write down, all the evil deeds of this man who is rightly called 'Thousand wiles' I will return to my subject.
>
> When, as I have said, it was rumoured abroad that Bricstan wished to put on the habit of religion, Robert, following the teaching of his master who always lies and deceives, appeared on the scene. He, beginning to heap falsehood on falsehood, said to us: 'Know that this man, Bricstan, is a thief, who has seized the king's money by larceny (*in latrocinio*) and hidden it, and is trying to take the habit to escape judgement and punishment for his crime, not for any other kind of salvation. For he found hidden treasure, and by secretly stealing from it has become a usurer. Since he is guilty of the crimes of larceny and usury (*Tantorum itaque reus criminum, latrocinii videlicet et usurae* ...), he fears to

32 *Leges Edwardi Confessoris*, 6.

33 *Leges Edwardi Confessoris*, 9.

come before the king or his judges.[34] Therefore I have been sent here to you at the king's command, and I forbid you to receive him into your community'. We therefore, hearing the king's prohibition and fearing to incur his wrath, refused to receive the man among us. What next? He was sent under surety to trial.[35]

The letter was manifestly designed to denigrate Robert *Malarteis*, for his wrongful accusation of Bricstan was the occasion for the miracle story which was the real message of this communication. The letter does, however, include some important points about the activity of royal representatives, and it connects with the impression given in the *Leges Henrici Primi* and the *Leges Edwardi Confessoris*. The passage above does not concern the debate in court, but rather the process by which Bricstan was brought into court. It starts by noting

[34] The text has *iudicum*, which Chibnall translated as justices. *Iudicum*, however, comes from *iudex*, judge, not *iustitia*, justice. The term *iudex* was commonly used for those who made judgements under traditional procedure, and who were suitors of the court rather than royal representatives. On these see Hudson, *Oxford History*, chapters 4 and 13.

[35] *Hoc cum a multis audiretur, nam licet maioris non esset, aliquantulæ tamen famæ homo ille erat, quidam Henrici regis minister, specialiter autem diaboli servus armatus lupinis dentibus accurrit.*

*Verum ut sciatis quis vel qualis iste esset, paululum a proposito digrediamur. Hic Rodbertus nominatur, et Malarteis cognominatur, quod nos latina lingua 'malum artificem' exponimus. Nec immerito. Ipse nanque nullum penitus aliud officium habebat, nisi tantum omnibus insidiari. Omnibus dico, monachis scilicet vel clericis, militibus et rusticis et totius ordinis hominibus tam religione famosis quam aliter viventibus, sed ne mendacium incurrere videar, frequenter hoc agebat quocumque suam maliciam dilatare valebat. Omnes itaque æqualiter pro posse accusabat, ut omnes in damnum mitteret totis viribus elaborabat. Cum alicui vel pluribus nocebat, inter illos numerabatur, de quibus dicitur, 'Letantur cum male fecerint, et exultant in rebus pessimis'. Si autem ex vero dampnare nequibat, per eum qui in illo loquebatur diabolum inventor falsitatis mendax et pater eius efficiebatur. Sed cum nullus etiam cum eo ab infantia inseparabiliter permanens huius viri mala non dico scribere, sed etiam referre valeat, nam iure mille artifex vocaretur, redeamus ad incepta.*

*Audito ut diximus rumore predicti viri religionis habitum arripere cupientis, magistri sui doctrinam qui semper mentitur aut decipit sequutus, advenit ille Rodbertus. Qui dicturus mendacium a mendacio incipiens, ait nobis 'Hunc hominem Bricstan videlicet furem esse, pecuniam regis propriam in latrocinio habere, celare, et ut criminis huius iudicium et pœnam evadere valeat, non causa alterius salutis monachatum quærere sciatis. Ipse nanque thesaurum occultum invenit, ex quo furtim sublato fœnerator effectus est. Tantorum itaque reus criminum, latrocinii videlicet et usuræ, presentiæ regis vel iudicum metuit assistere. Quapropter huc ad vos ex regis imperio missus, interdico ne illum in vestro collegio audeatis recipere'. Nos autem audita regis defensione, timentes iram eius incurrere, noluimus hunc hominum cœtui nostro coniungere. Quid plura? Sub fideiussoribus missus, ducitur ad iudicium.*

Orderic Vitalis, *Historia Ecclesiastica*, ed. and trans. Marjorie Chibnall, *The Ecclesiastical History of Orderic Vitalis* (6 volumes, Oxford, 1969–81), iii. 346–60; thence in Van Caenegem, *Lawsuits*, no. 204. This extract is at pp. 168–9.

that Bricstan was moderately well known; repute and reputation had long been important in the transaction of legal business. Robert *Malarteis* interested himself in Bricstan's dealings because he had heard rumours about them. On this basis, Robert *Malarteis* accused Bricstan of theft, robbery and usury, and on this basis prevented Bricstan from achieving his ambition of being received as a monk at Ely; instead, he summoned him to a formal trial in a court. The narrative proceeds to give an account of that trial, with the implication that Robert *Malarteis* carried out the actual pleading. It was held before eminent men of the district, including the bishop who wrote the letter from which the case is known, two local abbots and others, though the nature of the assembly is not actually stated; the eminence of those present might be taken as an indication that it was more likely to be the shire than the hundred, though it is hardly conclusive. What is significant is that Robert *Malarteis* accused someone of matters which clearly fell within the categories of the king's pleas – theft and robbery – and that, just as described in the *Leges Henrici Primi*, the initiation of a claim or accusation by the king's representative took precedence over claims and arrangements made by others; thus Bricstan was prevented from becoming a monk. The kinds of functions carried out by Robert *Malarteis* in this plea, and by the justices in the *Leges Henrici Primi* and the *Leges Edwardi Confessoris*, both involved the active pursuit of the king's claims by individuals based locally who would have been able to initiate and manage legal business, and who would have been aware of local gossip and local knowledge sufficiently to be able to identify and pursue the interests of the king. While these sources from the early twelfth century are consistent in noting that such arrangements were in place, and are corroborated by others which mention aspects of these kinds of activity, there is nothing like this in earlier sources. Sources from before the early twelfth century are not consistent in identifying figures such as justices and Robert *Malarteis* who might have claimed some of the king's claims, nor of the methods for claiming claims that appear in these sources.

The legal books and the narrative cited above are united on one point; the role of these royal functionaries was to pursue cases, to accuse people and summon them to court – one of the king's courts, for preference – and use that opportunity as a means for enforcing the king's claims and extracting some profit thence. They differed from later justices in that their role was not judicial, and they did not make judgements. Their presence did not disrupt traditional procedure from before the Norman Conquest, for the procedure adopted in courts was still dominated by the attendees or suitors, who still embodied the custom of their districts and formulated judgements in terms of the acquired knowledge of those who comprised the court.[36] A good example can be seen in the much discussed

[36] Hudson, *Oxford History*, chapter 13.

1127 plea between the archbishop of Canterbury and the abbot of St Augustine's, Canterbury, over claims in the port of Sandwich;[37] the narrative draws attention to the presence of a justice, who in this case was William, sheriff of Kent, but he seemingly said nothing during the plea and did not contribute to its settlement. Instead, the claims of the two competing sides were determined by a panel of locals, carefully drawn from different lands. They declared what they thought the rightful situation was, and their statement was accepted by the others present at the meeting of the court.

The particular role of royal functionaries has been noted before. In a powerful though relatively neglected article from 1976 titled 'Public Prosecution of Crime in Twelfth-Century England', Raoul Van Caenegem argued that the early twelfth century saw the appearance of a class of royal prosecutors, who worked within the traditional courts to bring pleas on behalf of the king.[38] The framework within which this idea was presented can be questioned in a number of ways – the idea that 'crime' was used as an organising principle in early twelfth-century England is particularly problematic[39] – but the basic idea links very well with much of the evidence from the early twelfth century. Thus, losing the references to crime, it would be more acceptable to claim that kings moved towards a model in which they actively pursued their claims through a network of local representatives, who could watch and listen for incidents that might bring profit for the king and then pursue those claims through actions in courts. All this was developed as a means for conserving royal claims in a fast-changing environment where traditional methods might no longer work.

## Justices and Pleas

The advent of these royal representatives as advocates and pursuers of the king's claims and interests occurred in Henry I's reign, and it can probably be connected with the decrees that were promulgated in 1108, and which were discussed in Chapter 6 above. It seems likely that the appearance of justices did not simply mean that a new functionary appeared in local courts; there is a strong likelihood that their appearance coincided with changes in procedure, so that these new figures were not simply there to pursue the king's claims in general terms, but

[37] Van Caenegem, *Lawsuits*, no. 254.

[38] Raoul C. Van Caenegem, 'Public Prosecution of Crime in Twelfth-Century England', in *Church and Government in the Middle Ages: Essays Presented to C. R. Cheney on his Seventieth Birthday*, ed. C. N. L. Brooke, D. E. Luscombe, G. H. Martin and D. Owen (Cambridge, 1976), 41–76, esp. 50–61.

[39] Paul R. Hyams, 'Does it Matter When the English Began to Distinguish Between Crime and Tort?', in *Violence in Medieval Society*, ed. Richard Kaeuper (Woodbridge, 2000), 107–28.

rather were meant to use particular means to pursue particular kinds of cases. The *Leges Henrici Primi* includes a reference to a new method of impleading in 1108–9.[40] The development of new functionaries and new procedures was almost certainly linked, so that the one was meant to be means by which the other was carried out and enforced.

The key text for this is a writ in favour of Gerard, archbishop of York, which has already been discussed above in Chapter 6, in relation to the 1108 decrees, for it matches and corroborates chronicle evidence that Henry I promulgated a decree on theft in that year. The key statement is worth considering in detail:

> I will and command that Gerard, archbishop of York, in the lands of his churches and in all lands of the archbishopric of York, has his pleas in his court about his moneyers and about robbers and about all others; and he has all his laws and customs and [those] of all his churches concerning all things and just as well as Archbishop Thomas had in the time of my father and brother. And he shall carry out my new establishments (*statuta*) concerning judgements or concerning the pleas of thieves and false moneyers, and he shall do this through his own justices in his court.[41]

The above extract from the writ starts with the basic distinction between courts and pleas that appears from Henry I's reign, and specifically grants that the archbishop should have pleas in his own court about moneyers, robbers and others. This document is not about the control of a court or claims in a court, but about particular kinds of business in a court. It is the last sentence of the extract which is the most puzzling. It states that the new establishments ('*statuta*') of the king should be carried out by the archbishop's justices; the establishments themselves were about judgements and the pleas of thieves and false moneyers. This is neither clear nor precise, but it seems that there was some action or were some actions that were to be carried out by the archbishop's justices, and that this was a concession from the king which allowed the continuation of the archbishop's claims but which also ensured that whatever was laid out in the king's new establishments ('*statuta*') would be carried out, but under the direction of the archbishop's justices rather than other functionaries. Or, to put the same point in other terms, the archbishop could keep his court, and he would be allowed to carry out judgements and pleas of thieves and false moneyers within them, through his own justices. The archbishop's justices would ensure that the archbishop's influence was preserved, and that judgements and pleas of thieves and false moneyers would be done in his name.

40 *Leges Henrici Primi*, 6.4.

41 *Regesta*, ii. no. 518. This is from the copy in *Calendar of the Patent Rolls Preserved in the Public Record Office*, ed. Deputy Keeper of the Records (75 vols, London, 1901–86), *1338–40*, 166. For the Latin text see footnote 33 to Chapter 6 above.

The York writ is not a decree that tried to change the law as a whole across the kingdom, but rather a particular concession, which created local exceptions to what was meant to have been a general pattern. The exceptions envisaged for York in relation to this business may have been unique, or may have been only one example of a wider class, but now there seem to be no other survivors if there were any. The importance of the York writ is not so much for what it indicates about local conditions on the lands of the archbishops of York, but rather for what the terms of the exemption say about the lost decree on theft and judgements, which is mentioned therein and in a number of chronicle references.[42] It shows that the lost decree was not simply one which ordered that thieves should be dealt with, as some Anglo-Saxon royal decrees had done, but that it also laid down that there were particular things that should be done. This may be why the chronicle reference which is the most specific evidence for the lost decree, describes it as one on theft and judgements; it laid down how matters of theft should be dealt with, in other words it laid down a procedure for dealing with these matters. This would also explain why the writ of exemption to the archbishop of York stated that he should have these matters dealt with in his court, but also specified that the pleas should be dealt with by his justice.

The argument advanced in the previous few paragraphs is a speculative one, for it is concerned with attempts to reconstruct from vague references the terms of a lost royal decree, whose existence is certain but whose content is not. The observations and inferences made above can be put together to provide a picture of a lost decree which brought about substantial change to the ways in which theft and maybe other matters were dealt with. It seems to have claimed that theft was a matter that pertained to the king, and that the management of it should be under the control of the king. The exemption granted to the archbishop of York was probably a mirror of the lost royal decree; it granted that the archbishop could deal with matters concerning theft in his court, and that the plea would then be his, and that his officer, the justice, would manage it. This should probably be taken as an indication that the lost royal decree laid down that theft would be heard in the king's court, and probably the hundred since it had just been claimed as the king's court, that the plea was the king's, and that it would be managed by the king's representative. What the plea involved is not stated; it might have meant that the king's representatives would manage any business involving theft that arose, or it might mean that there were specific processes designed to identify and manage instances of theft, much as in the later Assize of Clarendon. The arrangements sketched out in the references to this lost royal decree envisage that there would be some royal representative who would manage business, even if that representative is not identified there. A solution might be found from the

[42] The evidence is set out and discussed in detail in Chapter 6 above.

context. Such arrangements in the early years of Henry I's reign might naturally be linked with the appearance of justices, which was noted and discussed earlier in this chapter. These were local representatives of the king who managed royal interests and pursued royal claims on the basis of local knowledge of the societies and populations within which they worked.

There is other evidence that, from the middle of Henry I's reign, certain categories of legal business were pursued more rigorously and consistently, whereas others were not treated in the same way. This can be seen in the rise of exemption clauses in royal acta. These are in principle similar to the document in favour of the archbishop of York discussed above; they were grants or recognitions in which the beneficiary was allowed exemption from the full implementation and claiming of the king's dues. These exemptions were granted in various forms in the early twelfth century, but developed a more consistent and organised form during the middle part of Henry I's reign, as can be seen in this writ from Barking Abbey:

> Henry king of the English to all his sheriffs and reeves and all his servants of all England in whose jurisdictions the abbess of Barking has lands, greeting! I command that Agnes,[43] abbess of Barking, holds all her land and men well and in peace, free of pleas and complaints and shires and hundreds and *warpeni* and all other things except murder and robbery (*excepto murdro et latrocinio*), so well and in peace and honourably as well as any of her predecessors held [them], and just as that church is accustomed and ought to have those customs and freedoms from of old. Witness, William d'Aubigny the Breton. At Cliffe.[44]

This grants to the abbey exemption from all kinds of pleas, but reserves to the king his interest in robbery and murder. The king's reservation of these while he surrendered other claims must represent a judgement that these matters were of greater meaning to him than the other matters allowed to the nuns. This focus on some matters which were kept under direct royal control is not seen before, and reflects rising royal interest in some matters to the exclusion of others. This

[43] Adelicia MS, but there was no abbess of Barking of this name; probably Agnes was meant; D. Knowles, C. N. L. Brooke and V. London, *The Heads of Religious Houses I: England and Wales, 940–1216* (second edition, Cambridge, 2001), 208, 290.

[44] *H(enricus) rex Angl(orum) omnibus uicecomitibus et prepositis et omnibus ministris suis totius Anglie in quorum balliuis abbatissa Berchingie terras habet salutem. Precipio quod A(gnes) abbatissa Berchingie teneat totam terram et homines suos bene et in pace quietos de placitis et querelis et sciris et hundredis et warpeni et omnibus aliis rebus excepto murdro et latrocinio ita bene et in pace et honorifice sicut aliqua antecessorum suarum melius tenuit et sicut ecclesia illa has consuetudines et quietationes ab antiquo solet et debet habere. Teste W(illelmo) de Alb(ini) Britone. Apud Cliuam. Regesta*, ii. no. 1453; *Calendar of the Charter Rolls Preserved in the Public Record Office*, ed. The Deputy Keeper of the Records (6 vols, London, 1903–27), *1341–1417*, 285.

is a very different approach from that seen in the *Leges Henrici Primi*, chapter 10, which treats the king's pleas as an accumulation of claims across a wide area; it should be noted that the *Leges Henrici Primi* seems to have been a work composed by someone who worked within the framework of the law, and does not necessarily represent the perspective of the king and his advisers. The royal focus on these matters seen from Henry I's reign represents the beginning of a significant tradition, in that it is reminiscent of later arrangements, for *murdrum* and *latrocinium* were also the main concerns of the 1166 Assize of Clarendon.[45]

The focus on these matters as the most important parts of the king's pleas seems to begin in the middle years of Henry I's reign. *Latrocinium* – robbery – must be linked to the deep concern over theft seen in the Anglo-Saxon laws, while *murdrum* must refer to the process for punishing a locality for the death of a Norman.[46] The strong focus on these as the most enforced claims of the king from the middle of Henry I's reign was entirely new. The linking of these two as special matters must be accounted a move towards the formulation of a distinct category of crime.[47] The focus on *latrocinium* might be linked to the 1108 decree on theft noted above; the emphasis on *murdrum* cannot be linked to any similar occurrence, but given the sudden appearance of the word in exemption clauses and the lack of any other clear impulse behind it, it might be suspected that there once was one.[48]

*Murdrum* and *latrocinium* appear as items from which exemption was *not* granted after 1108, so that the phrase *excepto murdro et latrocinio* appears regularly.[49] It does not appear in documents from the times of the Anglo-Saxon

45 http://www.earlyenglishlaws.ac.uk/laws/texts/ass-clar/view/#edition/apparatus-1. Note that clause 8 specifically overrides liberties in this matter.

46 Bruce R. O'Brien, 'From Morðor to Murdrum: The Preconquest Origin and Norman Revival of the Murder Fine', *Speculum* 71 (1996), 321–57.

47 T. B. Lambert, 'Royal Protections and Private Justice: A Reassessment of Cnut's "Reserved Pleas"', in *English Law before Magna Carta: Felix Liebermann and* Die Gesetze der Angelsachsen, ed. Stefan Jurasinski, Lisi Oliver and Andrew Rabin (Leiden and Boston, 2010), 157–75. On the early absence of a distinct category of crime see T. B. Lambert, 'Theft, Homicide and Crime in Late Anglo-Saxon Law', *Past and Present* 214 (2012), 3–43.

48 If there were a lost decree on *murdrum* it might explain why it was transformed in Henry I's time; the earliest references indicate that *murdrum* was levied against the lord on whose land the body was found, whereas by the time of the 1129–30 Pipe Roll at latest it was levied on the hundred in which the body was found. See Bruce R. O'Brien, 'From Morðor to Murdrum: The Preconquest Origin and Norman Revival of the Murder Fine', *Speculum* 71 (1996), 321–57, at 337–41.

49 *Regesta*, ii. nos. 593, 738, 940, 968, 986, 1165, 1384, 1453, 1468, 1470, 1537, 1636, 1659, 1726, 1956. There may have been some grants of *murdrum* and *latrocinium*, see *Regesta*, ii. nos. 1282 and 1618 for Cluny, 637 for Ramsey, and 1427, 1471 and 1789 for Reading. *Regesta*, iii. nos. 31, 217, 295, 467. Possible genuine grants are *Regesta*, iii. nos. 687 for Reading and 866 for the Templars.

kings or from those of William the Conqueror or William Rufus, except in clear forgeries.[50] There are also a few forged charters which specified that *murdrum* and *latrocinium* had been granted to a beneficiary, in defiance of the usual pattern.[51]

These exemption clauses were not the norm. The grant of exemption from the shire, as in the document from Barking Abbey above, was only granted to small numbers of very privileged and well-connected beneficiaries. The positive grants and exemptions in the charter meant that the lands of the Barking nuns were remarkably free from intrusions by royal agents, and the nuns had unusual scope for running them as they saw fit. Yet, despite this, *murdrum* and *latrocinium* were not allowed to them.

There is a practical problem here; the lands of the nuns were not exempted from *murdrum* and *latrocinium*, but they were exempted from shires and hundreds. How were cases of *murdrum* and *latrocinium* dealt with? The answer is perhaps provided by a charter discussed above in Chapter 4. In this, Baldwin de Redvers, earl of Devon, as lord of the Isle of Wight, granted to those on the lands of the monks of Quarr Abbey that:

> Also I concede this liberty to the men residing in the alms of the said church,[52] that they should go to no hundred except to the hundred of theft (*latrocinii*), and if it happens that they fall into any forfeiture, the justice thence is mine and the compensation and fine belong to the abbot and monks.[53]

This sets up a distinction between the hundred, which presumably exercised its ordinary functions as an arena for the settlement of local disputes, and the hundred of *latrocinium*. It might be assumed that the latter was an occasional

[50] Bates, *Regesta*, nos. 19.1, 19.2, 22 (for Battle), 99, 100 (for Chertsey), 150 (for Gent), 290, 298, 305, 314, 324 (for Westminster). Forged grants of *latrocinium* are Bates, *Regesta*, nos. 22 (Chertsey), 290, 293, 294, 298, 301, 302, 306, 307, 318, 319, 320, 321, 322, 324, 328, 331, 332 and 333 (for Westminster).

[51] *Regesta*, ii. nos. 489, 735, 1099, 1174, 1178, 1204, 1205, 1238, 1251, 1739, 1787, 1804, 1896, 1794; *Regesta*, iii. 371, 592, 928, 929.

[52] This presumably means that the grant was made to those men who lived on those lands that the abbey held in free alms tenure.

[53] *Item hominibus in elemosina predicte ecclesie manentibus talem libertatem concedo, ut ad nullum hundredum eant nisi ad hundredum latrocinii et si contigerit eos cadere in aliquod forisfactum, iusticia inde sit mea et emendatio et catelum sit abbatis et monachorum*: Robert Bearman, *Charters of the Redvers Family and the Earldom of Devon, 1090–1217*, Devon and Cornwall Record Society, new series 37 (1994), 68, no. 17 extract; phrase shown in frontispiece plate; translation in S. F. Hockey, *Quarr Abbey and its Lands, 1132–1631* (Leicester, 1970), 6–8 and in Latin at 257–8 appendix A; calendared in S. F. Hockey, *The Charters of Quarr Abbey*, Isle of Wight Records Series 3 (1991), 1, no. 1; and facsimile in V. H. Galbraith, 'Monastic Foundation Charters of the Eleventh Centuries', *Cambridge Historical Journal* 4 (1934), 205–22, with facsimile facing p. 222, and discussion at 215–18. See discussion in Chapter 4 above.

session which dealt with matters linked to *latrocinium*, and maybe *murdrum* as well, and which lay somewhat outside the usual business of the hundred. The phrase used on the Isle of Wight is not common, but it suggests that references to *excepto murdro et latrocinio* might be read as 'except the assemblies of *murdrum* and *latrocinium*' just as easily as it might be read as 'except the procedures of *murdrum* and *latrocinium*'. Some sort of reading along these lines is necessary; it would not be credible that Henry I believed that he could grant exemption from the occurrences of murder and robbery. If these references do indeed point to how from Henry I's reign there were occasional special sessions of the hundreds which were obligatory even for those who normally did not attend, and which were run by royal officers in the direct interest in the king. It might be linked with the statement in the 1108 decree on shire and hundred courts, which barred sheriffs from holding special sessions of the shires and hundreds.[54]

## Justices and their Organisation

The chapter so far has been concerned with what justices did, and the remainder will focus instead on who they were and how they were organised. Much of the historiography suggests that there were at least two kinds of justices in circulation in the early twelfth century. One kind is the itinerant justice, and the other was the local justice.[55] The former is held to have moved around the country on something like the model of the itinerant justices of the thirteenth century, where itinerant justices held sessions of the king's court as they travelled.[56] Much of the later model is inapplicable to the twelfth century because it assumes that justices were judicial figures, as was discussed above. The other kind or justice posited is the idea of the local justice, that there were officials at shire or even hundred level who acted alongside or in concert with the itinerant justices.[57] The model of the

[54] *Regesta*, ii. no. 892, and discussed in detail in Chapter 6 above.

[55] H. A. Cronne, 'The Office of Local Justiciar in England under the Norman Kings', *University of Birmingham Historical Journal* 6 (1957–8), 18–38, at 18–19; H. G. Richardson and G. O. Sayles, *The Governance of Medieval England from the Conquest to Magna Carta* (Edinburgh, 1963), 173–190; C. Warren Hollister and John W. Baldwin, 'The Rise of Administrative Kingship: Henry I and Philip Augustus', *The American Historical Review* 83 (1978), 867–905, esp. 882–87; also a later version of this is C. Warren Hollister, 'The Rise of Administrative Kingship: Henry I', in his *Monarchy, Magnates and Institutions in the Anglo-Norman World* (London, 1986), 223–45, esp. 236–9; John Hudson, *The Formation of the English Common Law: Law and Society in England from King Alfred to Magna Carta* (second edition, Abingdon, 2018), 24–5.

[56] This is emphasised by the opening line of the final concords made by these itinerant justices: *Hec est finalis concordia facta in curia domini regis apud ...*

[57] H. A. Cronne, 'The Office of Local Justiciar in England under the Norman Kings',

itinerant justice has attracted much more historiographical attention, principally because it allows early twelfth-century justices to be depicted as the precursors of the later itinerant justices.[58]

Apparent mentions of justices can be found in many different kinds of sources, and have usually been treated as though they are of equal value. Often, this does not take into account the composition and contexts of the different kinds of source. Words are used in different patterns in different kinds of sources, and these distinctions tell us more about differences between the sources than about the ways in which justices actually worked in the early twelfth century. Most importantly, there is a major difference between the impression created by administrative sources – especially royal charters and writs – which sought to place early justices of whatever status in a specific local administrative context, and the impression created by narrative sources, which showed no real concern with the actual administrative context of the work of justices, and instead depicted a cabal that directly served the kings, and tended to use titles in a creative and impressionistic way to stress the personal power of certain favoured individuals. These contrasting approaches mean that the administrative sources mostly use *iustitia*, whereas the narrative sources use grander variants thereof and use them inconsistently. They also mean that the administrative sources name many justices, whereas the narrative sources tend to focus on a small group of men who enjoyed the special favour of Henry I in particular.

Charters and writs were the principal means by which the king and his immediate servants and advisers could influence how government was actually done across the kingdom, how they could dispense patronage, how they could co-ordinate business, and how they could access resources of all kinds. Such documents were, with only a few exceptions, designed to be used; they were not abstract manifestoes, but instead were addressed to specific individuals or to specific bodies which were expected to take action on the basis of these documents, or to acknowledge and recognise some change that had already been made. Charters and writs are the most important sources for identifying local hierarchies and the occupants of specific offices, and indeed provide more evidence for the identities and work of justices than any other class of sources. Their evidence is especially useful because it exposes the basis of the office, on which otherwise there has been much uncertainty.

---

*University of Birmingham Historical Journal* 6 (1957–8), 18–38; Hudson, *Oxford History*, 266–9. Their roles might be linked with those of the later coroners; see R. F. Hunnisett, 'The Origins of the Office of Coroner', *Transactions of the Royal Historical Society* fifth series 8 (1958), 85–104.

58 Doris M. Stenton, *English Justice between the Norman Conquest and the Great Charter, 1066–1215* (London, 1965), 65–7; W. T. Reedy, 'The Origins of the General Eyre in the Reign of Henry I', *Speculum* 41 (1966), 688–724, at 688–90.

Given that the charters and writs were used within the governmental system, and were specifically actionable by those who held different kinds of authority within it, these documents must necessarily have been based upon a precise and up-to-date knowledge of what offices were in place in particular shires, and who filled those offices. They were, moreover, written by the king's clerks, a small group of men who worked to fixed standards, and who seemingly had some fund of knowledge which provided them with precise and up-to-date details of who held office in particular places, and about the jurisdictional map of England, and who worked as part of a hierarchy in which their work was overseen and in which the most challenging and innovative material was reserved to the most senior within their office.[59] The precision with which these documents were written has already been used and emphasised by Judith Green, who has compiled lists of sheriffs up to 1154 largely based on the names which appear in the address clauses of particular documents.[60] For the purposes of identifying who was involved, the address clauses are especially useful, because they identify which shire was involved in any particular transaction, and who were the executive officers in that shire. Charters and writs, after all, seem to have been read out before the shire court as a means of appraising the assembled landholders of the transaction and so committing it to the memory of the shire as a means of generating testimony which could be used in the future in the event of dispute or uncertainty. The charters and writs present problems of their own, but the manner in which they were used means that they give precise information about the roles of justices in the governmental system.

Addresses to the shire court normally named the bishop whose diocese included the shire in question, then named the earl in those shires where an earl had a proprietorial interest, and either named the sheriff or included a vaguer address to the unnamed sheriff of the shire in question, and then finally addressed the remainder of the king's men as a broad class. From Henry I's reign shire addresses additionally included mention of the office of justice, which usually was placed between the bishop and the sheriff, or sometimes the name of an individual in that position. Long ago, William Stubbs noted that there are many occurrences in writs and writ-charters where a *iustitia* or *iustitiarius* is described as a member of a shire court, and thus by definition could not have been an itinerant justice representing the king's court;[61] there is a great deal of significance behind the ways in which justices were included in administrative documents.

[59] My view of the king's clerks is set out in Nicholas Karn, 'Robert de Sigillo: An Unruly Head of the Royal Scriptorium in the 1120s and 1130s', *English Historical Review* 123 (2008), 539–53. These pages on royal charters draw extensively on the expertise of Richard Sharpe.

[60] Judith A. Green, *English Sheriffs to 1154* (London, 1990).

[61] William Stubbs, *The Constitutional History of England: its Origins and Development*

The evidence for the spread of justices is set out in detail in the Appendix to this book. There it can be seen how references to justices can be found in almost every shire, and brings together evidence for who the justices were. There is a limitation to that evidence. For it seems that there were different grades of justice.[62] If the most senior ones appear in the royal acta, it seems there were others who worked at a more detailed and local level. In the narrative about Bricstan of Chatteris discussed above, most of the practical work was done by Robert *Malarteis*. Yet, at the final trial, Ralph Basset was present in a position of honour, even though he seemingly did not speak. Ralph is noted often in the Appendix to this volume as a royal justice; it may be that he held some kind of authority over Robert *Malarteis*. The idea that there may have been a hierarchy of justices appears also in a much-discussed charter of the Empress Matilda for Geoffrey de Mandeville, in which she provided that, among other offices, he should be *capitalis iusticia in Essexa*,[63] which implies that there were other, lesser justices in Essex.

## The First Appearance of Justices

The general pattern can be summarised straightforwardly. Words such as *iustitia* and *iustitiarius* (justice and justiciar) were used occasionally and irregularly in the later eleventh century, though most apparent instances of the use of the title at that point come from later forgeries. Early in Henry I's reign, that king appointed trusted individuals who could provide local oversight of the sheriffs in some shires, especially those more distant from the usual centres of royal power and which were rarely visited by kings. Evidently this policy was considered a success, for by 1108–9 these rather *ad hoc* forms of supervision were developed into a more regular one, in which justices were appointed to every shire as permanent members of the shire court and the title came into use.[64] There was,

(fifth edition, Oxford, 1891), i. 424; also J. H. Round, *The Commune of London and Other Studies* (London, 1899), 109, whose analysis of the charters is accepted here.

62 Raoul C. Van Caenegem, 'Public Prosecution of Crime in Twelfth-Century England', in *Church and Government in the Middle Ages: Essays Presented to C. R. Cheney on his Seventieth Birthday*, ed. C. N. L. Brooke, D. E. Luscombe, G. H. Martin and D. Owen (Cambridge, 1976), 41–76, at 52–3 suggests that the lesser justices might have been called serjeants, though this runs against the evidence of the *Leges Henrici Primi* and *Leges Edwardi Confessoris*. The evidence for this is the reference in *The Great Roll of the Pipe for the Thirty First Year of the Reign of King Henry I, Michaelmas 1130*, ed. Judith A. Green, Pipe Roll Society 95, new series 57 (2012), 72, where Benjamin the serjeant accounted for the ability to manage the king's pleas.

63 *Regesta*, iii. no. 274.

64 Evidence for this is set out in the Appendix.

at this point, no itineration because justices were members of the shire court, not visitors relying on the authority of the king's court.[65] This is really the heart of the matter; regardless of the inconsistencies of the chronicle evidence, the charters incontrovertibly show an office of justice in almost every shire, alongside the sheriff, and most of the references to justices concern these shire justices.[66] Sometimes justices were appointed to more than one shire, but so far as the king's clerks were concerned this made them no different from the sheriffs who were appointed to more than one shire; they were still addressed as integral parts of the various shire courts concerned. Indeed, those who served as justice for more than one shire in the later 1120s were usually the same men who served as sheriff of more than one shire, and in both cases their multiple jobs did not lead to a reconceptualisation of their offices as those of itinerant justices or itinerant sheriffs. The concentration of posts in the hand of a limited number of individuals was a feature of the later part of Henry I's reign, and most justices before that were relatively less conspicuous men. The shire model of justices remained the only one until itinerant justices as representatives of the king's court appeared in the 1160s.[67]

From pre-Conquest times to the end of the eleventh century, most royal writs were addressed to the shire or shire courts, and generally took a standard form, in which the diocesan bishop, local sheriff and the suitors of the shire or shire court were all named. The following example in the name of William II can stand as an example:

> W(illelmus) rex Anglie Th(ome) archiepiscopo et H. uicecomiti et omnibus baronibus et fidelibus suis de Ewerwicscira salutem.[68]

From Henry I's reign, the form of address to shire courts changed. Other individuals were included in the shire address clause, and picked out for special

65 William Stubbs, *The Constitutional History of England: its Origins and Development* (fifth edition, Oxford, 1891), i. 424.

66 On these see the evidence set out in the Appendix.

67 The earliest clear evidence for itinerant justices is the 1166 Assize of Clarendon (ed. Nicholas Vincent, http://www.earlyenglishlaws.ac.uk/laws/texts/ass-clar/). What happened between Henry II's accession in 1154 and the Assize is much less clear. William of Newburgh, *Historia rerum Anglicarum*, 2.1: ed. P. G. Walsh and M. J. Kennedy, *The History of English Affairs* (2 volumes, Warminster and Oxford, 1988–2007), ii. 14–17, states that Henry II appointed justices to all parts of the kingdom on his accession, which might indicate that shire justices remained in use. In contrast, John of Salisbury, *Policraticus*, 5.15: trans. Cary J. Nederman (Cambridge, 1990), 96–7, indicates that the phrase itinerant justices was known by the end of the 1150s, if the dating of *Policraticus* is secure. Exactly what was happening cannot be tested because Henry II's scribes abandoned the use of the address to the shire court, and so justices are not readily identifiable after 1154.

68 *Regesta*, i. no. 480.

mention in the same way that the bishop and the sheriff were. The clear implication is that those so named were members of the shire court, and were acting alongside the bishop and the sheriff.[69] The regular appearance of such men in address clauses is hard to date precisely. Yorkshire offers a good test case due to the abundance of royal documents addressed to its shire court from the first half of Henry I's reign. There is a clear pattern that addresses to the Yorkshire shire court and others did not include named individuals or offices other than the archbishop and sheriff in the archiepiscopate of Gerard (1101–1108); thus it must be meaningful, when in the archiepiscopate of Thomas II Nigel d'Aubigny[70] appears frequently between archbishop and sheriff. The Yorkshire data is full and helpful, and indicates that the composition of shire courts had been changed before the death of Thomas II of York. The Yorkshire pattern largely seems to parallel what is seen elsewhere, for about 1108 the same arrangements came to pass, and extra individuals were inserted into the address clause in addition to the bishop or archbishop and sheriff. The evidence for this is set out in more detail in the Appendix. The following few address clauses are offered as examples of the form used, and all are early and forms had not yet settled; Nigel d'Aubigny's name appears in these after that of Thomas II, archbishop of York, and so must have been written during the archbishop's short occupation of the office, from his nomination in May 1108[71] to his death in February 1114. In almost all of these, d'Aubigny is set between the archbishop of York and Osbert, sheriff of Yorkshire, even though he is not given a title in any of these addresses:

> H(enricus) rex Angl(orum) Thome archiepiscopo et Nigello de Albini et Osberto uicecomiti et omnibus baronibus et fidelibus francis et anglicis de Euewicscira salutem.[72]

> Henricus rex Anglorum T(home) archiepiscopo et Nigello de Albini et Osberto uicecomiti et omnibus fidelibus suis salutem.[73]

> Henricus rex Anglorum Tome archiepiscopo de Eboracho et Osberto uicecomiti et Nigello de Albeny et Aschetillo de Bulemer et omnibus baronibus et ministris suis et omnibus fidelibus suis francis et anglis de Eboraciscyra salutem.[74]

[69] William Stubbs, *The Constitutional History of England: its Origins and Development* (fifth edition, Oxford, 1891), i. 424; J. H. Round, *The Commune of London and Other Studies* (London, 1899), 109.

[70] D. E. Greenway, *Charters of the Honour of Mowbray, 1107–1191*, Records of Social and Economic History new series 1 (Oxford, 1972), xvii–xxvi.

[71] Royal scribes seem to have counted episcopal and archiepiscopal appointments from nomination or election rather than consecration, in defiance of the usual ecclesiastical habits.

[72] *Regesta*, ii. no. 977 of 1108 May 27 x 1114 Feb 24.

[73] *Regesta*, ii. no. 927 of 1108 May 27 x 1114 Feb 24.

[74] *Regesta*, ii. no. 995 of 1108 May 27 x 1114 Feb 24.

> Henricus rex Anglorum T(home) archiepiscopo et Nigello de Albini et Osberto uicecomiti et omnibus fidelibus suis salutem.[75]

> Henricus rex Angl(orum) Os(berto) uicecomiti et Nigello de Albeneio et omnibus baronibus francis et anglis de Euerwicscira salutem.[76]

> Henricus rex Anglorum Os(berto) uicecomiti et Nigello de Albinni et omnibus baronibus et omnibus fidelibus suis francis et anglis de Euerwik syra salutem.[77]

One early instance of the appearance of a name in this position is datable quite precisely, and is a little earlier than the Yorkshire examples.[78] A writ-charter in favour of Abingdon Abbey is datable to summer 1107, on the grounds that it confirmed a private deed dated internally to the seventh year of Henry I (1 August 1106–1 August 1107), while Henry I's charter is witnessed by Roger Bigod, who died in 1107.[79] Given that the royal charter is itself dated to Whitsun at Westminster, the only occasion when it could have been written was around Whitsun, 2 June 1107. The royal writ-charter was addressed to Oxfordshire and Buckinghamshire in the following terms:

> Henricus rex Anglorum Roberto episcopo Linc', et Nigello de Oili, et Hugoni de Bochelanda, et Willelmo uicecomiti de Oxeneford, et omnibus baronibus suis et fidelibus suis de Oxenefordscira et de Buchingehamscira, salutem.

Robert, bishop of Lincoln, was diocesan for both shires; William, described here specifically as sheriff of Oxford, is frequently mentioned in that office and served from the start of Henry I's reign to about 1110.[80] The other two are not titled, but their roles can be identified. Hugh of Buckland was one of the most prominent and long-serving of sheriffs in the first half of Henry I's reign, and was at various times sheriff of Berkshire, Buckinghamshire, Essex, Hertfordshire and Middlesex;[81] given that the document concerned some interests in Buckinghamshire and was addressed to its shire court, Hugh of Buckland must surely appear here as sheriff of Buckinghamshire.[82] Nigel d'Oilly appears in a number of address clauses concerning Oxfordshire, but in those is never given a title; rather, the profile of his activity very closely matches that for his near-namesake Nigel d'Aubigny in Yorkshire. He is named in three

75 *Regesta*, ii. no. 926 of 1108 May 27 x 1114 Feb 24.
76 *Regesta*, ii. no. 917 of 1108 May 27 x 1114 Feb 24.
77 *Regesta*, ii. no. 923 of 1108 May 27 x 1114 Feb 24.
78 *Regesta*, ii. no. 813, *Abingdon Chronicle*, ii. 154–7.
79 I. J. Sanders, *English Baronies: A Study of their Origin and Descent, 1086–1327* (Oxford, 1960), 47.
80 Judith A. Green, *English Sheriffs to 1154* (London, 1990), 69.
81 Judith A. Green, *English Sheriffs to 1154* (London, 1990), 26, 28, 39–40, 47, 57.
82 Judith A. Green, *English Sheriffs to 1154* (London, 1990), 28.

address-clauses, one being that just discussed, and two more surviving from Abingdon Abbey:

> Henricus rex Anglorum Nigello de Oilli et Willelmo uicecomiti de Oxen', salutem.[83]

> Henricus rex Anglorum Roberto episcopo Linc', et Thome de Sancto Iohanne, et Nigello de Oilleio, et omnibus baronibus, Francis et Anglis, de Oxenefordscira, salutem.[84]

In two of these, Nigel appeared before William, sheriff of Oxford, so that he cannot have been sheriff himself; in the third, he appears after Thomas de St John, who is known from other evidence as sheriff of Oxford between about 1111 and 1116. There seems no special significance in that Nigel d'Oilly appears after Thomas de St John, for, as in the examples of addresses including Nigel d'Aubigny in Yorkshire discussed earlier, the order of the participants seems to have been relatively fluid at this point.

The examples of Nigel d'Aubigny in Yorkshire and Nigel d'Oilly in Oxfordshire have been introduced to make the point that from 1107 or so the composition of shire courts changed, and it became common that names appeared of individuals who were not sheriff or bishop or earl, who had been addressed in royal writs and writ-charters since the early eleventh century. In the cases discussed here and in much of the other relevant evidence, names were used rather than titles, and this practice seems to have been a common one for the king's clerks. Sheriffs are usually addressed using their names, and sometimes even bishops are denoted simply as 'Bishop Robert' or similar, without naming the see. Yet sometimes those individuals who were so addressed were linked with a specific title, and the title which occurs is that of *iustitia*. For instance, Nigel d'Aubigny had a role in the shire court of Yorkshire and those of some other northern shires, for he was specifically named as justice in a writ concerning Northumberland.[85] Here, the two joint sheriffs of Northumberland[86] were ordered to see that Ranulf Flambard, bishop of Durham, was put into possession of the land at Ross in County Durham (then part of Northumberland rather than a shire)[87] which had been occupied

[83] *Regesta*, ii. no. 814, *Abingdon Chronicle*, ii. 134–5.

[84] *Regesta*, ii. no. 1128, *Abingdon Chronicle*, ii. 114–15.

[85] *Regesta*, ii. no. 993. *Quod nisi feceritis tunc precipio ut Nigellus de Albini et alia iusticia mea hoc faciat.*

[86] Judith A. Green, *English Sheriffs to 1154* (London, 1990), 65.

[87] Apart from this instance where a sheriff of Northumberland dealt with business in Durham, there is the division between Durham and Northumberland from the 1120s (noted *Regesta*, ii. no. 1561). This only survives in much later copies, which themselves report only a later description of that settlement. The copies of this differ substantially. Perhaps the earliest is the less detailed version in *Registrum Palatinum Dunelmense: The Register of Richard de Kellawe, Lord Palatine and Bishop of Durham, 1311–1316*,

by Robert de Muschamp, but which the bishop had shown should belong to his church. The sheriffs had either been unable to put the bishop into possession, perhaps due to opposition from de Muschamp, or had been unwilling to execute the sentence, for reasons not stated and not now readily inferred. The importance of this writ lies in its later stipulation that if the sheriffs did not act, then Nigel d'Aubigny and another justice were to put the bishop into possession. Clearly, Nigel was acting as justice in Northumberland at this point.

If the years before 1110 saw the appearance of extra individuals with a privileged role in shire courts, then by 1110 they became widespread to all parts of England.[88] Especially later in the reign of Henry I, it became commoner that address clauses specified the office rather than the individual. This is a trend rather than a marked change, and there still remained many instances in which named individuals were addressed, often when some man of special eminence occupied a shire office. In such addresses, it became the convention that the *iustitia* was placed in front of the sheriff and others, though after the bishop. The following examples illustrate how this was presented, and these are fairly standard for royal documents addressed to shire courts in the later years of Henry I's reign:

> H(enricus) rex Angl(orum) iustic' uicecomiti baronibus forestariis et ministris et omnibus fidelibus suis de Berchsir' salutem.[89]

> Henricus rex Angl<orum> episcopo Herefordensi et iusticiariis et uicecomitibus et omnibus baronibus et fidelibus suis francis et anglis de Gloucestrescira et Herefortscira salutem.[90]

> H(enricus) rex Angl(orum) iustic' et uicecomiti et ministris suis de Wirec'scira salutem.[91]

> Henricus rex Anglorum iusticiariis baronibus uicecomitibus et omnibus ministris et fidelibus suis francis et anglis de Essexia salutem.[92]

ed. Thomas Duffus Hardy (four volumes, London, 1873–8), i. 8, which describes the settlement as a division between the earl of Northumberland and the bishop of Durham; only the expanded version in *Registrum Palatinum Dunelmense: The Register of Richard de Kellawe, Lord Palatine and Bishop of Durham, 1311–1316*, ed. Thomas Duffus Hardy (four volumes, London, 1873–8), i. 39–41 treats the division as one between shires, by changing *comitem* to *comitatum*.

88 See the evidence set out in the Appendix below.

89 *Regesta*, ii. no. 1526.

90 *Regesta*, ii. no. 1723.

91 Not in *Regesta*, ed. R. R. Darlington, *The Cartulary of Worcester Cathedral Priory (Register I)*, Pipe Roll Society 76, new series 38 (1968), 24, no. 35.

92 *Regesta*, ii. no. 1835.

H(enricus) rex Angl(orum) Ricardo Basset et A(lberico) de Ver et uicecomiti et omnibus burgensibus suis de Geldefort salutem.[93]

The above examples vary in their use of the forms *iustitia* and *iustitiarius*, or in their use of shortened forms which could represent either. Most texts survive through copies in cartularies or other places, and might have been subject to the kinds of low-level interventions and modifications commonly undertaken by copyists. Only those writs and writ-charters which survive as originals in the hand of a recognised royal clerk can provide useful evidence for the spelling, and these indicate that variety was tolerated. Most original documents use shortened forms which are ambiguous between the two spellings,[94] but among those which did include a choice, *iustitia* was much the more common,[95] though *iustitiarius* also occurred.[96] There is no obvious point made in the variation between the two forms; it seems to be based on nothing more than personal preference.

The discussion over the last few pages has had one end in mind; the demonstration that mentions of justices in royal acta of various kinds emerged just before 1110, and that these mentions were mostly designed to fit a situation in which justices were members of local shire courts, and operated within that setting or in relation to it, much as did the sheriff. The evidence that justices were local figures goes beyond this, for a significant minority of the royal acta extends the parallel between justices and sheriffs by showing that they conceived of justices as being in relation to a particular shire, so that there was a justice of Northumberland in the same way that there was a sheriff of Northumberland, both of whom derived their title and power from their placing within the shire court. There are a few examples where someone is described as a justice within a specific shire or shires within royal acta of the early twelfth century:

H(enricus) rex Angl(orum) episcopo Exon(ie) et iustic(ie) sue Deuonie salutem.[97]

H(enricus) rex Angl(orum) episcopo Dunelm(ensi) et iusticiar(io) de

93 *Regesta*, ii. no. 1655; an original in the hand of scribe xi (Bishop, *Scriptores regis,* no. 294).

94 *Regesta*, ii. nos. 866 (Bishop, *Scriptores regis*, no. 468, scribe xiii), 1468 (Bishop, *Scriptores regis*, no. 597, a beneficiary scribe), 1919 (Bishop, *Scriptores regis*, no. 84, scribe xiv) have *iustic'*, as does H. S. Offler, 'A Northumberland Charter of King Henry I', in his *North of the Tees: Studies in Medieval British History* (Aldershot, 1996), no. VIII, 182 (not in *Regesta*). Three probable Westminster forgeries, *Regesta*, ii. nos. 1174, 1176, 1838 (Bishop, *Scriptores regis*, nos. 548, 550, 520, all beneficiary scribes), also have *iustic'*.

95 *Regesta*, ii. no. 1585 (Bishop, *Scriptores regis*, no. 317, not identified) has *iusticiis*.

96 *Regesta*, ii. no. 1563 (Bishop, *Scriptores regis*, no. 184, scribe ii) has *iusticiar'*.

97 *Regesta*, ii. no. 866 (Bishop, *Scriptores regis*, no. 468, scribe xiii).

Norhtnumbrelanda et uicecomiti et omnibus baronibus et fidelibus suis francis et anglis salutem.[98]

... Et ipse abbas teneat terram suam de Antigham ita bene et iuste et libere sicut predictus Adam ei clamauit terram illam quietam coram iusticia mea de Northfolch, scilicet coram A(lberico) de Ver et Roberto filio Walteri.[99]

... Et nisi feceritis iusticia mea Cantebrigeschire faciat fieri, ne super hoc inde clamorem audiam pro penuria iusticie. [100]

S(tephanus) rex Angl(orum) iustic(ie) de Warwic(scira) et uic(ecomiti) salutem.[101]

The king's clerks in the time of Henry I and Stephen conceived of the existence of an office of shire justice, and this accounts for a very high proportion of the mentions of justices in acta of those kings. Most of the addresses including justices are to shire courts, and must necessarily indicate that the persons so addressed were justices who operated within shires and who were part of their courts. This must apply to the addresses made to well-known individuals who have often been called itinerant justices.

## Conclusion

Royal justices appeared in 1107/8 as a result of royal initiative, and they seem to have been innovations; at least, there was no single one that prefigured that of the justice based in the shire court. These early justices worked to bring and manage pleas in the interest of the king, so that the king's claims to some kinds of plea and to the financial consequences arising from them would not be lost once lords took much business into their own courts. They should thus be understood as a response to the proliferation of lordly courts, and a means for ensuring that royal claims were still preserved. These justices seem to have been numerous and were based locally, so that they could keep track of pleas and events as they arose. In the early twelfth century they had not yet acquired judicial functions, but were closer to the later model of coroners.[102]

[98] *Regesta*, ii. no. 1563 (Bishop, *Scriptores regis*, no. 184, scribe ii).

[99] *Regesta*, ii. no. 1714.

[100] *Regesta*, iii. no. 269.

[101] *Regesta*, iii. no. 135, written in the hand of *scriptor* xviii: see Bishop, *Scriptores regis,* no. 50 and p1. xix (b) (facs.).

[102] R. F. Hunnisett, 'The Origins of the Office of Coroner', *Transactions of the Royal Historical Society* fifth series 8 (1958), 85–104.

# Conclusion

Shires and hundreds were created across England during the tenth century, and their operations were recorded in detail in the Anglo-Saxon laws, which have done so much to form ideas about how the new kingdom of England worked. Hundreds in particular had an important role as local assemblies, in which people would gather to see justice done to one another, and in which local communities, with all their dysfunctions and intimacies, sat in judgement upon themselves. The model set out in the laws was not long-lived, however. By the middle of the eleventh century it seems that already the unitary model of the hundred was starting to break down, and decay accelerated and became general into the twelfth century. The pattern of hundreds was remodelled as lords seized control of parts of it; either they claimed whole hundreds themselves, or they created lesser units which were originally subsets of hundreds and which were accountable to them, which came to be known as the *halimota*. The hundred managed by a lord and the *halimota* were mechanisms which allowed lords to raise exclusive claims over their dependents, and to monopolise lordship.

The *halimota* represented not just a change in how courts worked, but was also a step, and probably an important step, in the process of manorialisation, in which lordship, society and economy were progressively reconfigured. Later Anglo-Saxon lordship was multiple and many-sided; it was possible for one individual to owe different things to many different lords, because they might exercise lordship in different forms, or might exercise lordship in relation to different pieces of land, among other possible variations. In negotiating relationships with multiple lords, many peasants had a measure of agency, and their relationship to any one lord meant that it would have been harder for another to assert exclusive claims of lordship, because such a claim would have implications not merely for the peasant, but also for the other lords. Such complex lordship only worked because peasants were visible to many lords in public arenas such as the hundreds. Yet, it seems to have been a widespread aspiration among lords that they should be able to monopolise claims over those who were beneath them. This meant that they would have had exclusive claims over their resources and labour, and would have needed to prevent other lords making demands over their dependents. All this changed in the eleventh and twelfth centuries. Lordly courts were a means of institutionalising, and so intensifying and transforming, the power of one lord over dependents, but also because they meant that other lords could be excluded, and that the relationships of peasants could be restricted and managed solely through the lords who ruled over them. If peasants could be drawn into such structures, then the claims of lordship were strengthened and intensified.

This had considerable consequences for the landholdings of peasants. In 1066 and 1086, hundreds had or expected to have detailed and precise knowledge about all who held land on freer terms, including lords and some peasants – though, of course, the interests of unfree dependents never received this kind of recognition. This meant that the status and holdings of the freer peasants were visible to the hundred, and the hundred acted as witnesses and warrantors for that tenure. If such peasants could be placed within a lord's *halimota*, then their tenure of land would depend upon the willingness of that lord to recognise it through that court. Tenure of land in these circumstances could only be validated through the framework of lordship, not through recognition in the public hundred courts; instead, the peasants were effectively hidden from the public courts, and had no remedy against the lords on whom they depended. Ultimately, those who held by such dependent tenures were not allowed access to the writs and procedures of the early common law, and so their dependence on their lords was cemented.

In this sense, the early kinds of lordship court known as *halimota* should be understood not simply as expressions of pure lordship, but also as courts that grew out from the communal hundred courts, and which carried on some of their functions. This claim has large implications. It means that the hundred, long acclaimed as an instance where Anglo-Saxon foundations had long significance, should be reconsidered; though the name persisted, many of the key points that defined the Anglo-Saxon hundred did not have a long history. Many, indeed, seem to have been waning by the end of the eleventh century. Twelfth-century kings were willing to look upon individual *halimota* as courts that could act in concert with hundreds in providing inquests, and which acted as subsets of them. Henry II was the last king to do so; after the early years of his reign, he and his successors did not interact with the *halimota*. The withdrawal of royal interest in the *halimotas* meant that there was no other mechanism for those who were parts of such courts to interact with the common law which developed over the following decades. The creation of the kind of court known as *halimota*, and the developing attitudes and practices of kings towards it, were among the key developments that allowed the creation of the legal status of serfdom.

Yet, while this story is mostly about lords and their dependents, it also has wide relevance for the greatest of lords, the king. The actions of lords in creating their own courts and in subtracting business from the hundred meant that the wide remit of that assembly became limited, and the role of the hundred declined. It is conceivable that the hundred might have faded away much as the earlier Frankish *mallus* had done. Clearly, this did not happen. What prevented this outcome was that in 1108 Henry I acted to insist on royal ownership of the hundred in stronger terms than his predecessors had, and on the obligations of others to interact with the hundred as an expression of the king's lordship, just as the *halimota* was an expression of other lords' influence. Henry I also created the distinction between *curia* and *placitum*, which allowed kings to claim some business as their own while still respecting the position of lords' courts. These clear categories allowed business to be classified and described more consistently. This meant that he was able to insist on royal oversight and control of certain matters, and his acta show a consistent interest in theft and murder. In this, he built on much older ideas and royal claims, but also pointed forward towards the idea that certain grave infractions of public order formed a class of matters that might be called crime.

Royal interest in these matters was also sustained through the creation of a class of locally based royal officers called the justices, who brought pleas in the king's interest. This meant that they gathered intelligence locally and even listened to gossip, so that instances of behaviour that implicated the king's claims would be brought into courts. They were not judges, but instead relied on traditional procedure, in which panels of locals or the ordeal process were responsible for making decisions. They summoned, initiated procedures, and so forth, and drew fines and profits where they could. Their work is set out clearly in the *Leges Henrici Primi* and the *Leges Edwardi Confessoris*, though the role set out in these and other sources does not match to any one later office. While it is possible to see individuals acting locally in the king's interest earlier, from about 1108 there seem to have been such officers consistently in every shire. The creation of the justices should probably be linked to the upsurge of royal proclamations in that year, and show consistent and developed royal interest in the maintenance of public order.

The discussion within this book has placed these developments within a framework that is essentially legal. It is about courts, about the claims and expectations of various parties, and about how those were handled and assessed. It has presented a model for how the changing framework of legal assemblies and changing ideas around them altered legal behaviour and how many kinds of people could perceive their legal claims and relationships, and thus their place in society as a whole. These changes were not legislated, but seemingly they arose by experimentation as lords tried different methods for managing their interests, and ultimately they seem to have spread by imitation thereafter. All strengthened the vertical relationship between lords and their dependents, and seem to owe much to developing attitudes towards lordship itself.

The consequences of these changes were enormous. They stretched far beyond the framework of the law, and contributed to making the social and economic order of high medieval and later medieval England. They underpinned the process of manorialisation, which reshaped rural society and economy into structures that persisted for centuries thereafter. They helped to shape how lords interacted with and looked upon their dependents. They did much to form the legal behaviour and expectations of the peasants, including their desire for assemblies as a forum for doing business, their expectations about process, and so forth. The developments described in this book also did much to redefine the boundary between the free and unfree, which had consequences not only for the structure of society but also for the content of the common law as it developed from the later twelfth century. The changes to hundreds and the creation of private courts were subtle changes, but formed a kind of deep change that impacted on society, law, culture and economy far from those localised starting places.

# Appendix: The Evidence for Justices, 1100–54

The evidence for justices is scattered and diffuse, at least before the survival of consistent and relevant evidence from the last years of the twelfth century onward.[1] It has never been brought together as rigorously as the evidence for sheriffs,[2] and this has meant that justices as a whole have been understood much less thoroughly than sheriffs. There have been four modern exercises in listing justices for the period in question, but all are incomplete. The first was by Doris Stenton,[3] and this was part of a larger exercise in tracing justices into the early thirteenth century. She based its contents on the kinds of sources which were of most importance for the thirteenth century, but carried those choices back into the early twelfth century. So, she discussed Anglo-Norman justices solely on the basis of the Pipe Roll for 1129–30, which meant that she could only cover a small part of the first half of the twelfth century, passed by other and more abundant kinds of evidence, and glossed over the simple ambiguity of so many entries in that Pipe Roll. A similar approach was followed in the list of justices by Warren Hollister.[4] This again is based on the Pipe Roll for 1129–30, but Hollister supplemented the data because there are obvious gaps and missing segments in that Pipe Roll; for instance, he noted that there is no account for Shropshire there, and suggested that Payn fitz John might have acted as justice in that shire. His supplementary conjectures are plausible, and some are corroborated below, but he does not explain the basis for them. He seems to assume that only those known at the king's court could have been justices. The third and fourth lists by Susan Reynolds, and by Christopher Brooke and Gillian Keir, covered the justices of London alone.[5] They make use of a fuller range of

1 David Crook, *Records of the General Eyre* (London, 1982), sets out the evidence that survives from the start of consistent enrolment in 1194, and which allows for systematic identification of justices.

2 Judith A. Green, *English Sheriffs to 1154* (London, 1990).

3 Doris Mary Stenton, 'The Development of the Judiciary 1100–1215', in her *Pleas Before the King or his Justices, 1198–1212*, iii: *Rolls or Fragments of Rolls from the Years 1199, 1201 and 1203–6*, Selden Society 83 (1967), xlvii–ccxciv, at xlvii–l.

4 C. Warren Hollister and John W. Baldwin, 'The Rise of Administrative Kingship: Henry I and Philip Augustus', *American Historical Review* 83 (1978), 867–905, at 886; another version in C. Warren Hollister, 'The Rise of Administrative Kingship: Henry I', in his *Monarchy, Magnates and Institutions in the Anglo-Norman World* (London, 1986), 223–45, at 240.

5 Susan Reynolds, 'The Rulers of London in the Twelfth Century', *History* 57 (1972),

sources, and draw extensively on royal and other charters to make these lists. They are the most successful list of justices hitherto published, though they are necessarily limited in geographical scope.

The lists below respond to the advantages and shortcomings of the previous lists, and to some of the ideas about justices set out in Chapter 7 above. In terms of sources, two of the lists are based overwhelmingly on charters, especially royal charters, and sideline the evidence of the Pipe Roll. The charters have considerable advantages over other sources. They are abundant where the financial records are not; charters survive from across the whole period from 1100 to the start of Henry II's reign, and so a list compiled from charters can take include coverage of all those years, not simply those just prior to 1130. They therefore give a longer list of individuals, and also mean that attention is not directed towards the years 1129–30, which were almost certainly anomalous. Then, a couple of well-connected and trusted individuals acted as sheriffs of multiple shires, somewhat at odds with the more usual pattern in which shires were distributed among many people.[6] There are indications that something similar happened in relation to justices, and that duties were committed to a few favoured individuals – indeed, the same favoured individuals who acted as sheriff many times over – and so 1129–30 is also an unusual period with regard to justices. Charters survive from all parts of the kingdom, and so it is possible to look at those shires which are not covered in the Pipe Roll. While coverage is general, there are nonetheless patterns with regard to where charters survive. Some shires with large populations and many powerful churches which could archive and preserve documents have much surviving evidence; yet other shires did not have these advantages, and so are covered much less fully. The former position applies to such places as Yorkshire; the latter to shires such as Buckinghamshire. The emphasis on royal charters here is not without problems, but it gives a broader overall impression than reliance on the Pipe Roll.

This list is based not on all charters, but on those that were written in the name of the king.[7] There are some notable advantages in limiting the evidence to royal charters. They were drafted with much consistency, because most of them were written by a fairly small group of scribes and secretaries who adhered to agreed norms. Those norms were developed because royal charters were not simple certificates, but instead were functional documents, which were meant to bring

---

337–57, at 354; Christopher Brooke and Gillian Keir, *London, 800–1216: The Shaping of a City* (London, 1975), 371–4, 'Appendix II: The Sheriffs and Justices of London and Middlesex, *c.* 1030–1216'. See also the longer discussion in Christopher Brooke and Gillian Keir, *London, 800–1216: The Shaping of a City* (London, 1975), 199–218.

6 Judith A. Green, *English Sheriffs to 1154* (London, 1990), 25, 28, 29, 40, 47, 48, 53, 61, 64, 77, 78.

7 See Chapter 7 above for comments on why royal charters should be read differently from those in the names of others.

about some effect through being implemented or recognised by royal servants of various kinds. That link to local structures of power is something that is not seen to the same extent for any other body of charter texts from twelfth-century England, and means that the royal charters have a particular importance in trying to understand those structures of power.

The royal charters present information about justices in various forms. At the simplest level, there are a few that specifically name someone as a justice, such as the grant of land to Gervase, justice of London, by Matilda, Stephen's queen (*dedi Geruasio iustic(ie) de Lond(onia)*).[8] There are relatively few of these. Most references to justices in royal charters occur instead in the opening address clause. These were among the functional elements of royal charters, in that they indicated to whom the document should be delivered, and by whom the instructions contained in the document should be implemented. In the vast majority of cases, this meant the local servants of the king, such as sheriffs or justices. Grants made or authorised by kings were notified to the whole shire court in question. These address clauses contribute the majority of the data tabulated in this appendix. Some royal charters included another clause nearer the end, which has become known as a *nisi feceris* clause. These contained instructions about enforcement, presumably where the king or the beneficiary of the charter felt there was a danger that the terms would not be implemented as expected. Such clauses occur most often where a charter was directed to someone other than the king's servants for implementation. These often specify that the local sheriff was to ensure that the terms were carried out, but sometimes a justice was specifically assigned this role. *Nisi feceris* clauses provide a few more instances of justices.

The address clauses provide data in various forms. In some cases they include the name of an individual which is linked to the title *iustitia* or *iustitiarius*, and in some cases there is only the title without the name of an actual person. Even these latter cases are useful in that they show that there was a justice of the shire in question at that time. Where titles and names occur in an address clause, the king's scribes imposed an order of precedence. The following example shows how they structured these address clauses:

> H(enricus) rex Anglorum episcopo Dunelmensi et iustic' et uic(ecomiti) et baronibus et omnibus ministris et fidelibus suis de Norhu(m)berlant francis et anglis salutem.[9]

8 *Regesta*, iii. no. 243; for comment see J. H. Round, *Geoffrey de Mandeville: A Study of the Anarchy* (London, 1892), 120.

9 Not in *Regesta*. From H. S. Offler, 'A Northumberland Charter of King Henry I', in his *North of the Tees: Studies in Medieval British History*, ed. A. J. Piper and A. I. Doyle (Aldershot, 1996), no. VIII, p. 182. Original; hand identified by Offler as *scriptor* xiii.

The document in this case is a notification addressed to the shire court of Northumberland as a whole, and includes only those who were part of the shire court. All the participants in the court are named in order of precedence; the bishop (in this case, of Durham), the justice, the sheriff, the barons of the shire, the king's servants (evidently those of lesser status) and the king's sworn men, otherwise the suitors of the shire court. In those shires where there was an earl, his name or title or both were inserted immediately after those of the relevant local bishop. This order of precedence was followed rigorously by the king's scribes; there are no instances where, say, the bishop follows the sheriff in such addresses. There are also a number of cases in which a name is inserted between the bishop and the sheriff, though without any title. Given the rigour and consistency with which the king's scribes observed their order of precedence, such cases have been included below among the likely instances of justices; it helps that in most such cases the person named is specifically identified as a justice in other sources.[10] The shire addresses of the charters issued in the names of the Anglo-Norman kings mean that justices can be seen with some clarity for the period up to 1154, but not thereafter; the address to the shire court was abandoned by Henry II, and so justices in the shire court cannot be seen so consistently from the point of his accession.

This appendix is made up of three sections, each of which addresses a key question about early justices. The first examines the regional distribution of references to justices in the early twelfth century, to make the point that almost every shire under direct royal lordship can be shown to have had a justice. The second sets out evidence for who these early justices were, to show that the justices were a larger and more local class than those who have been identified from the 1129–30 Pipe Roll. The third brings together the evidence from the Pipe Roll itself.

## Section 1: The Geographical Distribution of Justices To 1154

The following table illustrates the geographical spread of the office of justice. It is based upon a very conservative reading of the evidence. After each shire name there may be found those instances in which a writ or writ-charter is addressed to the shire court of that shire and which includes specific mention of a justice. All these locate the justice in the shire court, and so show that the office described here had a different basis from the later itinerant justices, who were not members of the shire courts when they heard pleas. There is little room

[10] The observation that additional names in such shire addresses likely denoted justices was first made in J. H. Round, *The Commune of London and Other Studies* (London, 1899), 109.

for doubt that mentions of justices in the address clauses of royal acta must refer to offices which were defined as being based within, and being exercised within, the setting of shire administration and especially the shire court. Such justices were, moreover, a normal part of administration in the early twelfth century. Royal acta which demanded the attention or action of justices were addressed to all parts of England, and in each case placed the justice very specifically in a local context. The references collected here show that, despite suggestions that the appearance of justices in shire courts was variable,[11] there was in fact a consistent system.

The evidence for this is set out in the following table, which includes only those instances where inclusion in an address to a shire court, or specific mention of the justice of a particular shire, makes it clear that the scribes responsible for the acta could only have conceived of the role in a shire context. More ambiguous mentions of justices have been excluded; only those which fit within these quite narrow criteria have been included.

| *Name of shire* | Regesta *number.*<br>*Those in* **bold** *survive as originals; those additionally underlined in the hands of recognised royal scribes, for whom the Bishop no. of the scribe is appended. Thus, for instance, (s.xxii) means that the original is in the hand of* scriptor *xxii.* |
|---|---|
| Bedfordshire | ii. 1449 |
| Berkshire | ii. 1111, 1174, 1477, 1478, 1526: iii. 3 (with Oxfordshire), 4, 5, 10 (with Oxfordshire) |
| Buckinghamshire | iii. 30, 586, 589, 649, 744, also 719 mentions a justice in a *nisi feceris* clause |
| Cambridgeshire | ii. 1543, 1629, ?1729, 1751, 1778: iii. **138 (*s.xxii*), 139 (*s.xxii*)**, 251, 268, 269 for a mention of a justice of Cambridgeshire in a *nisi feceris* clause |
| Cornwall | ii. 1068 (with Devon): iii. 572 (with Devon) |
| Cumberland | ii. 1617, 1752 (as Carlisle, with Yorkshire), 1753 (as Carlisle, with Yorkshire) |
| Devon | ii. **866 (*s.xiii*)**, 1068 (with Cornwall): iii. 1 (with Dorset), 572 (with Cornwall) |
| Dorset | ii. 754: iii. 1 (with Devon) |

[11] For instance, John Hudson, *The Formation of the English Common Law: Law and Society in England from King Alfred to Magna Carta* (second edition, Abingdon, 2018), 24–5.

| *Name of Shire* | *Regesta number* |
|---|---|
| Essex | ii. 577, 1362: iii. **40 (*s.xiv*), 41 (*s.xx*), 42 (*s.xx*)**, 137, **147 (*s.xxi*), 148 (*s.xxi*)**, 207c, 218, 222, 223, 227, 230, 231, 232, 236, 237, 239, 240, 307, **308 (*s.xx*)**, 374, 520, **538 (*s.xxi*)**, 545 in a *nisi feceris* clause, 546, 547, 549, 559, 565, 566, 613, 733, 761, 769, 770, 844, **877 (*s.xxi*)**, 914, 931, 932 |
| Gloucestershire | ii. **1723 (*s.xiii*) (with Herefordshire)**: iii. 192, 357, 361, **389 (*s.xvii*), 390 (*s.xx*)** |
| Hampshire | ii. 1759 (with Yorkshire), 1762, 1872, 1873: iii. 827, 828 |
| Herefordshire | ii. **1723 (*s.xiii*) (with Gloucestershire)**: iii. 384, 385, 396 |
| Hertfordshire | iii. 219, **244 (*s.xxi*), 508 (*s.xxi*), 510 (*s.xxi*)**, 511, 514, **515 (*s.xxii*)**, 742, 856, 857, 858, 860 |
| Huntingdonshire | ii. 1659, 1766, 1788, 1860b, 1860c, 1860d, 1916, 1960: iii. 410, **669 (*s.xxi*)**, 881, 884, 889 |
| Kent | iii. 160, 161, 340 (with London), 482 (with Lincolnshire), **519 (*s.xxii*)**, 573, 720, 743 (not identified) |
| Lincolnshire | ii. 1253, 1465, 1566, 1770 (with Nottinghamshire), 1841: iii. 85, 87, 125, 412, 463, 464, 467, 468, 469, **471 (*s.xxii*)**, 473, 474, 475, 480 (city of Lincoln), 482 (with Kent), 483, **488 (*s.xxii*)** (city of Lincoln), 605, 606, 652, 656, 985 (with Yorkshire) |
| London/ Middlesex | ii. 556, 1106, 1761: iii. 14 (with Middlesex), **317 (*s.xxii*)**, 340 (with Kent), 502, **507 (*s.xxi*)**, 523, 526, 532, 534 (with Middlesex), 535, 536, 693, 829, 849, **935 (*s.xx*) (Middlesex, with Sussex)**, 925 (Middlesex only), 930 |
| Norfolk | ii. ?830, 833, 954, 1094 (with Suffolk), 1159 (with Suffolk), 1443 (with Suffolk), 1444 (with Suffolk), 1608 (with Suffolk), 1714, 1866 (with Suffolk), 1888, 1914 (with Suffolk), 1954, charter for William Buttevilain (with Suffolk and Northamptonshire):[a] iii. **15 (*s.xiv*) (with Suffolk)**, 106 (with Suffolk), 110 (with Suffolk), **150 (*s.xxii*) (with Suffolk), 176 (*s.xx*), 177 (*s.xxi*) (with Suffolk)**, 247, 248, 279 (with Suffolk), 287 (with Suffolk), 289 (with Suffolk), 291, 402 (with Suffolk), 405, 619 (with city of Norwich), **670 (*s.xxii*) (with Suffolk)**, 762 (with Suffolk), 763 (with Suffolk), 767 (with Suffolk), 772 (with Suffolk), 802 (with Suffolk), 822 (with Suffolk), 837 (with Suffolk), 876, 974 |
| Northamptonshire | ii. 1318, 1318 note, charter for William Buttevilain (with Suffolk and Norfolk),[b] charter for Fawsley church:[c] iii. 611, 660, 661 |
| Northumberland | ii. 1323, 1339, **1563 (*s.xi*)**, 1849, **writ for Ralph de Chalgio (?*s. xiii*)**[d]: iii. 373, 603, 904, 905, 907 |
| Nottinghamshire | ii. 1770 (with Lincolnshire), 1870, 1871: iii. 107 (with Yorkshire), 109 (with Yorkshire), **256 (*s.xiv*)**, 442, 737, 738 |

| *Name of Shire* | *Regesta number* |
|---|---|
| Oxfordshire | ii. 1838, 1957: iii. 3 (with Berkshire), 10 (with Berkshire), 191, 238, 293, 367, 590, 637, 638, 639, 641, 852, 855 |
| Shropshire | iii. 376 |
| Somerset | ii. 1763: iii. 27, 924, 954 |
| Staffordshire | iii. 454, 456, 457, 714, 715 |
| Suffolk | *See under Norfolk: the two* shires *were run together:* **see iii. 201 for a specific mention of a justice of Suffolk**, 229 (Suffolk only), 235 (Suffolk only), 278 (Suffolk only) |
| Surrey | ii. 1718, 1743, 1818: iii. 33, 171, 172, 173, 202, 830, 957 |
| Sussex | ii. 859, 1404, 1670: iii. **935 (*s.xx*) (with Middlesex). Also iii. 448 (*s.xxii*) addr. to the Rape of Pevensey, incl. a justice** |
| Warwickshire | ii. 1789; iii. **135 (*s.xviii*)**, 570, 662, **688 (*s.xiii*)**, 965 (with Worcestershire) |
| Wiltshire | iii. **786 (*s.x*)**: iii. 789 |
| Worcestershire | Writ for Worcester:[e] iii. 965 (with Warwickshire), 970 |
| Yorkshire | ii. 711, 1328, 1429, 1454, **1730 (*s.xiv*)**, 1749, 1752 (with Carlisle), 1753 (with Carlisle), 1759 (with Hampshire), 1809, 1889: iii. 100, 101, 102, 107 (with Nottinghamshire), 109 (with Nottinghamshire), 120, 121, 123, **258 (*s.xxii*)**, 307 (city of York), 560, 561, 620, 625, 664, 797, 816, 923, 976, 977, 978, 981, 982 (city of York), 984, 985 (with Lincolnshire), 986, 987, 988, 993, 994 |

a From Bodleian ms. Dodsworth 75, fo. 188r, calendared in Francis Blomefield, *An Essay towards a Topographical History of the Shire of Norfolk* (11 volumes, London, 1805–10), iii. 47.

b From Bodleian ms. Dodsworth 75, fo. 188r, calendared in Francis Blomefield, *An Essay towards a Topographical History of the Shire of Norfolk* (11 volumes, London, 1805–10), iii. 47.

c *The Cartulary of Daventry Priory*, ed. M. J. Franklin, Northamptonshire Record Society 35 (1988), 331, no. 644.

d H. S. Offler, 'A Northumberland charter of King Henry I', in his *North of the Tees: Studies in Medieval British History*, ed. A. J. Piper and A. I. Doyle (Aldershot, 1996), no. VIII, p. 182.

e *The Cartulary of Worcester Cathedral Priory (Register I)*, ed. R. R. Darlington, Pipe Roll Society 76, new series 38 (1968), 24, no. 35.

The table shows that justices were imposed almost uniformly across the shires. Some of the omitted shires – Lancashire, Rutland, Westmorland – had not yet been created in the earlier twelfth century. One other shire – Cheshire – was held as a delegated jurisdiction by an earl, and so, though a fully constituted unit with a shire court, was not addressed by the king in writ-charters. There was one anomalous case, Derbyshire. It was paired with Nottinghamshire for most administrative purposes, but its pairing went much further than those seen elsewhere, such as those between Somerset and Dorset; Derbyshire did not have its own shire court in the early twelfth century, and there may not have been a separate office of sheriff of Derbyshire, for the post may in effect have been little more than an appendix to that of sheriff of Nottinghamshire.[12] The only missing shire where there is no clear explanation is Leicestershire, and the lack of evidence here reflects how few royal acta survive from that shire, perhaps because it had so few major ecclesiastical beneficiaries which might have preserved documents.

Durham is not included in this table because it was not at this point a full shire, but rather was an unusually extensive liberty within the shire of Northumberland.[13] There was a court which exercised jurisdiction over Durham, and it had important parallels with normal shire courts, but it was a private court held under the aegis of the bishops of Durham. There seems to be only one instance in which it was addressed by a king in the period under examination, where the justice was presumably one of the bishop of Durham rather than of the king.[14]

Putting these exceptions to one side, there is a clear pattern that emerges from this table; that almost every normally constituted shire court included among its members a justice by the start of King Stephen's reign at latest, and probably for some years before. Such officers were a regular and probably essential part of the proceedings of any such court.

## Section 2: The Identity of Justices to 1154

The list in Section 1 set out the evidence for the use of the title of justice in England between 1100 and 1154, and showed that the title was used in relation to almost every shire. This strongly suggests that there was a justice in almost every shire, and that the justice was a key part of the shire court. This list differs from the earlier one in that it sets out the evidence for who were the individuals who acted as justices in the shires. Once again, royal charters form the evidence for doing this because they were designed to be used within these courts, and so are precise and specific in addressing these individuals; when someone was addressed as justice in relation to a particular shire and shire court, it meant that they acted in that role. Many individuals can be identified as justices from the

12 Judith A. Green, *English Sheriffs to 1154* (London, 1990), 14, 34. The shire court of Derbyshire was held at Nottingham, and presumably was identical with the shire court of Nottinghamshire, until Henry II ordered that a separate court should be established. See *Placita de Quo Warranto Temporibus Edw. I, II & III in Curia Receptæ Scaccarii Westm. Asservata*, ed. W. Illingworth (London, 1818), 158–9; Frederick Pollock and Frederic Maitland, *The History of English Law Before the Time of Edward I* (second edition, Cambridge, 1898), i. 555; Robert C. Palmer, *The County Courts of Medieval England, 1150–1350* (Princeton, 1982), 29.

13 See Chapter 7 footnote 86 above.

14 *Regesta*, iii. no. 166, in the hand of *scriptor* xiii.

royal charters. Sometimes their names are paired with the title *iustitia*, though in other cases justices can be identified where their names were included between those of the bishop and sheriff, as noted above. In addition, there are cases where someone other than a sheriff is named in a *nisi feceris* clause, and these at least merit consideration as an occurrence of a justice.

The list presented here is a minimal one. It is dependent on patterns of survival in the evidence, most obviously, so that some shires are much better represented than others. The list is also affected by the ways in which the position of justice was filled. Not all address clauses include bishop, justice and sheriff; some have only two names, for it was possible for one person to hold more than one role. Sometimes, a bishop acted as justice in a shire,[15] and sometimes a sheriff was justice.[16] In such cases the individual would have been named only once in any one document. The existence of such duplications can be identified in some cases, but it can only be suspected that there were many more similar occurrences.

| | |
|---|---|
| Bedfordshire | Ralph Basset<br>August 1100 x 21 November 1129<br>Mentioned in a *nisi feceris* clause, *Regesta*, ii. no. 1533. He is not known as sheriff of Bedfordshire. Dated before the death of Nigel d'Aubigny. |
| Berkshire | There are no identifiable justices of Berkshire. It is possible that Roger, bishop of Salisbury, was justice, because Berkshire fell within his diocese. |
| Buckinghamshire | Nigel d'Oilli<br>1107<br>Addressed before the sheriffs of Buckinghamshire and Oxfordshire in *Regesta*, ii. no. 813. Dated after the grant that was confirmed therein, and before the death of Roger Bigod. |
| Cambridgeshire | Geoffrey de Mandeville<br>1140<br>He may be addressed as justice in *Regesta*, iii. no. 265, which is a command to enforce *Regesta*, iii. no. 264 if the addressees did not do so. He has not been identified as a sheriff of Cambridgeshire. Dated after *Regesta*, iii. no. 264 and before Geoffrey was earl. |
| Cheshire | There are no identifiable justices of Cheshire in this period. |

15 For instance, *Regesta*, iii. no. 490 made the bishop of Lincoln justice of Lincoln and Lincolnshire.

16 For instance, *Regesta*, iii. nos. 274–5 made the sheriff of Essex the justice as well; Van Caenegem, *Lawsuits*, no. 254, states that William, sheriff of Kent, was also justice in an 1127 plea.

| | |
|---|---|
| Cornwall | Geoffrey de Furnellis and William fitz John<br>1129 x 1130<br>Addressed as justices of Devon and Cornwall, *Regesta*, ii. no. 1663. Dated by the mention of a justice in the Pipe Roll. |
| Cumberland | Walter Espec and Eustace fitz John<br>1128 x 1130<br>Addressed before the sheriff, *Regesta*, ii. no. 1560 and 1685. Dated in the period for which Hildred of Carlisle and Odard account for the farm in the Pipe Roll, which also mentions the pleas of these two men. |
| Derbyshire | There are no identifiable justices of Derbyshire. |
| Devon | Ralph Basset<br>29 September 1102 x 1129<br>Mentioned in a writ to the sheriff, *Regesta*, ii. no. 1488. Dated after Plympton was founded and before Ralph Basset died. Mentions the geld and assizes of Ralph Basset.<br>Robert Arundel, Durand de Moiun and Herbert de Alneto<br>1123 x 1130<br>Described as king's justices in an account of a case in the court of the bishop of Exeter.[a] Many of the witnesses were canons of Exeter, so it might be presumed that the plea was held there. Dated during Bernard's activity, and before the Pipe Roll records Herbert to have been dead. For Durand see also under Somerset, where he was justice.<br>Robert Arundel and William fitz John<br>1129 x 1130<br>Addressed before the sheriff, *Regesta*, ii. no. 1667. Dated by the Pipe Roll.<br>William fitz John<br>1129 x 1130<br>Addressed as justice of Devon and Cornwall before the sheriff, *Regesta*, ii. no. 1663. Dated by the mention of this justice in the Pipe Roll. |
| Dorset | Bishop Roger of Salisbury and Alfred of Lincoln<br>29 September 1102 x 1129<br>Mentioned as justices ('sicut iusticiarii mei'), *Regesta*, ii. no. 754. Dated after Roger was bishop of Salisbury and before the Pipe Roll. |
| Essex | Geoffrey de Mandeville<br>1135 x 1137<br>Probably addressed as justice, *Regesta*, iii. 40: *S(tephanus) rex Angl(orum) iustic(ie) et Gaufr(ido) de Magnauilla et uic(ecomiti) et ministr(is) suis de Essexa salutem.* Dated after Stephen's accession and before the death of Robert fitz Richard de Clare, who witnessed it. |

| | |
|---|---|
| Essex *cont.* | Matilda's first grant of justiceship, midsummer 1141, *Regesta*, iii. no. 274, *capitalis iusticia in Essexa*.<br>The Empress Matilda granted the office of justice of Essex to Geoffrey de Mandeville, earl of Essex, along with the justiceships of Hertfordshire, London and Middlesex, with the offices of sheriff in those shires, in July 1141: *Regesta*, iii. no. 275. The same grants were then confirmed by Stephen at Christmas 1141: *Regesta*, iii. no. 276.<br>Richard de Lucy<br>1143 x 1154<br>Addressed as justice, *Regesta*, iii. nos. 546, 547, 548, 549, 550, 552, 559; after the fall of Geoffrey de Mandeville and his replacement as sheriff of Essex by Maurice; before the death of Stephen.<br>1147 x 1154<br>Probably addressed as justice, *Regesta*, iii. no. 848, in a *nisi feceris* role. Not otherwise identified as sheriff of Essex |
| Gloucestershire | Miles of Gloucester<br>1136<br>Described as justice in a grant to him; the position of justice was already held by him, and was not part of the grant, *Regesta*, iii. no. 386. Before the death of Payn fitz John in 1137. |
| Hampshire | There are no identifiable justices of Hampshire; but see under Isle of Wight, which was originally a portion of Hampshire. It might be conjectured that the bishops of Winchester acted as justices of Hampshire, which might explain why no other justices appear. |
| Herefordshire | Walter of Gloucester<br>10 April 1121<br>Addressed as sheriff, *Regesta*, ii. no. 1265. Dated by the mention of Easter being spent at Berkeley. |
| Hertfordshire | Geoffrey de Mandeville<br>July 1141<br>The Empress Matilda granted the office of justice of Hertfordshire to Geoffrey de Mandeville, earl of Essex, along with the justiceships of Essex, London and Middlesex, with the offices of sheriff in those shires, in July 1141: *Regesta*, iii. no. 275. The same grants were then confirmed by Stephen at Christmas 1141: *Regesta*, iii. no. 276. |
| Huntingdonshire | *Regesta*, ii. no. 1751 mentions a justice sent to the abbot of Ramsey's court at St Ives, October 1109 x 1112, after there was a bishop of Ely and before Bernard, abbot of Ramsey, died.<br>Bishop of Lincoln (unnamed – Robert or Alexander)<br>August 1100 x July 1133<br>Mentioned in a writ, *Regesta*, ii. no. 1837, in a *nisi feceris* clause if the sheriff failed to act. Dated only while Henry I was in England. |

| | |
|---|---|
| Isle of Wight | ?Alfred of Lincoln<br>[12 March x 3 September] 1101 x 29 September 1102<br>Mentioned as enforcer in a writ addressed to Richard de Redvers as lord of the island, *Regesta*, ii. no. 603. Dated while Roger was chancellor. |
| Kent | Aubrey de Vere<br>1135 x 1141<br>Mentioned in a *nisi feceris* clause, *Regesta*, iii. no. 143. Dated after Stephen's accession and before the death of Aubrey de Vere. |
| Leicestershire | There are no identifiable justices of Leicestershire. |
| Lincolnshire | William d'Aubigny<br>May x July 1133<br>Addressed before the sheriff, *Regesta*, ii. no. 1784. Dated after Nigel was elected bishop of Ely and before Henry I was last in England.<br>Earl William (probably de Roumare, earl of Lincoln)<br>1140 x 1147<br>Named as justice in a *nisi feceris* clause (*Et nisi feceris, iusticia mea comes Willelmus faciat*), *Regesta*, iii. no. 472. Dated after Robert became chancellor, and before William left for Normandy.<br>Robert de Chesney, bishop of Lincoln<br>1154<br>Granted the post of justice of Lincoln and of Lincolnshire (Sciatis me concessisse *Roberto episcopo Linc(olniensi) iustitiam meam de Linc(olnia) et de Linc(olne)scira)*, *Regesta*, iii. no. 490. |
| London | J. H. Round argued that the justiciarship of London was created through the terms of Henry I's charter for the burgesses of London.[b] The London charter itself is not likely to be entirely authentic.[c] The charter instead probably reflects the desire of the townsmen to protect themselves from the claims of Geoffrey de Mandeville.[d] The justices of London often seem to have formed an oligarchy linked by family and commercial interests.[e] The post of justice of London seems to have been separate from that of justice of Middlesex from an early date.<br>Fulcher fitz Walter<br>December 1113 x 1131.<br>Addressed before Eustace the sheriff, *Regesta*, ii. no. 1610a. Dated while Reginald was abbot of Ramsey.<br>Richard Basset and Aubrey de Vere<br>August 1100 x July 1133<br>Addressed before the sheriffs, *Regesta*, ii. no. 1781. Dated before Henry I was last in England<br>Andrew Bucca Uncta<br>1135 x 1139<br>Addressed as justice, *Regesta*, iii. nos. 445, 524, before Bishop Henry of Winchester was papal legate. |

| | |
|---|---|
| London *cont.* | Named as justice in a plea partly before the king, *Regesta*, iii. no. 506<br>1139, addressed as justice, *Regesta*, iii. no. 525<br>Osbert Eightpence/Huitdeniers<br>June 1139 x June 1141<br>Addressed as justice, after the arrest of Roger of Salisbury and before the Empress's arrival at Westminster, *Regesta*, iii. nos. 527, 528, 531; same addressed as justice by the empress, summer 1141, *Regesta*, iii. no. 529<br>Geoffrey de Mandeville<br>The Empress Matilda granted the office of justice of London and Middlesex to Geoffrey de Mandeville, earl of Essex, along with the justiceships of Essex and Hertfordshire, with the offices of sheriff in those shires, in July 1141: *Regesta*, iii. no. 275. The same grants were then confirmed by Stephen at Christmas 1141: *Regesta*, iii. no. 276. Geoffrey identified himself as *iusticiarius London'* in one of his charters.[f]<br>Gervase of Cornhill<br>It is not entirely clear when Gervase was justice, though the evidence for his use of the title in the 1140s is very strong. Matilda, Stephen's queen, described him as *Geruasio iustic(ie) de Lond(onia)* in a charter perhaps of 1141, though potentially as late as 1147: *Regesta*, iii. no. 243. He also used the title on his seal.[g]<br>Richard de Lucy and Theodoric son of Deorman<br>After 1143<br>Addressed as joint justices of London *(R(icardo) de Lucy et Teor(ico) filio Derm(ani) iusticiar(iis) London(ie))*, *Regesta*, iii. no. 534. The charter refers to Bishop Henry of Winchester's journey to Rome, probably that of 1143. |
| Middlesex | Roger, bishop of Salisbury, and Geoffrey de Clinton<br>January 1121 x July 1133<br>Addressed before the sheriffs, *Regesta*, ii. no. 1881. Dated after Herbert was abbot of Westminster.<br>Geoffrey de Mandeville<br>July 1141<br>The Empress Matilda granted the office of justice of London and Middlesex to Geoffrey de Mandeville, earl of Essex, along with the justiceships of Essex and Hertfordshire, with the offices of sheriff in those shires, in July 1141: *Regesta*, iii. no. 275. The same grants were then confirmed by Stephen at Christmas 1141: *Regesta*, iii. no. 276. Geoffrey identified himself as *iusticiarius London'* in one of his charters.[h] |
| Norfolk | Ralph Basset<br>August 1100 x August 1127<br>His intervention is threatened in a *nisi feceris* clause, *Regesta*, ii. no. 1520. Dated after Henry was king and before Ralph was last in England. |

| | |
|---|---|
| Norfolk *cont.* | R. Basset and others<br>26 April 1114 x 1 September 1117<br>Addressed before Robert fitz Walter as sheriff, *Regesta*, ii. no. 1094. Dated after Ralph was translated to Canterbury and before Bishop Robert of Chester died; his see was then vacant until after the death of Herbert of Norwich.<br>R. Basset and Aubrey de Vere<br>August 1131 x July 1133<br>Addressed in an unconventional way, iusticiariis suis R' Basset et *A(lberico) de Ver et burgensibus de Norwyco et ministris suis de Norfolc' et Suthf'*, *Regesta*, ii. no. 1608. Dated while Henry I was in England after the 1129 Pipe Roll, which does not mention this transaction.<br>Aubrey de Vere and Robert fitz Walter<br>March x July 1133<br>Mentioned as justices of Norfolk only and having recently heard a plea ( ... *coram iusticia mea de Northfolch, scilicet coram A(lberico) de Ver et Roberto filio Walteri* ... ), *Regesta*, ii. no. 1714. Dated while Anselm was abbot of Hulme.<br>Richard Basset and Aubrey de Vere<br>July 1133<br>Mentioned as custodians of the king's claims in Suffolk, *Regesta*, ii. no. 1783. Dated by the likely association with Henry I's last crossing. |
| Northamptonshire | According to an extract from a royal writ in the Daventry cartulary, the justices at some point in Henry I's reign were the bishop of Lincoln and the sheriff (unnamed).[i] |
| Northumberland | Nigel d'Aubigny<br>[March x April] 1107 x April 1116<br>Mentioned in a *nisi feceris* clause, *Regesta*, ii. no. 993. Dated while Ranulf was chancellor and before he was last in England before the death of Queen Matilda.<br>[March x April] 1107 x 1 May 1118<br>Addressed as justice in a writ of Queen Matilda further to the above, *Regesta*, ii. no. 1001. Dated after the above might have been issued and before the death of Matilda.<br>2 February 1115 or 1116<br>Addressed before the sheriff, *Regesta*, ii. no. 1124. Dated on a Candlemas when Henry I was in England, Thurstan was archbishop and when Count Robert of Meulan was alive.<br>Walter Espec and Forne son of Sigulf<br>August 1100 x August 1127<br>Addressed before the sheriffs, *Regesta*, ii. no. 1279. Dated before Henry I was last in England before the death of Flambard.<br>1100 x 1116 |

| | |
|---|---|
| Northumberland *cont.* | *Regesta*, ii. no. 1339 seems to indicate that Northumberland had more than one justice simultaneously.<br>November 1120 x July 1133<br>Addressed before the sheriff, *Regesta*, ii. no. 1264. Dated after Henry I was first in England after the death of Abbot Richard of St Albans, and before he was last there.<br><u>Walter Espec and Eustace fitz John</u><br>1130<br>Addressed, *Regesta*, ii. no. 1685. Dated by the mention of the transaction on the Pipe Roll. |
| Nottinghamshire | <u>Richard Basset and Aubrey de Vere</u><br>April 1123 x May 1133<br>Addressed before the sheriff (unnamed), *Regesta*, ii. no. 1660. Dated after Alexander was bishop of Lincoln and before Geoffrey the chancellor was made a bishop.<br><u>William Peverell</u><br>1136 x 1154<br>Addressed before the sheriff, *Regesta*, iii. no. 831, datable only while Stephen was in England. |
| Oxfordshire | <u>Nigel d'Oilly</u><br>1107<br>Addressed before the sheriffs of Buckinghamshire and Oxfordshire in *Regesta*, ii. no. 813. Dated after the grant that was confirmed therein, and before the death of Roger Bigod.<br>1109 x 1121<br>Addressed *after* Thomas de St John, sheriff of Oxford, in *Regesta*, ii. no. 1128, after Hervey was bishop of Ely and before Robert was made earl of Gloucester.<br><u>Roger, bishop of Salisbury</u><br>April 1123 x August 1131<br>Addressed before the sheriff (unnamed), *Regesta*, ii. no. 1707. Dated after Alexander was elected bishop of Lincoln and before Henry I was last in Normandy before Nigel was elected bishop of Ely.<br><u>Roger, bishop of Salisbury, and Geoffrey de Clinton</u><br>January 1121 x July 1133<br>Addressed probably as justices, *Regesta*, ii. no. 1881. Dated after Herbert was abbot of Westminster.<br><u>Richard Basset</u><br>July 1129 x July 1133<br>Mentioned in a *nisi feceris* clause as enforcer, *Regesta*, ii. no. 1882. Dated while Henry I was in England after the death of Earl Ranulf of Chester. |
| Pembroke | <u>Bernard, bishop of St Davids</u><br>1130 x July 1133<br>Mentioned in a *nisi feceris* clause, *Regesta*, ii. no. 1754. Dated after the Pipe Roll and before Henry I was last in England. |

| | |
|---|---|
| Pembroke *cont.* | Writ to Bernard ordering this, *Regesta*, ii. no. 1755, same dating. |
| Shropshire | The evidence for Shropshire differs substantially from that seen elsewhere. There had been an earldom of Shropshire in William the Conqueror's time, in the hands of the Montgomery family, which would have meant that addresses to the shire court would have included bishop, earl and sheriff. After their rebellion and expulsion in 1102, Richard de Belmeis, one of their former servants, was addressed between bishop and sheriff, presumably managing their former claims; *Regesta*, ii. no. 1102. This is much earlier than any justices seen elsewhere. Otherwise, there are no identifiable justices of Shropshire. |
| Somerset | <u>Walter of Gloucester</u><br>[26 x 30] December 1122 x 25 March 1123<br>Addressed before the sheriff, *Regesta*, ii. no. 1384. Dated after the death of Bishop John and before the election of Godfrey; the writ makes clear that the see was vacant.<br>29 September 1102 x 1128<br>Mentioned in a *Per* clause concerning Somerset, *Regesta*, ii. no. 1519; it is not clear why he was the informant here, except as sheriff. Dated after Roger of Salisbury was bishop and before Walter died.<br><u>Durand de Moiun</u><br>29 July 1121 x July 1133<br>Mentioned in writ alongside Warin as enforcer of judgement, *Regesta*, ii. no. 1302. Dated after the judgement that the writ enforces and before Henry was last in England.<br>See also under Devon, where he was justice |
| Staffordshire | There are no identifiable justices of Staffordshire. |
| Suffolk | See under Norfolk |
| Surrey | <u>Roger, bishop of Salisbury, and Geoffrey de Clinton</u><br>January 1121 x July 1133<br>Addressed before the sheriffs, *Regesta*, ii. no. 1881. Dated after Herbert was abbot of Westminster.<br><u>Richard Basset and Aubrey de Vere</u><br>1129 x July 1133<br>Addressed before the (unnamed) sheriff, *Regesta*, ii. no. 1655. Dated after the inheritance of Geoffrey Purcell, the beneficiary, and before Henry I was last in England. |
| Sussex | Much like Shropshire, the Montgomery family had extensive claims here before their rebellion and expulsion in 1102. One of their former functionaries, Richard de Belmeis, appears in addresses for Sussex in an undefined role, but presumably as manager of the former Montgomery claims: *Regesta*, ii. nos. 614 and 810. All must be dated before he was made bishop of London in 1108; *Regesta*, ii. no. 810 must be dated to 1107 or 1108 |

| | |
|---|---|
| Sussex *cont.* | because it was witnessed by Ranulf the chancellor. This shows that this arrangement persisted for some years after the expulsion of the Montgomeries.<br>Hamo dapifer<br>August 1100 x November 1135<br>Mentioned in a *nisi feceris* clause, *Regesta*, ii. no. 1669. Dated only by Henry's reign. |
| Warwickshire | Ralph Basset<br>November 1120 x 1129<br>Mentioned in a *nisi feceris* clause, *Regesta*, ii. no. 1033. Dated after the fourth seal came into use and before the death of Ralph Basset. |
| Wiltshire | There are no identifiable justices of Wiltshire. It is possible that Roger, bishop of Salisbury, was justice, because Wiltshire fell within his diocese. |
| Worcestershire | There are no identifiable justices of Worcestershire. |
| Yorkshire | Nigel d'Aubigny<br>27 May 1108 x [21 x 24] February 1114.<br>Addressed as justice, *Regesta*, ii. nos. 917, 923, 927, 977. Dated while Thomas II was archbishop.<br>2 February 1115 or 1116<br>Addressed before the sheriff, *Regesta*, ii. no. 1124. Dated on a Candlemas when Henry I was in England, Thurstan was archbishop and when Count Robert of Meulan was alive.<br>[15 x 16] August 1114 x January 1123<br>Addressed before the sheriff, *Regesta*, ii. no. 1357. Dated after Thurstan was elected and before the death of Ranulf the chancellor.<br>[15 x 16] August 1114 x 21 November 1129<br>Mentioned as justice in a *nisi feceris* clause, *Regesta*, ii. no. 1630. Dated after Thurstan was archbishop and before Nigel died.<br>Nigel d'Aubigny and Anschetillus de Bulmer<br>27 May 1108 x [21 x 24] February 1114.<br>Addressed after Osbert the sheriff, *Regesta*, ii. no. 995. Dated while Thomas II was archbishop.<br>Nigel d'Aubigny and Ranulf Bucel<br>27 May 1108 x 21 November 1129<br>Addressed, role uncertain, *Regesta*, ii. no. 1330. Dated after the election of an Archbishop T. and before the death of Nigel d'Aubigny.<br>Eustace fitz John and Walter Espec<br>January 1123 x 14 May 1133<br>Addressed in *Regesta*, ii. no. 1756. Dated while Geoffrey was chancellor.<br>January 1123 x May 1133 (Walter Espec alone) |

| | |
|---|---|
| Yorkshire *cont.* | Addressed before the sheriff with Anschitillus de Bulmer as sheriff, *Regesta*, ii. no. 1532. Dated while Geoffrey was chancellor.<br>1129 x July 1133<br>Addressed as sheriff with Eustace fitz John as sheriff, *Regesta*, ii. no. 1662. Dated after the death of Anschetillus de Bulmer and before Henry I was last in England.<br><u>Walter Espec, Eustace fitz John and Forne (son of Sigulf)</u><br>1119 x 1129<br>Addressed before a sheriff is mentioned, *Regesta*, ii. no. 1557. Dated after Abbot Geoffrey of St Mary's was elected and before Forne died. |

[a] J. H. Round ed., 'Bernard, the King's Scribe', *English Historical Review* 14 (1899), 417–30, at 421.

[b] J. H. Round, *Geoffrey de Mandeville: A Study of the Anarchy* (London, 1892), 373.

[c] See comments in Nicholas Karn, 'Robert de Sigillo: An Unruly Head of the Royal Scriptorium in the 1120s and 1130s', *English Historical Review* 123 (2008), 539–53, at 549, and literature cited there.

[d] For an earlier list of London justices see Susan Reynolds, 'The Rulers of London in the Twelfth Century', *History* 57 (1972), 337–57, at 354, and Christopher Brooke and Gillian Keir, London, *800–1216: The Shaping of a City* (London, 1975), 371–4, 'Appendix II: The Sheriffs and Justices of London and Middlesex, c. 1030–1216'.

[e] Christopher Brooke and Gillian Keir, *London, 800–1216: The Shaping of a City* (London, 1975), 199–218

[f] J. H. Round, *The Commune of London and Other Studies* (London, 1899), 118.

[g] J. H. Round, *Geoffrey de Mandeville: A Study of the Anarchy* (London, 1892), 305.

[h] J. H. Round, *The Commune of London and Other Studies* (London, 1899), 118.

[i] *The Cartulary of Daventry Priory*, ed. M. J. Franklin, Northamptonshire Record Society 35 (1988), 331, no. 644

## Section 3: The Evidence for Pleas and Justices in the 1129–30 Pipe Roll

Though, as noted above, the Pipe Roll has been used more often than any other source of group of sources in setting out who the justices were in that year and the years immediately preceding, it is in fact rather unsuitable for assessing the spread of justices or their activities. It does not identify individuals using their titles, but merely uses their names. From the perspective of the exchequer, it probably mattered little who the justices actually were; the concern of the exchequer was in identifying who was liable for a debt, and what that debt was. The Pipe Roll is consistent in noting who was liable, but is much less rigorous in noting where the plea came from. The fixed conventions seen from the last decades of the twelfth century had not yet appeared. Thus, an extensive set of pleas is sometimes noted in the Yorkshire account as the pleas of Blyth (presumably, they were held there), and sometimes as the pleas of Geoffrey de Clinton at Blyth.[17] Elsewhere debts are attributed to vague occurrences, such as pleas or pleas of deer, without any indication of who might have been involved in conducting them. The Pipe Roll may well hide much activity by justices.

The relationship of justices to pleas must have been different in 1129–30 from what it became towards the end of the twelfth century, because early justices lacked the authoritative position of later ones, and were participants in court proceedings rather than those who dominated it.[18] This can probably be seen in the Pipe Roll. The account for Oxfordshire notes that Walter the archdeacon was responsible for the proceeds of a plea between him and Restold, the former sheriff of Oxford (*... pro placito quod fuit inter eum et Restoldum vicecomitem*).[19] Walter was accountable for the plea to the exchequer, which means that this could not be simply a private plea between Walter and Restold; the sums of money are very large, and might relate to Restold's misdeeds as sheriff.[20] Elsewhere, Walter acted as the king's representative, advocate and agent, in other words as justice.[21] The description of his involvement in this case does not match how the work of justices was described later in the twelfth century, but the links here suggest that he was acting as justice. Pleas do not need to be described as 'of' someone to indicate that justices were at work, at least in the first half of the twelfth century.[22]

The Pipe Roll includes many references to some prominent individuals whose role as justices has often been mentioned, such as Richard Basset and Geoffrey de Clinton. They were clearly active, and their widespread roles in many shires parallel the ways in which Basset and Aubrey de Vere operated as sheriffs across many shires. Yet, alongside these, the Pipe Roll shows that there were other men

17 *The Great Roll of the Pipe for the Thirty-First Year of the Reign of King Henry I, Michaelmas 1130*, ed. Judith A. Green, Pipe Roll Society 95, new series 57 (2012), 21–2.

18 See Chapter 7 for all this.

19 *The Great Roll of the Pipe for the Thirty-First Year of the Reign of King Henry I, Michaelmas 1130*, ed. Judith A. Green, Pipe Roll Society 95, new series 57 (2012), 3.

20 For Restold's other debts for his actions as sheriff of Oxford see *The Great Roll of the Pipe for the Thirty-First Year of the Reign of King Henry I, Michaelmas 1130*, ed. Judith A. Green, Pipe Roll Society 95, new series 57 (2012), 2.

21 J. C. Crick, 'Oxford, Walter of (*d.* in or before 1151?)', *ODNB*. For his work at the exchequer see *Regesta*, ii. no. 1000; *Abingdon Chronicle*, ii. 170–1. For his work as administrator of a vacant abbey see *Chronicon Petroburgense*, ed. Thomas Stapleton, Camden Society (1849), 157–83, and Hugh Candidus, *Chronicle*, ed. W. T. Mellows, *The Chronicle of Hugh Candidus, a Monk of Peterborough* (Oxford, 1949), 99.

22 Note also *The Great Roll of the Pipe for the Thirty-First Year of the Reign of King Henry I, Michaelmas 1130*, ed. Judith A. Green, Pipe Roll Society 95, new series 57 (2012), 56, where the abbot of Fécamp accounted *Et xx m. argenti de placitis Ricardi Bass' pro Salida homine suo*, which seems to show pleas of a justice on behalf of one of his men.

who took part in pleas in the interest of the king, yet who have not attracted the same level of attention as their more eminent colleagues. These included such men as Anfrid the collector in Bedfordshire, Walchelin Visdelup in Berkshire and Surrey, Robert Arundel in Cornwall, Devon and Dorset, and so forth. Their appearance here points to how the eminent men must in practice have depended on locals, because they could not have committed much time to any particular shire.

| **County** | **Pipe Roll mentions of justices, cited by page.**[a] |
|---|---|
| Bedfordshire | 82 pleas of Anfrid the collector, pleas of Geoffrey de Clinton of the jurors and lesser men of the shire |
| Berkshire | 97 old pleas of Ralph Basset of the common shire, pleas of Geoffrey de Clinton<br>98 pleas of Ralph Basset for the mutilation of his men, pleas of Geoffrey de Clinton, new plea of Walchelin Visdelup of assarts |
| Buckinghamshire | 80 old pleas of Ralph Basset, pleas of Geoffrey de Clinton of the lawmen of Buckingham<br>81, Richard son of Alured the butler paid 15m that he sit with Ralph Basset at the king's pleas |
| Cambridgeshire | None named |
| Carlisle | 112 pleas of Walter Espec and Eustace fitz John |
| Cornwall | 125 pleas of Robert Arundel and his associates of the forest |
| Derbyshire | See under Nottinghamshire |
| Devon | 121 pleas of Robert Arundel of the burgesses of Exeter<br>122 pleas of Robert Arundel of the men of Ralph Taisson of the men of Wonford, pleas of Robert Arundel of the forest |
| Dorset and Wiltshire | 11 pleas of Robert Arundel and his associates of the forest<br>13 pleas of Geoffrey de Clinton.<br>14 pleas of Ralph Basset about treasure. |
| Durham | 104 pleas of Eustace fitz John |
| Essex | 43 pleas of G Clinton<br>44 pleas of Geoffrey de Clinton of the small men<br>45 pleas of William d'Aubigny and his associates of the forest<br>47 pleas of Geoffrey de Clinton |
| Gloucestershire | 61 pleas of Miles of Gloucester and Payn fitz John, plea of the money of Roger of Berkeley, plea of the treasure of Roger of Berkeley, plea of Payn fitz John<br>62 plea of wife of John of Sudeley |
| Hampshire | 30 pleas of the king at Eling, pleas of Miles of Gloucester |
| Hertfordshire | 48 pleas of Richard Basset |
| Huntingdonshire | 37 pleas of Geoffrey de Clinton |
| Kent | 51 pleas of Henry de Port and his associaties<br>51–2 pleas of Geoffrey de Clinton and jurors of shire |

| | |
|---|---|
| Leicestershire | 70 pleas of Richard Basset |
| Lincolnshire | 87 pleas of Ralph Basset<br>88 pleas of Geoffrey de Clinton<br>89 pleas of William d'Aubigny<br>90 pleas of Ralph Basset, Anschetill collector accounted for money from pleas of William d'Aubigny, pleas of William d'Aubigny<br>91 pleas of Richard Basset and William d'Aubigny<br>92 pleas of Richard Basset of the small men, pleas of William d'Aubigny<br>93 pleas of William d'Aubigny<br>95 pleas of William d'Aubigny, pleas of William d'Aubigny of Boston |
| London | 114 pleas of Ralph Basset |
| Norfolk | 72 Benjamin returned account for having custody of pleas of the Crown<br>73 pleas of Ralph Basset, pleas of Geoffrey de Clinton<br>74 pleas of Richard Basset, pleas of Geoffrey de Clinton, plea of money of Benjamin, pleas of Richard Basset at Thetford<br>75 plea of Richard Basset |
| Northamptonshire | 66 pleas of Geoffrey de Clinton |
| Northumberland | 28 pleas of Walter Espec and Eustace fitz John |
| Nottinghamshire and Derbyshire | 7 pleas of Geoffrey de Clinton; pleas of Ralph Basset<br>8 pleas of Geoffrey de Clinton. |
| Oxfordshire | 3 Walter the archdeacon (of Oxford) accounted for a plea between himself and Restold the sheriff. |
| Pembroke | 107 pleas of Miles of Gloucester and Payn fitz John |
| Staffordshire | 58 pleas of Geoffrey de Clinton, pleas of Miles of Gloucester of the forest of bishopric of Chester, pleas of Miles of Gloucester and Payn fitz John, pleas of Geoffrey de Clinton for breach of the peace |
| Suffolk | 76 pleas of Ralph Basset<br>77 pleas of William of Houghton, pleas of Richard Basset<br>78 pleas of Geoffrey de Clinton, new pleas of Richard Basset |
| Surrey | 39 pleas of Ralph Basset of the forest, old pleas of Ralph Basset of the common shire<br>39 pleas of Geoffrey de Clinton<br>40 pleas of Walchelin Visdeloup for assarts |
| Sussex | 54 pleas of Geoffrey de Clinton and jurors of shire<br>55 pleas of Richard Basset<br>56 plea of Richard Basset for Salida his man, pleas of Richard Basset for the small men for default of hundreds |
| Warwickshire | 84 plea of William Hubold, pleas of Geoffrey de Clinton<br>85 plea of W(alter) of Gloucester |

| | |
|---|---|
| Westmorland | 112 small pleas of Walter Espec and Eustace fitz John, pleas of Eustace fitz John for the small men |
| Wiltshire | See under Dorset |
| Yorkshire | 20 pleas of Eustace fitz John<br>21 pleas of Geoffrey de Clinton and his associates; pleas of Walter Espec and Eustace fitz John; pleas of Geoffrey de Clinton and his associates of Blyth.<br>25 pleas of Ralph Basset<br>26 pleas of Walter Espec, Walter Espec and Eustace [fitz John]<br>27 Heading – Pleas of W. Espec and Eustace fitz John<br>Pleas of Serlo de Burg and Osbert his nephew |

[a] Cited from *The Great Roll of the Pipe for the Thirty-First Year of the Reign of King Henry I, Michaelmas 1130*, ed. Judith A. Green, Pipe Roll Society 95, new series 57 (2012).

# Bibliography

## Manuscripts

*Cambridge*

Corpus Christi College, ms. 139 (collection of chronicles from Sawley Abbey, s.xii).

The University Library ms. Additional 3020 (Red Book of Thorney; s.xiv ex. general cartulary).

*London*

The British Library, ms. Additional 38816 (compilation from St Mary's Abbey, York, s.xii).

The British Library, ms. Additional Roll 34933 (Manor court roll for Ramsey Abbey's manor of Lawshall, Suffolk, 1466).

The National Archives, C66/224 (Patent Roll 22 Edward III).

The National Archives, SC 2/203/96 (Manor court roll for Ramsey Abbey's manor of Lawshall, Suffolk, 1364–8).

The National Archives, SC 2/203/97 (Manor court rolls for Ramsey Abbey's manor of Lawshall, Suffolk, 1484–9 and 1498–9).

*Oxford*

The Bodleian Library, ms. Arch. Selden B 16 (William of Malmesbury's copy of the Breviary of Alaric, s.xii in.).

The Bodleian Library, ms. Bodley 39 (later thirteenth-century register from St Mary's Abbey York).

The Bodleian Library, ms. Dodsworth 63 (notes and transcripts by Roger Dodsworth, s. xvii med.).

The Bodleian Library, ms. Dodsworth 75 (notes and transcripts by Roger Dodsworth, s. xvii med.).

The Bodleian Library, ms. Trinity College 85 (Cartulary of Montacute Priory, *c.* 1300).

## Printed Primary Sources

*Accounts of the Manor and Hundred of Macclesfield, Cheshire, Michaelmas 1361 to Michaelmas 1362*, edited by P. H. W. Booth, The Record Society of Lancashire and Cheshire 138 (2003).

Anglo-Saxon Charters indexes via http://www.esawyer.org.uk/.

*Anglo-Saxon Charters* 7–8: *The Charters of Abingdon Abbey*, ed. Susan Kelly (two vols, Oxford, 2000–1).

*Anglo-Saxon Charters* 14: *Charters of Peterborough Abbey*, ed. Susan Kelly (Oxford, 2009).

*The Anglo-Saxon Chronicle: A Revised Translation*, ed. Dorothy Whitelock, David C. Douglas and Susie I. Tucker (London, 1961); *The Peterborough Chronicle, 1070–1154*, ed. Cecily Clark (second edition, Oxford, 1970).

Anselm, *letters*, ed. F. S. Schmitt, *Sancti Anselmi Cantuariensis Archiepiscopi Opera Omnia* (6 vols, Edinburgh, 1946–61); trans. W. Fröhlich, *The Letters of Saint Anselm of Canterbury*, Cistercian Series 96–7, 142 (3 vols, Kalamazoo, 1990–4).

Assize of Clarendon: ed. William Stubbs, *Select Charters and Other Illustrations of English Constitutional History* (ninth edition, Oxford, 1913), 170–3.

Battle of Maldon, *English Historical Documents, c. 500–1042*, ed. and trans. Dorothy Whitelock (London, 1955), 293–7.

Bede, *Historia ecclesiastica*, ed. and trans. B. Colgrave and R. A. B. Mynors (Oxford, 1969).

Blomefield, Francis, *An Essay towards a Topographical History of the Shire of Norfolk* (11 vols, London, 1805–10).

*Calendar of the Charter Rolls Preserved in the Public Record Office*, ed. The Deputy Keeper of the Records (6 vols, London, 1903–27).

*Calendar of the Patent Rolls Preserved in the Public Record Office*, ed. Deputy Keeper of the Records (75 vols, London, 1901–86).

*The Cartulary of Daventry Priory*, ed. M. J. Franklin, Northamptonshire Record Society 35 (1988).

*The Cartulary of Worcester Cathedral Priory (Register I)*, ed. R. R. Darlington, Pipe Roll Society 76, new series 38 (1968).

*The Charters of the Anglo-Norman Earls of Chester, c. 1071–1237*, ed. Geoffrey Barraclough, Record Society of Lancashire and Cheshire 126 (1988).

*Charters of the Honour of Mowbray, 1107–1191*, ed. D. E. Greenway, Records of Social and Economic History new series 1 (Oxford, 1972).

*The Charters of Quarr Abbey*, ed. S. F. Hockey, Isle of Wight Records Series 3 (1991).

*Charters of the Redvers Family and the Earldom of Devon, 1090–1217*, ed. Robert Bearman, Devon and Cornwall Record Society, new series 37 (1994).

The Charters of William II and Henry I: https://actswilliam2henry1.wordpress.com/.

*The Chronicle of Battle Abbey*, ed. and trans. Eleanor Searle (Oxford, 1980).

*Chronicon Petroburgense*, ed. Thomas Stapleton, Camden Society (1849).

*Councils and Synods with other Documents relating to the English Church: Part*

*1, AD 871–1204*, ed. D. Whitelock, M. Brett and C. N. L. Brooke (2 vols, Oxford, 1981).

*The Court Rolls of the Honor of Clitheroe in the County of Lancaster*, ed. William Farrer (three vols, Manchester, 1897–1912).

*De iniusta uexacione Willelmi episcopi primi per Willelmum regem filium Willelmi magni regis*, ed. H. S. Offler, A. J. Piper and A. I. Doyle, *Camden Miscellany* xxxiv: *Chronology, Conquest and Conflict in Medieval Britain*, Camden fifth series 10 (Cambridge, 1997), 49–104.

Domesday Book: *Domesday Book: Text and Translation*, ed. and trans. J. Morris (38 vols, Chichester, 1975–86) *also*, the Alecto edition of Domesday Book, *Great Domesday Book*, ed. and trans. R. W. H. Erskine and G. H. Martin (62 vols, London, 1987–92).

Eadmer of Canterbury, *Historia Nouorum in Anglia*, ed. Martin Rule (London, 1884); trans. Geoffrey Bosanquet (London, 1964).

*Earldom of Gloucester Charters: The Charters and Scribes of the Earls and Countesses of Gloucester to AD 1217*, ed. Robert B. Patterson (Oxford, 1973).

*The Early Charters of Waltham Abbey, 1062–1230*, ed. Rosalind Ransford (Woodbridge, 1989).

Early English Laws: http://www.earlyenglishlaws.ac.uk/

*Early Yorkshire Charters*: VIII, *The Honour of Warenne*, edited by Charles Travis Clay, Yorkshire Archaeological Society, Extra Series 6 (1949).

*English Episcopal Acta* 1: *Lincoln, 1076–1185*, ed. David M. Smith (Oxford, 1980).

*English Episcopal Acta* 31: *Ely, 1109–1197*, ed. Nicholas Karn (Oxford, 2005).

*English Episcopal Acta* 33: *Worcester, 1062–1185*, ed. Mary Cheney, David Smith, Christopher Brooke and Philippa M. Hoskin (Oxford, 2007).

*English Episcopal Acta* 42: *Ely, 1198–1256*, ed. Nicholas Karn (Oxford, 2013).

*English Royal Lawsuits from William I to Richard I*, ed. and trans. R. C. van Caenegem, 2 vols, Selden Society, 106–7 (1990–1).

'*Epistulae Fiscannenses*: lettres d'amitié, de gouvernement et d'affaires', ed. J. Laporte, *Revue Mabillon* 44 (1953), 5–31.

*Feudal Documents from the Abbey of Bury St Edmunds*, ed. D. C. Douglas (London, 1932).

*Die Gesetze der Angelsachsen*, ed. Felix Liebermann (3 vols, Halle, 1903–16).

Glanvill: *The Treatise on the Laws and Customs of the Realm of England Commonly Called Glanvill*, ed. and trans. G. D. G. Hall and M. T. Clanchy (Oxford, 1993)

*The Great Roll of the Pipe for the Thirty First Year of the Reign of King Henry I, Michaelmas 1130*, ed. Judith A. Green, Pipe Roll Society 95, new series 57 (2012).

*The Great Rolls of the Pipe for the Second, Third, and Fourth Years of the Reign of King Henry II, AD 1155, 1156, 1157, 1158*, ed. Joseph Hunter (London, 1844).

*The Great Roll of the Pipe for the Twelfth Year of the Reign of King Henry the Second*, Pipe Roll Society 9 (1888).

*The Great Roll of the Pipe for the Thirteenth Year of the Reign of King Henry II, AD 1166–1167*, Pipe Roll Society 11 (1889).

*Halmota Prioratus Dunelmensis, Containing Extracts from the Halmote Court or Manor Rolls of the Prior and Convent of Durham, AD 1296–AD 1384*, edited by W. H. D. Longstaffe and John Booth, Surtees Society 82 (1889).

*Historia Ecclesie Abbendonensis/The History of the Church of Abingdon*, ed. and trans. John Hudson (two vols, Oxford, 2002–7).

Hugh Candidus, *Chronicle*, ed. W. T. Mellows, *The Chronicle of Hugh Candidus, a Monk of Peterborough* (Oxford, 1949).

*Inquisitio Eliensis*, ed. N. E. S. A. Hamilton, *Inquisitio Comitatus Cantabrigiensis* (London, 1876), 97–195.

Jocelin of Brakelond, *Chronicle*, ed. and trans. H. E. Butler (Edinburgh, 1949).

John of Salisbury, *Policraticus*: trans. Cary J. Nederman (Cambridge, 1990).

John of Worcester, *Chronicle*, ed. and trans. R. R. Darlington and P. McGurk (two vols of three published, Oxford, 1995–8).

Kalendar of Abbot Samson, in *The Kalendar of Abbot Samson of Bury St Edmunds and Related Documents*, ed. R. H. C. Davis, Camden Third Series 84 (1954).

Lanfranc, *letters*, ed. and trans. Helen Clover and Margaret Gibson, *The Letters of Lanfranc, Archbishop of Canterbury* (Oxford, 1979).

Lantfred of Winchester, 'Miracles of St Swithun', ed. and trans. Michael Lapidge, *The Cult of St Swithun*, Winchester Studies 4.1 (Oxford, 2003).

*The Laws of the Earliest English Kings*, ed. and trans. F. L. Attenborough (Cambridge, 1922)

*The Laws of the Kings of England from Edmund to Henry I*, ed. and trans. A. J. Robertson (Cambridge, 1925).

*Leet Jurisdiction in the City of Norwich during the XIIIth and XIVth Centuries*, ed. William Hudson, Selden Society 5 (1892).

*Leges Anglorum*: F. Liebermann, *Über die Leges Anglorum saeculo xiii. ineunte Londoniis collectae* (Halle, 1892).

*Leges Edward Confessoris*: ed. and trans. Bruce R. O'Brien, *God's Peace and King's Peace: The Laws of Edward the Confessor* (Philadelphia, 1999).

*Leges Henrici Primi*: ed. and trans. L. J. Downer, *Leges Henrici Primi* (Oxford, 1972).

*The Leicestershire Survey* c. *AD 1130*, ed. C. F. Slade (Leicester, 1956).

*Liber Eliensis*, ed. E. O. Blake, Camden Third Series 92 (1962); *Liber Eliensis: A History of the Isle of Ely from the Seventh Century to the Twelfth*, trans. Janet Fairweather (Woodbridge, 2005).

*Monasticon Anglicanum*, William Dugdale and Roger Dodsworth, ed. and revised J. Caley, H. Ellis and B. Bandinel (6 vols in 8 parts, London, 1817–30, reprinted 1846).

'A Northumberland Charter of King Henry I', ed. H. S. Offler, in his *North of the Tees: Studies in Medieval British History*, ed. A. J. Piper and A. I. Doyle (Aldershot, 1996), no. VIII.

Orderic Vitalis, *Historia Ecclesiastica*, ed. and trans. Marjorie Chibnall, *The Ecclesiastical History of Orderic Vitalis* (6 vols, Oxford, 1969–81).

*Peterborough Medieval Court Rolls*, translated by Margaret Briston with an introduction by Nicholas Karn, Northamptonshire Record Society 48 (2015).

*Placita de Quo Warranto Temporibus Edw. I, II & III in Curia Receptæ Scaccarii Westm. Asservata*, ed. W. Illingworth (London, 1818).

*Quadripartitus, ein Englisches Rechtsbuch von 1114*, ed. Felix Liebermann (Halle, 1892).

*Regesta Regum Anglo-Normannorum, 1066–1154*; i: *Regesta Willelmi Conquestoris et Willelmi Rufi, 1066–1100*, ed. H. W. C. Davis and R. J. Whitwell (Oxford, 1913); ii: *Regesta Henrici Primi, 1100–1135*, ed. C. Johnson and H. A. Cronne (Oxford, 1956); iii: *Regesta Regis Stephani ac Mathildis Imperatricis ac Gaufridi et Henrici Ducum Normannorum, 1135–1154*, ed. H. A. Cronne and R. H. C. Davis (Oxford, 1968).

*Regesta Regum Anglo-Normannorum: The Acta of William I, 1066–1087*, ed. David Bates (Oxford, 1998).

*Registrum Palatinum Dunelmense: The Register of Richard de Kellawe, Lord Palatine and Bishop of Durham, 1311–1316*, ed. Thomas Duffus Hardy (four vols, London, 1873–8).

*Registrum sive Liber Irrotularius et Consuetudinarius Prioratus Beatæ Mariæ Wigorniensis*, ed. William Hale Hale [*sic*], Camden Society 91 (1865).

*St Benet of Holme, 1020-1210: The Eleventh and Twelfth Century Sections of Cotton MS Galba E. ii.: The Register of the Abbey of St Benet of Holme*, ed. J. R. West, Norfolk Record Society 2–3 (1934).

Stephen of Whitby, Roger Dodsworth and William Dugdale, *Monasticon Anglicanum, sive Pandectae coenobiorum* (3 vols, London, 1655–73), i. 383–6, and thence in W. Dugdale and R. Dodsworth, *Monasticon Anglicanum*, ed. and revised J. Caley, H. Ellis and B. Bandinel (6 vols in 8 parts, London, 1817–30, reprinted 1846), iii. 544–6.

Symeon of Durham, *Libellus de exordio atque procursu istius, hoc est Dunhelmensis, ecclesie/Tract on the origins and progress of this the Church of Durham*, ed. and trans. David Rollason (Oxford, 2000).

Thomas of Marlborough, *History of the Abbey of Evesham*, ed. and trans. by Jane Sayers and Leslie Watkiss (Oxford, 2003).

*Two Cartularies of the Augustinian Priory of Bruton and the Cluniac Priory of Montacute*, ed. Members of the Council, Somerset Record Society 8 (1894).

*Vetus liber archidiaconi Eliensis*, ed. C. L. Feltoe and E. H. Minns, Octavo Publications of the Cambridge Antiquarian Society 48 (1917).

William of Malmesbury, *De Antiquitate Glastonie ecclesie*, ed. and trans. John Scott (Woodbridge, 1981).

William of Malmesbury, *Gesta Regum Anglorum/The History of the English Kings*, ed. and trans. R. A. B. Mynors, R. M. Thomson and M. Winterbottom (two vols, Oxford, 1998–9).

William of Newburgh, *Historia rerum Anglicarum*: ed. and trans. P. G. Walsh and M. J. Kennedy, *The History of English Affairs* (2 vols, Warminster and Oxford, 1988–2007).

*Wulfstan's Canon Law Collection*, ed. J. E. Cross and Andrew Hamer (Woodbridge, 1999).

## Secondary Sources

Abels, R. P., 'Sheriffs, Lord-Seeking and the Norman Settlement of the South-East Midlands', *Anglo-Norman Studies* XIX (1997), 19–50.

Aird, W. M., 'An Absent Friend: The Career of Bishop William of St Calais', in *Anglo-Norman Durham, 1093–1193*, ed. David Rollason, Margaret Harvey and Michael Prestwich (Woodbridge, 1994), 283–97.

Alexander, James W., 'New Evidence on the Palatinate of Chester', *English Historical Review* 85 (1970), 715–29.

——, 'The Alleged Palatinates of Norman England', *Speculum* 56 (1981), 17–27.

Alvarez de las Asturias, Nicolás, 'The Use of the *Collectio Lanfranci*: The Evidence of the Manuscripts', in *Bishops, Texts and the Use of Canon Law around 1100: Essays in Honour of Martin Brett*, ed. Bruce C. Brasington, and Kathleen G. Cushing (Aldershot, 2008), 121–7.

——, 'Lanfranc of Bec's Version of Decretals in a Canonistic Context', *Catholic Historical Review* 98 (2012), 649–78.

Ault, Warren Ortman, *Private Jurisdiction in England* (New Haven, 1923).

Bailey, Mark, *The English Manor,* c. *1200*–c. *1500* (Manchester, 2002).

Barlow, Frank, 'St Calais [St Carilef], William de (*c.* 1030–1096)', *ODNB.*

Barrow, Julia, 'How the Twelfth-Century Monks of Worcester Perceived their Past', in *The Perception of the Past in Twelfth-Century Europe*, ed. Paul Magdalino (London, 1992), 53–74.

Bartlett, Robert, *Trial by Fire and Water: The Medieval Judicial Ordeal* (Oxford, 1986).

——, *The Making of Europe: Conquest, Colonization and Cultural Change, 950–1350* (London, 1993).

Bates, David R., 'The Character and Career of Odo, Bishop of Bayeux (1049/50–1097', *Speculum* 50 (1975), 1–20.

——, 'The Origins of the Justiciarship', *Anglo-Norman Studies* IV (1981), 1–12, 167–71.

——, *The Normans and Empire: The Ford Lectures delivered in the University of Oxford during Hilary Term 2010* (Oxford, 2013).

——, *William the Conqueror* (New Haven, 2016).

Baxter, Stephen, 'The Representation of Lordship and Land Tenure in Domesday Book', in *Domesday Book*, ed. Elizabeth M. Hallam and David Bates (Stroud, 2001), 73–102, 203–8.

——, *The Earls of Mercia: Lordship and Power in Late Anglo-Saxon England* (Oxford, 2007).

——, 'Lordship and Justice in Late Anglo-Saxon England: The Judicial Functions of Soke and Commendation Revisited', in *Early Medieval Studies in Memory of Patrick Wormald*, ed. Stephen Baxter, Catherine Karkov, Janet L. Nelson and David Pelteret (Farnham, 2009), 383–419.

Baxter, Stephen, and John Blair, 'Land Tenure and Royal Patronage in the Early English Kingdom: A Model and a Case Study', *Anglo-Norman Studies* XXVIII (2006), 19–46.

Bishop, T. A. M., and Pierre Chaplais, *Facsimiles of English Royal Writs to AD 1100* (Oxford, 1957).

Bishop, T. A. M., *Scriptores Regis*: *Facsimiles to Identify and Illustrate the Hands of Royal Scribes in Original Charters of Henry I, Stephen and Henry II* (Oxford, 1961).

Bisson, Thomas N., 'The "Feudal Revolution"', *Past and Present* 142 (1994), 6–42.

——, 'Medieval Lordship', *Speculum* 70 (1995), 743–59.

——, *The Crisis of the Twelfth Century: Power, Lordship and the Origins of European Government* (Princeton, 2009).

Blair, John, 'Parish Churches in the Eleventh Century', in *Domesday Studies*, ed. G. H. Martin, Ann Williams and R. W. H. Erskine (London, 1987), 65–8.

——, ed., *Minsters and Parish Churches: The Local Church in Transition, 950–1200* (Oxford, 1988).

——, 'Introduction: from Minster to Parish Church', in *Minsters and Parish Churches: The Local Church in Transition, 950–1200*, ed. John Blair (Oxford, 1988), 1–19.

Brand, Paul, *The Origins of the English Legal Profession* (Oxford, 1992).

——, 'The Origins of the English Legal Profession', rpt in his *The Making of the Common Law* (London, 1992), 1–20.

Brett, Martin, 'The *Collectio Lanfranci* and its Competitors', in *Intellectual Life in the Middle Ages: Essays Presented to Margaret Gibson*, ed. Lesley Smith and Benedicta Ward (1992), 157–71.

Brooke, C. N. L., and Gillian Keir, *London, 800–1216: The Shaping of a City* (London, 1975).

Brooke, Z. N., *The English Church and the Papacy from the Conquest to the Reign of John* (Cambridge, 1931).

Brooks, Nicholas P., 'The Fonthill Letter, Ealdorman Ordlaf and Anglo-Saxon Law in Practice', in *Early Medieval Studies in Memory of Patrick Wormald*, ed. Stephen Baxter, Catherine Karkov, Janet L. Nelson and David Pelteret (Farnham, 2009), 301–17.

Burton, Janet, 'The Monastic Revival in Yorkshire: Whitby and St Mary's, York', in *Anglo-Norman Durham, 1093–1193*, ed. David Rollason, Margaret Harvey and Michael Prestwich (Woodbridge, 1994), 41–51.

——, *The Monastic Order in Yorkshire, 1069–1215* (Cambridge, 1999).

Cam, H. M., 'An East Anglian Shire-Moot of Stephen's Reign, 1148–1153', *English Historical Review* 39 (1924), 569–71.

——, '*Manerium cum Hundredo*: The Hundred and the Hundredal Manor', rpt in her *Liberties and Communities in Medieval England: Collected Studies in Local Administration and Topography* (Cambridge, 1944), 64–90.

——, 'Early Groups of Hundreds', rpt in her *Liberties and Communities in Medieval England: Collected Studies in Local Administration and Topography* (Cambridge, 1944), 91–106.

Cambridge, E., and D. Rollason, 'The Pastoral Organization of the Anglo-Saxon Church: A Review of the "Minster Hypothesis"', *Early Medieval Europe* 4 (1995), 87–104.

Campbell, James, 'Observations on English Government from the Tenth to the Twelfth Century', rpt in his *Essays in Anglo-Saxon History* (London, 1986), 155–70.

——, 'Hundreds and Leets: A Survey with Suggestions, in *Medieval East Anglia*, ed. Christopher Harper-Bill (Woodbridge, 2005), 153–67.

Chadwick, H. Munro, *Studies on Anglo-Saxon Institutions* (Cambridge, 1905).

Chaplais, Pierre, 'William of Saint-Calais and the Domesday Survey', *Domesday Studies*, ed. J. C. Holt (Woodbridge, 1987), 65–77.

Cheney, C. R., *From Becket to Langton: English Church Government, 1170–1213* (Manchester, 1956).

Clanchy, M. T., *From Memory to Written Record: England, 1066–1307* (third edition, Chichester, 2013).

Cooper, Alan, 'Extraordinary Privilege: The Trial of Penenden Heath and the Domesday Inquest', *English Historical Review* (2001), 1167–92.

——, *Bridges, Law and Power in Medieval England, 700–1400* (Woodbridge, 2006).

Crick, J. C., 'Oxford, Walter of (*d.* in or before 1151?)', *ODNB*.

Cronne, H. A., 'The Office of Local Justiciar in England under the Norman Kings', *University of Birmingham Historical Journal* 6 (1957–8), 18–38.

Crook, David, *Records of the General Eyre* (London, 1982).

Crosby, Everett U., *Bishop and Chapter in Twelfth-Century England: A Study of the 'Mensa Episcopalis'* (Cambridge, 1994).

Crouch, David, 'The Administration of the Norman Earldom', in *The Earldom of Chester and its Charters: A Tribute to Geoffrey Barraclough*, ed. A. T. Thacker, , *Journal of the Chester Archaeological Society* 71 (1991), 69–95.

Dalton, Paul, 'Ranulf II and Lincolnshire', in *The Earldom of Chester and its Charters: A Tribute to Geoffrey Barraclough*, ed. A. T. Thacker, *Journal of the Chester Archaeological Society* 71 (Chester, 1991), 109–34.

Davies, Wendy, and Paul Fouracre, 'Introduction', in *The Settlement of Disputes in Early Medieval Europe*, ed. Wendy Davies and Paul Fouracre (Cambridge, 1986), 1–5.

Davis, R. H. C., 'Bede after Bede', in *Studies in Medieval History Presented to R. Allen Brown*, ed. C. Harper-Bill, C. J. Holdsworth and J. L. Nelson (Woodbridge, 1989), 103–16.

——, *King Stephen, 1135–1154* (third edition, London, 1990).

Demarest, E. B., 'The Hundred-Pennies', *English Historical Review* 33 (1918), 62–72.

Denholm-Young, N., *Seignorial Administration in England* (London, 1937).

*Dictionary of Medieval Latin from British Sources*, ed. Richard Ashdowne, David Howlett and Ronald Latham (three vols, Oxford, 2018).

Douglas, D. C., *The Social Structure of Medieval East Anglia*, Oxford Studies in Social and Legal History 9 (Oxford, 1927).

Dyer, Christopher, *Lords and Peasants in a Changing Society: The Estates of the Bishopric of Worcester, 680–1540* (Cambridge, 1980).

Eales, Richard, 'Royal Power and Castles in Norman England', rpt in *Anglo-Norman Castles*, ed. Robert Liddiard (Woodbridge, 2003), 41–67.

Faith, Rosamund, *The English Peasantry and the Growth of Lordship* (Leicester, 1997).

Finberg, H. P. R., 'The Early History of Werrington', *English Historical Review* 59 (1944), 237–51.

Fleming, Robin, *Kings and Lords in Conquest England* (Cambridge, 1991).

——, *Domesday Book and the Law: Society and Legal Custom in Early Medieval England* (Cambridge, 1998).

Foot, Sarah, 'The Abbey's Armoury of Charters', in *Bury St Edmunds and the Norman Conquest*, ed. Tom Licence (Woodbridge, 2014), 31–52.

Galbraith, V. H., 'Monastic Foundation Charters of the Eleventh Centuries', *Cambridge Historical Journal* 4 (1934), 205–22.

Garnett, George, *Conquered England: Kingship, Succession and Tenure, 1066–1166* (Oxford, 2007).

Goebel, Julius, *Felony and Misdemeanor: A Study in the History of Criminal Law* (New York, 1937).

Green, Judith A., 'The Last Century of Danegeld', *English Historical Review* 96 (1981), 241–58.
——, *The Government of England under Henry I* (Cambridge, 1986).
——, *English Sheriffs to 1154* (London, 1990).
——, *Henry I, King of England and Duke of Normandy* (Cambridge, 2006).
Greenway, D. E., *Fasti Ecclesiae Anglicanae, 1066–1300*: i, *St Paul's, London* (London, 1968)
——, *Fasti ecclesiae Anglicanae, 1066–1300*, ii: *Monastic Cathedrals: Northern and Southern Provinces* (London, 1971).
——, *Fasti Ecclesiae Anglicanae, 1066–1300*: iv, *Salisbury* (London, 1991).
——, *Fasti Ecclesiae Anglicanae, 1066–1300*: vi, *York* (London, 1996).
——, *Fasti ecclesiae Anglicanae, 1066–1300*: vii, *Bath and Wells* (London, 2001).
Gullick, Michael, 'Lanfranc and the Oldest Manuscript of the *Collectio Lanfranci*', in *Bishops, Texts and the Use of Canon Law around 1100: Essays in Honour of Martin Brett*, ed. Bruce C. Brasington, and Kathleen G. Cushing (Aldershot, 2008), 79–89.
Hagger, Mark, *Norman Rule in Normandy, 911–1144* (Woodbridge, 2017).
Haines, R. M., 'Patronage and Appropriation in Ely Diocese: The Share of the Benedictines', *Revue Bénédictine* 108 (1998), 298–314.
Harmer, Florence E., *Anglo-Saxon Writs* (second edition, Stamford, 1989).
Hart, C. R., *The Danelaw* (London, 1992).
Harvey, P. D. A. 'Rectitudines Singularum Personarum and Gerefa', *English Historical Review* 108 (1993), 1–22.
——, *Manors and Maps in Rural England, from the Tenth Century to the Seventeenth* (Farnham, 2010).
——, 'The Manorial Reeve in Twelfth-Century England', rpt in his *Manors and Maps in Rural England, from the Tenth Century to the Seventeenth* (Farnham, 2010), no. II.
Harvey, Sally, 'Domesday Book and its Predecessors', *English Historical Review* 86 (1971), 753–73.
——, *Domesday: Book of Judgement* (Oxford, 2014).
Hase, P. H., 'The Mother Churches of Hampshire', in *Minsters and Parish Churches: The Local Church in Transition, 950–1200*, ed. John Blair (Oxford, 1988), 45–66.
Haskins, Charles Homer, *Norman Institutions* (Cambridge, 1918).
Hearnshaw, F. J. C., *Leet Jurisdiction in England, especially as Illustrated by the Records of the Court Leet of Southampton* (Southampton, 1908).
Helmholz, R. H., *The Oxford History of the Laws of England*: 1, *The Canon Law and Ecclesiastical Jurisdiction from 597 to the 1640s* (Oxford, 2004).
Henderson, Charles, 'Records of the Borough of Truro before AD 1300', *Journal of the Royal Institution of Cornwall* 23 (1929), 103–36.

Hockey, S. F., *Quarr Abbey and its Lands, 1132–1631* (Leicester, 1970).

Hollister, C. Warren, 'The Norman Conquest and the Genesis of English Feudalism', *American Historical Review* 66 (1961), 641–63.

——, 'The Rise of Administrative Kingship: Henry I', in his *Monarchy, Magnates and Institutions in the Anglo-Norman World* (London, 1986), 223–45.

Hollister, C. Warren, and John W. Baldwin, 'The Rise of Administrative Kingship: Henry I and Philip Augustus', *The American Historical Review* 83 (1978), 867–905.

Holt, J. C., 'Politics and Property in Early Medieval England', *Past and Present* 57 (1972), 3–52.

——, '1086', *Domesday Studies*, ed. J. C. Holt (Woodbridge, 1987), 41–64.

Hudson, John, *Land, Law and Lordship in Anglo-Norman England* (Oxford, 1994).

——, 'Court Cases and Legal Arguments in England, *c.* 1066–1166', *Transactions of the Royal Historical Society* sixth series 10 (2000), 91–115.

——, 'The Fate of Earl Waltheof and the Idea of Personal Law in England after 1066', in *Normandy and its Neighbours, 900–1250: Essays for David Bates*, ed. David Crouch and Kathleen Thompson (Turnhout, 2011), 223–35.

——, *The Oxford History of the Laws of England*: ii, *871–1215* (Oxford, 2012).

——, *The Formation of the English Common Law: Law and Society in England from King Alfred to Magna Carta* (second edition, Abingdon, 2018).

Hunnisett, R. F., 'The Origins of the Office of Coroner', *Transactions of the Royal Historical Society* fifth series 8 (1958), 85–104.

Hutchins, John, *The History and Antiquities of the County of Dorset ... with a Copy of Domesday Book and the Inquisitio Gheldi for the County*, third edition ed. William Shipp and James Whitworth Hodson (London, 1861–70).

Hyams, Paul, *Kings, Lords and Peasants in Medieval England: The Common Law of Villeinage in the Twelfth and Thirteenth Centuries* (Oxford, 1980).

——, 'Trial by Ordeal: The Key to Proof in the Early Common Law', in *On the Laws and Customs of England: Essays in Honour of Samuel E. Thorne*, ed. Morris S. Arnold, Thomas Andrew Green, S. A. Scully and S. D. White (Chapel Hill, 1981), 90–126.

——, 'Does it Matter When the English Began to Distinguish Between Crime and Tort?', in *Violence in Medieval Society*, ed. Richard Kaeuper (Woodbridge, 2000), 107–28.

——, *Rancor and Reconciliation in Medieval England* (Ithaca, 2003).

——, 'Property Talk in Old English: Did Anglo-Saxon England Know the Concept of Seisin?', forthcoming.

John, Eric, 'An Alleged Worcester Charter of the Reign of Edgar', *Bulletin of the John Rylands Library* 41 (1958), 54–80.

——, *Land Tenure in Early England* (Leicester, 1964).

——, 'The Church of Worcester and St Oswald', in *Belief and Culture in the*

*Middle Ages: Studies Presented to Henry Mayr-Harting*, ed. Richard Gameson and Henrietta Leyser (Oxford, 2001), 142–57

Karn, Nicholas, 'Robert de Sigillo: An Unruly Head of the Royal Scriptorium in the 1120s and 1130s', *English Historical Review* 123 (2008), 539–53.

——, 'Secular Power and its Rewards in Dorset in the Late Eleventh and Early Twelfth Centuries', *Historical Research* 82 (2009), 2–16.

——, 'Rethinking the *Leges Henrici Primi*', in *English Law before Magna Carta: Felix Liebermann and* Die Gesetze der Angelsachsen, ed. Stefan Jurasinski, Lisi Oliver and Andrew Rabin (Leiden and Boston, 2010), 199–220.

Kemp, Brian, 'Some Aspects of the *Parochia* of Leominster in the 12th Century', in *Minsters and Parish Churches: The Local Church in Transition, 950–1200*, ed. John Blair (Oxford, 1988), 83–95.

Kennedy, A. G., 'Disputes about *Bocland*: The Forum for their Adjudication', *Anglo-Saxon England* 14 (1985), 175–95.

King, Edmund, *King Stephen* (New Haven, 2010).

Knowles, D., C. N. L. Brooke and V. London, *The Heads of Religious Houses I: England and Wales, 940–1216* (second edition, Cambridge, 2001).

Lambert, T. B., 'Royal Protections and Private Justice: A Reassessment of Cnut's "Reserved Pleas"', in *English Law before Magna Carta: Felix Liebermann and* Die Gesetze der Angelsachsen, ed. Stefan Jurasinski, Lisi Oliver and Andrew Rabin (Leiden and Boston, 2010), 157–75.

——, 'Theft, Homicide and Crime in Late Anglo-Saxon Law', *Past and Present* 214 (2012), 3–43.

——, *Law and Order in Anglo-Saxon England* (Oxford, 2017).

Larson, Peter L., 'Village Voice or Village Oligarchy? The Jurors of the Durham Halmote Court, 1349–1424', *Law and History Review* 28 (2010), 675–709.

Latham, R. E., *Revised Medieval Latin Word-List from British and Irish Sources* (Oxford, 1965).

Lawson, M. K., *Cnut, England's Viking King, 1016–35* (second edition, Stroud, 2011).

Le Patourel, John, 'The Date of the Trial on Penenden Heath', *English Historical Review* 61 (1946), 378–88.

Levett, Ada, *Studies in Manorial History*, edited by H. M. Cam, M. Coate and L. S. Sutherland (Oxford, 1938).

Levison, W., 'A Report on the Penenden Trial', *English Historical Review* 27 (1912), 717–20.

Lewis, C. P., 'Herefordshire under William I', *Anglo-Norman Studies* VII (1985), 195–213.

——, 'The Formation of the Honor of Chester, 1066–1100', *The Earldom of Chester and its Charters: A Tribute to Geoffrey Barraclough*, ed. A. T. Thacker, *Journal of the Chester Archaeological Society* 71 (1991), 37–68.

——, 'Avranches, Hugh d', First Earl of Chester (d. 1101)', *ODNB*.

Loyn, H. R., 'The Hundred in England in the Tenth and Early Eleventh Centuries', in *British Government and Administration: Studies Presented to S. B. Chrimes*, ed. H. Hearder and H. R. Loyn (Cardiff, 1974), 1–15.

——, *The Governance of Anglo-Saxon England, 500–1087* (London, 1984).

Maitland, F. W., *Select Pleas in Manorial and Other Seignorial Courts: Volume 1, Reigns of Henry III and Edward I*, Selden Society 2 (1889).

——, 'Leet and Tourn', rpt in *Selected Historical Essays of F. W. Maitland, Chosen and Introduced by Helen M. Cam* (Cambridge, 1957), 41–51.

——, *Domesday Book and Beyond: Three Essays in the Early History of England* (revised edition with an introduction by Edward Miller, London, 1960).

Mason, J. F. A., 'The Norman Earls of Shrewsbury', *Transactions of the Shropshire Archaeological Society* 57 (1964 for 1962–3), 152–61.

——, 'The Officers and Clerks of the Norman Earls of Shrewsbury', *Transactions of the Shropshire Archaeological Society* 56 (1961) 244–57.

——, 'Roger de Montgomery and His Sons (1067–1102)', *Transactions of the Royal Historical Society* fifth series 13 (1963), 1–28.

——, 'Montgomery, Roger de, First Earl of Shrewsbury (d. 1094)', *ODNB*.

Miller, Edward, *The Abbey and Bishopric of Ely: The Social History of an Ecclesiastical Estate from the Tenth Century to the Early Fourteenth Century* (Cambridge, 1951).

Milsom, S. F. C., *The Legal Framework of English Feudalism* (Cambridge, 1976).

Molyneaux, George, *The Formation of the English Kingdom in the Tenth Century* (Oxford, 2015).

Morris, Colin, 'William I and the Church Courts', *English Historical Review* 82 (1967), 449–63.

Morris, William Alfred, *The Frankpledge System* (New York, 1910).

Nightingale, Pamela, 'The Origin of the Court of Husting and Danish Influence on London's Development into a Capital City', *English Historical Review* 102 (1987), 559–78.

Niles, John D., 'The Myth of the Feud in Anglo-Saxon England', *The Journal of English and Germanic Philology* 114 (2015), 163–200.

O'Brien, Bruce R., 'From Morðor to Murdrum: The Preconquest Origin and Norman Revival of the Murder Fine', *Speculum* 71 (1996), 321–57.

——, 'The Instituta Cnuti and the Translation of English Law', *Anglo-Norman Studies* XXV (2003), 177–97.

Oliver, Lisi, *The Body Legal in Barbarian Law* (Toronto, 2011).

*Oxford Dictionary of National Biography*, ed. Colin Matthew and Brian Harrison (60 vols, Oxford, 2004); online with supplements at https://www.oxforddnb.com/.

Page, William, ed., *Victoria History of the Counties of England: Hampshire*, iii. (London, 1908).

——, ed., *Victoria History of the Counties of England: A History of the County of Worcester*, iii. (London, 1913).

Palliser, D. M., 'Review Article: The 'Minster Hypothesis'', *Early Medieval Europe* 5 (1996), 207–14.

Palmer, Robert C., *The County Courts of Medieval England, 1150–1350* (Princeton, 1982).

Pantos, Aliki, 'The Location and Form of Anglo-Saxon Assembly-Places: Some "Moot Points"', in *Assembly Places and Practices in Medieval Europe*, ed. Aliki Pantos and Sarah Semple (Dublin, 2004), 155–80.

Philpott, Mark, 'The *De iniusta uexacione Willelmi episcopi primi* and Canon Law in Anglo-Norman Durham', in *Anglo-Norman Durham, 1093–1193*, ed. David Rollason, Margaret Harvey and Michael Prestwich (Woodbridge, 1994), 125–37.

Pollock, Frederick, and Frederic Maitland, *The History of English Law Before the Time of Edward I* (second edition, Cambridge, 1898).

Rabin, Andrew, 'Ritual Magic or Legal Performance? Reconsidering an Old English Charm against Theft', in *English Law before Magna Carta: Felix Liebermann and* Die Gesetze der Angelsachsen, ed. Stefan Jurasinski, Lisi Oliver and Andrew Rabin (Leiden and Boston, 2010), 177–95.

Razi, Zvi, and Richard M. Smith, eds., *Medieval Society and the Manor Court* (Oxford, 1996).

Razi, Zvi, and Richard M. Smith, 'The Origins of the English Manorial Court Rolls', in their *Medieval Society and the Manor Court* (Oxford, 1996), 36–68.

Reedy, W. T., 'The Origins of the General Eyre in the Reign of Henry I', *Speculum* 41 (1966), 688–724.

Reynolds, Andrew, *Anglo-Saxon Deviant Burial Customs* (Oxford, 2009).

Reynolds, Susan, 'The Rulers of London in the Twelfth Century', *History* 57 (1972), 337–57.

Richardson, H. G., and G. O. Sayles, *The Governance of Medieval England from the Conquest to Magna Carta* (Edinburgh, 1963).

Roffe, David, 'From Thegnage to Barony: Sake and Soke, Title and Tenants-in-Chief', *Anglo-Norman Studies* XII (1989), 157–76.

——, 'Introduction to the Nottinghamshire Domesday', *The Nottinghamshire Domesday* [introduction and translation] (London, 1990), 1–31.

——, 'Hundreds and Wapentakes', in *The Lincolnshire Domesday* [introduction and translation] (London, 1992), 32–42.

——, 'The Historia Croylandensis: a Plea for Reassessment', *English Historical Review* 110 (1995), 93–108.

Rosser, Gervase, 'The Anglo-Saxon Gilds', in John Blair, ed., *Minsters and Parish Churches: The Local Church in Transition, 950–1200* (Oxford, 1988), 31–4.

Round, J. H., *Geoffrey de Mandeville: A Study of the Anarchy* (London, 1892).

——, 'Bernard, the King's Scribe', *English Historical Review* 14 (1899), 417–30.
——, *The Commune of London and Other Studies* (London, 1899).
——, *Feudal England: Historical Studies on the Eleventh and Twelfth Centuries* (reset edition, London, 1964).
Rubin, Stanley, 'The *Bot*, or Composition in Anglo-Saxon Law: A Reassessment', *The Journal of Legal History* 17 (1996), 144–54.
Sabapathy, John, *Officers and Accountability in Medieval England,* c. *1170–1300* (Oxford, 2014).
Saltman, Avrom, *Theobald, Archbishop of Canterbury* (London, 1956).
Salzman, L. F., J. P. C. Roach, A. W. Mabbs, R. B. Pugh, C. R. Elrington, A. P. M. Wright, J. J. Wilkes, C. P. Lewis and A. F. Wareham, eds., *The Victoria History of the Counties of England: A History of Cambridgeshire and the Isle of Ely* (10 vols and index, London and Oxford, 1938–2002).
Sanders, I. J., *English Baronies: A Study of their Origin and Descent, 1086–1327* (Oxford, 1960).
Sawyer, Peter, 'The Royal *Tun* in Pre-Conquest England', in *Ideal and Reality in Frankish and Anglo-Saxon Society*, ed. Patrick Wormald, Donald Bullough and R. Collins (Oxford, 1983), 273–99.
Scammell, Jean, 'The Origins and Limitations of the Liberty of Durham', *English Historical Review* 81 (1966), 449–73.
Searle, Eleanor, *Lordship and Community: Battle Abbey and its Banlieu, 1066–1538* (Toronto, 1974).
Semple, Sarah, 'Locations of Assembly in Early Anglo–Saxon England', in *Assembly Places and Practices in Medieval Europe*, ed. Aliki Pantos and Sarah Semple (Dublin, 2004), 135–54.
Sharpe, Richard, 'The Use of Writs in the Eleventh Century', *Anglo-Saxon England* 32 (2003), 247–91.
——, '1088—William II and the Rebels', *Anglo-Norman Studies* XXVI (2004), 139–58.
——, *Norman Rule in Cumbria, 1092–1136* (Carlisle, 2006).
——, 'The Dating of *Quadripartitus* Again', in *English Law before Magna Carta: Felix Liebermann and* Die Gesetze der Angelsachsen, ed. Stefan Jurasinski, Lisi Oliver and Andrew Rabin (Leiden and Boston, 2010), 81–93.
Stenton, Doris M., *English Justice between the Norman Conquest and the Great Charter, 1066–1215* (London, 1965).
——, 'The Development of the Judiciary 1100–1215', in her *Pleas Before the King or his Justices, 1198–1212*, iii: *Rolls or Fragments of Rolls from the Years 1199, 1201 and 1203–6*, Selden Society 83 (1967), xlvii–ccxciv.
Stenton, F. M., 'St Benet of Hulme and the Norman Conquest', *English Historical Review* 37 (1922), 225–35.
——, 'Acta Episcoporum', *The Cambridge Historical Journal* 3 (1929), 1–14.

——, *The First Century of English Feudalism 1066–1166: The Ford Lectures Delivered in the University of Oxford 1929* (second edition, Oxford, 1961).

Stubbs, William, *The Constitutional History of England: its Origins and Development* (fifth edition, Oxford, 1891).

Sutherland, Donald W., *Quo Warranto Proceedings in the Reign of Edward I, 1278–1294* (Oxford, 1963).

Thomson, Rodney, *The Archives of the Abbey of Bury St Edmunds*, Suffolk Records Society 21 (1980).

——, *William of Malmesbury* (revised edition, Woodbridge, 2003).

Thorn, F. R., 'Hundreds and Wapentakes', in *The Worcestershire Domesday* [introduction and translation] (London, 1986), 32–7.

——, 'Hundreds and Wapentakes', *The Northamptonshire and Rutland Domesday* [introduction and translation] (London, 1987), 35–39.

——, 'Hundreds and Wapentakes', in *The Hampshire Domesday* [introduction and translation] (London, 1989), 28–39.

——, 'Hundreds and Wapentakes', *The Leicestershire Domesday* [introduction and translation] (London, 1990), 22–30.

——, 'Hundreds and Wapentakes', *The Nottinghamshire Domesday* [introduction and translation] (London, 1990), 32–43.

Vallerani, Massimo, *Medieval Public Justice*, translated by Sarah Rubin Blanshei (Washington, 2012).

Van Caenegem, Raoul C., 'Public Prosecution of Crime in Twelfth-Century England', in *Church and Government in the Middle Ages: Essays Presented to C. R. Cheney on his Seventieth Birthday*, ed. C. N. L. Brooke, D. E. Luscombe, G. H. Martin and D. Owen (Cambridge, 1976), 41–76.

Vincent, Nicholas, 'King Henry II and the Monks of Battle: The Battle Chronicle Unmasked', in *Belief and Culture in the Middle Ages: Studies Presented to Henry Mayr-Harting*, ed. Richard Gameson and Henrietta Leyser (Oxford, 2001), 264–86.

West, F., *The Justiciarship in England, 1066–1232* (Cambridge, 1966).

White, Graeme J., *The Magna Carta of Cheshire* (Chester, 2015).

Wightman, W. E., 'The Palatine Earldom of William fitz Osbern in Gloucestershire and Worcestershire (1066–1071)', *English Historical Review* 77 (1962), 6–17.

Williams, Ann, 'A Bell House and a Burh-Geat: Lordly Residences in England before the Norman Conquest', rpt in *Anglo-Norman Castles*, ed. Robert Liddiard (Woodbridge, 2003), 23–40.

Wormald, Patrick, 'Maitland and Anglo-Saxon Law: Beyond Domesday Book', in *The History of English Law: Centenary Essays on 'Pollock and Maitland'*, ed. John Hudson, *Proceedings of the British Academy* 89 (1996), 1–20.

—— '*Lex Scripta* and *Verbum Regis*: Legislation and Germanic Kingship from Euric to Cnut', rpt in his *Legal Culture in the Early Medieval West: Law as Text, Image and Experience* (London, 1999), 1–43.

——, 'A Handlist of Anglo-Saxon Lawsuits', rpt in his *Legal Culture in the Early Medieval West: Law as Text, Image and Experience* (London, 1999), 253–87.

——, 'Charters, Law and the Settlement of Disputes in Anglo-Saxon England', rpt in his *Legal Culture in the Early Medieval West: Law as Text, Image and Experience* (London, 1999), 289–311.

——, 'Law and Justice in the Early English Kingdom: Oswaldslow Revisited', rpt in his *Legal Culture in the Early Medieval West: Law as Text, Image and Experience* (London, 1999), 313–32.

——, '*Engla Lond*: the Making of an Allegiance', rpt in his *Legal Culture in the Early Medieval West: Law as Text, Image and Experience* (London, 1999), 359–82.

——, *The Making of English Law: King Alfred to the Twelfth Century* (Oxford, 1999).

# Index

Printed and bound by CPI Group (UK) Ltd, Croydon, CR0 4YY

15/09/2026

14962417-0004